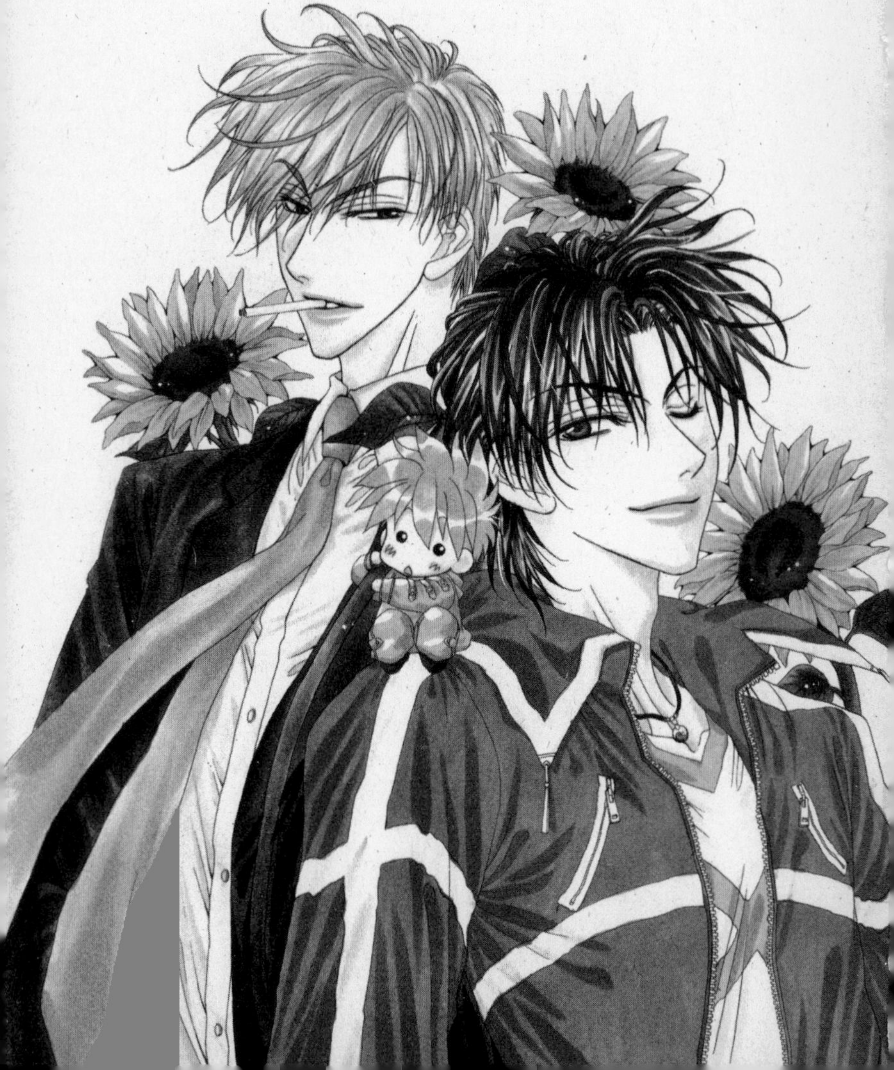

Translator - Heidi Yamaguchi
English Adaptation - Jackie Medel
Contributing Editor - Jodi Bryson
Retouch and Lettering - James Dashiell
Cover Layout - Anna Kernbaum
Graphic Designer - John Lo

Editor - Nora Wong
Managing Editor - Jill Freshney
Production Coordinator - Antonio DePietro
Production Manager - Jennifer Miller, Mutsumi Miyazaki
Art Director - Matt Alford
Editorial Director - Jeremy Ross
VP of Production - Ron Klamert
President & C.O.O. - John Parker
Publisher & C.E.O. - Stuart Levy

E-mail: editor@TOKYOPOP.com

Come visit us online at www.TOKYOPOP.com

A  Manga

TOKYOPOP Inc.
5900 Wilshire Blvd. Suite 2000
Los Angeles, CA 90036

Eerie Queerie! Vol. 1

ISBN: 1-59182-719-1

First TOKYOPOP printing: March 2004

10 9 8 7 6 5 4

Printed in the USA

Eerie Queerie!

Vol. 1

by Shuri Shiozu

TOKYOPOP®

Los Angeles • Tokyo • London

For more
information visit
www.TOKYOPOP.com

12.20.03T

ALSO AVAILABLE FROM 🌐 TOKYOPOP®

MANGA

.HACK//LEGEND OF THE TWILIGHT
@LARGE
A.I. LOVE YOU
AI YORI AOSHI
ANGELIC LAYER
ARM OF KANNON
BABY BIRTH
BATTLE ROYALE
BATTLE VIXENS
BRAIN POWERED
BRIGADOON
B'TX
CANDIDATE FOR GODDESS, THE
CARDCAPTOR SAKURA
CARDCAPTOR SAKURA - MASTER OF THE CLOW

CHOBITS
CHRONICLES OF THE CURSED SWORD
CLAMP SCHOOL DETECTIVES
CLOVER
COMIC PARTY
CONFIDENTIAL CONFESSIONS
CORRECTOR YUI
COWBOY BEBOP
COWBOY BEBOP: SHOOTING STAR
CRESCENT MOON
CYBORG 009
D.N. ANGEL
DEMON DIARY
DEMON ORORON, THE
DEUS VITAE
DIGIMON
DIGIMON ZERO TWO
DIGIMON TAMERS
DOLL May 2004
DRAGON HUNTER
DRAGON KNIGHTS
DUKLYON: CLAMP SCHOOL DEFENDERS
ERICA SAKURAZAWA COLLECTED WORKS
EERIE QUEERIE!
FAERIES' LANDING
FAKE
FLCL
FORBIDDEN DANCE
FRUITS BASKET
G GUNDAM
GATE KEEPERS
GETBACKERS
GIRL GOT GAME
GRAVITATION
GTO
GUNDAM SEED ASTRAY

GUNDAM WING
GUNDAM WING: BATTLEFIELD OF PACIFISTS
GUNDAM WING: ENDLESS WALTZ
GUNDAM WING: THE LAST OUTPOST (G-UNIT)
HAPPY MANIA
HARLEM BEAT
I.N.V.U.
IMMORTAL RAIN
INITIAL D
ISLAND
JING: KING OF BANDITS
JULINE
JUROR 13
KARE KANO
KILL ME, KISS ME
KINDAICHI CASE FILES, THE
KING OF HELL
KODOCHA: SANA'S STAGE
LAMENT OF THE LAMB
LES BIJOUX
LOVE HINA
LUPIN III
MAGIC KNIGHT RAYEARTH I
MAGIC KNIGHT RAYEARTH II
MAHOROMATIC: AUTOMATIC MAIDEN
MAN OF MANY FACES
MARMALADE BOY
MARS
MINK
MIRACLE GIRLS
MIYUKI-CHAN IN WONDERLAND
MODEL
ONE
PARADISE KISS
PARASYTE
PEACH GIRL
PEACH GIRL: CHANGE OF HEART
PET SHOP OF HORRORS
PITA-TEN
PLANET LADDER
PLANETES
PRIEST
PRINCESS AI
PSYCHIC ACADEMY
RAGNAROK
RAVE MASTER
REALITY CHECK
REBIRTH
REBOUND
REMOTE
RISING STARS OF MANGA
SABER MARIONETTE J
SAILOR MOON

12.20.03T

CONTENTS

Eerie Queerie! Vol.1

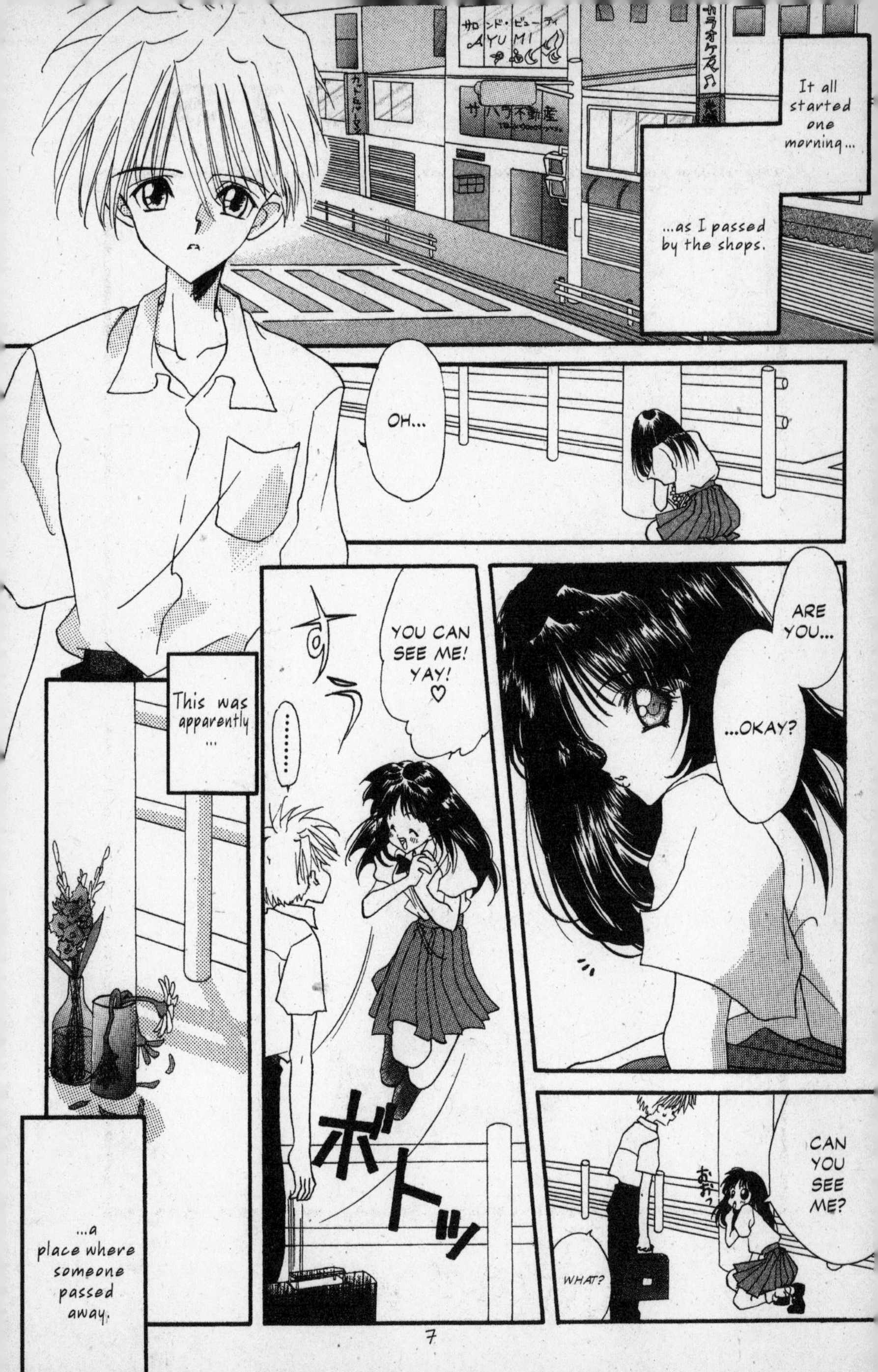
サロン・ド・ビューティ AYUMI
サハラ不動産
It all started one morning...
...as I passed by the shops.
OH...
ARE YOU...
...OKAY?
YOU CAN SEE ME! YAY! ♡
......
ボトッ
CAN YOU SEE ME?
WHAT?
This was apparently ...
...a place where someone passed away.

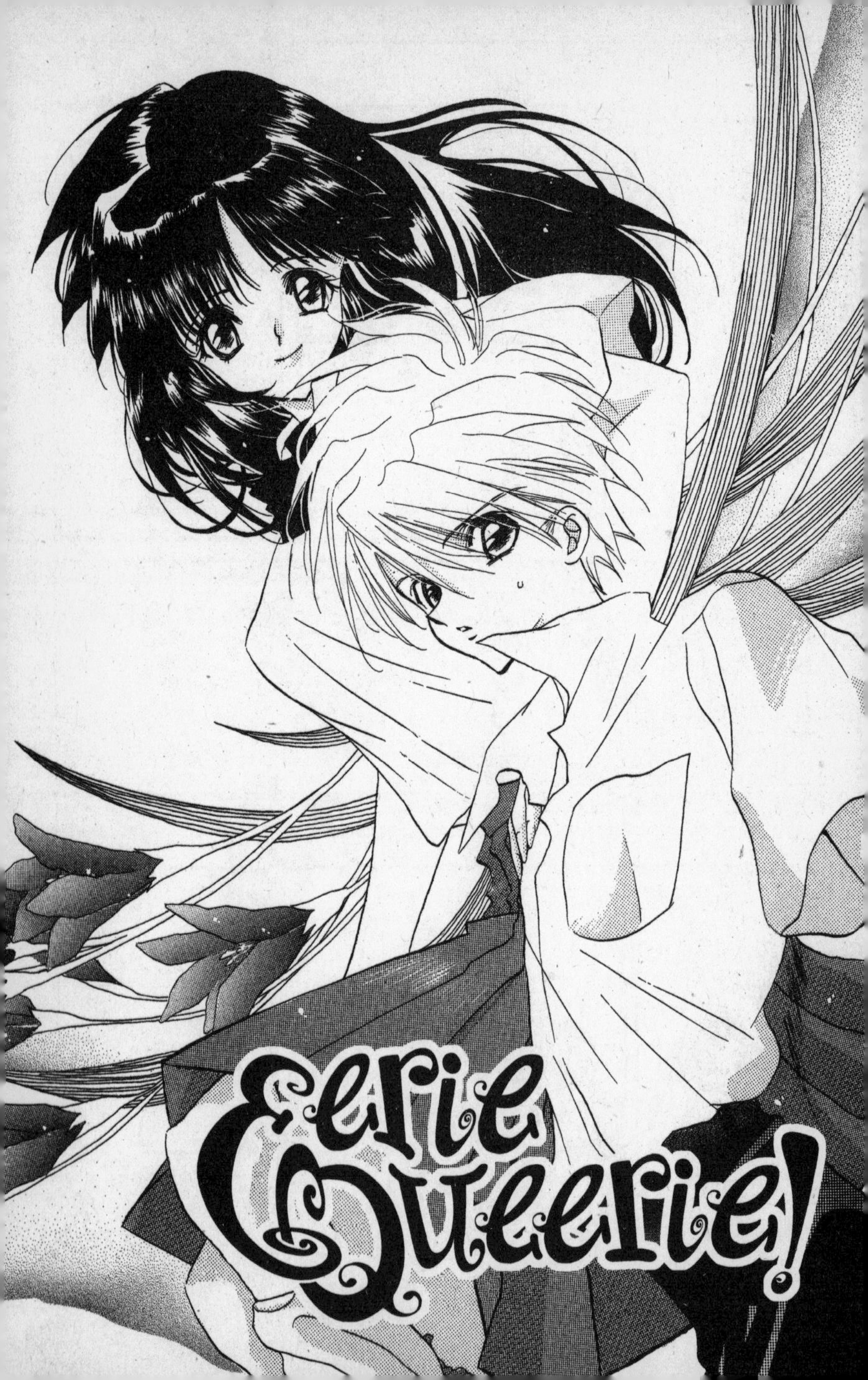
Eerie Queerie!

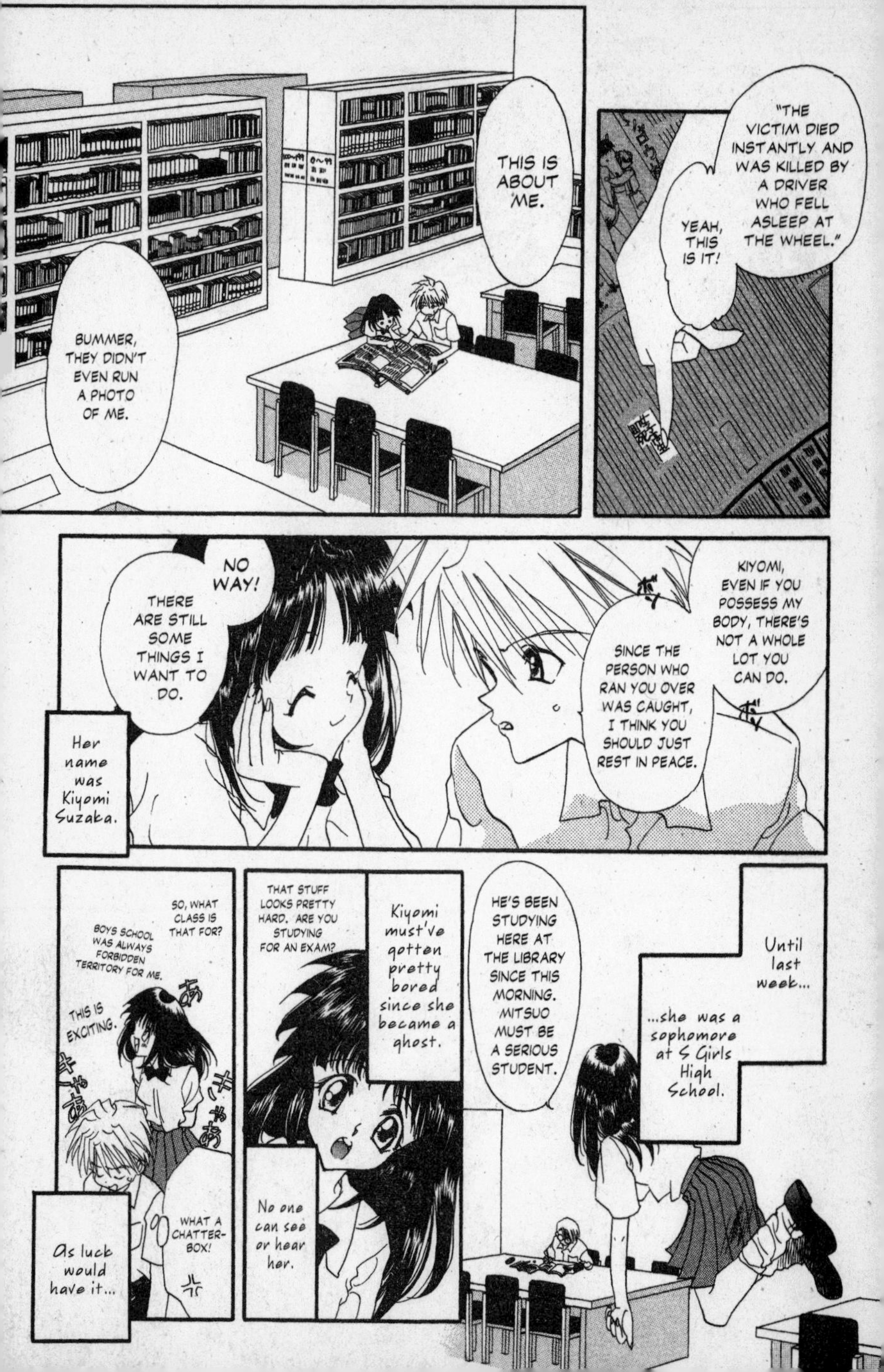
"THE VICTIM DIED INSTANTLY AND WAS KILLED BY A DRIVER WHO FELL ASLEEP AT THE WHEEL."
YEAH, THIS IS IT!
THIS IS ABOUT ME.
BUMMER, THEY DIDN'T EVEN RUN A PHOTO OF ME.
KIYOMI, EVEN IF YOU POSSESS MY BODY, THERE'S NOT A WHOLE LOT YOU CAN DO.
SINCE THE PERSON WHO RAN YOU OVER WAS CAUGHT, I THINK YOU SHOULD JUST REST IN PEACE.
NO WAY!
THERE ARE STILL SOME THINGS I WANT TO DO.
Her name was Kiyomi Suzaka.
Until last week...
...she was a sophomore at S Girls High School.
HE'S BEEN STUDYING HERE AT THE LIBRARY SINCE THIS MORNING. MITSUO MUST BE A SERIOUS STUDENT.
Kiyomi must've gotten pretty bored since she became a ghost.
THAT STUFF LOOKS PRETTY HARD. ARE YOU STUDYING FOR AN EXAM?
No one can see or hear her.
SO, WHAT CLASS IS THAT FOR?
BOYS SCHOOL WAS ALWAYS FORBIDDEN TERRITORY FOR ME.
THIS IS EXCITING.
WHAT A CHATTER-BOX!
As luck would have it...

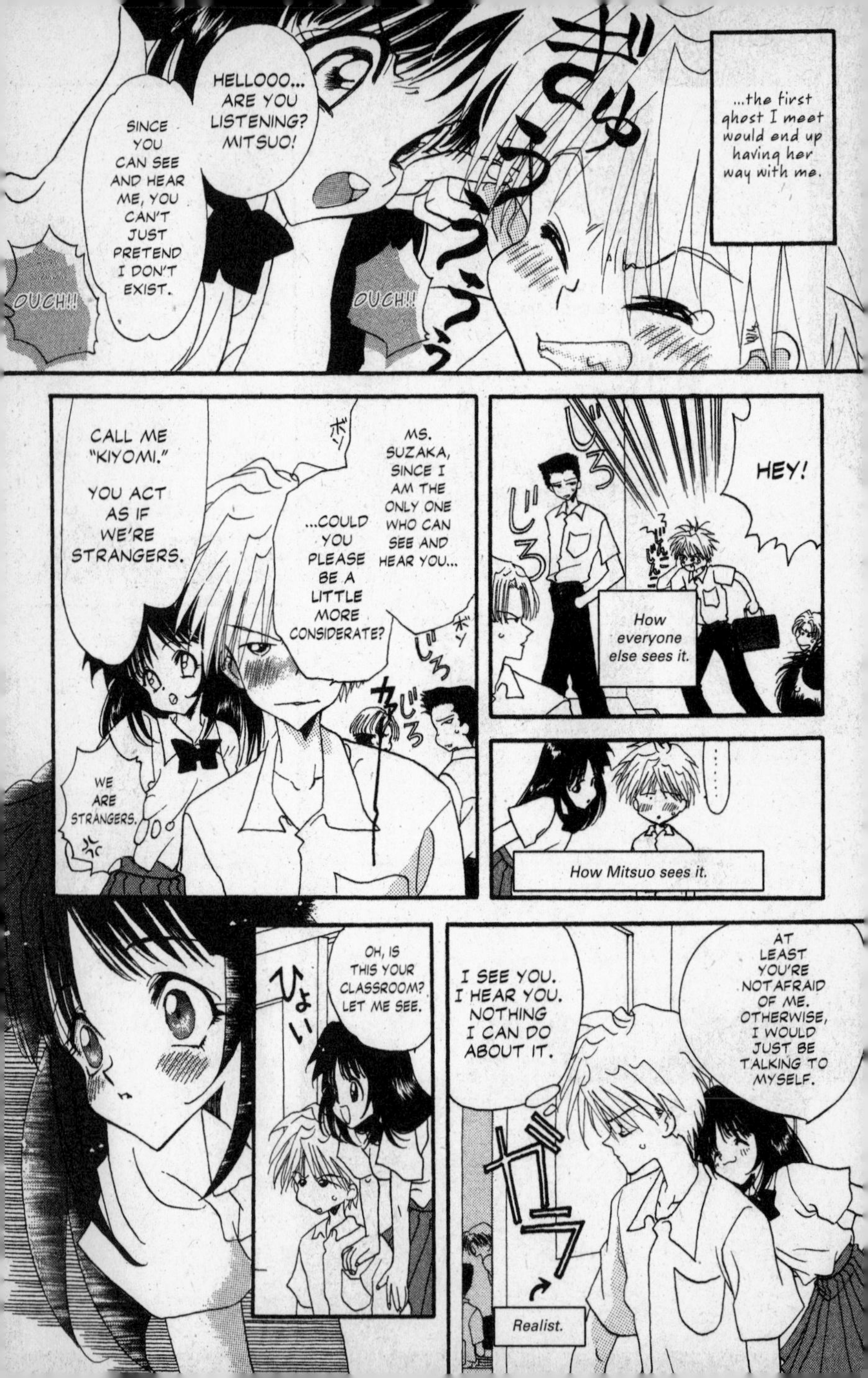
...the first ghost I meet would end up having her way with me.
HELLOOO... ARE YOU LISTENING? MITSUO!
SINCE YOU CAN SEE AND HEAR ME, YOU CAN'T JUST PRETEND I DON'T EXIST.
OUCH!!
OUCH!!
HEY!
じろじろ
How everyone else sees it.
......
How Mitsuo sees it.
MS. SUZAKA, SINCE I AM THE ONLY ONE WHO CAN SEE AND HEAR YOU...
...COULD YOU PLEASE BE A LITTLE MORE CONSIDERATE?
CALL ME "KIYOMI." YOU ACT AS IF WE'RE STRANGERS.
WE ARE STRANGERS.
AT LEAST YOU'RE NOTAFRAID OF ME. OTHERWISE, I WOULD JUST BE TALKING TO MYSELF.
I SEE YOU. I HEAR YOU. NOTHING I CAN DO ABOUT IT.
Realist.
OH, IS THIS YOUR CLASSROOM? LET ME SEE.
ひょい

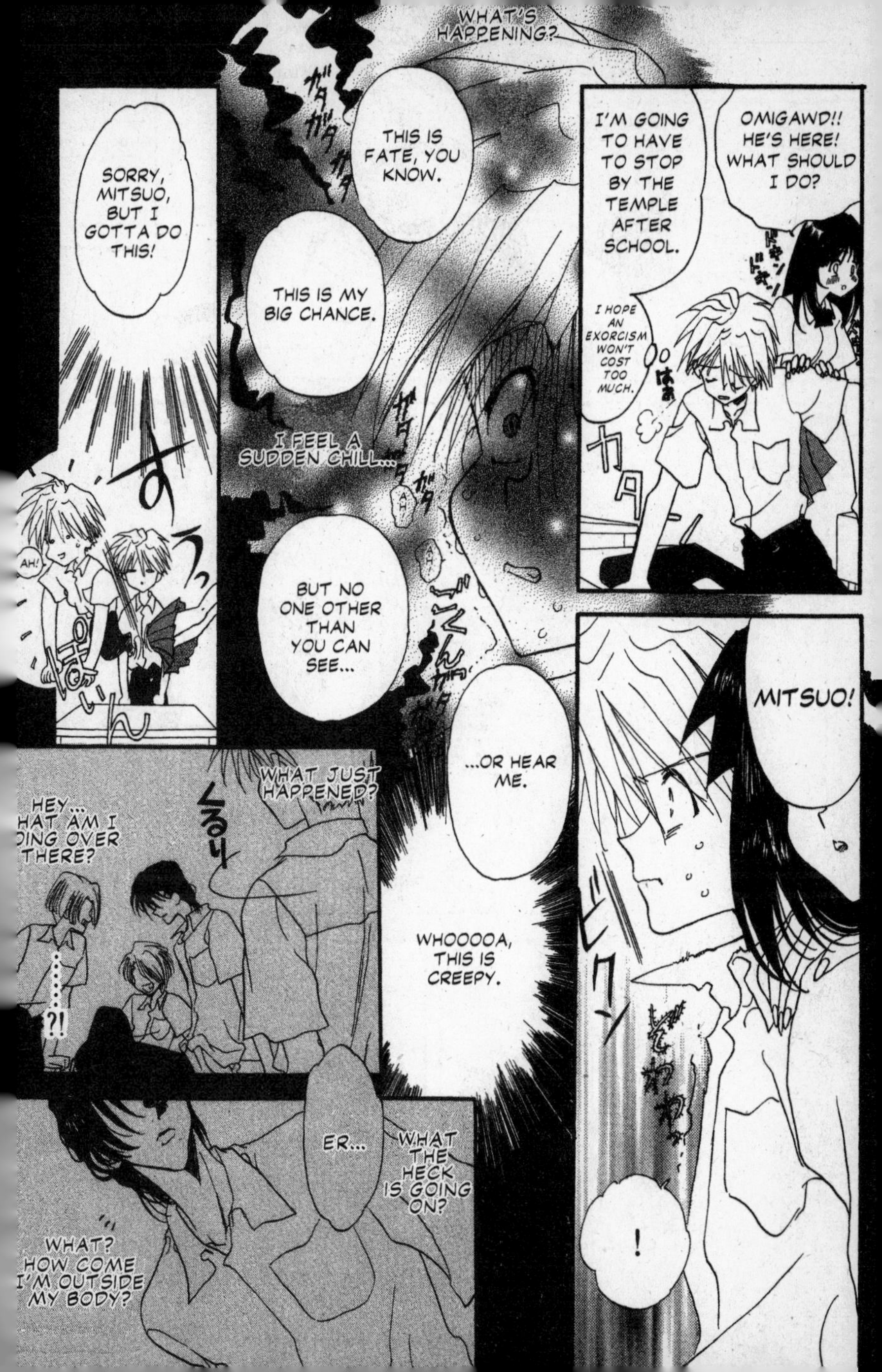
OMIGAWD!! HE'S HERE! WHAT SHOULD I DO?
I'M GOING TO HAVE TO STOP BY THE TEMPLE AFTER SCHOOL.
I HOPE AN EXORCISM WON'T COST TOO MUCH.
MITSUO!
!
WHAT'S HAPPENING?
THIS IS FATE, YOU KNOW.
THIS IS MY BIG CHANCE.
I FEEL A SUDDEN CHILL...
AH!
AH!
BUT NO ONE OTHER THAN YOU CAN SEE...
...OR HEAR ME.
WHOOOOA, THIS IS CREEPY.
SORRY, MITSUO, BUT I GOTTA DO THIS!
AH!
WHAT JUST HAPPENED?
HEY... HAT AM I OING OVER THERE?
......
?!
ER...
WHAT THE HECK IS GOING ON?
WHAT? HOW COME I'M OUTSIDE MY BODY?

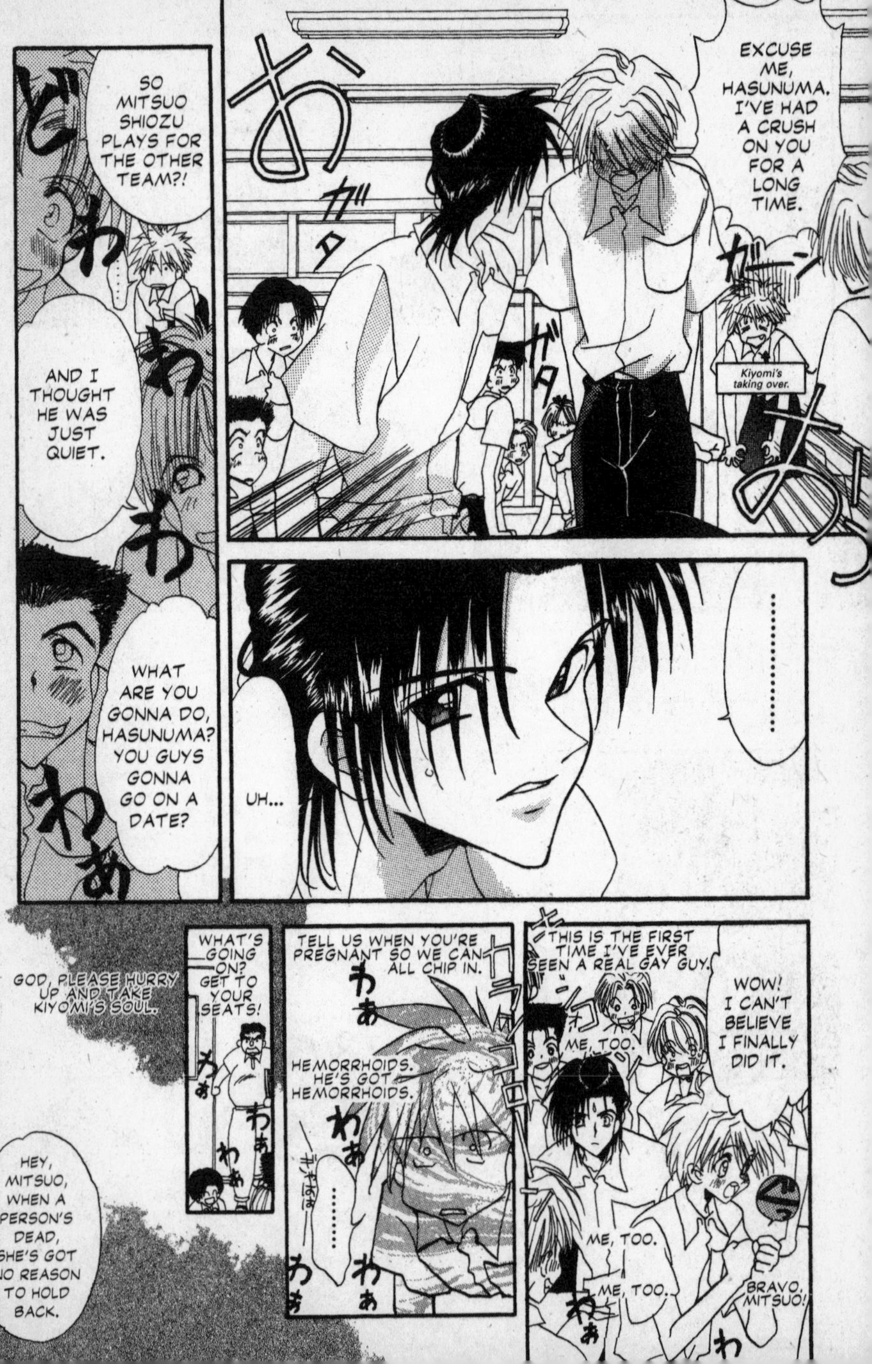
EXCUSE ME, HASUNUMA. I'VE HAD A CRUSH ON YOU FOR A LONG TIME.
Kiyomi's taking over.
......
UH...
SO MITSUO SHIOZU PLAYS FOR THE OTHER TEAM?!
AND I THOUGHT HE WAS JUST QUIET.
WHAT ARE YOU GONNA DO, HASUNUMA? YOU GUYS GONNA GO ON A DATE?
WOW! I CAN'T BELIEVE I FINALLY DID IT.
THIS IS THE FIRST TIME I'VE EVER SEEN A REAL GAY GUY.
ME, TOO.
ME, TOO.
ME, TOO.
BRAVO, MITSUO!
TELL US WHEN YOU'RE PREGNANT SO WE CAN ALL CHIP IN.
HEMORRHOIDS. HE'S GOT HEMORRHOIDS.
......
WHAT'S GOING ON? GET TO YOUR SEATS!
GOD, PLEASE HURRY UP AND TAKE KIYOMI'S SOUL.
HEY, MITSUO, WHEN A PERSON'S DEAD, SHE'S GOT NO REASON TO HOLD BACK.

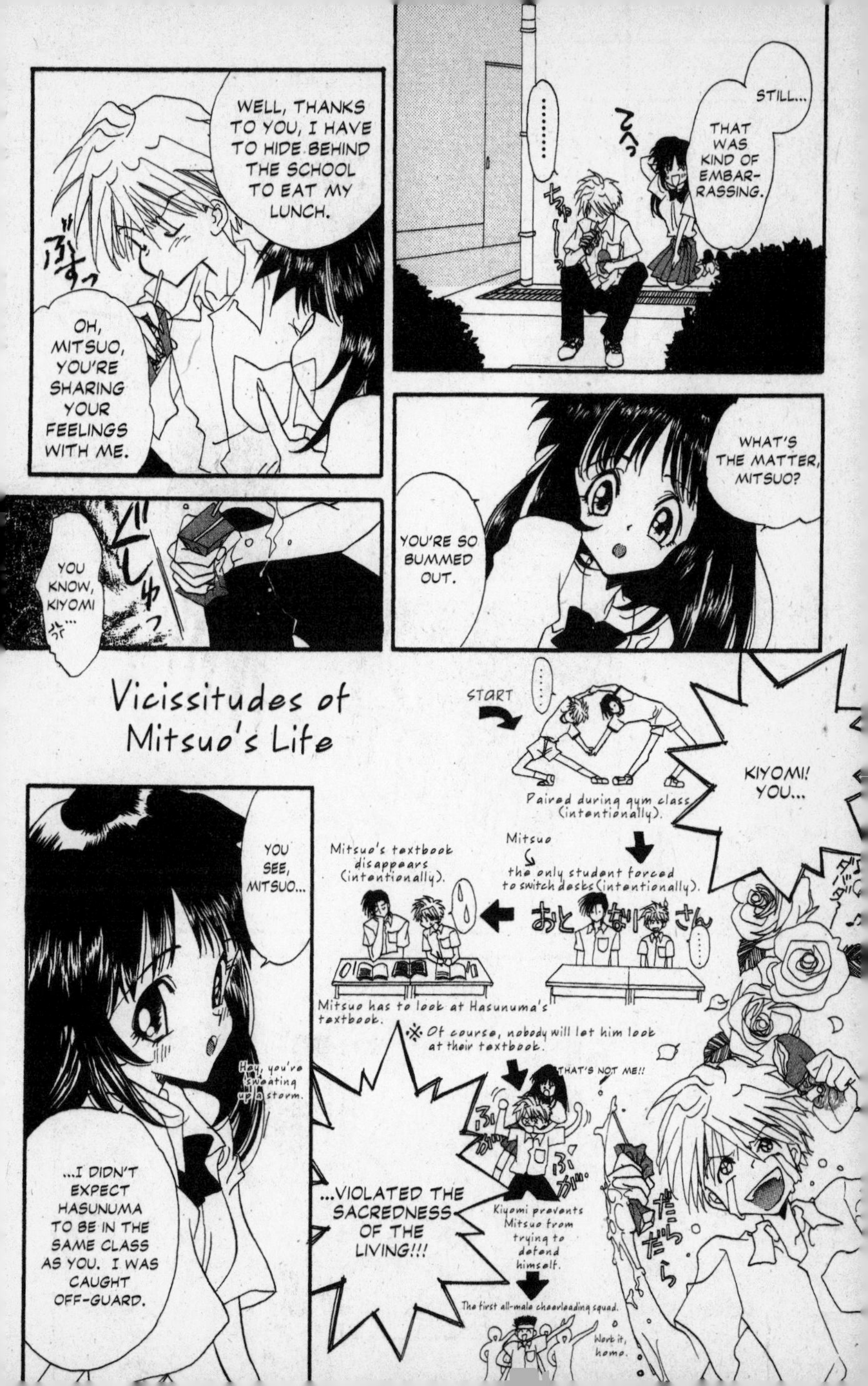

......
STILL... THAT WAS KIND OF EMBARRASSING.
WELL, THANKS TO YOU, I HAVE TO HIDE BEHIND THE SCHOOL TO EAT MY LUNCH.
OH, MITSUO, YOU'RE SHARING YOUR FEELINGS WITH ME.
WHAT'S THE MATTER, MITSUO?
YOU'RE SO BUMMED OUT.
YOU KNOW, KIYOMI...
KIYOMI! YOU...
Vicissitudes of Mitsuo's Life
START
......
Paired during gym class (intentionally).
Mitsuo
the only student forced to switch desks (intentionally).
Mitsuo's textbook disappears (intentionally).
Mitsuo has to look at Hasunuma's textbook.
※ Of course, nobody will let him look at their textbook.
THAT'S NOT ME!!
Kiyomi prevents Mitsuo from trying to defend himself.
The first all-male cheerleading squad.
Work it, homo.
...VIOLATED THE SACREDNESS OF THE LIVING!!!
YOU SEE, MITSUO...
Hey, you're sweating up a storm.
...I DIDN'T EXPECT HASUNUMA TO BE IN THE SAME CLASS AS YOU. I WAS CAUGHT OFF-GUARD.

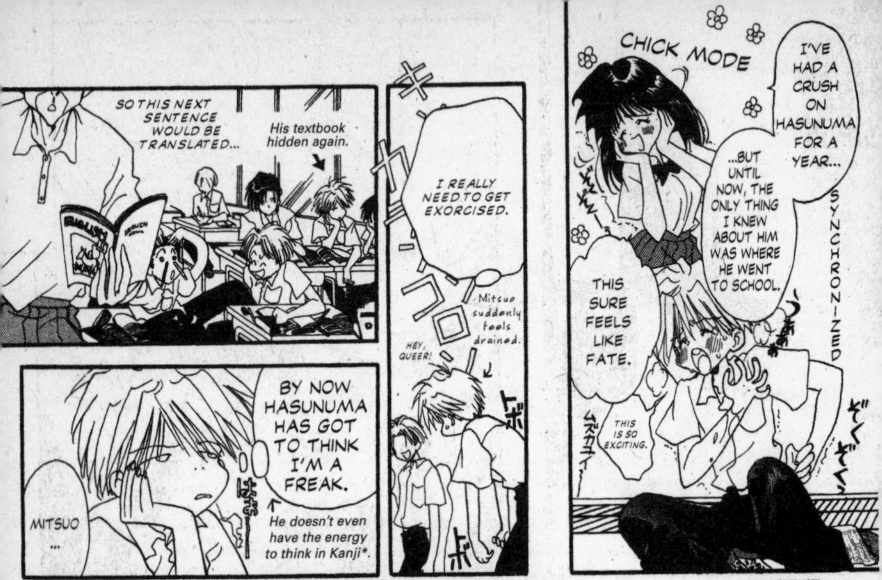
CHICK MODE
I'VE HAD A CRUSH ON HASUNUMA FOR A YEAR...
...BUT UNTIL NOW, THE ONLY THING I KNEW ABOUT HIM WAS WHERE HE WENT TO SCHOOL.
SYNCHRONIZED
THIS SURE FEELS LIKE FATE.
THIS IS SO EXCITING.
I REALLY NEED TO GET EXORCISED.
Mitsuo suddenly feels drained.
HEY, QUEER!
SO THIS NEXT SENTENCE WOULD BE TRANSLATED...
His textbook hidden again.
BY NOW HASUNUMA HAS GOT TO THINK I'M A FREAK.
He doesn't even have the energy to think in Kanji*.
MITSUO ...

*A Japanese form of writing based on Chinese characters.

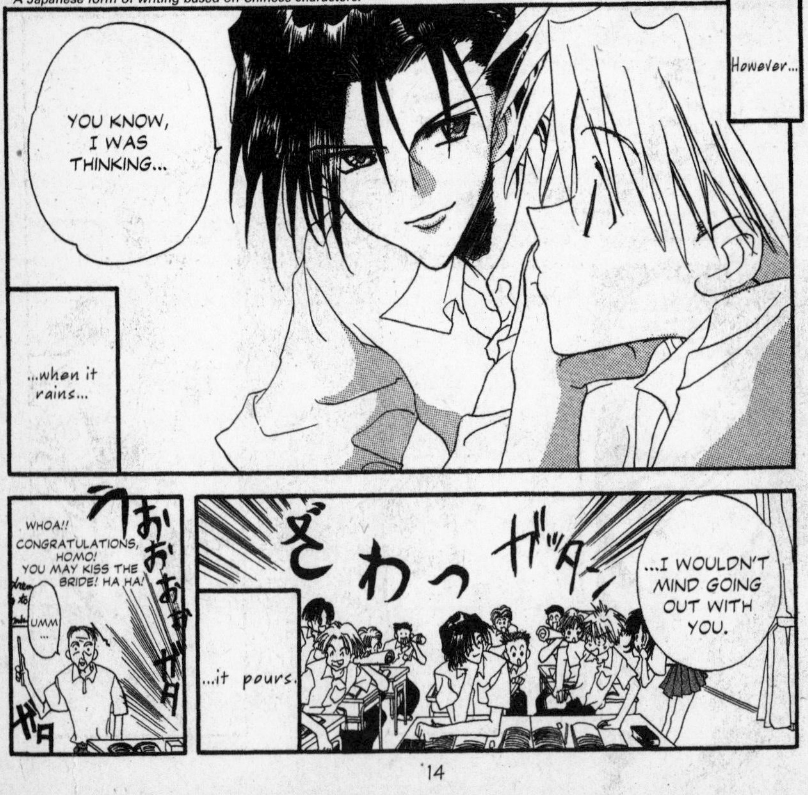
However...
YOU KNOW, I WAS THINKING...
...when it rains...
...I WOULDN'T MIND GOING OUT WITH YOU.
...it pours.
WHOA!! CONGRATULATIONS, HOMO! YOU MAY KISS THE BRIDE! HA HA!
UMM ...

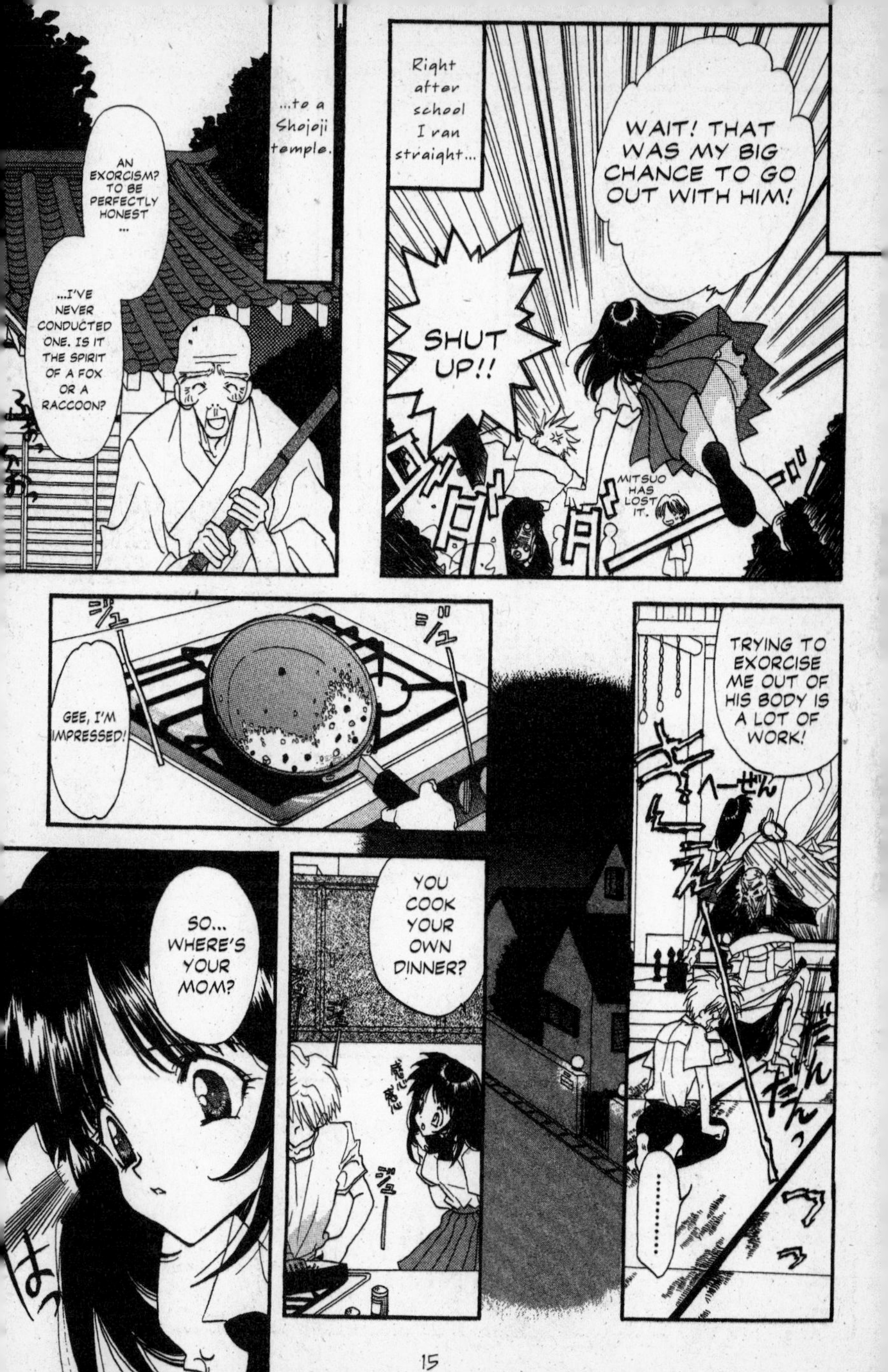
WAIT! THAT WAS MY BIG CHANCE TO GO OUT WITH HIM!
Right after school I ran straight...
SHUT UP!!
MITSUO HAS LOST IT.
...to a Shojoji temple.
AN EXORCISM? TO BE PERFECTLY HONEST ...
...I'VE NEVER CONDUCTED ONE. IS IT THE SPIRIT OF A FOX OR A RACCOON?
TRYING TO EXORCISE ME OUT OF HIS BODY IS A LOT OF WORK!
へーぜん
......
ジュ
ジュ
GEE, I'M IMPRESSED!
YOU COOK YOUR OWN DINNER?
SO... WHERE'S YOUR MOM?

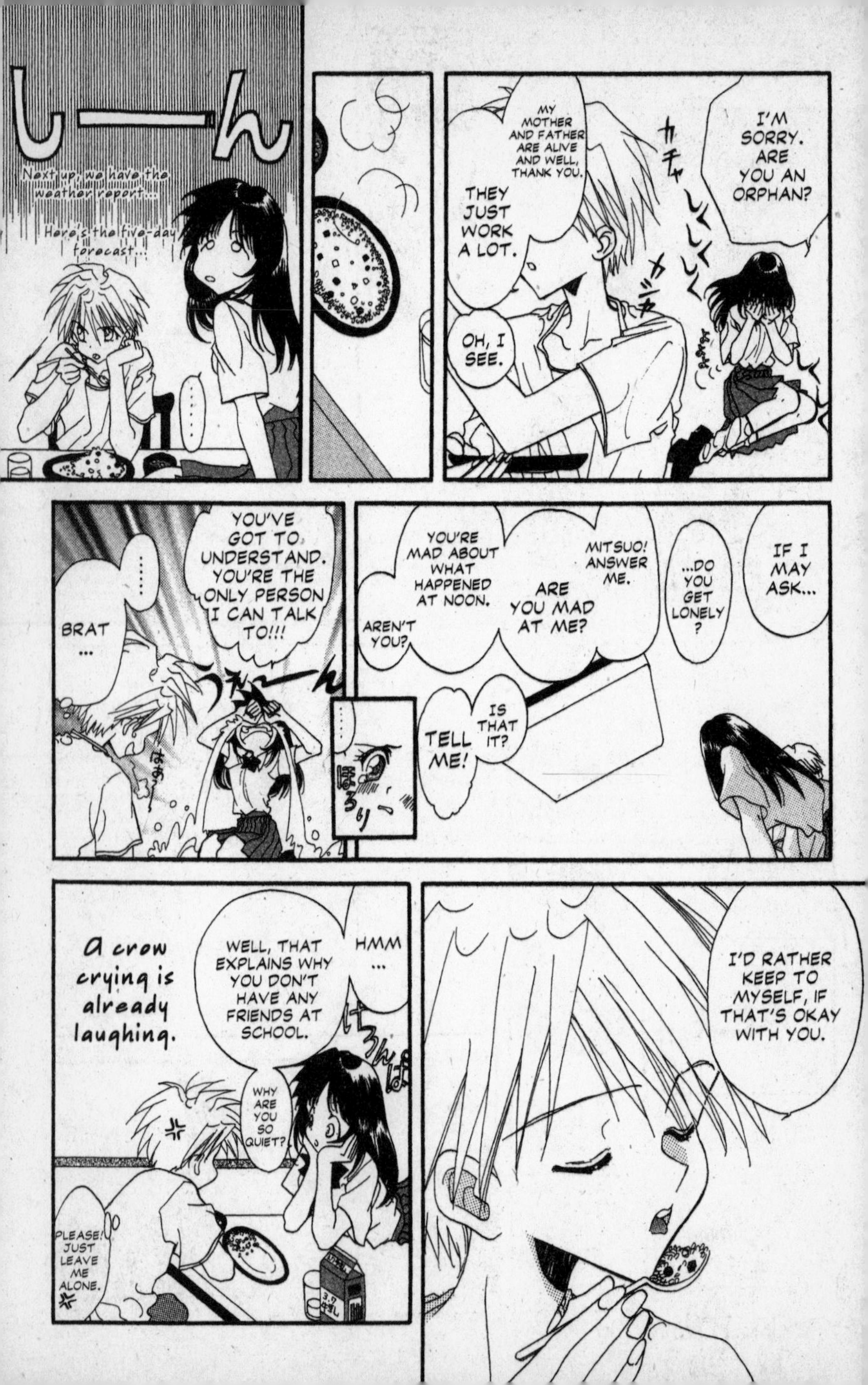
I'M SORRY. ARE YOU AN ORPHAN?
MY MOTHER AND FATHER ARE ALIVE AND WELL, THANK YOU.
THEY JUST WORK A LOT.
OH, I SEE.
しーん
Next up, we have the weather report...
Here's the five-day forecast...
......
IF I MAY ASK...
...DO YOU GET LONELY?
MITSUO! ANSWER ME.
ARE YOU MAD AT ME?
YOU'RE MAD ABOUT WHAT HAPPENED AT NOON.
AREN'T YOU?
IS THAT IT?
TELL ME!
......
YOU'VE GOT TO UNDERSTAND. YOU'RE THE ONLY PERSON I CAN TALK TO!!!
......
BRAT...
I'D RATHER KEEP TO MYSELF, IF THAT'S OKAY WITH YOU.
HMM...
WELL, THAT EXPLAINS WHY YOU DON'T HAVE ANY FRIENDS AT SCHOOL.
WHY ARE YOU SO QUIET?
PLEASE! JUST LEAVE ME ALONE.
A crow crying is already laughing.

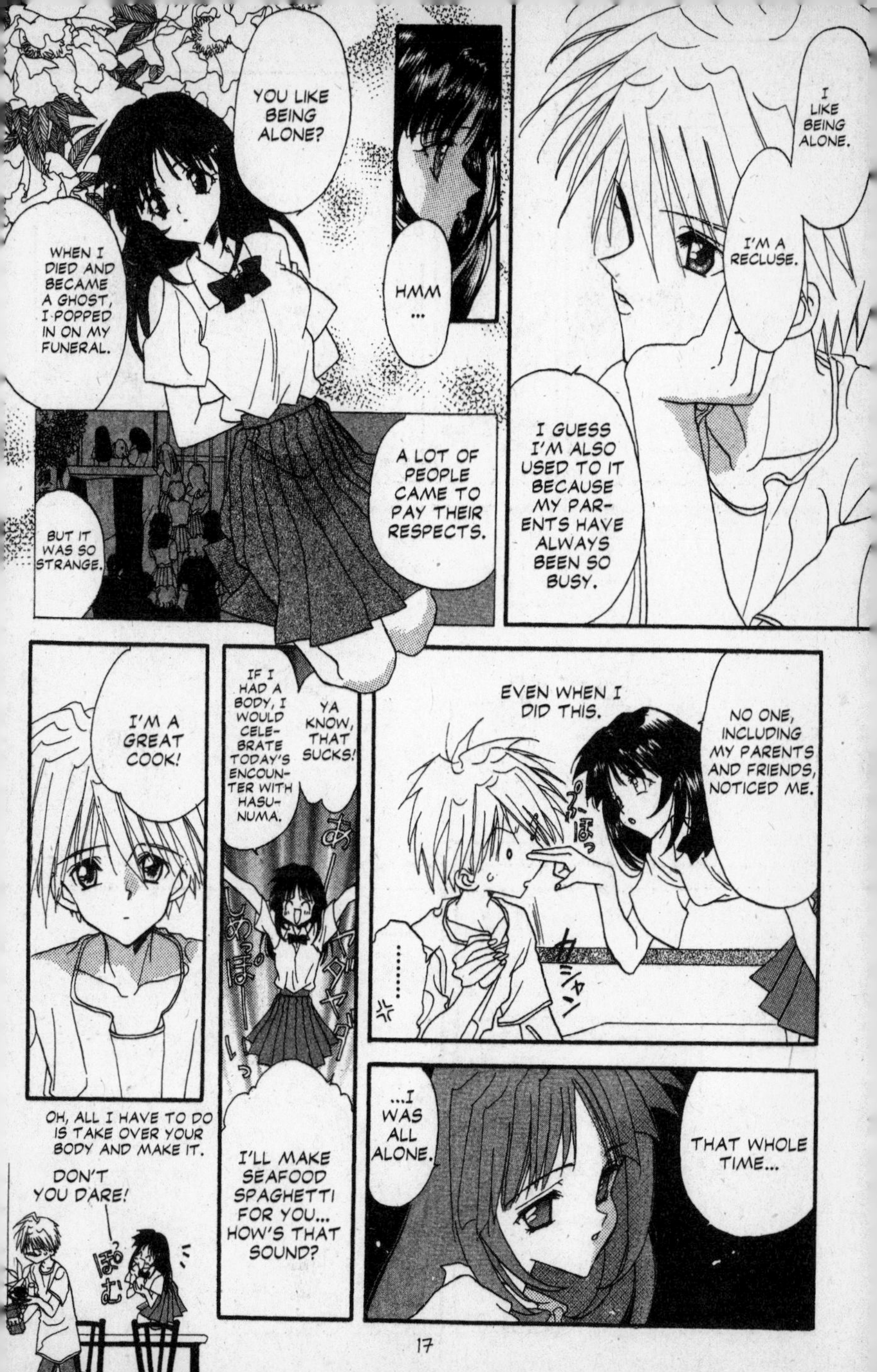
I LIKE BEING ALONE.
I'M A RECLUSE.
I GUESS I'M ALSO USED TO IT BECAUSE MY PARENTS HAVE ALWAYS BEEN SO BUSY.
HMM ...
YOU LIKE BEING ALONE?
WHEN I DIED AND BECAME A GHOST, I POPPED IN ON MY FUNERAL.
A LOT OF PEOPLE CAME TO PAY THEIR RESPECTS.
BUT IT WAS SO STRANGE.
NO ONE, INCLUDING MY PARENTS AND FRIENDS, NOTICED ME.
EVEN WHEN I DID THIS.
......
THAT WHOLE TIME...
...I WAS ALL ALONE.
YA KNOW, THAT SUCKS!
IF I HAD A BODY, I WOULD CELEBRATE TODAY'S ENCOUNTER WITH HASUNUMA.
I'LL MAKE SEAFOOD SPAGHETTI FOR YOU... HOW'S THAT SOUND?
I'M A GREAT COOK!
OH, ALL I HAVE TO DO IS TAKE OVER YOUR BODY AND MAKE IT.
DON'T YOU DARE!

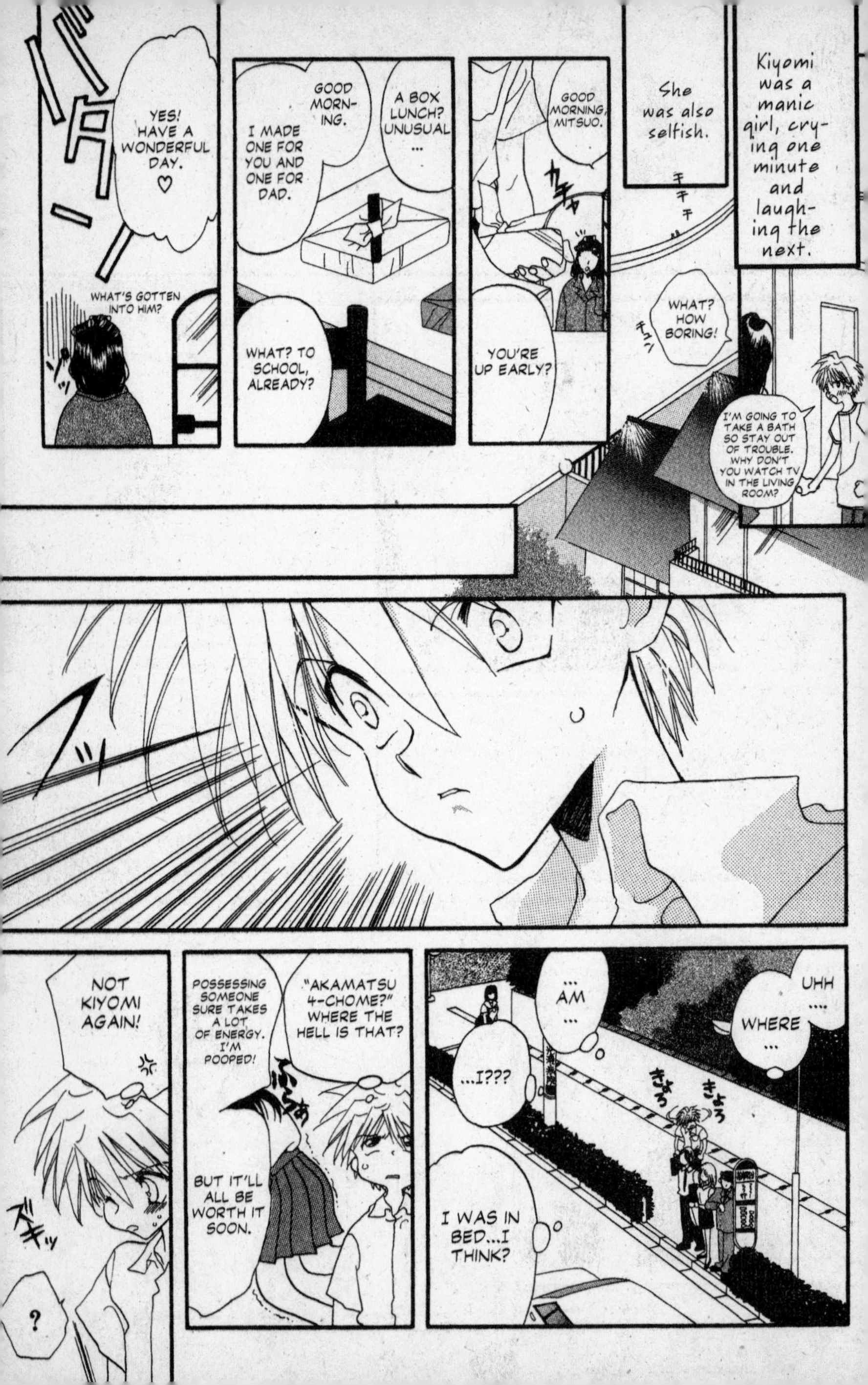
Kiyomi was a manic girl, crying one minute and laughing the next.
She was also selfish.
I'M GOING TO TAKE A BATH SO STAY OUT OF TROUBLE. WHY DON'T YOU WATCH TV IN THE LIVING ROOM?
WHAT? HOW BORING!
GOOD MORNING, MITSUO.
YOU'RE UP EARLY?
A BOX LUNCH? UNUSUAL...
GOOD MORNING.
I MADE ONE FOR YOU AND ONE FOR DAD.
WHAT? TO SCHOOL, ALREADY?
YES! HAVE A WONDERFUL DAY. ♡
WHAT'S GOTTEN INTO HIM?
UHH .... WHERE ...
... AM ...
...I???
I WAS IN BED...I THINK?
"AKAMATSU 4-CHOME?" WHERE THE HELL IS THAT?
POSSESSING SOMEONE SURE TAKES A LOT OF ENERGY. I'M POOPED!
BUT IT'LL ALL BE WORTH IT SOON.
NOT KIYOMI AGAIN!
?

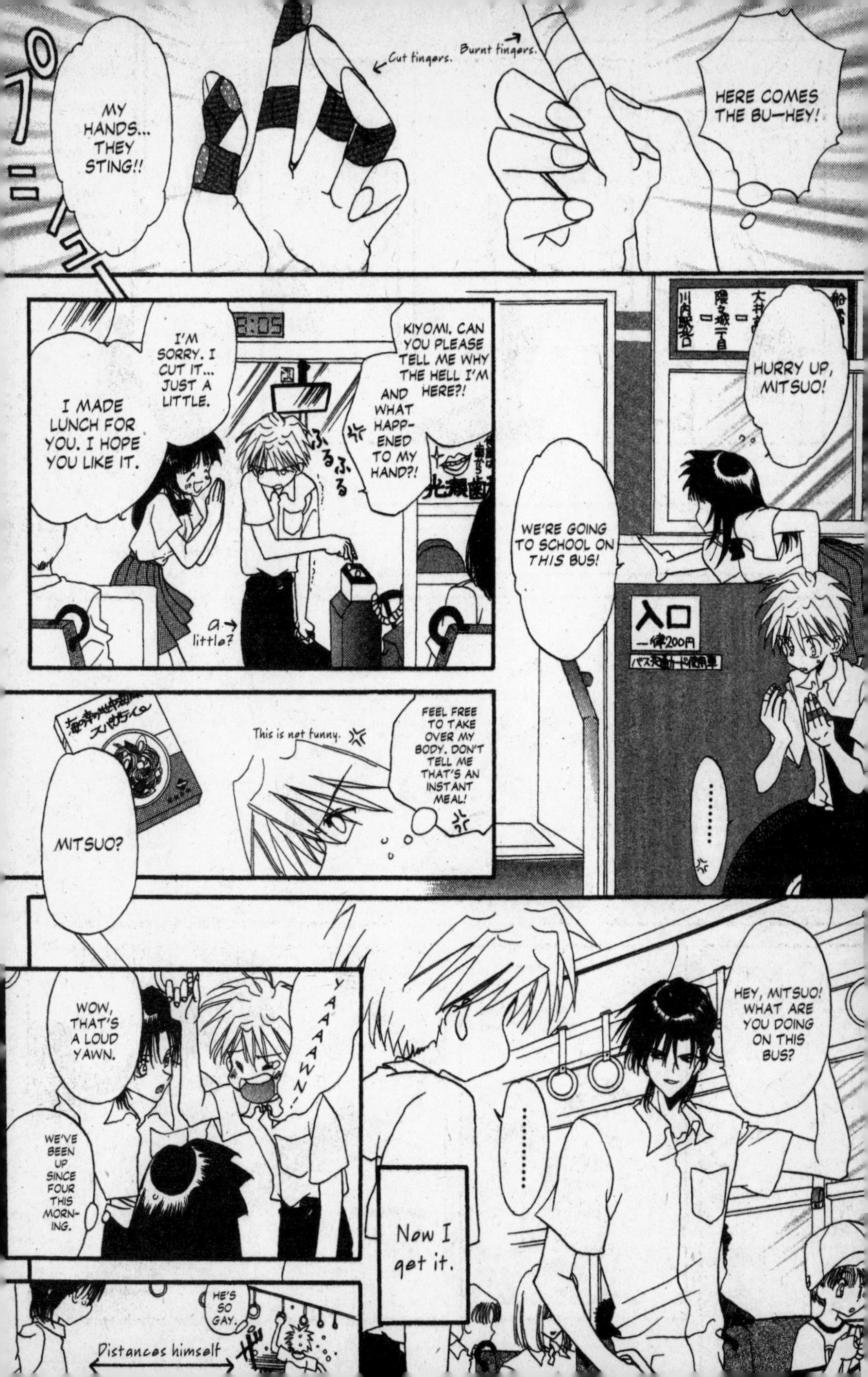
HERE COMES THE BU—HEY!
Burnt fingers.
Cut fingers.
MY HANDS... THEY STING!!
HURRY UP, MITSUO!
WE'RE GOING TO SCHOOL ON THIS BUS!
入口
一律200円
......
KIYOMI. CAN YOU PLEASE TELL ME WHY THE HELL I'M HERE?!
AND WHAT HAPPENED TO MY HAND?!
ふるふる
I'M SORRY. I CUT IT... JUST A LITTLE.
I MADE LUNCH FOR YOU. I HOPE YOU LIKE IT.
a little?
FEEL FREE TO TAKE OVER MY BODY. DON'T TELL ME THAT'S AN INSTANT MEAL!
This is not funny.
MITSUO?
HEY, MITSUO! WHAT ARE YOU DOING ON THIS BUS?
......
Now I get it.
YAAAAAWN!
WOW, THAT'S A LOUD YAWN.
WE'VE BEEN UP SINCE FOUR THIS MORNING.
HE'S SO GAY.
Distances himself

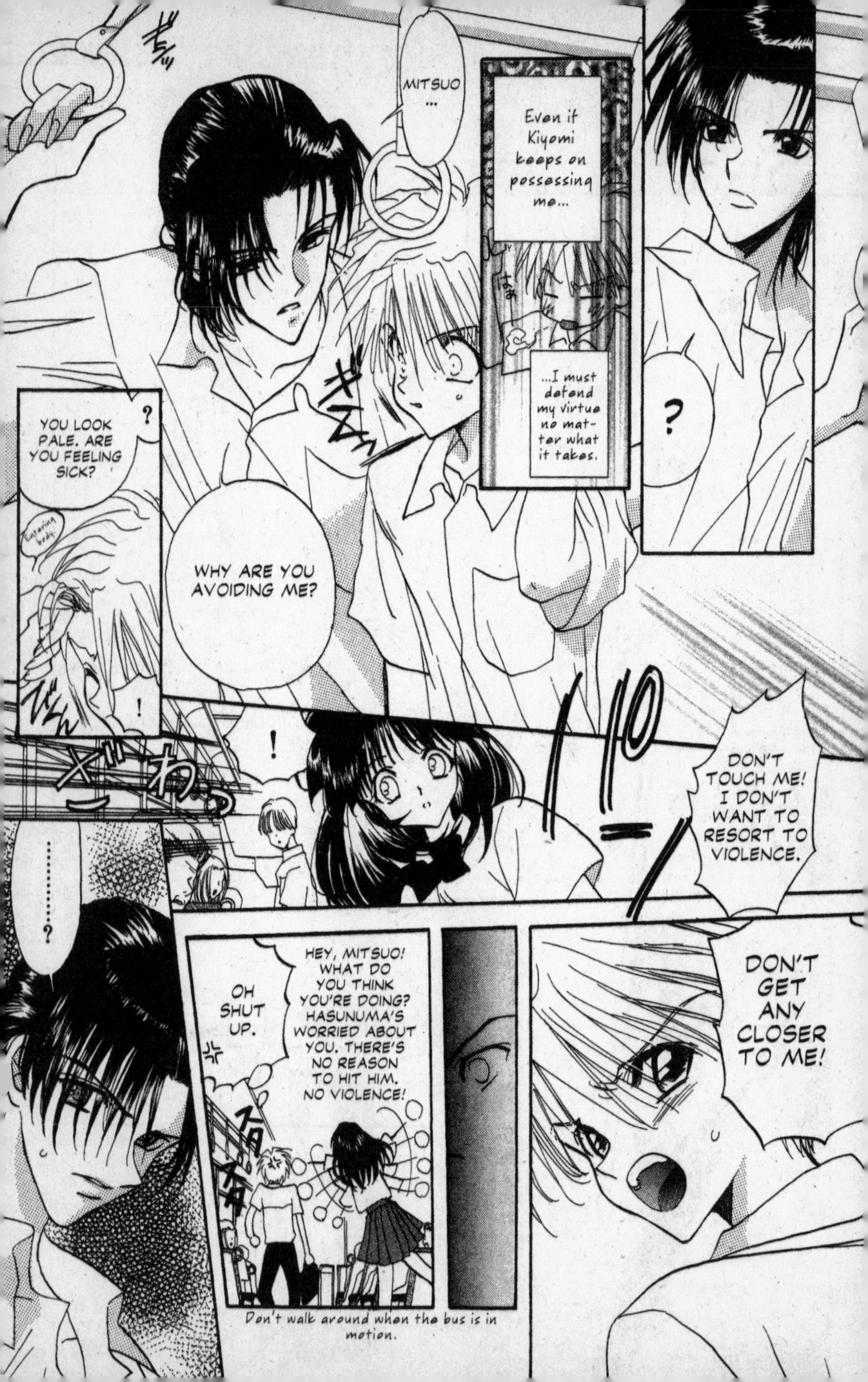
MITSUO ...
Even if Kiyomi keeps on possessing me...
?
...I must defend my virtue no matter what it takes.
YOU LOOK PALE. ARE YOU FEELING SICK?
?
Entering body.
WHY ARE YOU AVOIDING ME?
!
DON'T TOUCH ME! I DON'T WANT TO RESORT TO VIOLENCE.
!
DON'T GET ANY CLOSER TO ME!
HEY, MITSUO! WHAT DO YOU THINK YOU'RE DOING? HASUNUMA'S WORRIED ABOUT YOU. THERE'S NO REASON TO HIT HIM. NO VIOLENCE!
OH SHUT UP.
Don't walk around when the bus is in motion.
......?

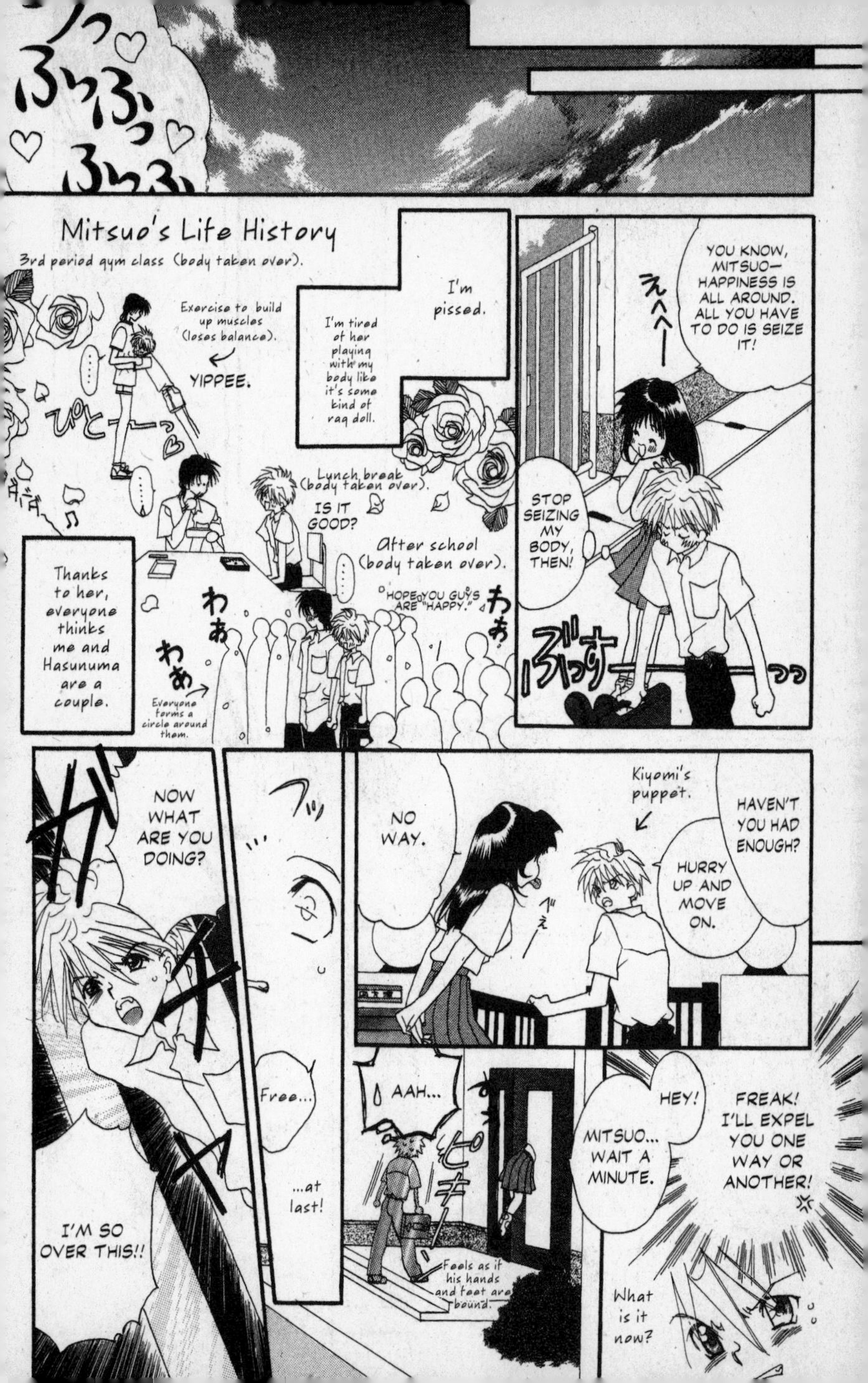

ふっふっ ふっふっ
YOU KNOW, MITSUO— HAPPINESS IS ALL AROUND. ALL YOU HAVE TO DO IS SEIZE IT!
えへへー
STOP SEIZING MY BODY, THEN!
ぶっすーっ
I'm pissed.
I'm tired of her playing with my body like it's some kind of rag doll.
Mitsuo's Life History
3rd period gym class (body taken over).
Exercise to build up muscles (loses balance).
YIPPEE.
......
ぴとーっ
......
Lunch break (body taken over).
IS IT GOOD?
......
After school (body taken over).
HOPE YOU GUYS ARE "HAPPY."
わあ
わあ
わあ
Everyone forms a circle around them.
Thanks to her, everyone thinks me and Hasunuma are a couple.
HAVEN'T YOU HAD ENOUGH?
Kiyomi's puppet.
HURRY UP AND MOVE ON.
NO WAY.
べぇー
FREAK! I'LL EXPEL YOU ONE WAY OR ANOTHER!
HEY!
MITSUO... WAIT A MINUTE.
What is it now?
AAH...
ピキーン
Feels as if his hands and feet are bound.
フッ
Free...
...at last!
NOW WHAT ARE YOU DOING?
I'M SO OVER THIS!!

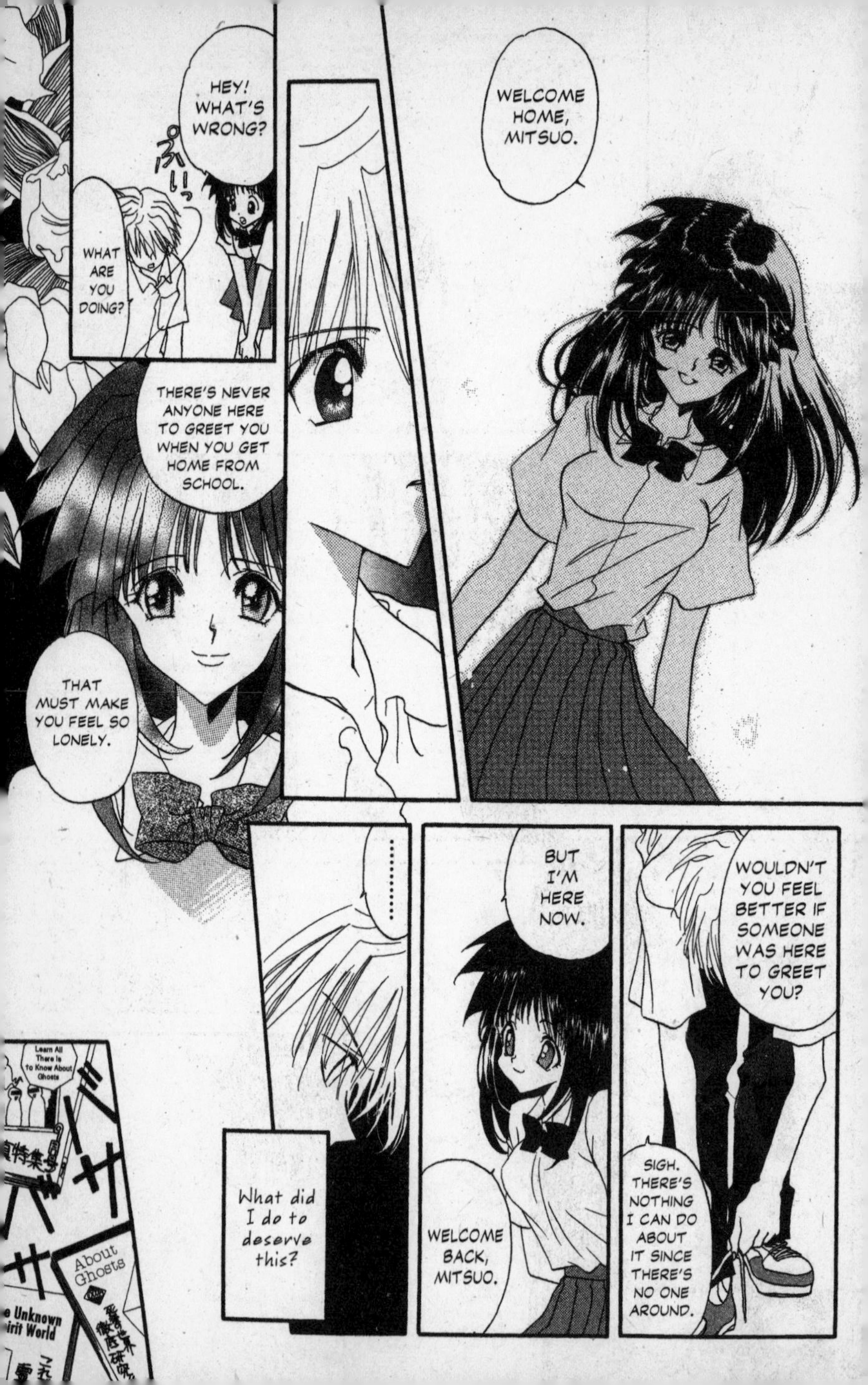
WELCOME HOME, MITSUO.
HEY! WHAT'S WRONG?
ぷいっ
WHAT ARE YOU DOING?
THERE'S NEVER ANYONE HERE TO GREET YOU WHEN YOU GET HOME FROM SCHOOL.
THAT MUST MAKE YOU FEEL SO LONELY.
WOULDN'T YOU FEEL BETTER IF SOMEONE WAS HERE TO GREET YOU?
SIGH. THERE'S NOTHING I CAN DO ABOUT IT SINCE THERE'S NO ONE AROUND.
BUT I'M HERE NOW.
WELCOME BACK, MITSUO.
......
What did I do to deserve this?
Learn All There Is to Know About Ghosts
About Ghosts

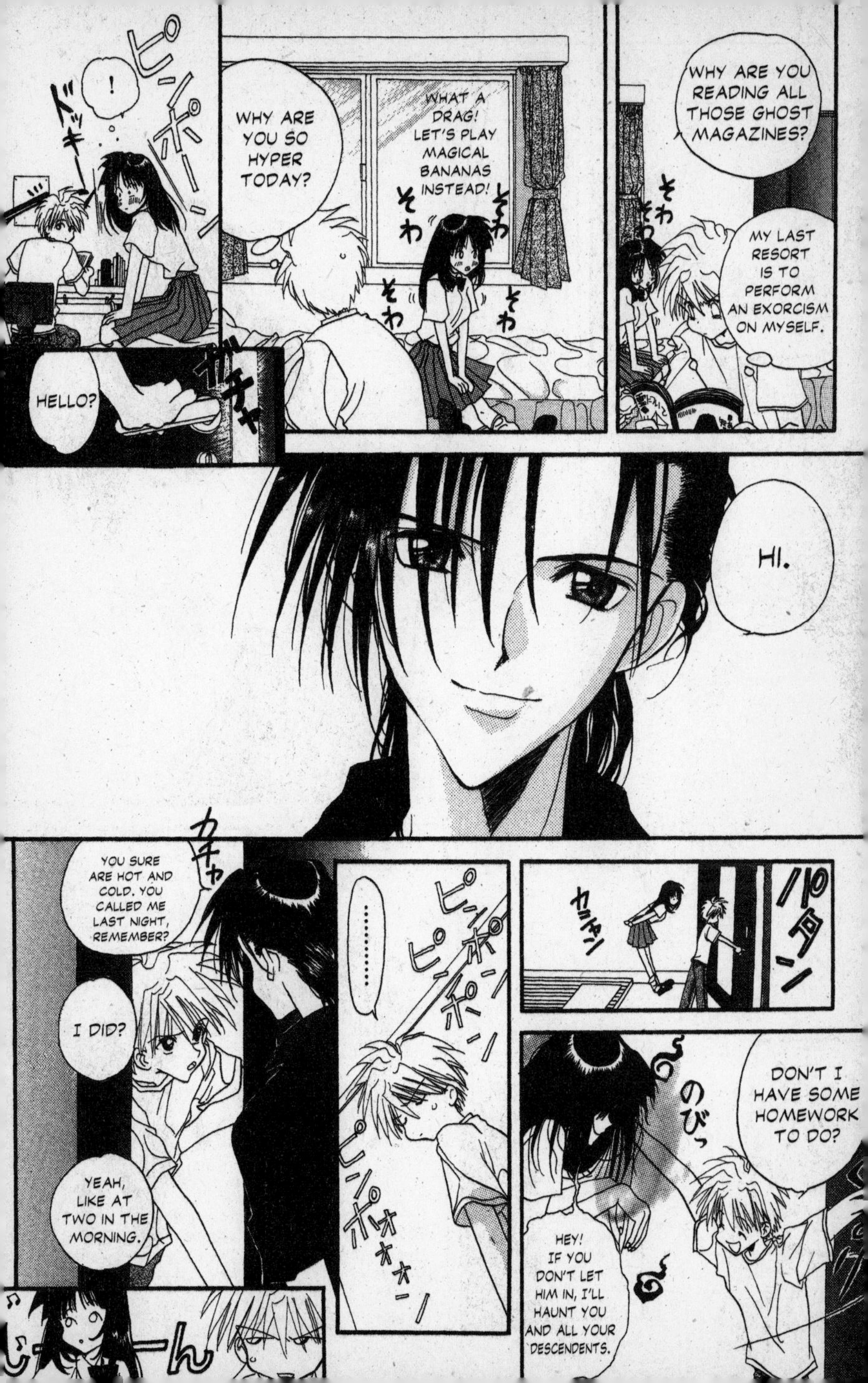
WHY ARE YOU READING ALL THOSE GHOST MAGAZINES?
そわそわ
MY LAST RESORT IS TO PERFORM AN EXORCISM ON MYSELF.
WHY ARE YOU SO HYPER TODAY?
WHAT A DRAG! LET'S PLAY MAGICAL BANANAS INSTEAD!
そわ
そわ
そわ
そわ
ピーンポーン
ドッキー
!
ガチャ
HELLO?
HI.
パタン
カチャン
DON'T I HAVE SOME HOMEWORK TO DO?
のびっ
HEY! IF YOU DON'T LET HIM IN, I'LL HAUNT YOU AND ALL YOUR DESCENDENTS.
……
ピンポーン
ピンポーン
ピンポオオオーン
カチャ
YOU SURE ARE HOT AND COLD. YOU CALLED ME LAST NIGHT, REMEMBER?
I DID?
YEAH, LIKE AT TWO IN THE MORNING.
じーん

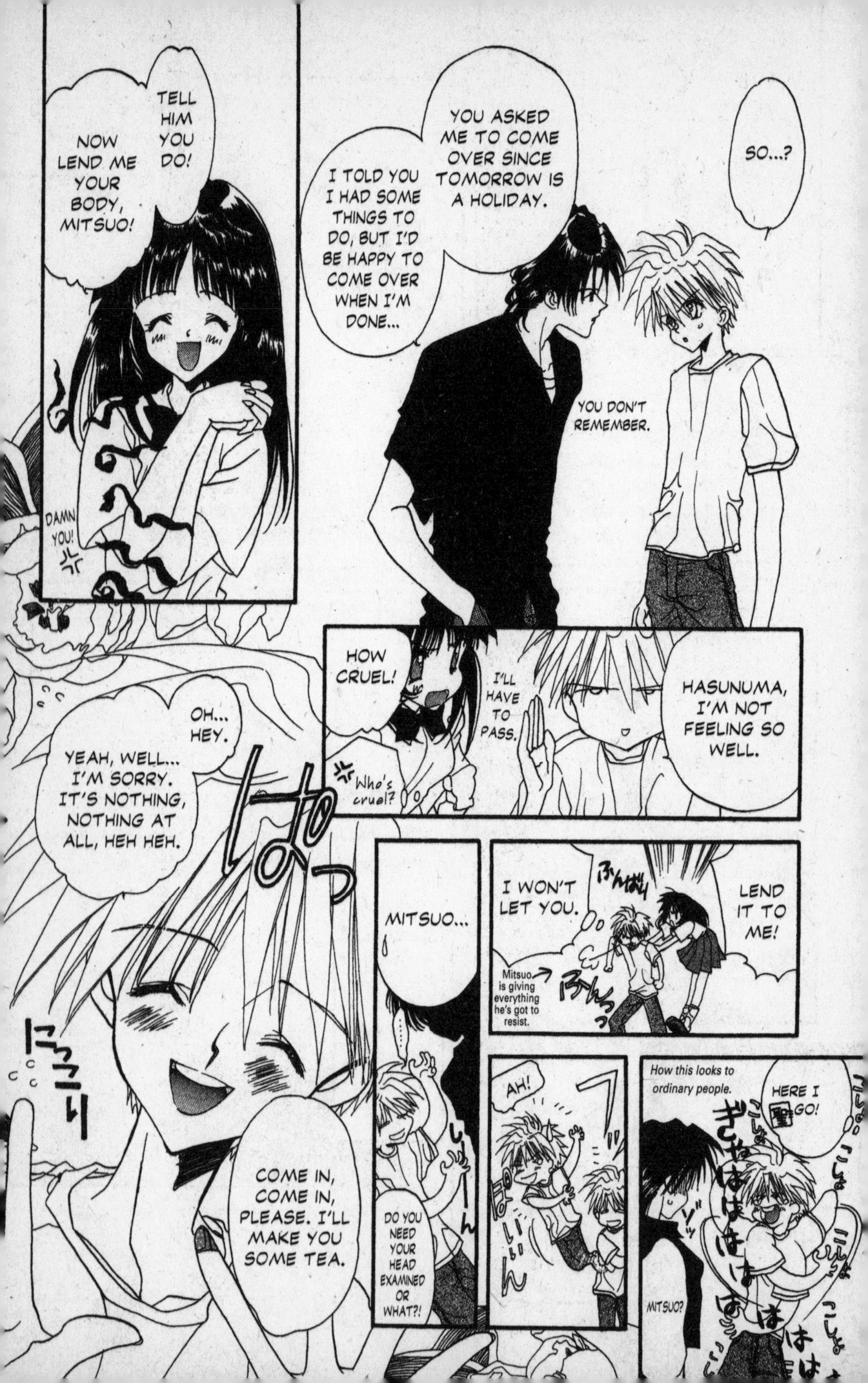
SO...?
YOU ASKED ME TO COME OVER SINCE TOMORROW IS A HOLIDAY.
I TOLD YOU I HAD SOME THINGS TO DO, BUT I'D BE HAPPY TO COME OVER WHEN I'M DONE...
YOU DON'T REMEMBER.
TELL HIM YOU DO!
NOW LEND ME YOUR BODY, MITSUO!
DAMN YOU!
HASUNUMA, I'M NOT FEELING SO WELL.
I'LL HAVE TO PASS.
HOW CRUEL!
Who's cruel?
LEND IT TO ME!
I WON'T LET YOU.
Mitsuo is giving everything he's got to resist.
MITSUO...
How this looks to ordinary people.
HERE I GO!
MITSUO?
AH!
DO YOU NEED YOUR HEAD EXAMINED OR WHAT?!
OH... HEY.
YEAH, WELL... I'M SORRY. IT'S NOTHING, NOTHING AT ALL, HEH HEH.
COME IN, COME IN, PLEASE. I'LL MAKE YOU SOME TEA.

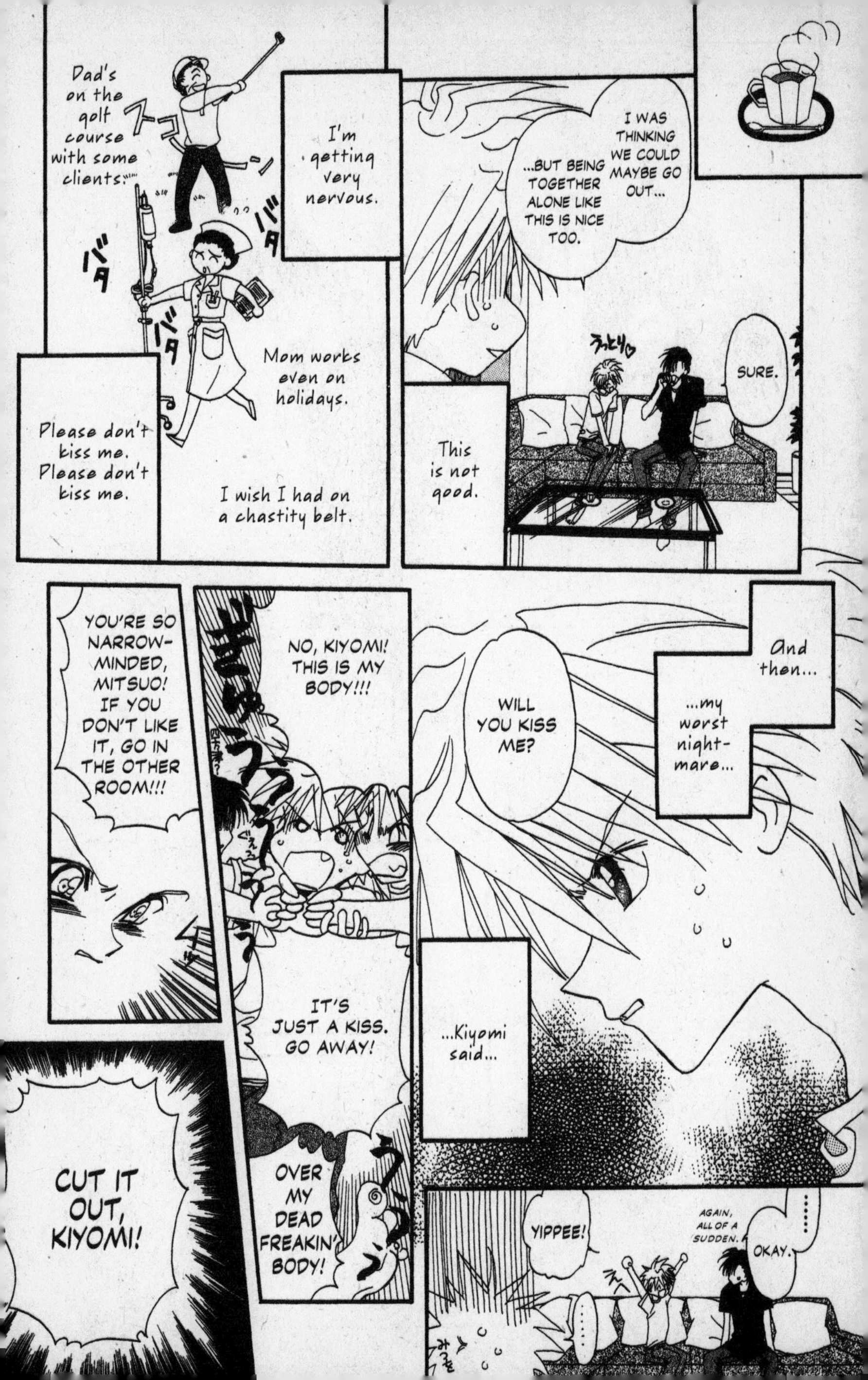
I WAS THINKING WE COULD MAYBE GO OUT...
...BUT BEING TOGETHER ALONE LIKE THIS IS NICE TOO.
I'm getting very nervous.
Dad's on the golf course with some clients...
Mom works even on holidays.
I wish I had on a chastity belt.
Please don't kiss me. Please don't kiss me.
SURE.
This is not good.
And then...
...my worst nightmare...
WILL YOU KISS ME?
...Kiyomi said...
......
AGAIN, ALL OF A SUDDEN.
OKAY.
YIPPEE!
NO, KIYOMI! THIS IS MY BODY!!!
IT'S JUST A KISS. GO AWAY!
OVER MY DEAD FREAKIN' BODY!
YOU'RE SO NARROW-MINDED, MITSUO! IF YOU DON'T LIKE IT, GO IN THE OTHER ROOM!!!
CUT IT OUT, KIYOMI!

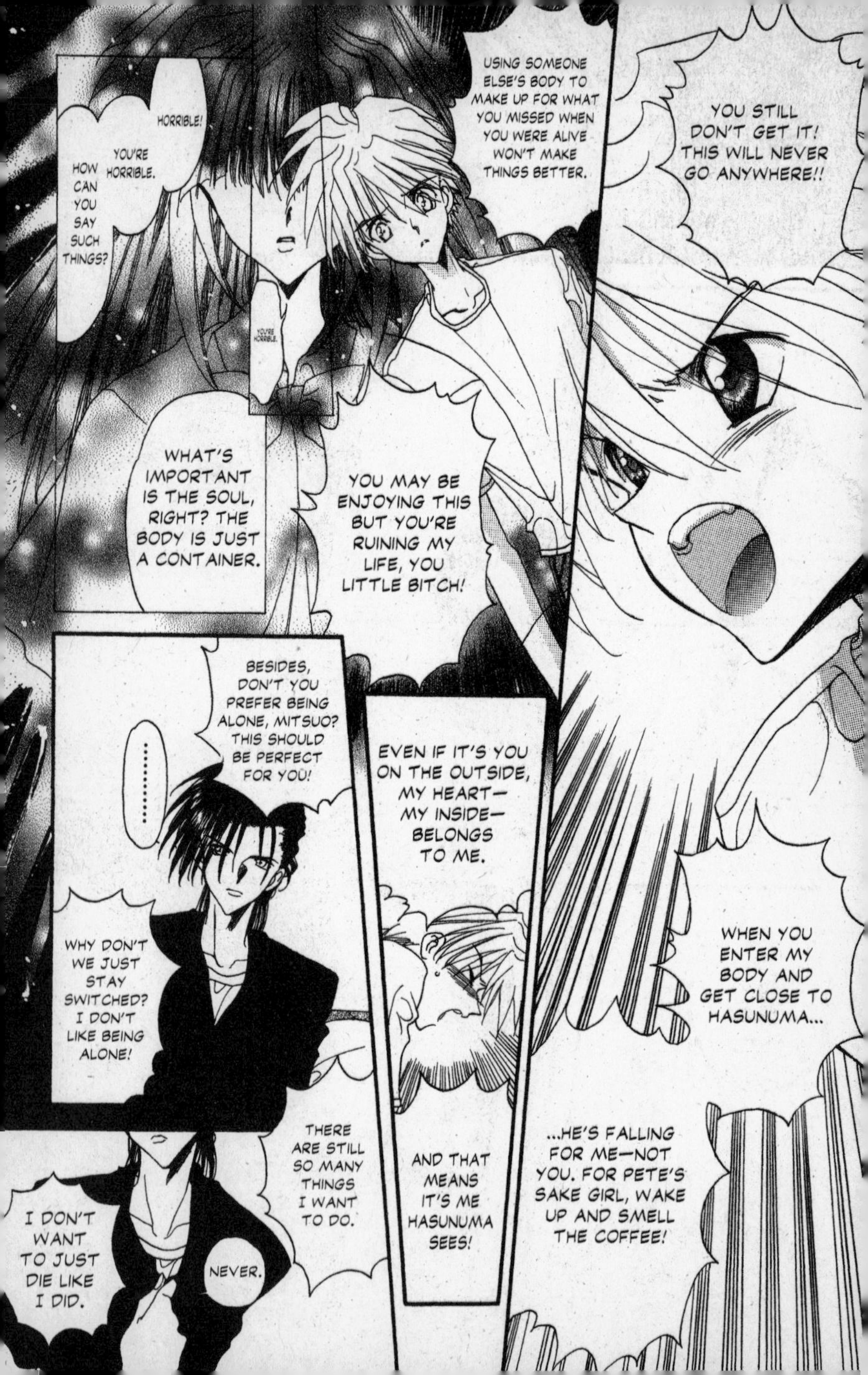
YOU STILL DON'T GET IT! THIS WILL NEVER GO ANYWHERE!!
WHEN YOU ENTER MY BODY AND GET CLOSE TO HASUNUMA...
...HE'S FALLING FOR ME—NOT YOU. FOR PETE'S SAKE GIRL, WAKE UP AND SMELL THE COFFEE!
USING SOMEONE ELSE'S BODY TO MAKE UP FOR WHAT YOU MISSED WHEN YOU WERE ALIVE WON'T MAKE THINGS BETTER.
HORRIBLE!
YOU'RE HORRIBLE.
HOW CAN YOU SAY SUCH THINGS?
YOU'RE HORRIBLE.
WHAT'S IMPORTANT IS THE SOUL, RIGHT? THE BODY IS JUST A CONTAINER.
YOU MAY BE ENJOYING THIS BUT YOU'RE RUINING MY LIFE, YOU LITTLE BITCH!
EVEN IF IT'S YOU ON THE OUTSIDE, MY HEART—MY INSIDE—BELONGS TO ME.
AND THAT MEANS IT'S ME HASUNUMA SEES!
BESIDES, DON'T YOU PREFER BEING ALONE, MITSUO? THIS SHOULD BE PERFECT FOR YOU!
....
WHY DON'T WE JUST STAY SWITCHED? I DON'T LIKE BEING ALONE!
THERE ARE STILL SO MANY THINGS I WANT TO DO.
I DON'T WANT TO JUST DIE LIKE I DID.
NEVER.

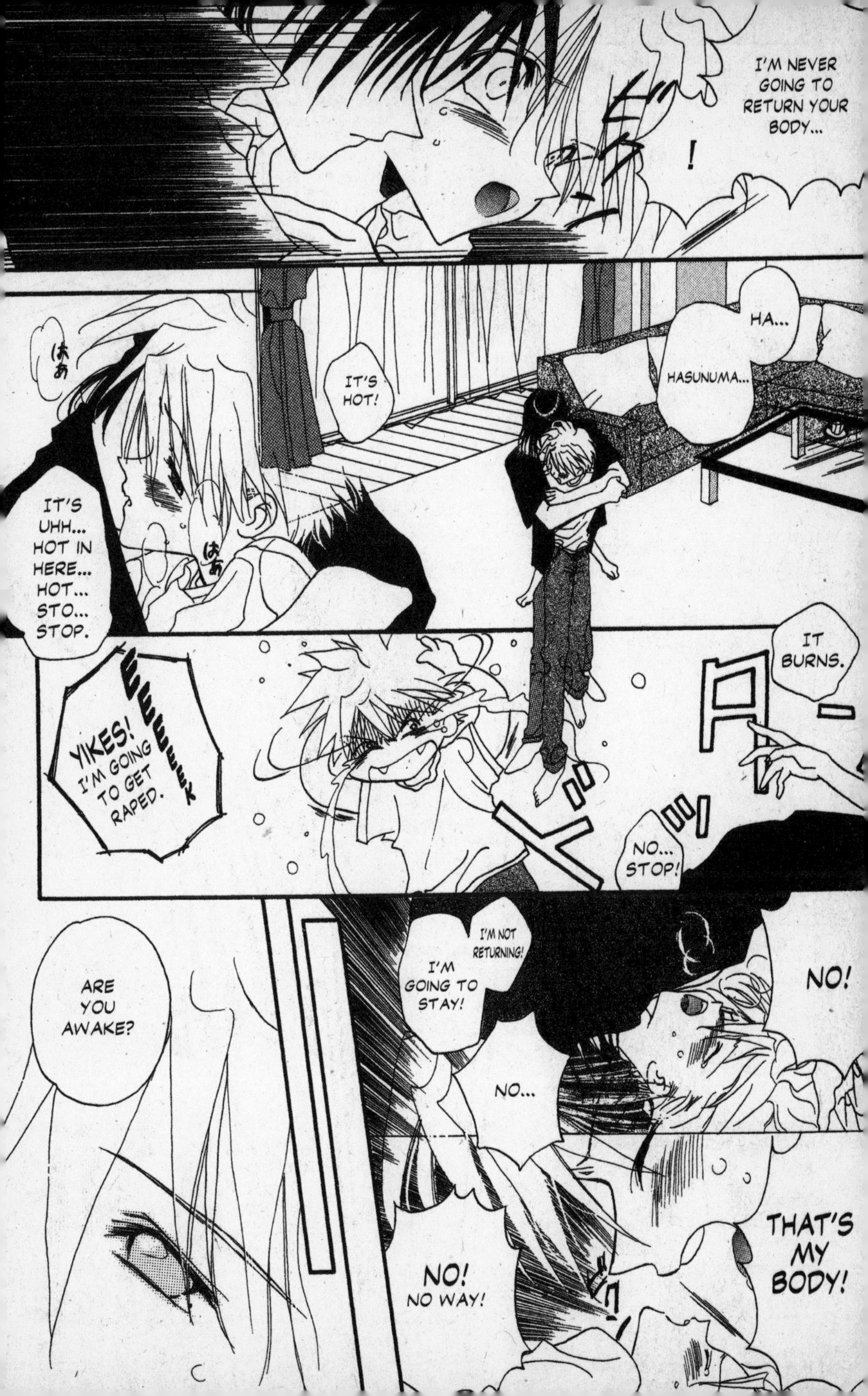
I'M NEVER GOING TO RETURN YOUR BODY...
!
HA... HASUNUMA...
IT'S HOT!
はあ
IT'S UHHH... HOT IN HERE... HOT... STO... STOP.
はあ
IT BURNS.
NO... STOP!
YIKES! I'M GOING TO GET RAPED.
NO!
I'M NOT RETURNING!
I'M GOING TO STAY!
NO...
THAT'S MY BODY!
NO! NO WAY!
ARE YOU AWAKE?

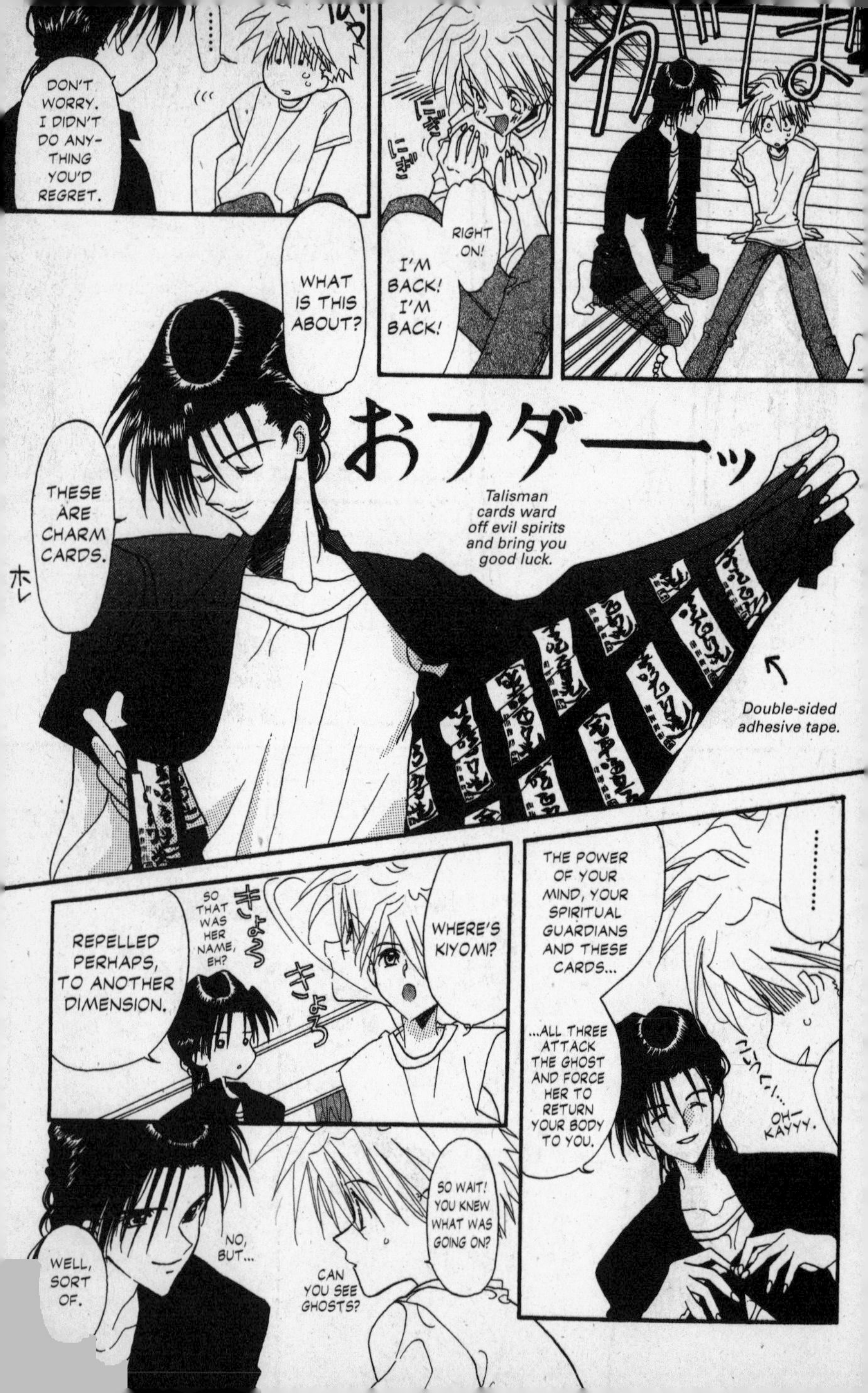
にぎにぎ
RIGHT ON!
I'M BACK! I'M BACK!
......
DON'T WORRY. I DIDN'T DO ANYTHING YOU'D REGRET.
WHAT IS THIS ABOUT?
おフダーッ
Talisman cards ward off evil spirits and bring you good luck.
THESE ARE CHARM CARDS.
ホレ
Double-sided adhesive tape.
......
THE POWER OF YOUR MIND, YOUR SPIRITUAL GUARDIANS AND THESE CARDS...
...ALL THREE ATTACK THE GHOST AND FORCE HER TO RETURN YOUR BODY TO YOU.
OH-KAYYY.
WHERE'S KIYOMI?
きょろきょろ
SO THAT WAS HER NAME, EH?
REPELLED PERHAPS, TO ANOTHER DIMENSION.
SO WAIT! YOU KNEW WHAT WAS GOING ON?
CAN YOU SEE GHOSTS?
NO, BUT...
WELL, SORT OF.

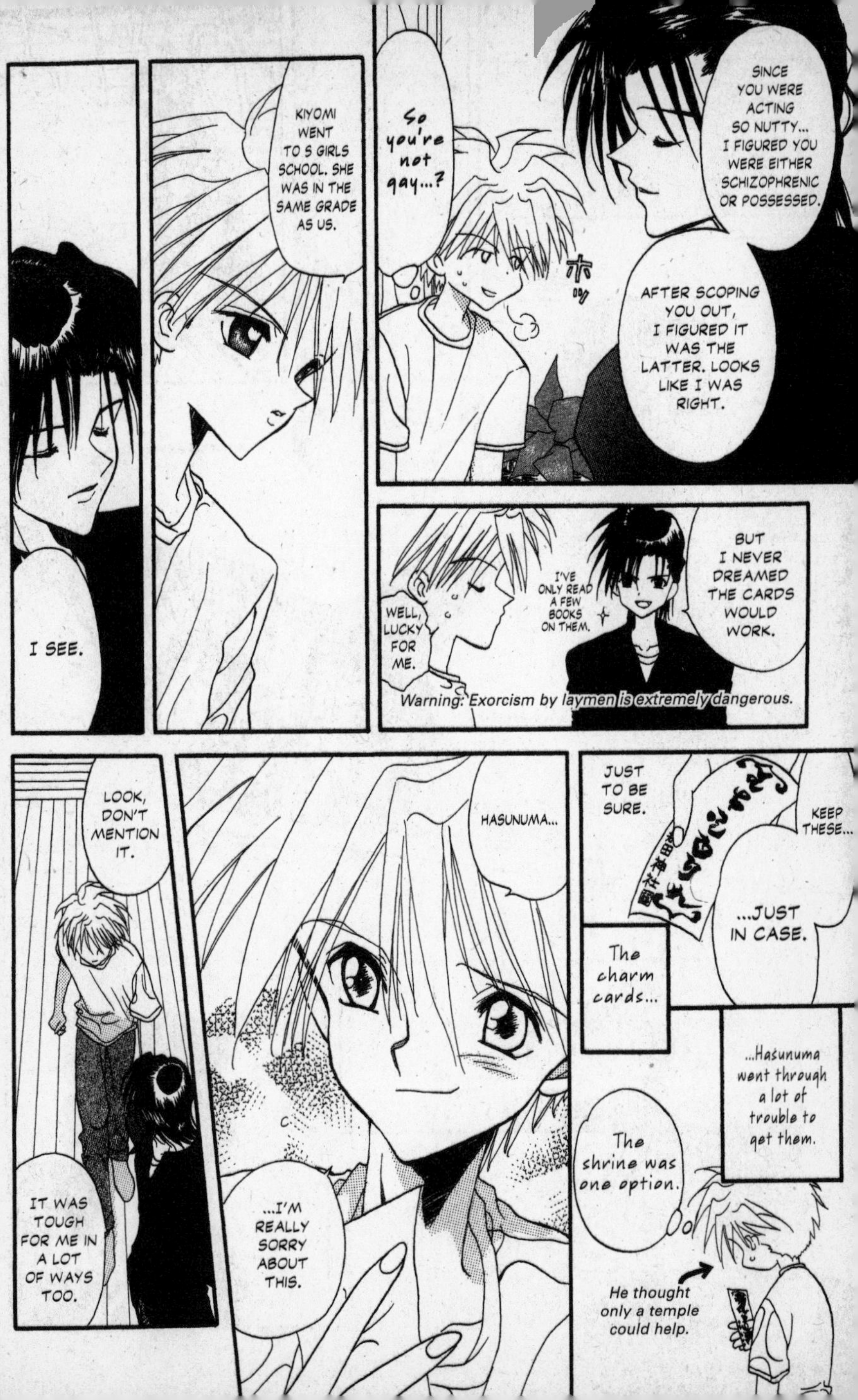
SINCE YOU WERE ACTING SO NUTTY... I FIGURED YOU WERE EITHER SCHIZOPHRENIC OR POSSESSED.
AFTER SCOPING YOU OUT, I FIGURED IT WAS THE LATTER. LOOKS LIKE I WAS RIGHT.
ホッ
So you're not gay...?
BUT I NEVER DREAMED THE CARDS WOULD WORK.
I'VE ONLY READ A FEW BOOKS ON THEM.
WELL, LUCKY FOR ME.
Warning: Exorcism by laymen is extremely dangerous.
KIYOMI WENT TO S GIRLS SCHOOL. SHE WAS IN THE SAME GRADE AS US.
I SEE.
KEEP THESE...
JUST TO BE SURE.
...JUST IN CASE.
The charm cards...
...Hasunuma went through a lot of trouble to get them.
The shrine was one option.
He thought only a temple could help.
HASUNUMA...
...I'M REALLY SORRY ABOUT THIS.
LOOK, DON'T MENTION IT.
IT WAS TOUGH FOR ME IN A LOT OF WAYS TOO.

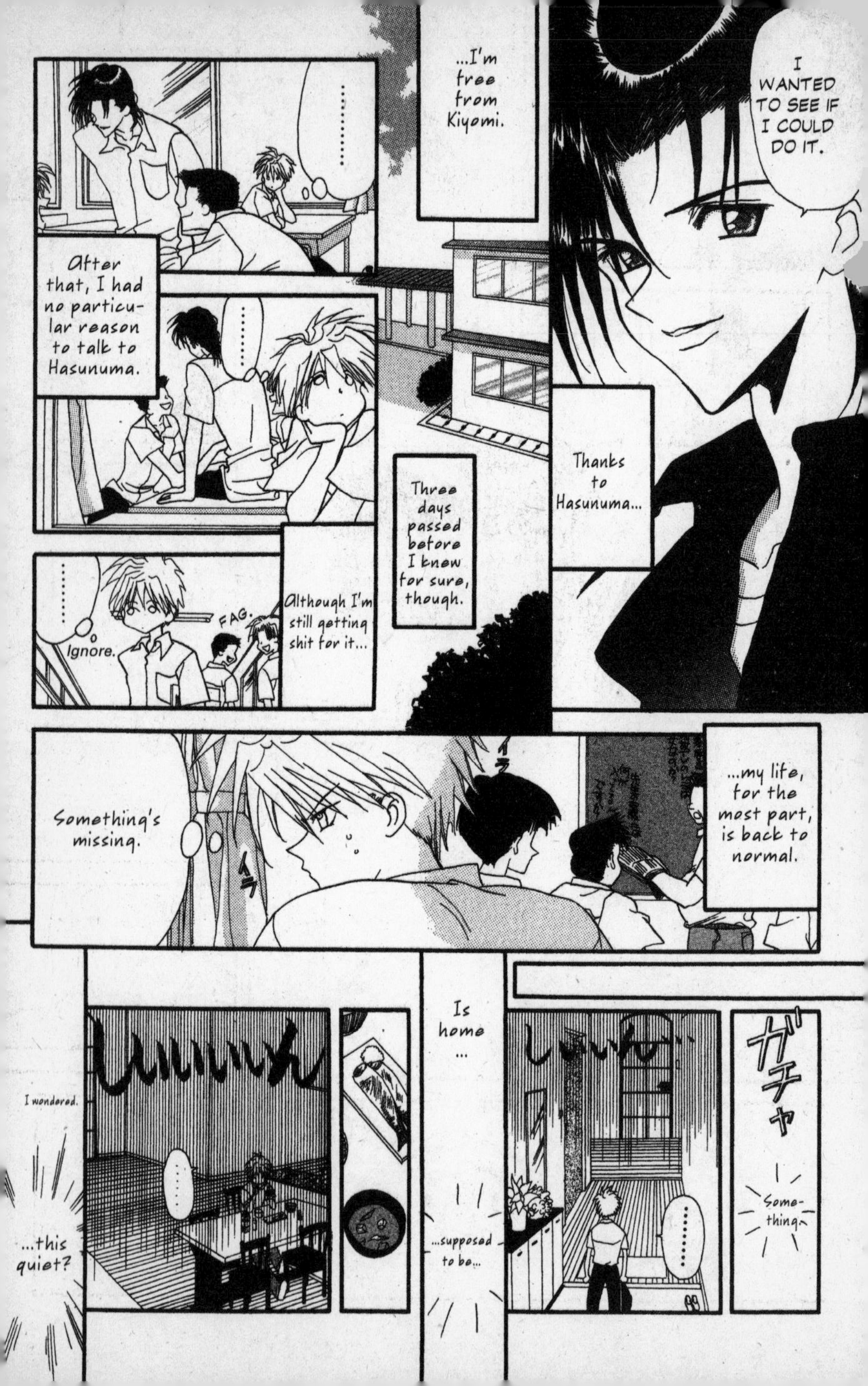
I WANTED TO SEE IF I COULD DO IT.
Thanks to Hasunuma...
...I'm free from Kiyomi.
Three days passed before I knew for sure, though.
......
After that, I had no particular reason to talk to Hasunuma.
......
Although I'm still getting shit for it...
FAG.
......
Ignore.
...my life, for the most part, is back to normal.
Something's missing.
ガチャ
Some-thing.
......
Is home ...
...supposed to be...
......
...this quiet?
I wondered.

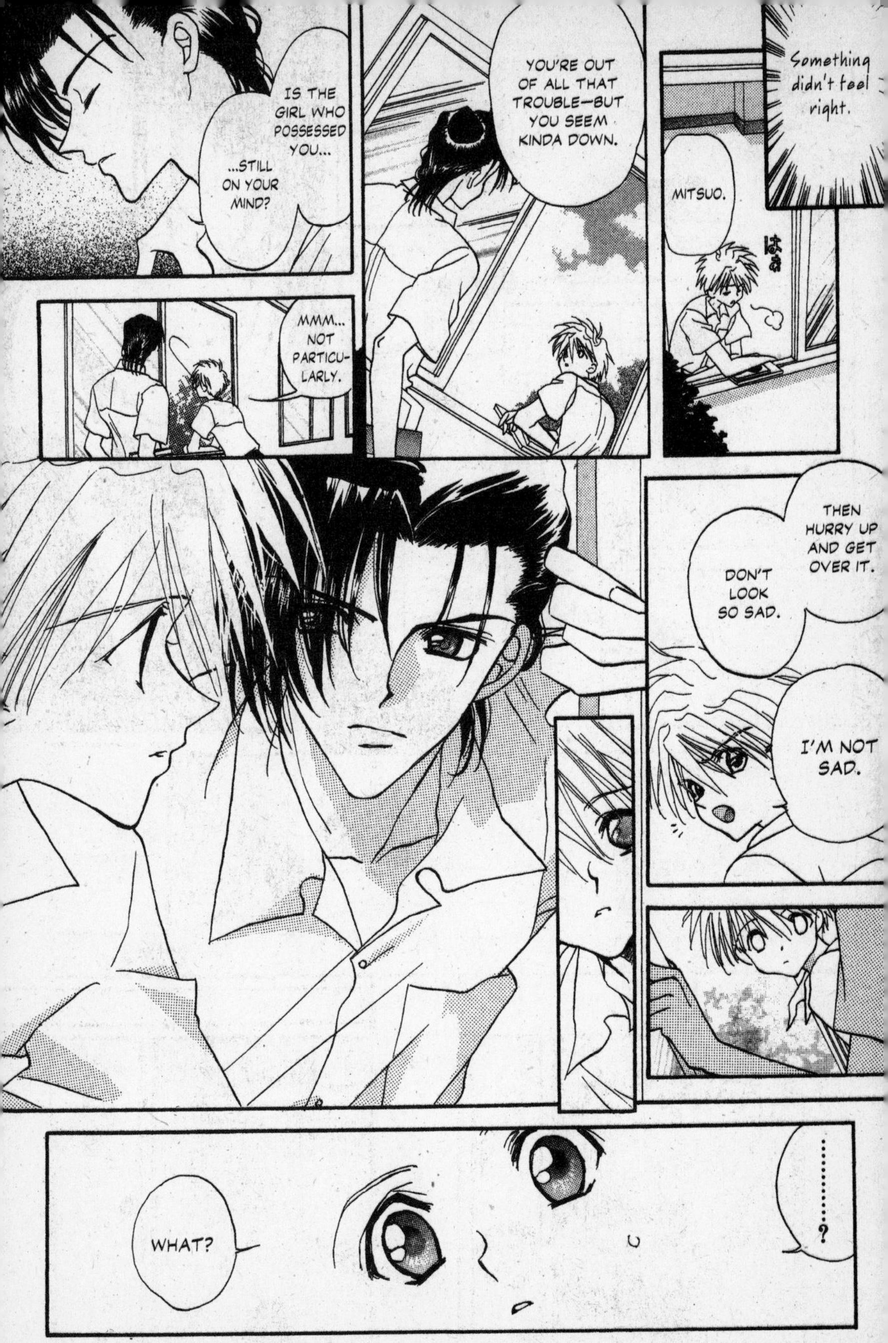
Something didn't feel right.
MITSUO.
はぁ
YOU'RE OUT OF ALL THAT TROUBLE—BUT YOU SEEM KINDA DOWN.
IS THE GIRL WHO POSSESSED YOU...
...STILL ON YOUR MIND?
MMM... NOT PARTICU-LARLY.
THEN HURRY UP AND GET OVER IT.
DON'T LOOK SO SAD.
I'M NOT SAD.
......?
WHAT?

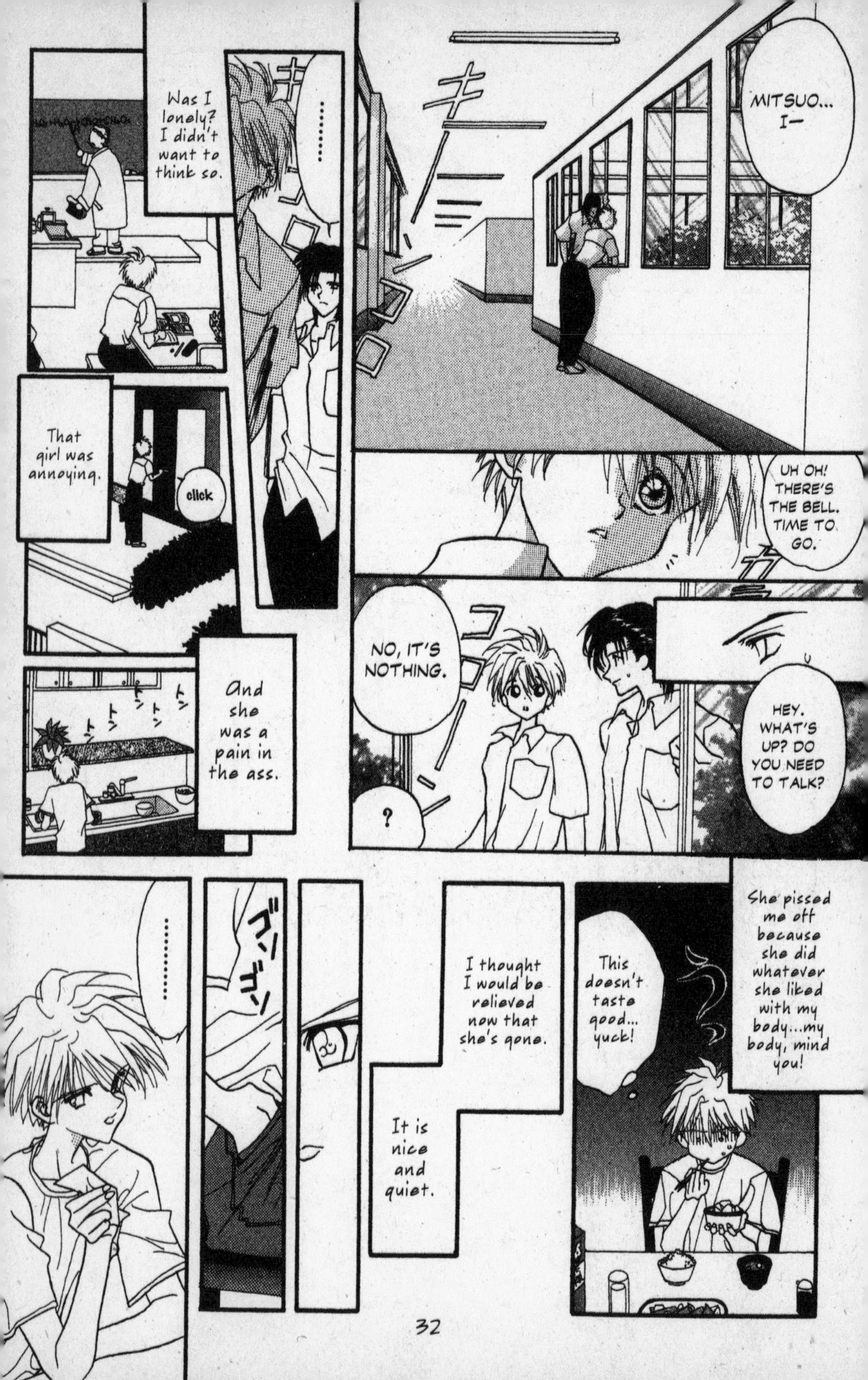
MITSUO... I—
UH OH! THERE'S THE BELL. TIME TO GO.
HEY. WHAT'S UP? DO YOU NEED TO TALK?
NO, IT'S NOTHING.
?
....
Was I lonely? I didn't want to think so.
That girl was annoying.
click
And she was a pain in the ass.
She pissed me off because she did whatever she liked with my body...my body, mind you!
This doesn't taste good... yuck!
I thought I would be relieved now that she's gone.
It is nice and quiet.
....

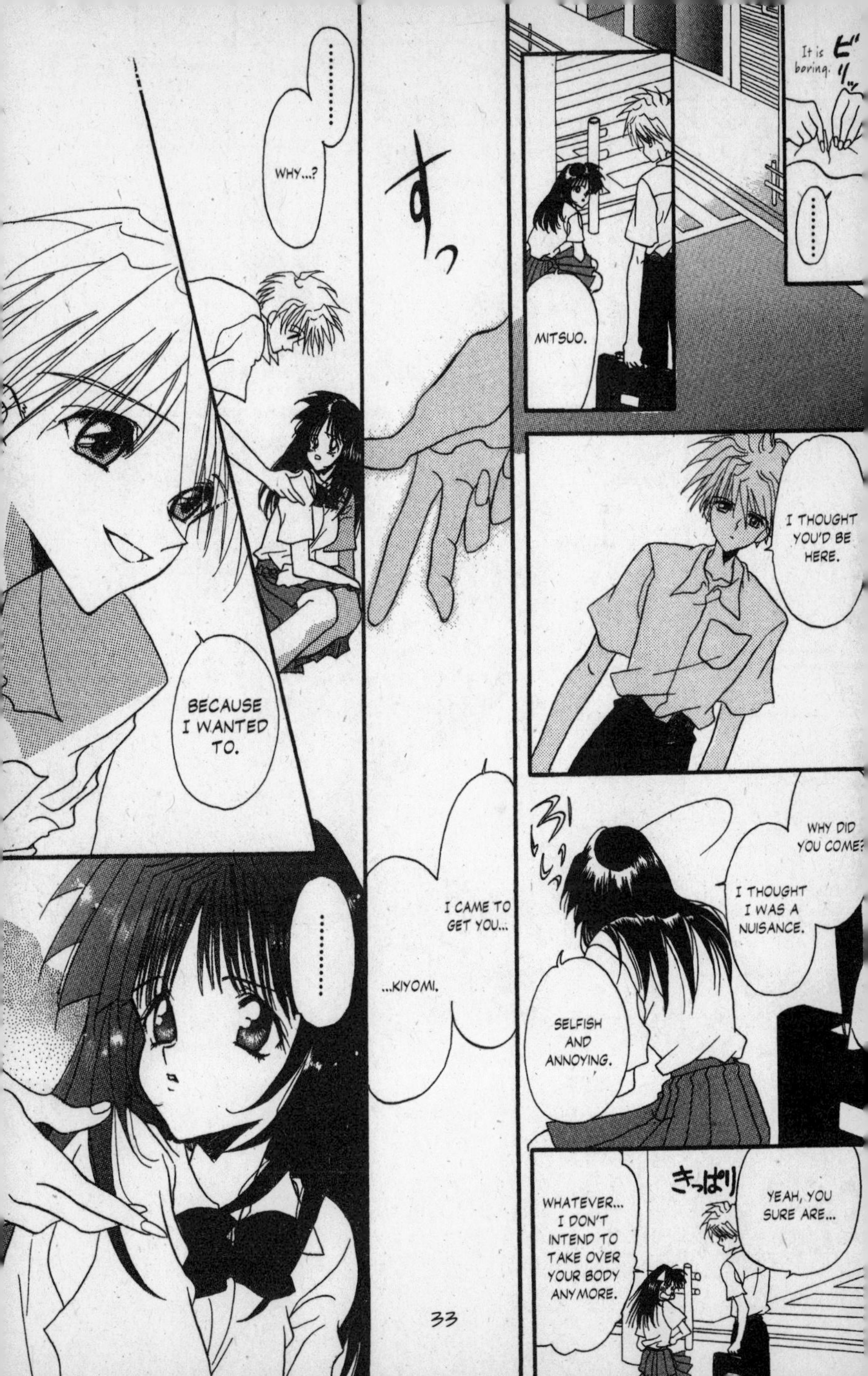
It is boring.
ビリッ
......
MITSUO.
I THOUGHT YOU'D BE HERE.
WHY DID YOU COME?
I THOUGHT I WAS A NUISANCE.
SELFISH AND ANNOYING.
YEAH, YOU SURE ARE...
きっぱり
WHATEVER... I DON'T INTEND TO TAKE OVER YOUR BODY ANYMORE.
すっ
I CAME TO GET YOU...
...KIYOMI.
......
WHY...?
BECAUSE I WANTED TO.
......

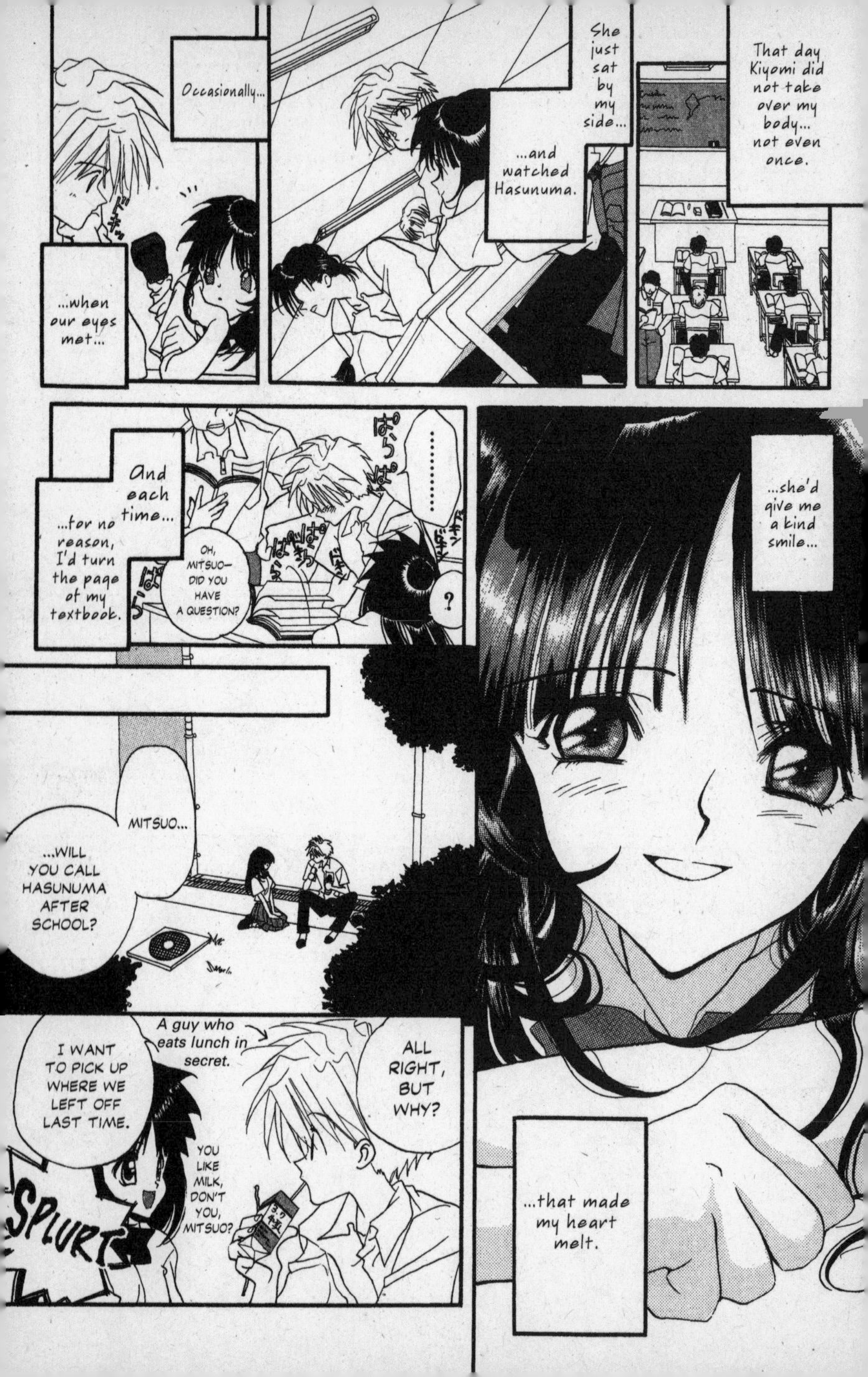
That day Kiyomi did not take over my body... not even once.
She just sat by my side...
...and watched Hasunuma.
Occasionally...
...when our eyes met...
...she'd give me a kind smile...
...that made my heart melt.
And each time...
...for no reason, I'd turn the page of my textbook.
......
OH, MITSUO—DID YOU HAVE A QUESTION?
?
MITSUO...
...WILL YOU CALL HASUNUMA AFTER SCHOOL?
ALL RIGHT, BUT WHY?
A guy who eats lunch in secret.
I WANT TO PICK UP WHERE WE LEFT OFF LAST TIME.
YOU LIKE MILK, DON'T YOU, MITSUO?
SPLURT

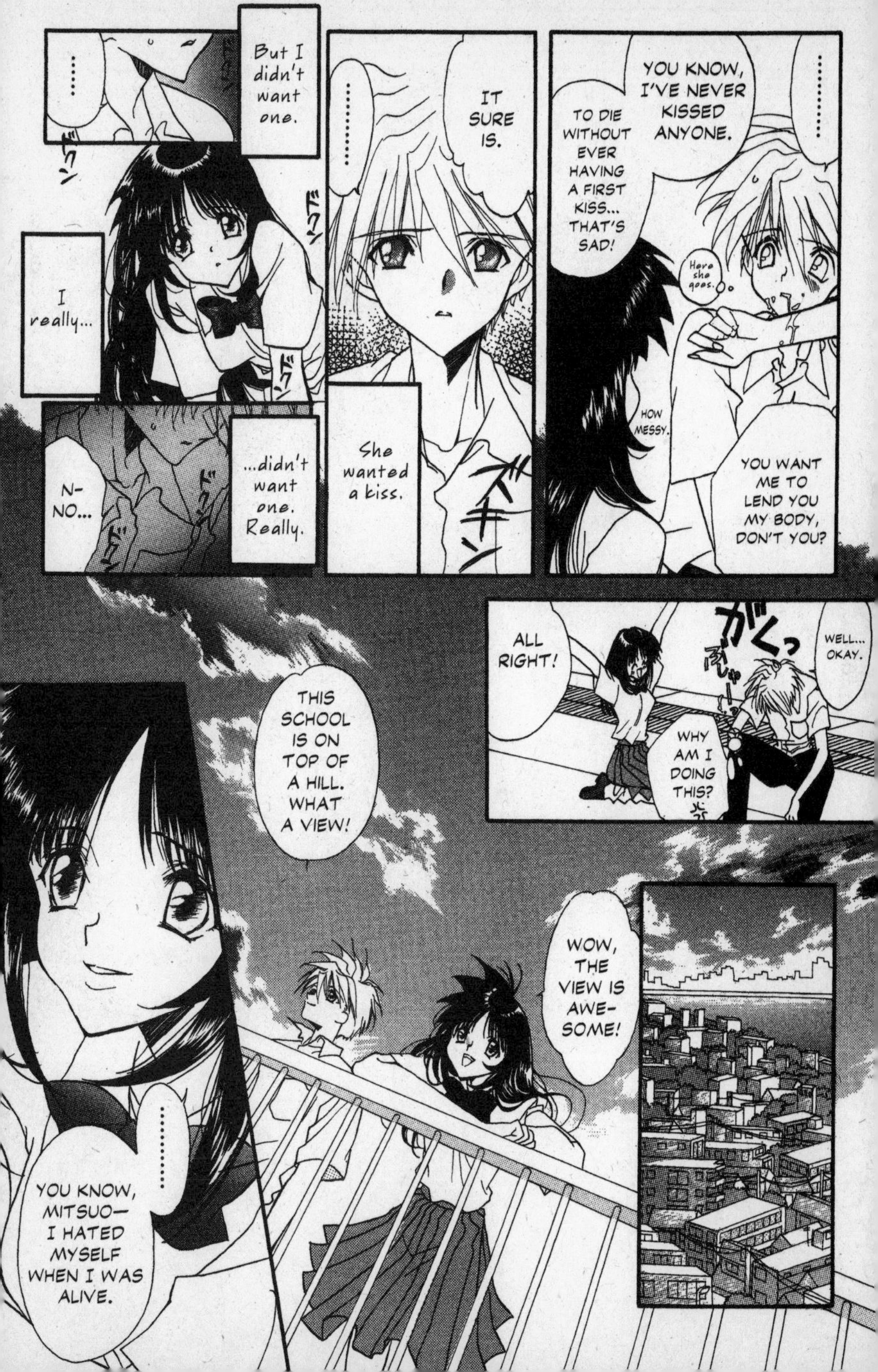
......
YOU KNOW, I'VE NEVER KISSED ANYONE.
TO DIE WITHOUT EVER HAVING A FIRST KISS... THAT'S SAD!
Here she goes.
HOW MESSY.
YOU WANT ME TO LEND YOU MY BODY, DON'T YOU?
IT SURE IS.
......
She wanted a kiss.
But I didn't want one.
......
I really...
...didn't want one. Really.
N-NO...
WELL... OKAY.
ALL RIGHT!
WHY AM I DOING THIS?
WOW, THE VIEW IS AWE-SOME!
THIS SCHOOL IS ON TOP OF A HILL. WHAT A VIEW!
......
YOU KNOW, MITSUO— I HATED MYSELF WHEN I WAS ALIVE.

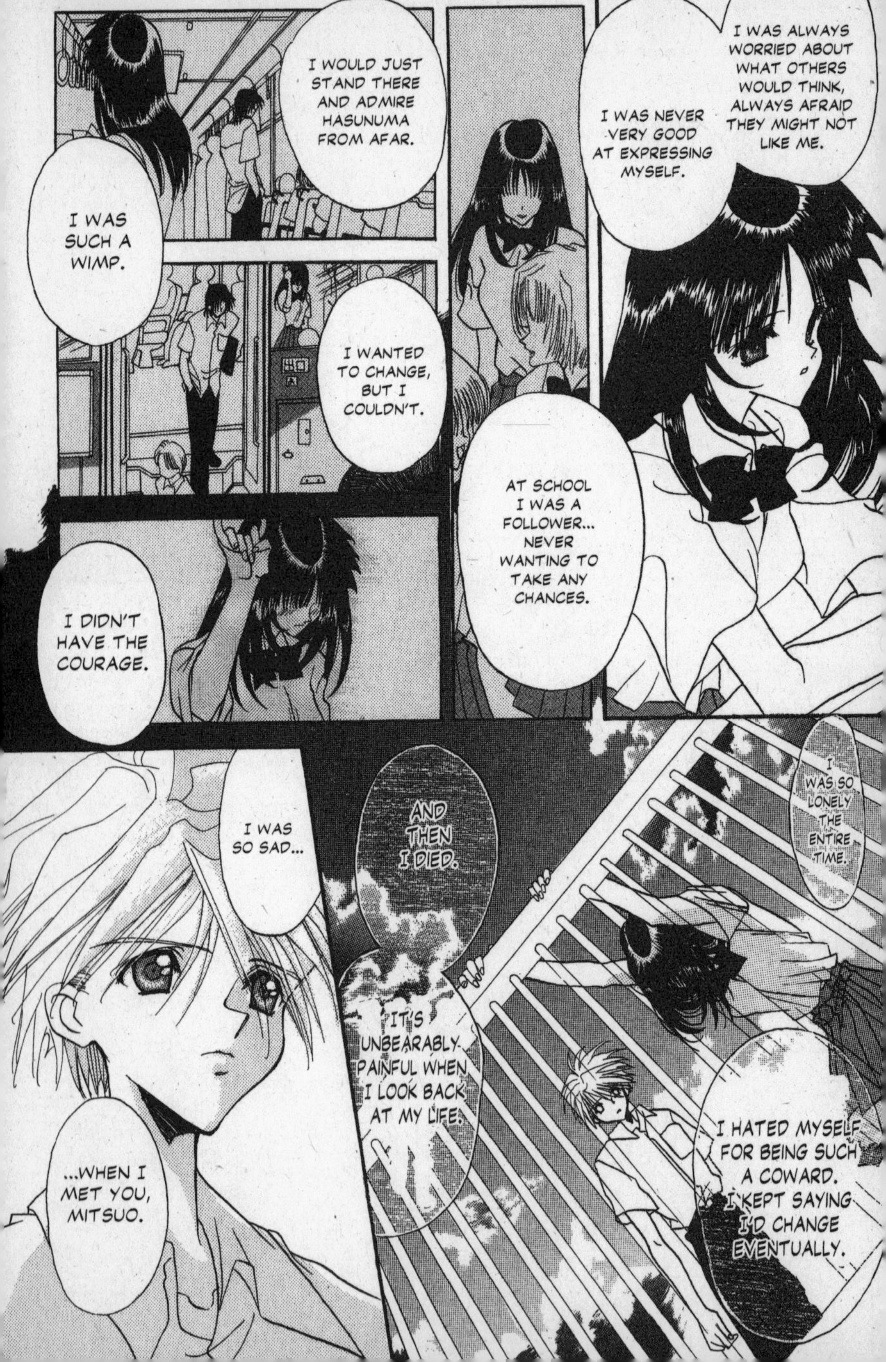
I WAS ALWAYS WORRIED ABOUT WHAT OTHERS WOULD THINK, ALWAYS AFRAID THEY MIGHT NOT LIKE ME.
I WAS NEVER VERY GOOD AT EXPRESSING MYSELF.
AT SCHOOL I WAS A FOLLOWER... NEVER WANTING TO TAKE ANY CHANCES.
I WOULD JUST STAND THERE AND ADMIRE HASUNUMA FROM AFAR.
I WAS SUCH A WIMP.
I WANTED TO CHANGE, BUT I COULDN'T.
I DIDN'T HAVE THE COURAGE.
I WAS SO LONELY THE ENTIRE TIME.
AND THEN I DIED.
I HATED MYSELF FOR BEING SUCH A COWARD. I KEPT SAYING I'D CHANGE EVENTUALLY.
IT'S UNBEARABLY PAINFUL WHEN I LOOK BACK AT MY LIFE.
I WAS SO SAD...
...WHEN I MET YOU, MITSUO.

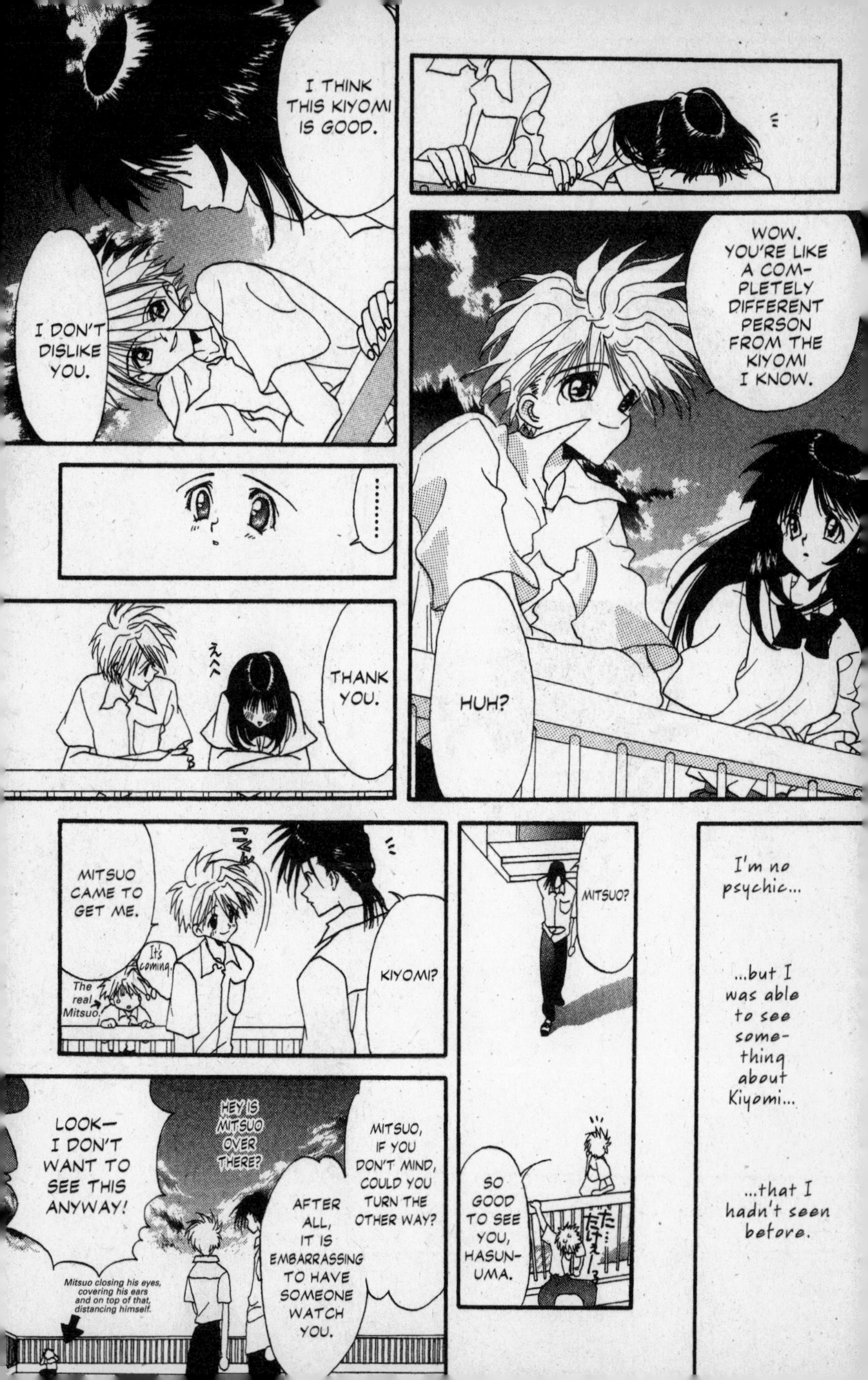
WOW. YOU'RE LIKE A COM-PLETELY DIFFERENT PERSON FROM THE KIYOMI I KNOW.
HUH?
I THINK THIS KIYOMI IS GOOD.
I DON'T DISLIKE YOU.
....
THANK YOU.
I'm no psychic...
...but I was able to see some-thing about Kiyomi...
...that I hadn't seen before.
MITSUO?
SO GOOD TO SEE YOU, HASUN-UMA.
KIYOMI?
MITSUO CAME TO GET ME.
It's coming.
The real Mitsuo.
MITSUO, IF YOU DON'T MIND, COULD YOU TURN THE OTHER WAY?
AFTER ALL, IT IS EMBARRASSING TO HAVE SOMEONE WATCH YOU.
HEY IS MITSUO OVER THERE?
LOOK— I DON'T WANT TO SEE THIS ANYWAY!
Mitsuo closing his eyes, covering his ears and on top of that, distancing himself.

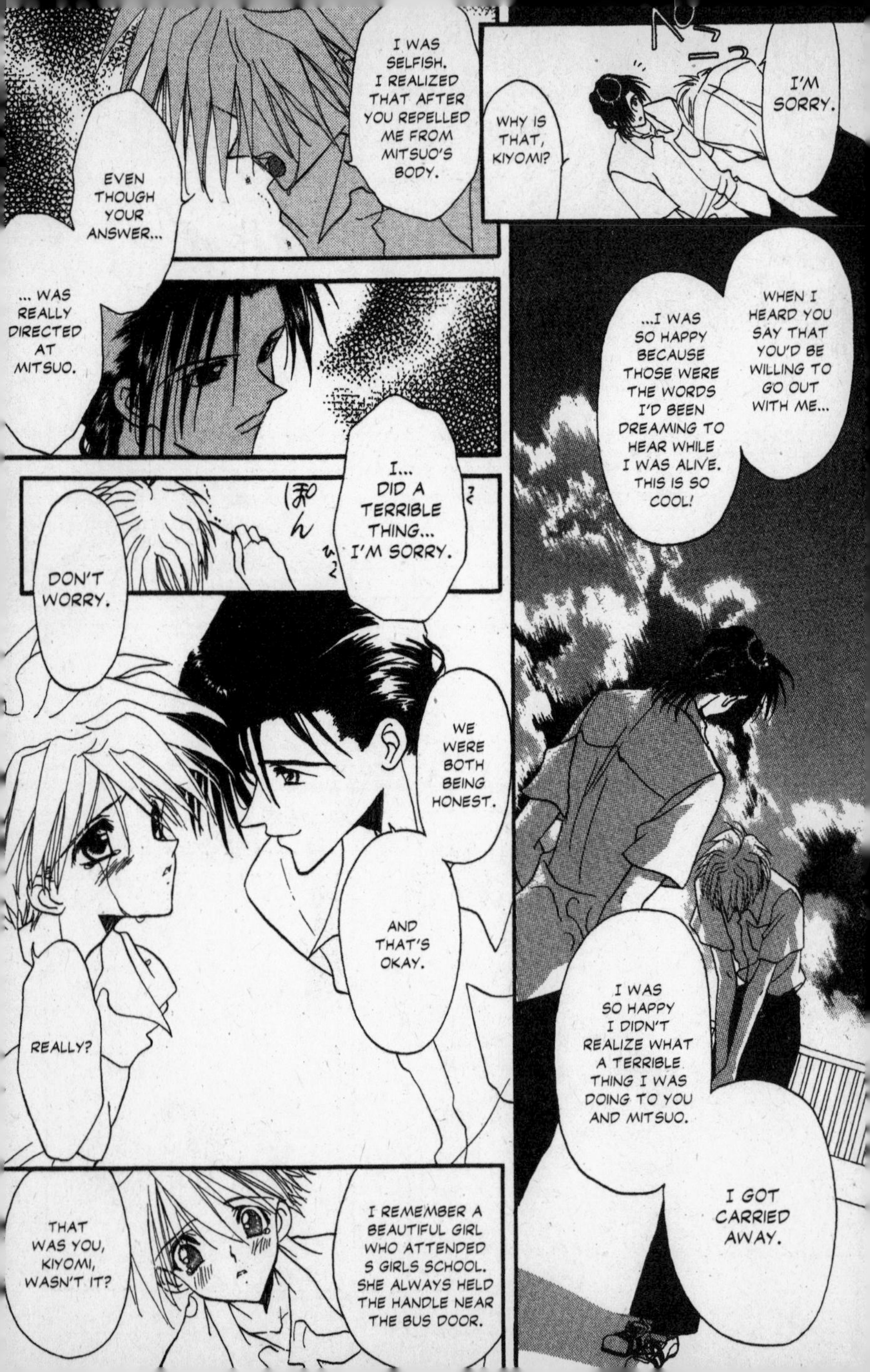
I'M SORRY.
WHY IS THAT, KIYOMI?
WHEN I HEARD YOU SAY THAT YOU'D BE WILLING TO GO OUT WITH ME...
...I WAS SO HAPPY BECAUSE THOSE WERE THE WORDS I'D BEEN DREAMING TO HEAR WHILE I WAS ALIVE. THIS IS SO COOL!
I WAS SO HAPPY I DIDN'T REALIZE WHAT A TERRIBLE THING I WAS DOING TO YOU AND MITSUO.
I GOT CARRIED AWAY.
I WAS SELFISH. I REALIZED THAT AFTER YOU REPELLED ME FROM MITSUO'S BODY.
EVEN THOUGH YOUR ANSWER...
... WAS REALLY DIRECTED AT MITSUO.
I... DID A TERRIBLE THING... I'M SORRY.
DON'T WORRY.
WE WERE BOTH BEING HONEST.
AND THAT'S OKAY.
REALLY?
I REMEMBER A BEAUTIFUL GIRL WHO ATTENDED S GIRLS SCHOOL. SHE ALWAYS HELD THE HANDLE NEAR THE BUS DOOR.
THAT WAS YOU, KIYOMI, WASN'T IT?

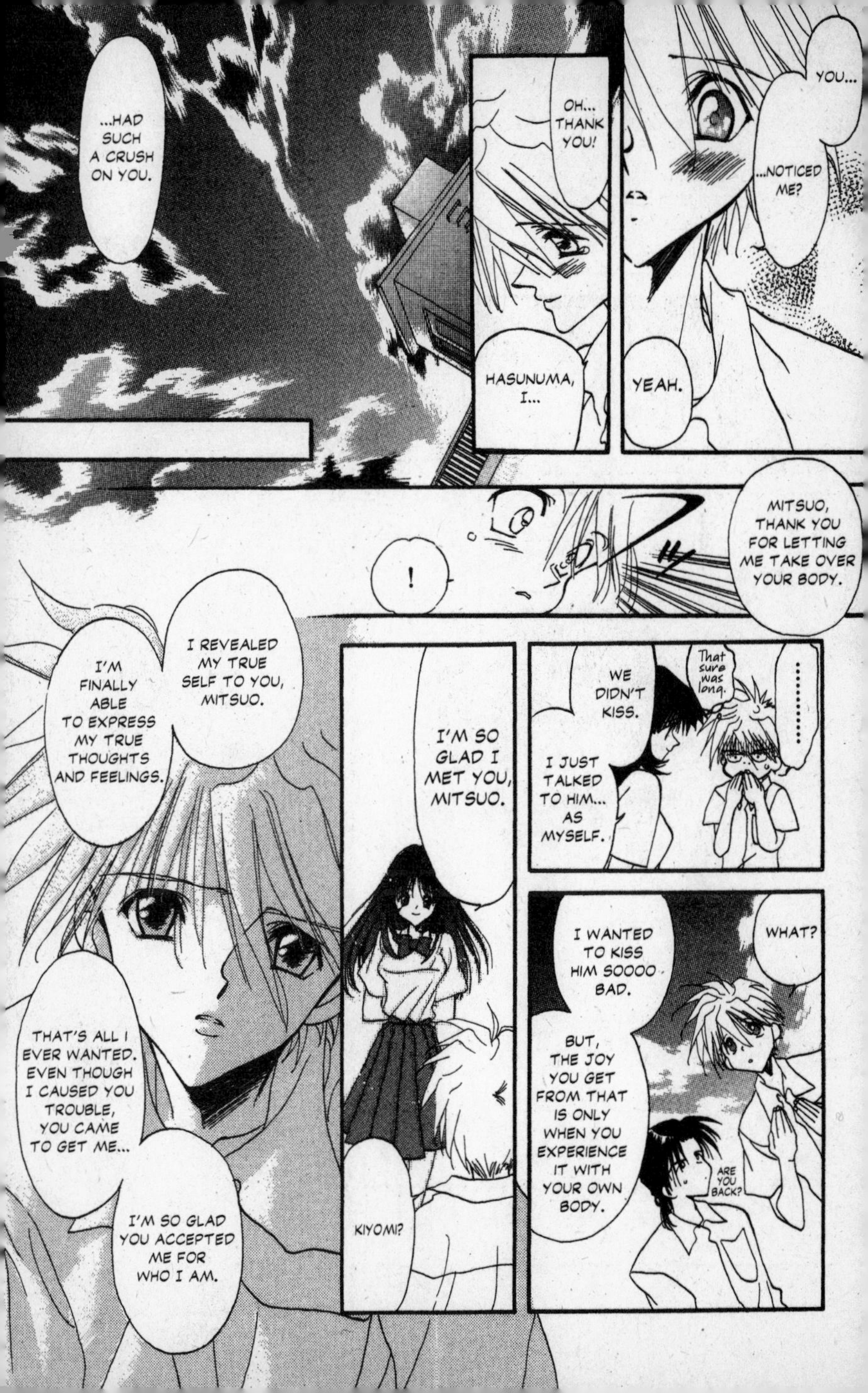
YOU...
...NOTICED ME?
YEAH.
OH... THANK YOU!
HASUNUMA, I...
...HAD SUCH A CRUSH ON YOU.
MITSUO, THANK YOU FOR LETTING ME TAKE OVER YOUR BODY.
!
......
That sure was long.
WE DIDN'T KISS.
I JUST TALKED TO HIM... AS MYSELF.
WHAT?
I WANTED TO KISS HIM SOOOO BAD.
BUT, THE JOY YOU GET FROM THAT IS ONLY WHEN YOU EXPERIENCE IT WITH YOUR OWN BODY.
ARE YOU BACK?
I'M SO GLAD I MET YOU, MITSUO.
KIYOMI?
I REVEALED MY TRUE SELF TO YOU, MITSUO.
I'M FINALLY ABLE TO EXPRESS MY TRUE THOUGHTS AND FEELINGS.
THAT'S ALL I EVER WANTED. EVEN THOUGH I CAUSED YOU TROUBLE, YOU CAME TO GET ME...
I'M SO GLAD YOU ACCEPTED ME FOR WHO I AM.

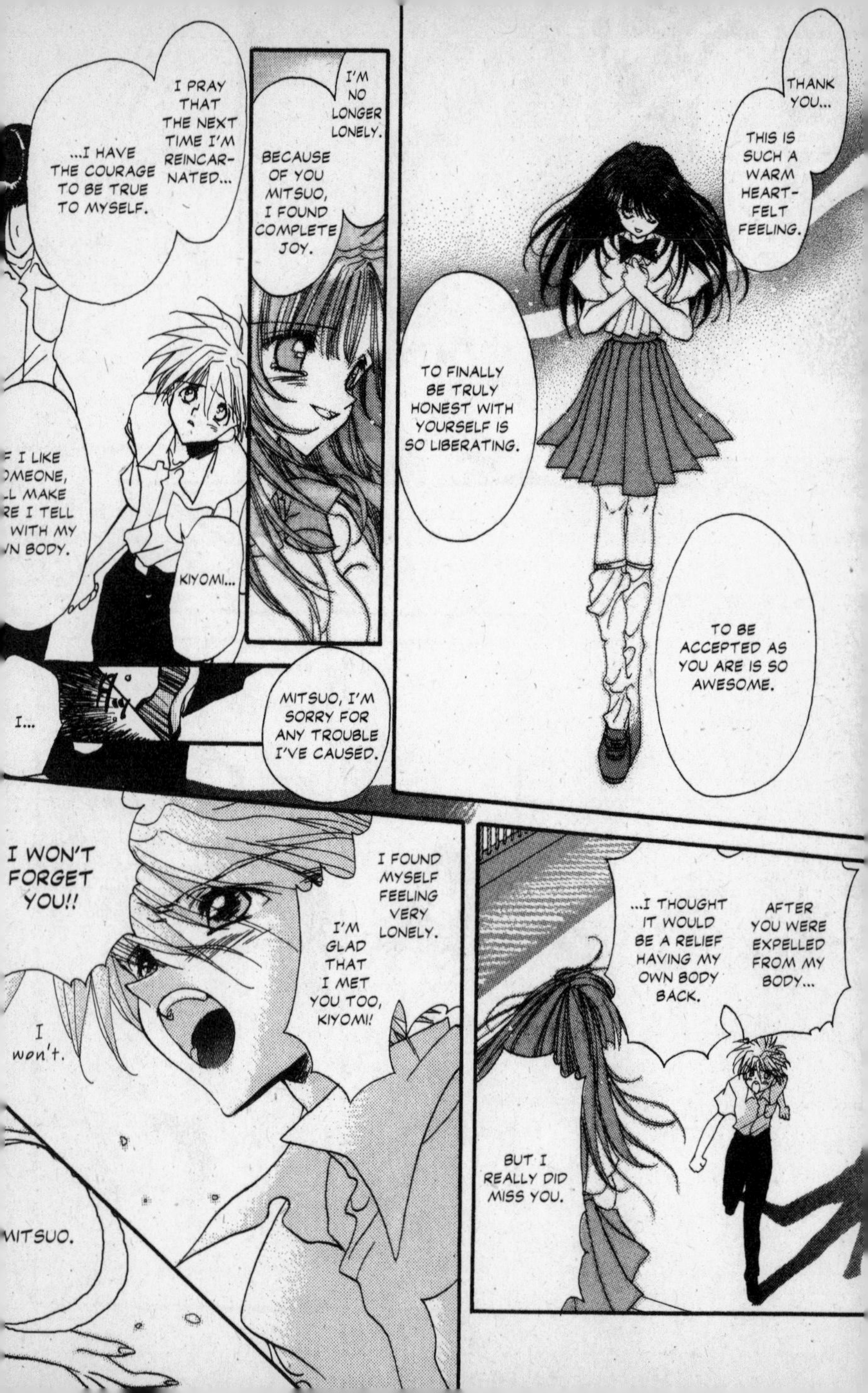
THANK YOU...
THIS IS SUCH A WARM HEART-FELT FEELING.
TO FINALLY BE TRULY HONEST WITH YOURSELF IS SO LIBERATING.
TO BE ACCEPTED AS YOU ARE IS SO AWESOME.
I'M NO LONGER LONELY.
BECAUSE OF YOU MITSUO, I FOUND COMPLETE JOY.
I PRAY THAT THE NEXT TIME I'M REINCARNATED...
...I HAVE THE COURAGE TO BE TRUE TO MYSELF.
KIYOMI...
F I LIKE OMEONE, LL MAKE RE I TELL WITH MY N BODY.
MITSUO, I'M SORRY FOR ANY TROUBLE I'VE CAUSED.
I...
AFTER YOU WERE EXPELLED FROM MY BODY...
...I THOUGHT IT WOULD BE A RELIEF HAVING MY OWN BODY BACK.
BUT I REALLY DID MISS YOU.
I FOUND MYSELF FEELING VERY LONELY.
I'M GLAD THAT I MET YOU TOO, KIYOMI!
I WON'T FORGET YOU!!
I won't.
MITSUO.

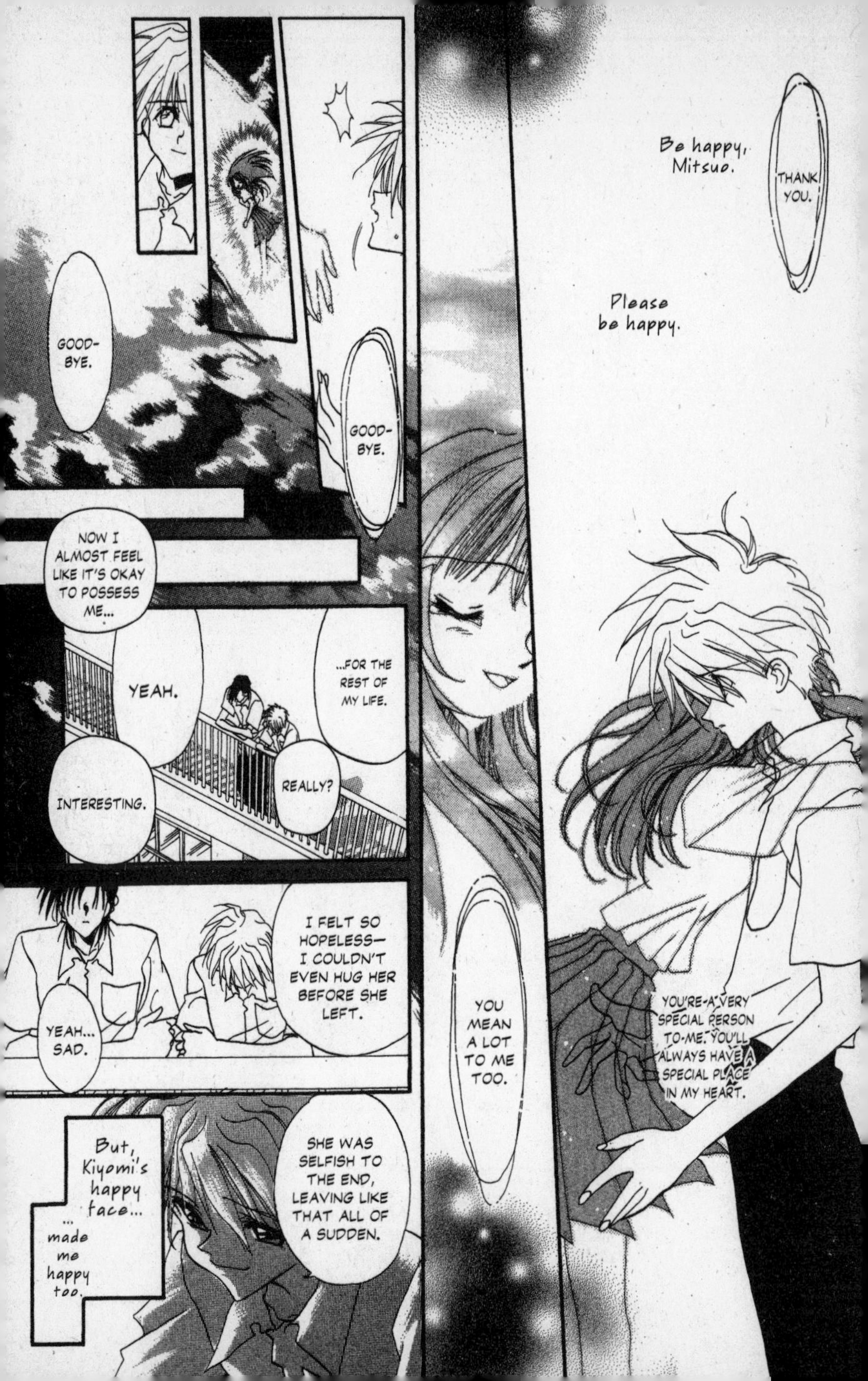
THANK YOU.
Be happy, Mitsuo.
Please be happy.
YOU'RE A VERY SPECIAL PERSON TO ME. YOU'LL ALWAYS HAVE A SPECIAL PLACE IN MY HEART.
YOU MEAN A LOT TO ME TOO.
GOOD-BYE.
GOOD-BYE.
NOW I ALMOST FEEL LIKE IT'S OKAY TO POSSESS ME...
...FOR THE REST OF MY LIFE.
YEAH.
REALLY?
INTERESTING.
I FELT SO HOPELESS— I COULDN'T EVEN HUG HER BEFORE SHE LEFT.
YEAH... SAD.
SHE WAS SELFISH TO THE END, LEAVING LIKE THAT ALL OF A SUDDEN.
But, Kiyomi's happy face...
...made me happy too.

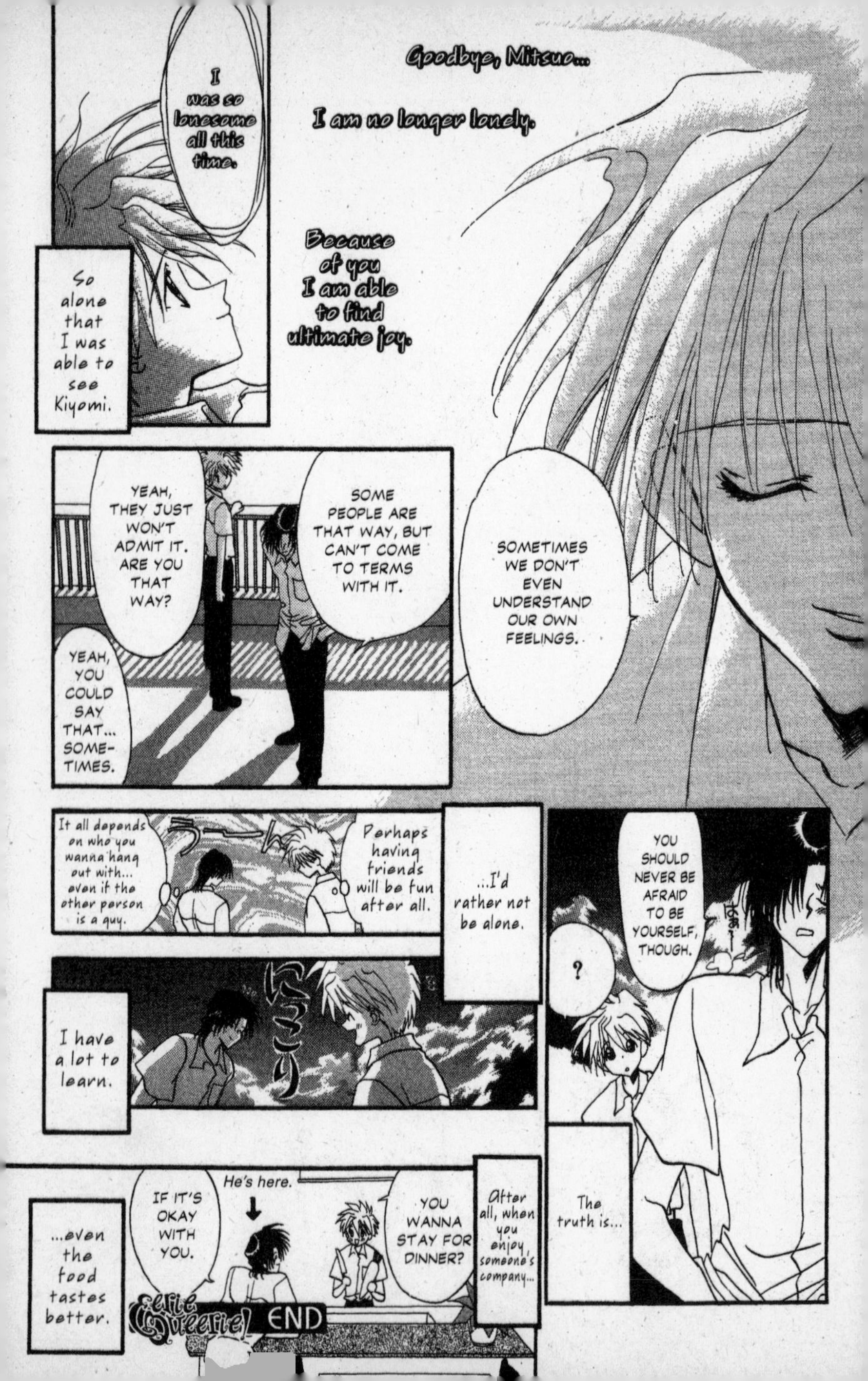
Goodbye, Mitsuo...
I am no longer lonely.
Because of you I am able to find ultimate joy.
SOMETIMES WE DON'T EVEN UNDERSTAND OUR OWN FEELINGS.
I was so lonesome all this time.
So alone that I was able to see Kiyomi.
SOME PEOPLE ARE THAT WAY, BUT CAN'T COME TO TERMS WITH IT.
YEAH, THEY JUST WON'T ADMIT IT. ARE YOU THAT WAY?
YEAH, YOU COULD SAY THAT... SOMETIMES.
YOU SHOULD NEVER BE AFRAID TO BE YOURSELF, THOUGH.
?
The truth is...
...I'd rather not be alone.
Perhaps having friends will be fun after all.
It all depends on who you wanna hang out with... even if the other person is a guy.
I have a lot to learn.
After all, when you enjoy someone's company...
YOU WANNA STAY FOR DINNER?
He's here.
IF IT'S OKAY WITH YOU.
...even the food tastes better.
Elite Queerie! END

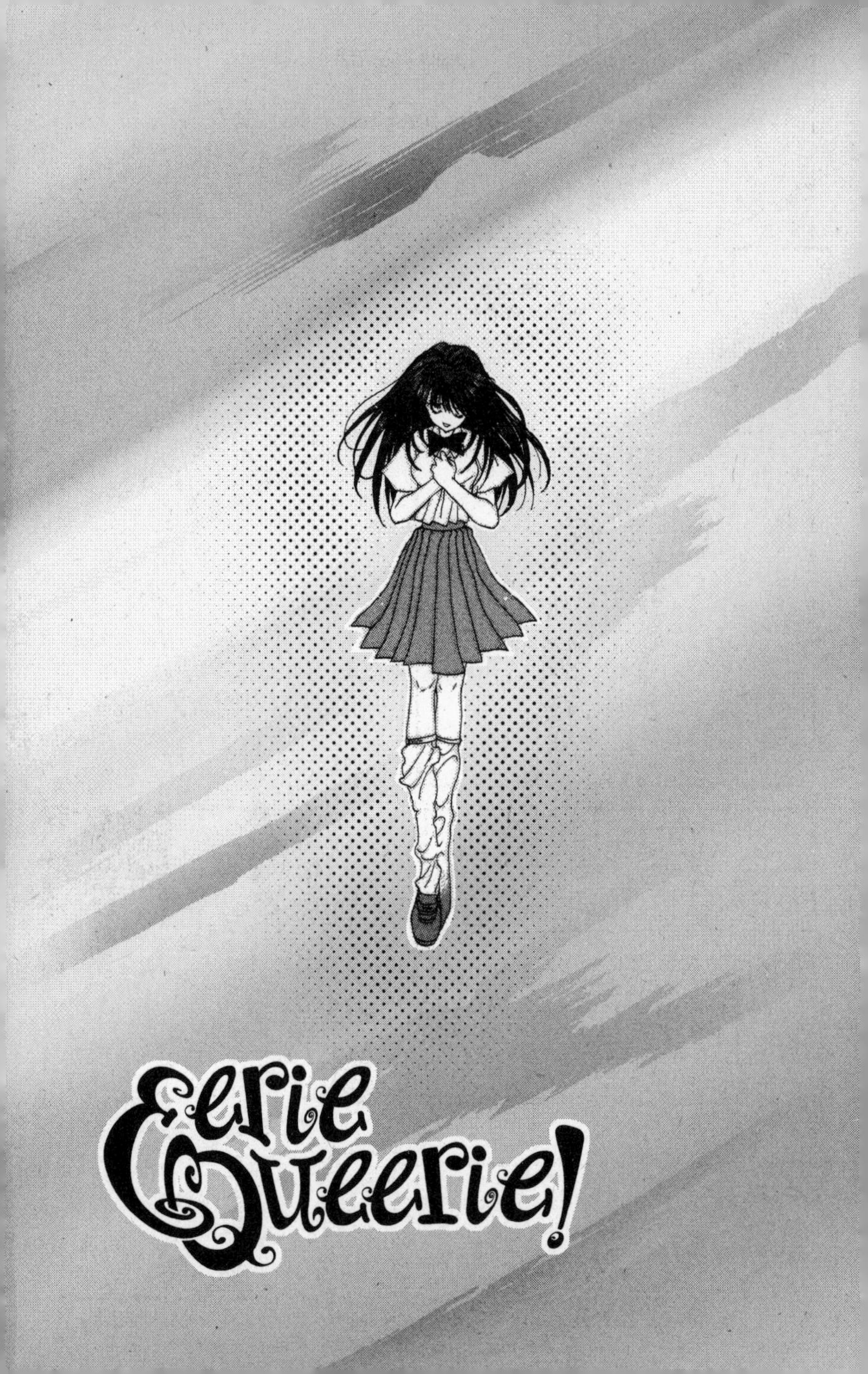
Eerie Queerie!

Trying very hard not to laugh.

にらめっこ
あっぷっぷ

Staring Contest

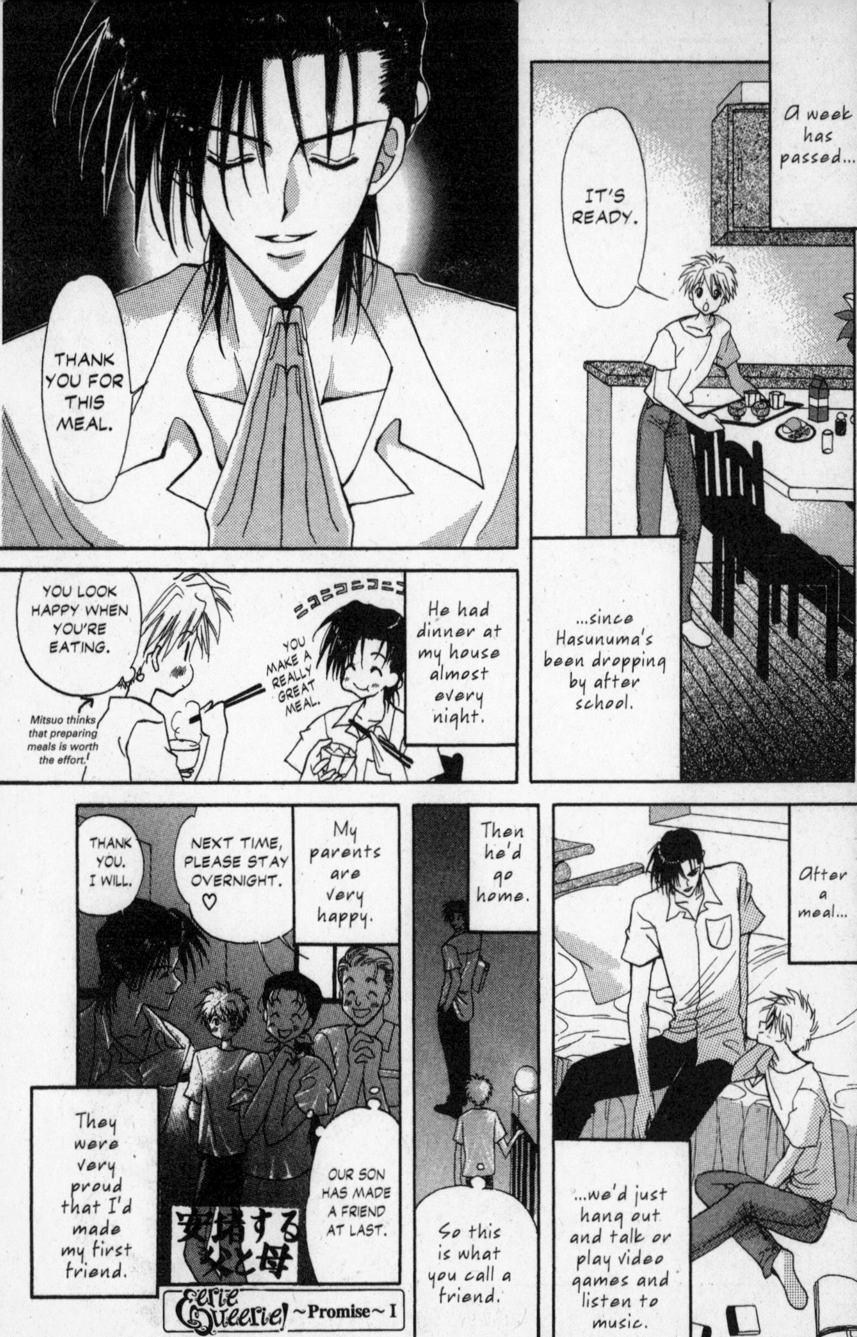
A week has passed...
IT'S READY.
...since Hasunuma's been dropping by after school.
THANK YOU FOR THIS MEAL.
He had dinner at my house almost every night.
ニコニコニコニ
YOU MAKE A REALLY GREAT MEAL.
YOU LOOK HAPPY WHEN YOU'RE EATING.
Mitsuo thinks that preparing meals is worth the effort.
After a meal...
...we'd just hang out and talk or play video games and listen to music.
Then he'd go home.
So this is what you call a friend.
My parents are very happy.
NEXT TIME, PLEASE STAY OVERNIGHT. ♡
THANK YOU. I WILL.
OUR SON HAS MADE A FRIEND AT LAST.
安堵する父と母
They were very proud that I'd made my first friend.

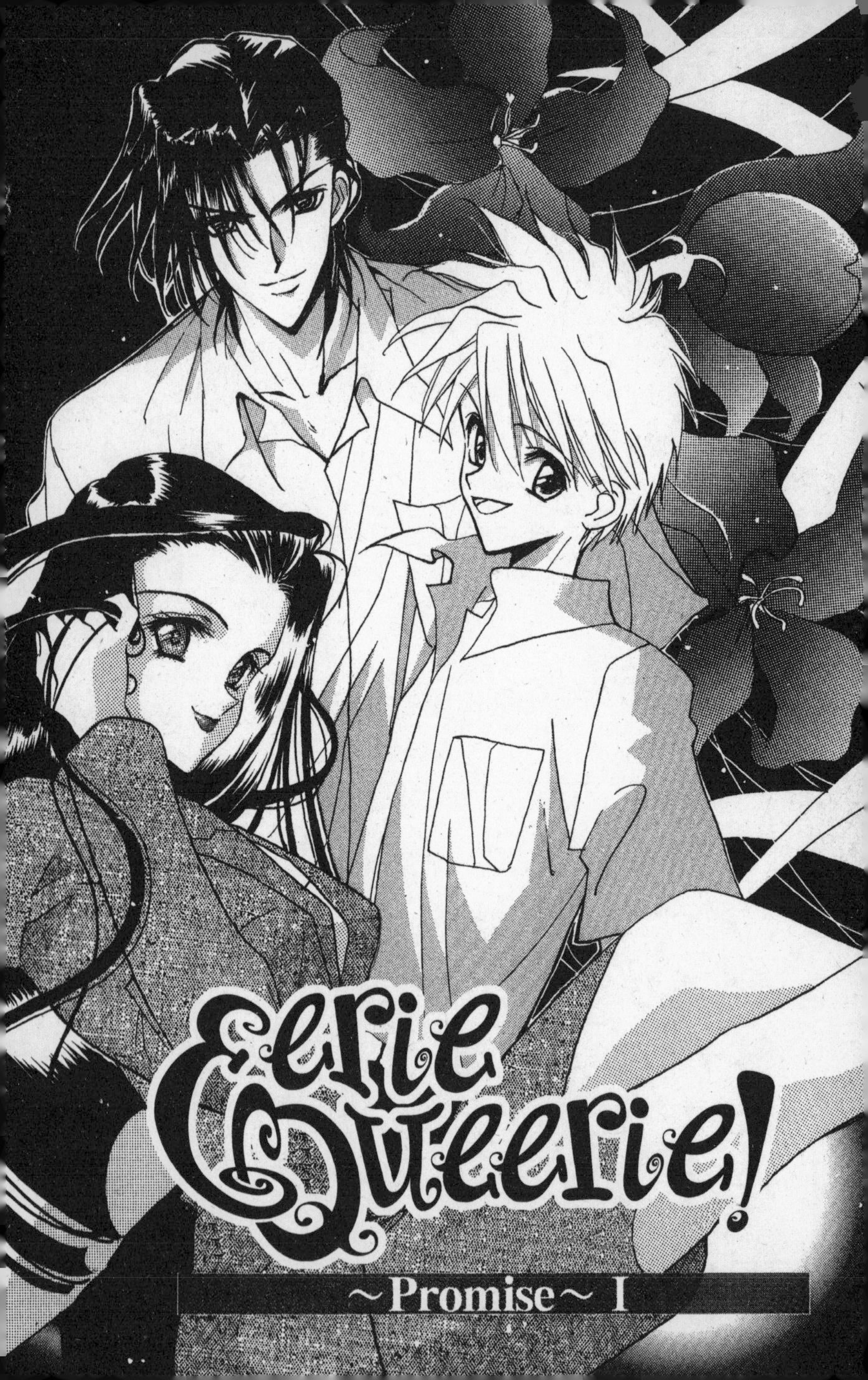
Eerie Queerie!
~Promise~ I

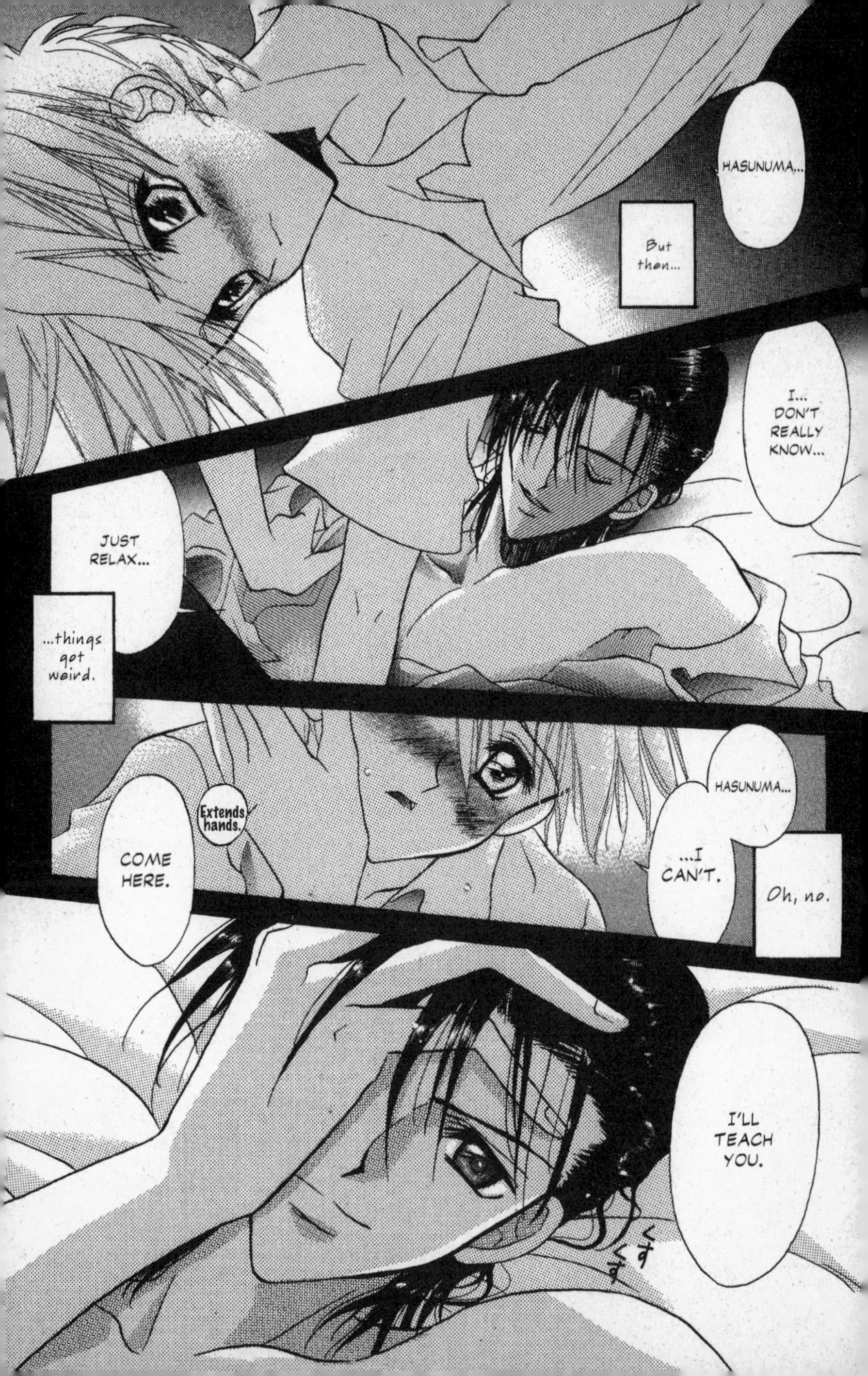
HASUNUMA...
But then...
I... DON'T REALLY KNOW...
JUST RELAX...
...things got weird.
HASUNUMA...
Oh, no.
...I CAN'T.
Extends hands.
COME HERE.
I'LL TEACH YOU.
くすくす

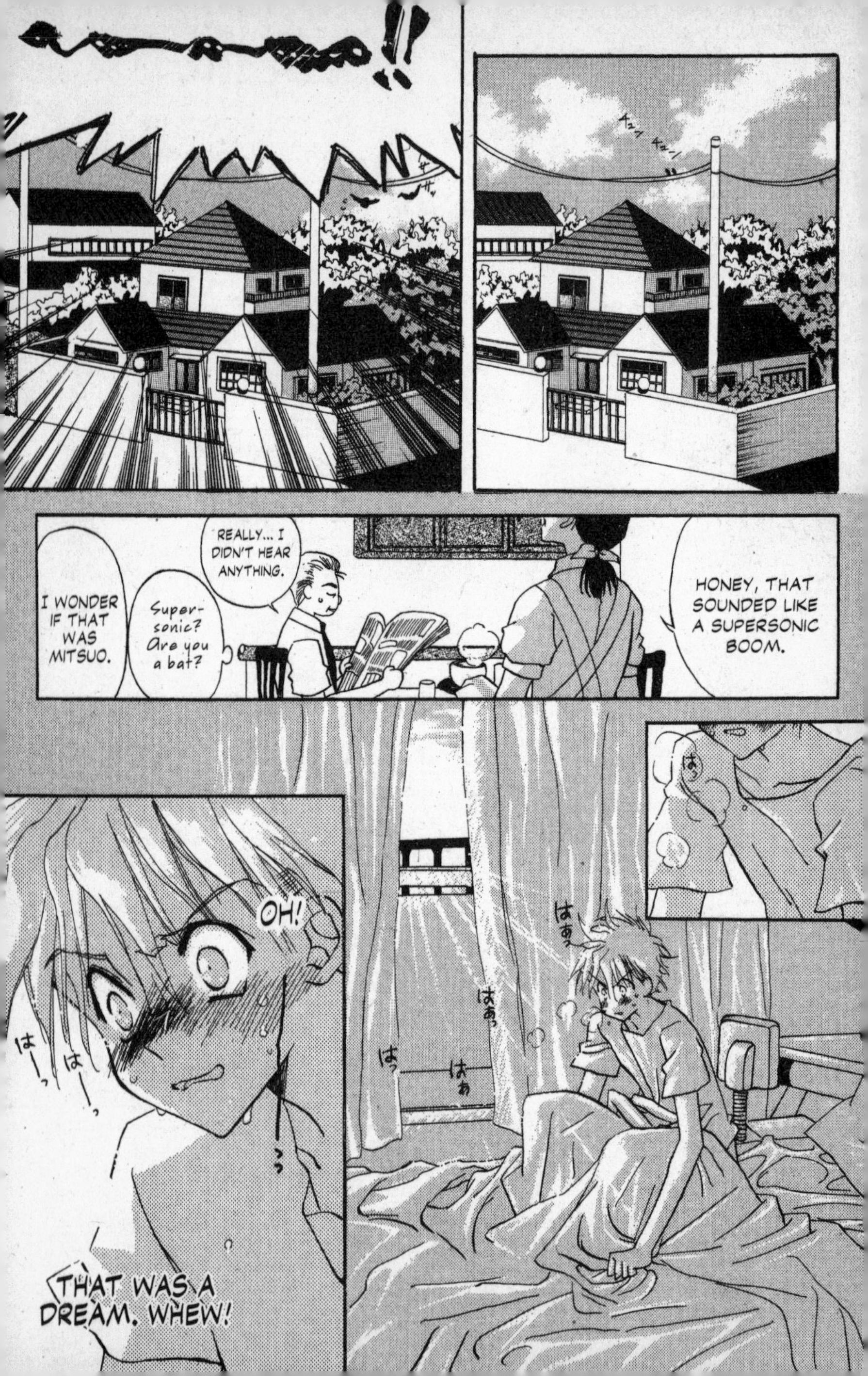
HONEY, THAT SOUNDED LIKE A SUPERSONIC BOOM.
REALLY... I DIDN'T HEAR ANYTHING.
Super-sonic? Are you a bat?
I WONDER IF THAT WAS MITSUO.
はっ
はぁっ
はぁっ
はっ
はぁ
OH!
は一っ
は一っ
THAT WAS A DREAM. WHEW!

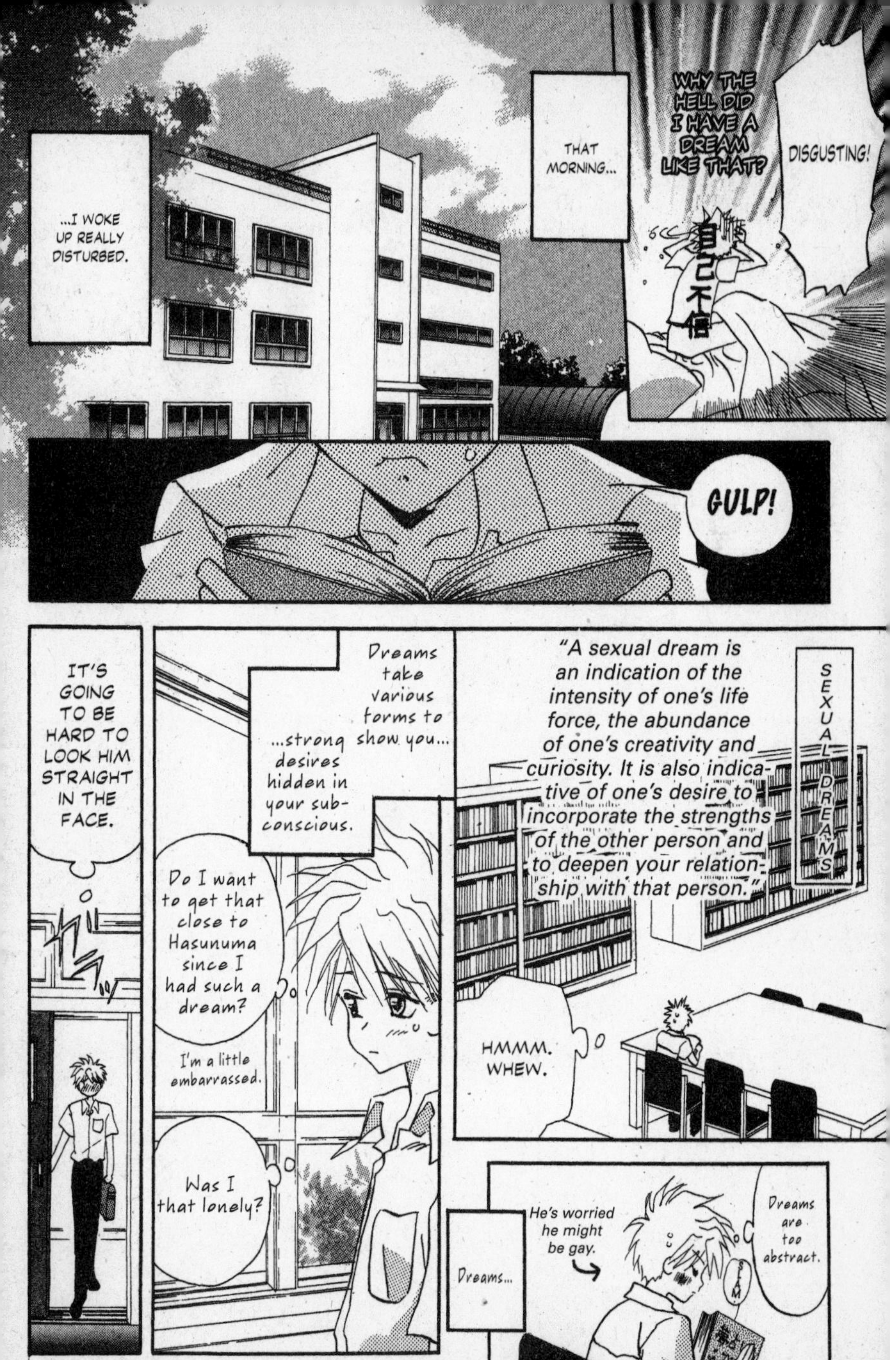
DISGUSTING!
WHY THE HELL DID I HAVE A DREAM LIKE THAT?
自己不信
THAT MORNING...
...I WOKE UP REALLY DISTURBED.
GULP!
SEXUAL DREAMS
"A sexual dream is an indication of the intensity of one's life force, the abundance of one's creativity and curiosity. It is also indicative of one's desire to incorporate the strengths of the other person and to deepen your relationship with that person."
HMMM. WHEW.
Dreams are too abstract.
SLAM
He's worried he might be gay.
Dreams...
Dreams take various forms to show you...
...strong desires hidden in your subconscious.
Do I want to get that close to Hasunuma since I had such a dream?
I'm a little embarrassed.
Was I that lonely?
IT'S GOING TO BE HARD TO LOOK HIM STRAIGHT IN THE FACE.

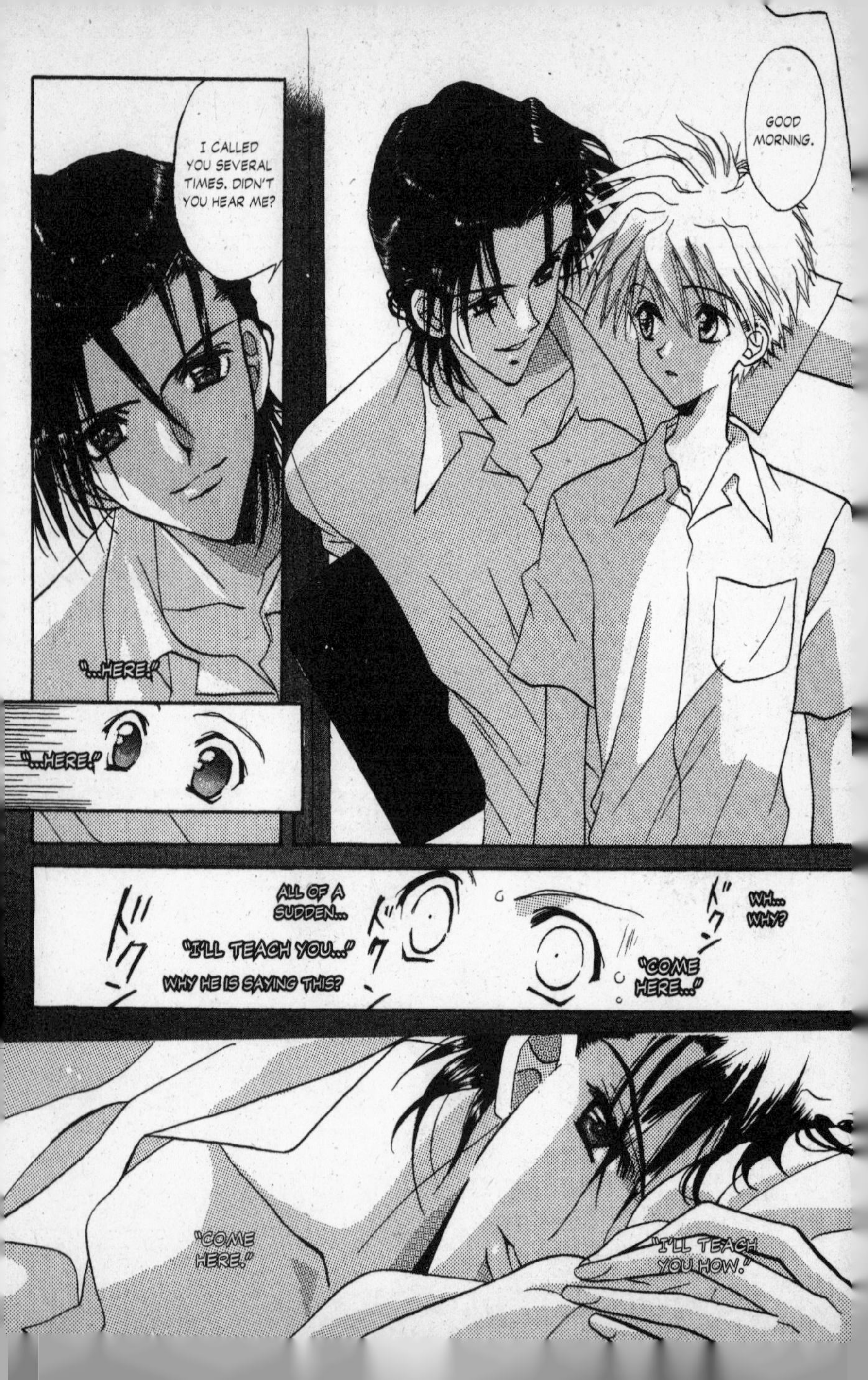
GOOD MORNING.
I CALLED YOU SEVERAL TIMES. DIDN'T YOU HEAR ME?
"...HERE."
"...HERE."
WH... WHY?
"COME HERE..."
ALL OF A SUDDEN...
"I'LL TEACH YOU..."
WHY HE IS SAYING THIS?
"I'LL TEACH YOU HOW."
"COME HERE."

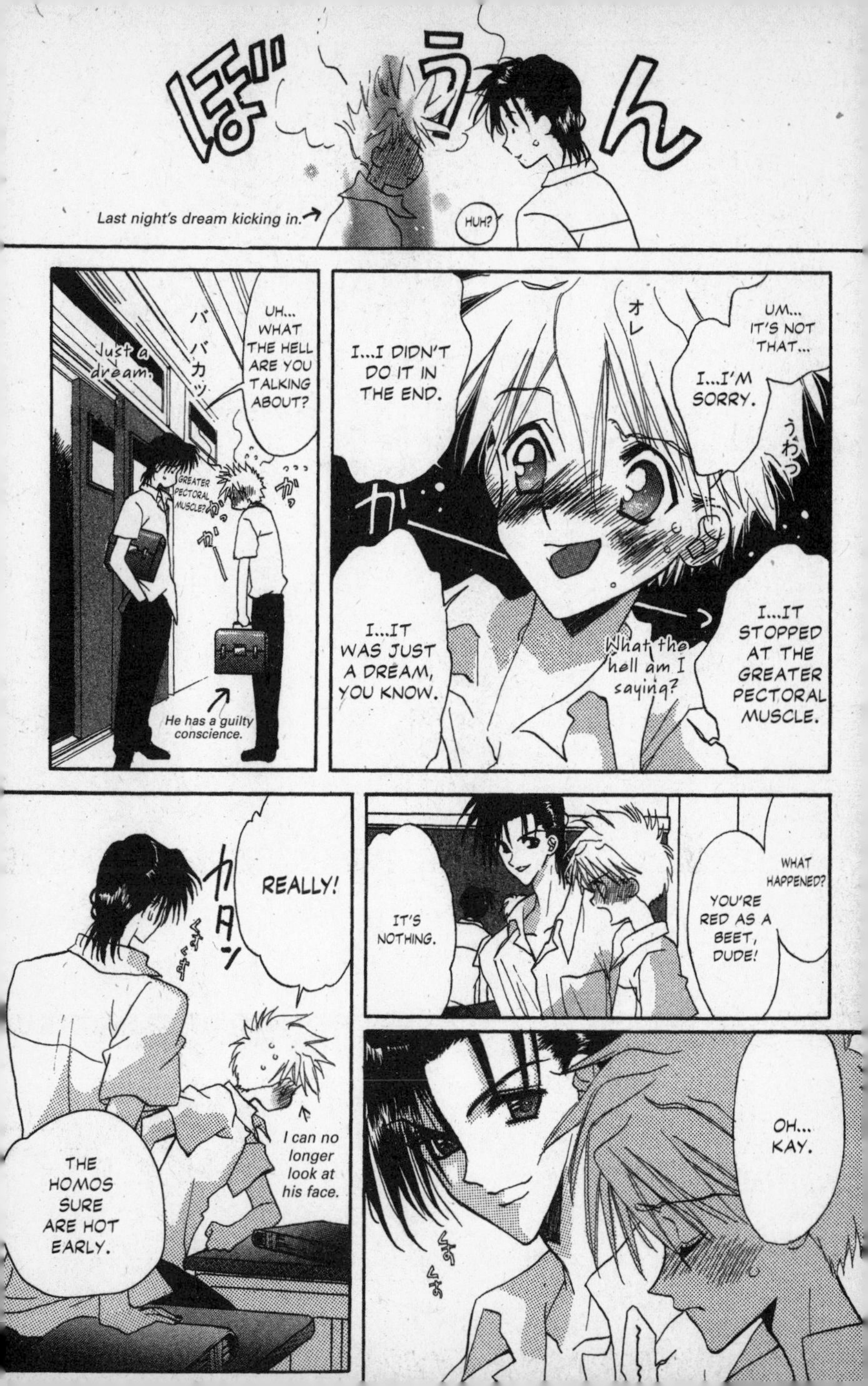
HUH?
Last night's dream kicking in.
UM... IT'S NOT THAT...
I...I'M SORRY.
I...I DIDN'T DO IT IN THE END.
I...IT STOPPED AT THE GREATER PECTORAL MUSCLE.
What the hell am I saying?
I...IT WAS JUST A DREAM, YOU KNOW.
UH... WHAT THE HELL ARE YOU TALKING ABOUT?
Just a dream.
GREATER PECTORAL MUSCLE?
He has a guilty conscience.
WHAT HAPPENED?
YOU'RE RED AS A BEET, DUDE!
IT'S NOTHING.
OH... KAY.
REALLY!
I can no longer look at his face.
THE HOMOS SURE ARE HOT EARLY.

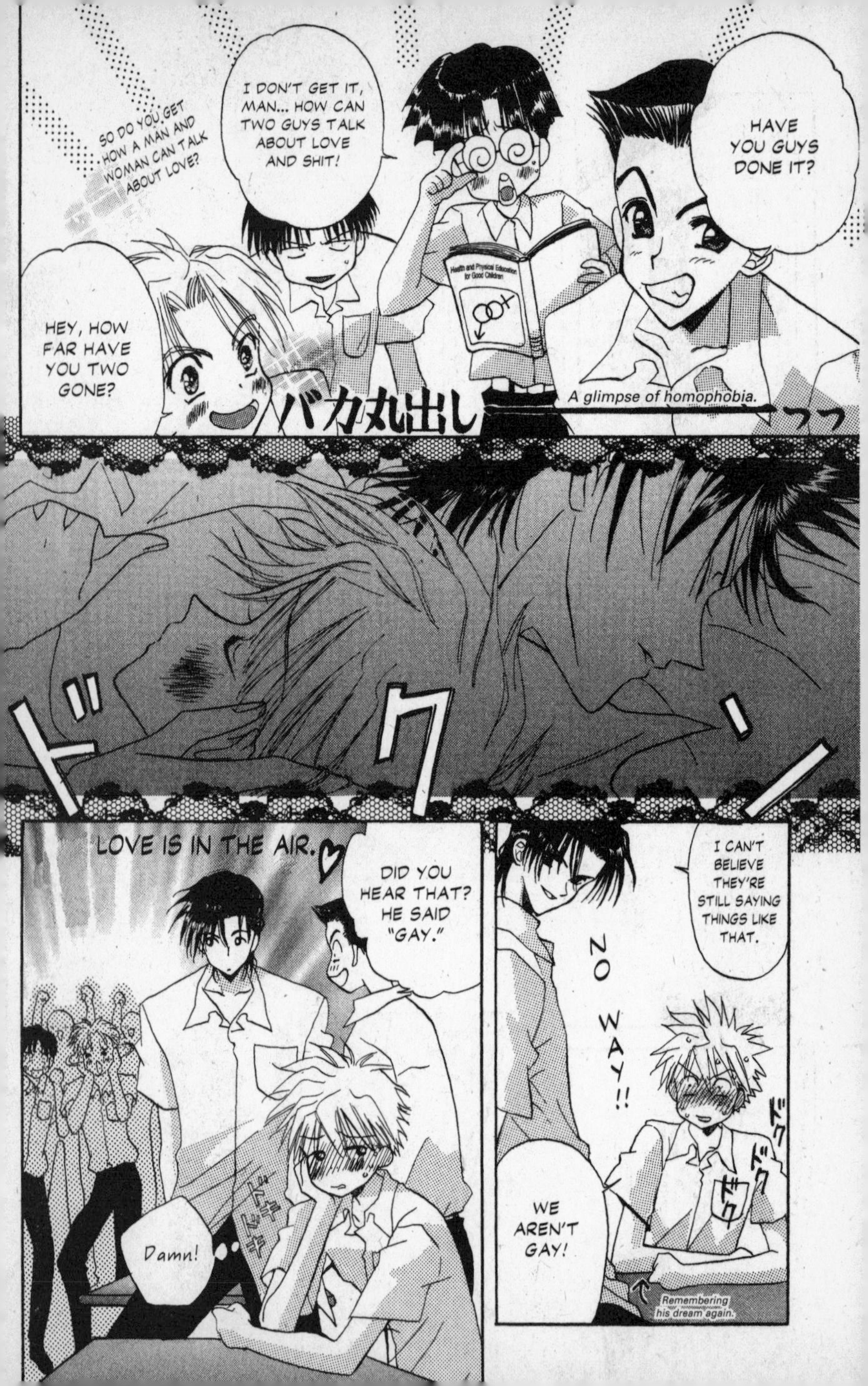

HAVE YOU GUYS DONE IT?
I DON'T GET IT, MAN... HOW CAN TWO GUYS TALK ABOUT LOVE AND SHIT!
SO DO YOU GET HOW A MAN AND WOMAN CAN TALK ABOUT LOVE?
Health and Physical Education for Good Children
HEY, HOW FAR HAVE YOU TWO GONE?
A glimpse of homophobia.
バカ丸出し
ドクン
I CAN'T BELIEVE THEY'RE STILL SAYING THINGS LIKE THAT.
NO WAY!!
WE AREN'T GAY!
ドクドクドク
Remembering his dream again.
LOVE IS IN THE AIR.♡
DID YOU HEAR THAT? HE SAID "GAY."
Damn!
ドキドキ

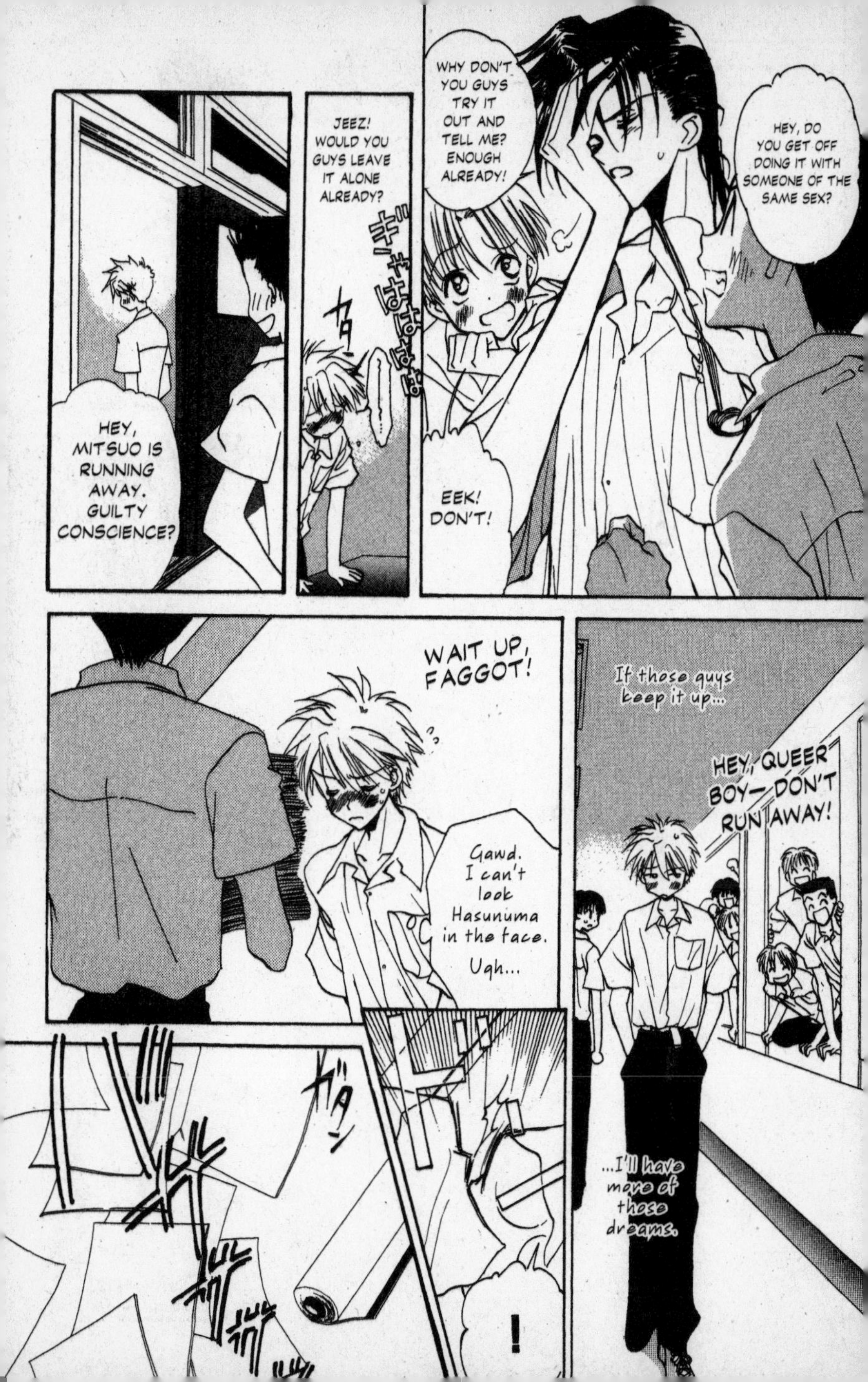
HEY, DO YOU GET OFF DOING IT WITH SOMEONE OF THE SAME SEX?
WHY DON'T YOU GUYS TRY IT OUT AND TELL ME? ENOUGH ALREADY!
EEK! DON'T!
JEEZ! WOULD YOU GUYS LEAVE IT ALONE ALREADY?
ぎゃはははは
カタ
HEY, MITSUO IS RUNNING AWAY. GUILTY CONSCIENCE?
If those guys keep it up...
HEY, QUEER BOY—DON'T RUN AWAY!
...I'll have more of those dreams.
WAIT UP, FAGGOT!
Gawd. I can't look Hasunuma in the face.
Ugh...
ガタン
!

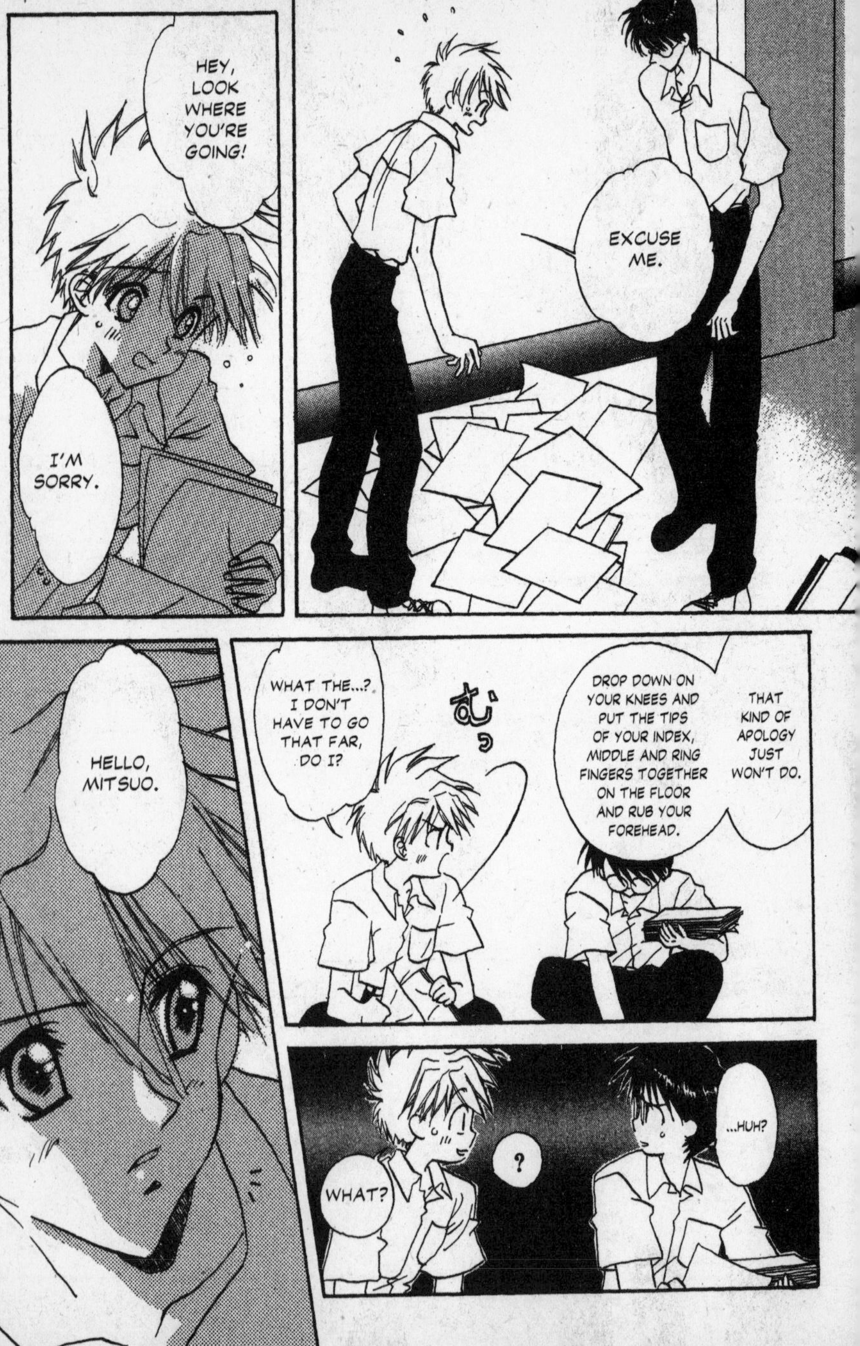
EXCUSE ME.
HEY, LOOK WHERE YOU'RE GOING!
I'M SORRY.
THAT KIND OF APOLOGY JUST WON'T DO.
DROP DOWN ON YOUR KNEES AND PUT THE TIPS OF YOUR INDEX, MIDDLE AND RING FINGERS TOGETHER ON THE FLOOR AND RUB YOUR FOREHEAD.
むっ
WHAT THE...? I DON'T HAVE TO GO THAT FAR, DO I?
...HUH?
?
WHAT?
HELLO, MITSUO.

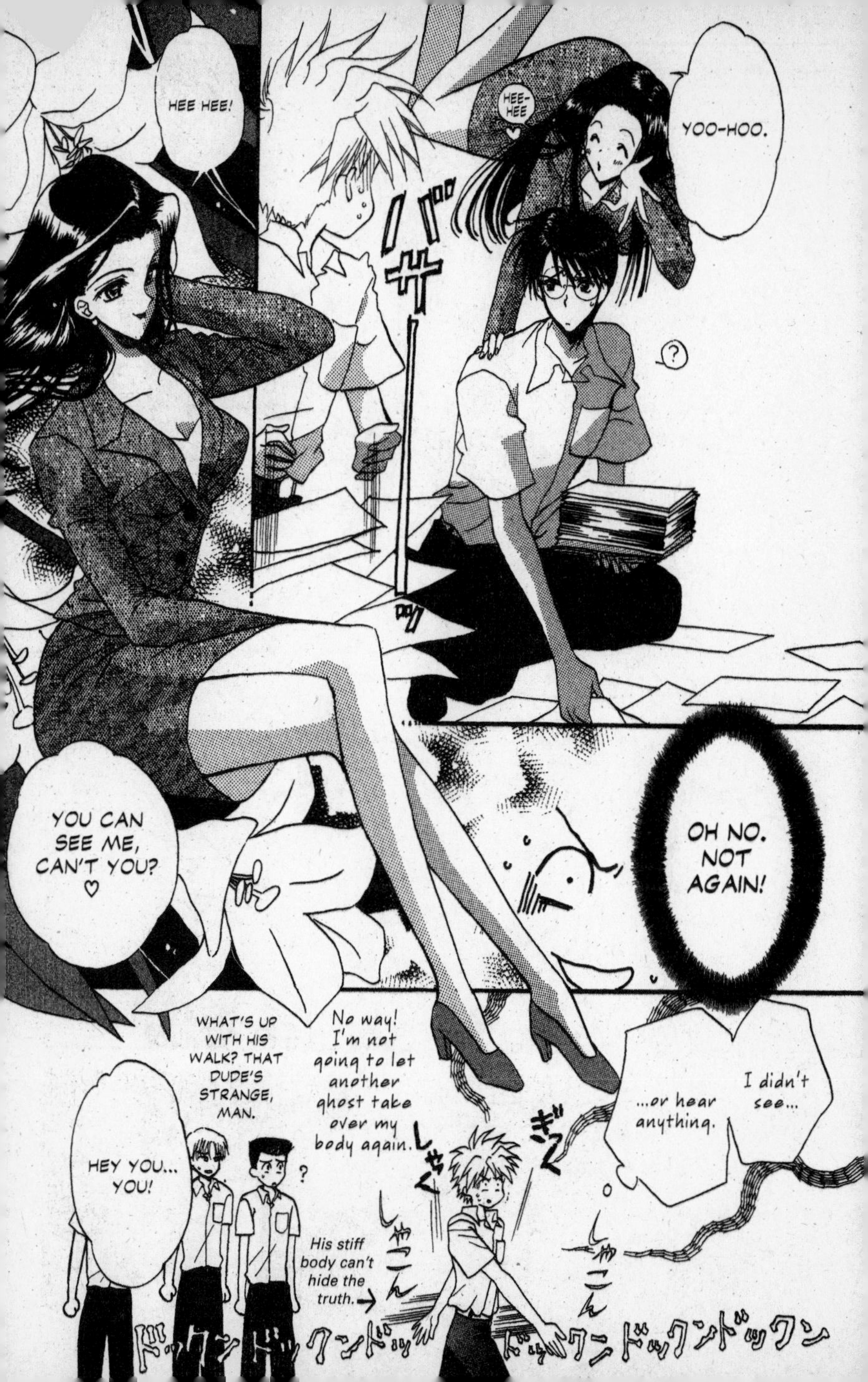
YOO-HOO.
HEE-HEE ♥
HEE HEE!
?
YOU CAN SEE ME, CAN'T YOU? ♥
OH NO. NOT AGAIN!
I didn't see...
...or hear anything.
No way! I'm not going to let another ghost take over my body again.
WHAT'S UP WITH HIS WALK? THAT DUDE'S STRANGE, MAN.
?
HEY YOU... YOU!
His stiff body can't hide the truth.

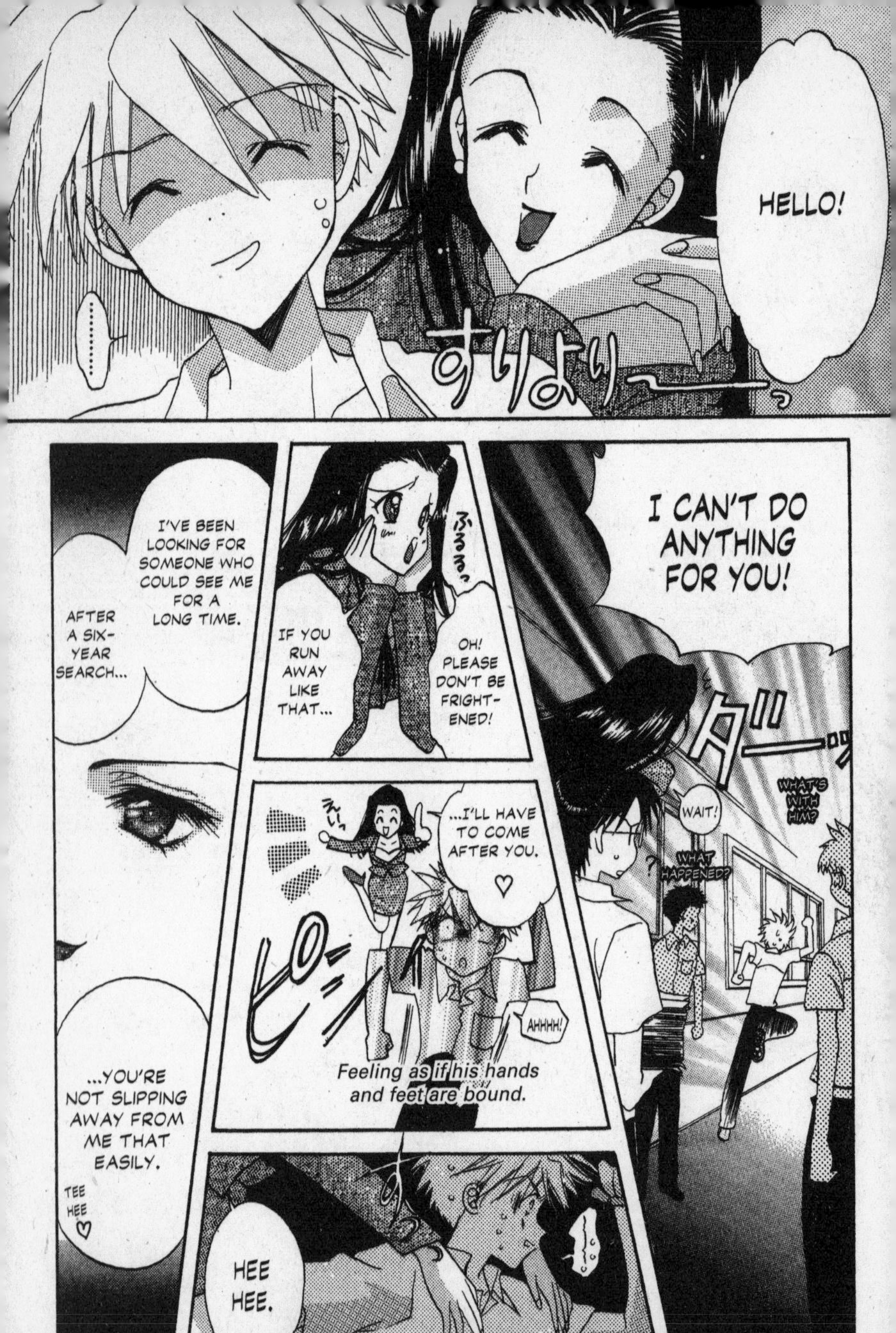
HELLO!
……
すりより
I CAN'T DO ANYTHING FOR YOU!
ダーーッ
WHAT'S WITH HIM?
WAIT!
WHAT HAPPENED?
OH! PLEASE DON'T BE FRIGHTENED!
ふるるっ
IF YOU RUN AWAY LIKE THAT...
...I'LL HAVE TO COME AFTER YOU. ♡
AHHHH!
Feeling as if his hands and feet are bound.
I'VE BEEN LOOKING FOR SOMEONE WHO COULD SEE ME FOR A LONG TIME.
AFTER A SIX-YEAR SEARCH...
...YOU'RE NOT SLIPPING AWAY FROM ME THAT EASILY.
TEE HEE ♡
……
HEE HEE.
EDITOR'S NOTE: ENTERING MITSUO'S BODY.

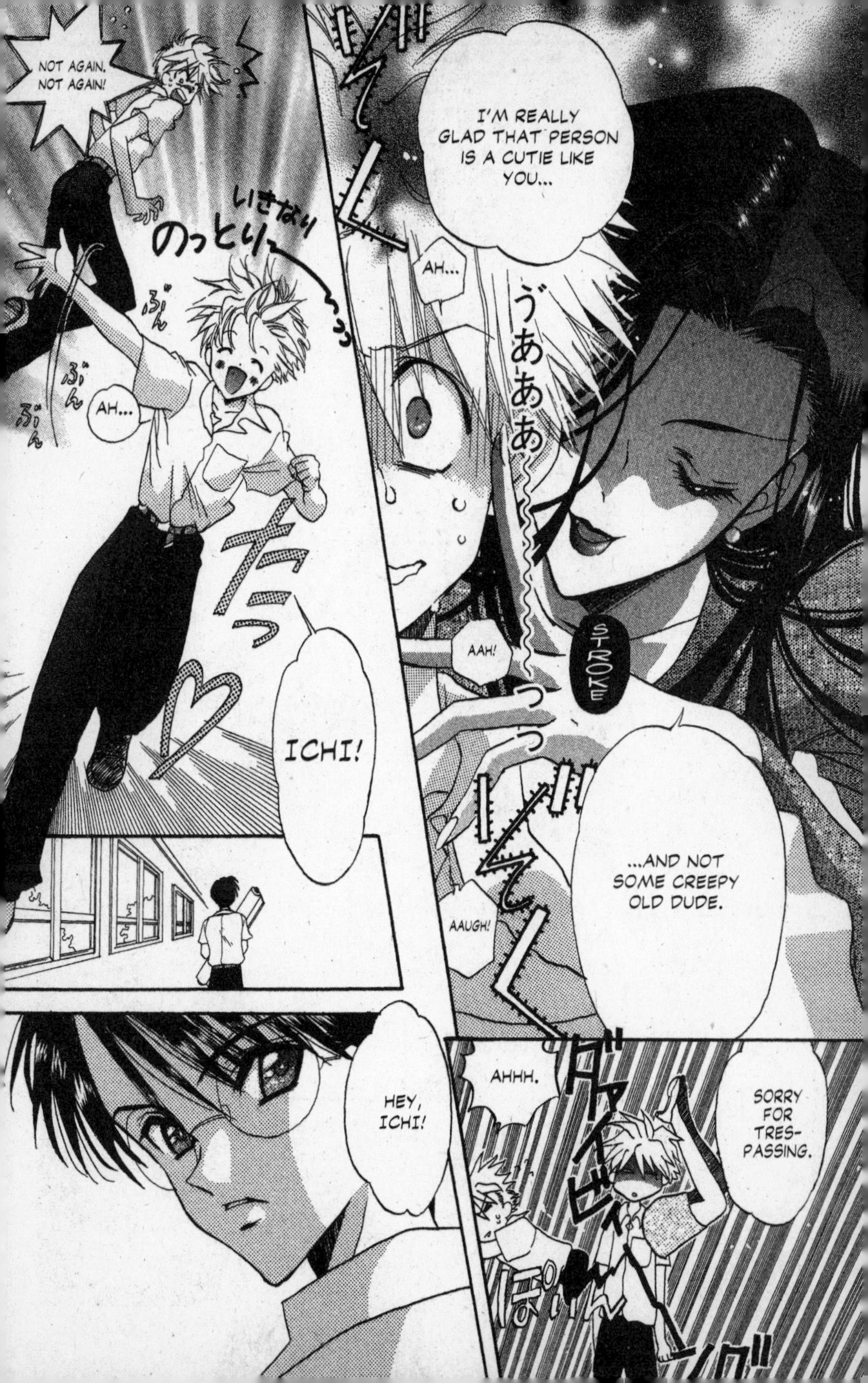
I'M REALLY GLAD THAT PERSON IS A CUTIE LIKE YOU...
AH...
うあああ〜
STROKE
AAH!
...AND NOT SOME CREEPY OLD DUDE.
AAUGH!
NOT AGAIN. NOT AGAIN!
いきなり
のっとり〜
ぶん
ぶん
ぶん
AH...
ICHI!
SORRY FOR TRES-PASSING.
AHHH.
HEY, ICHI!

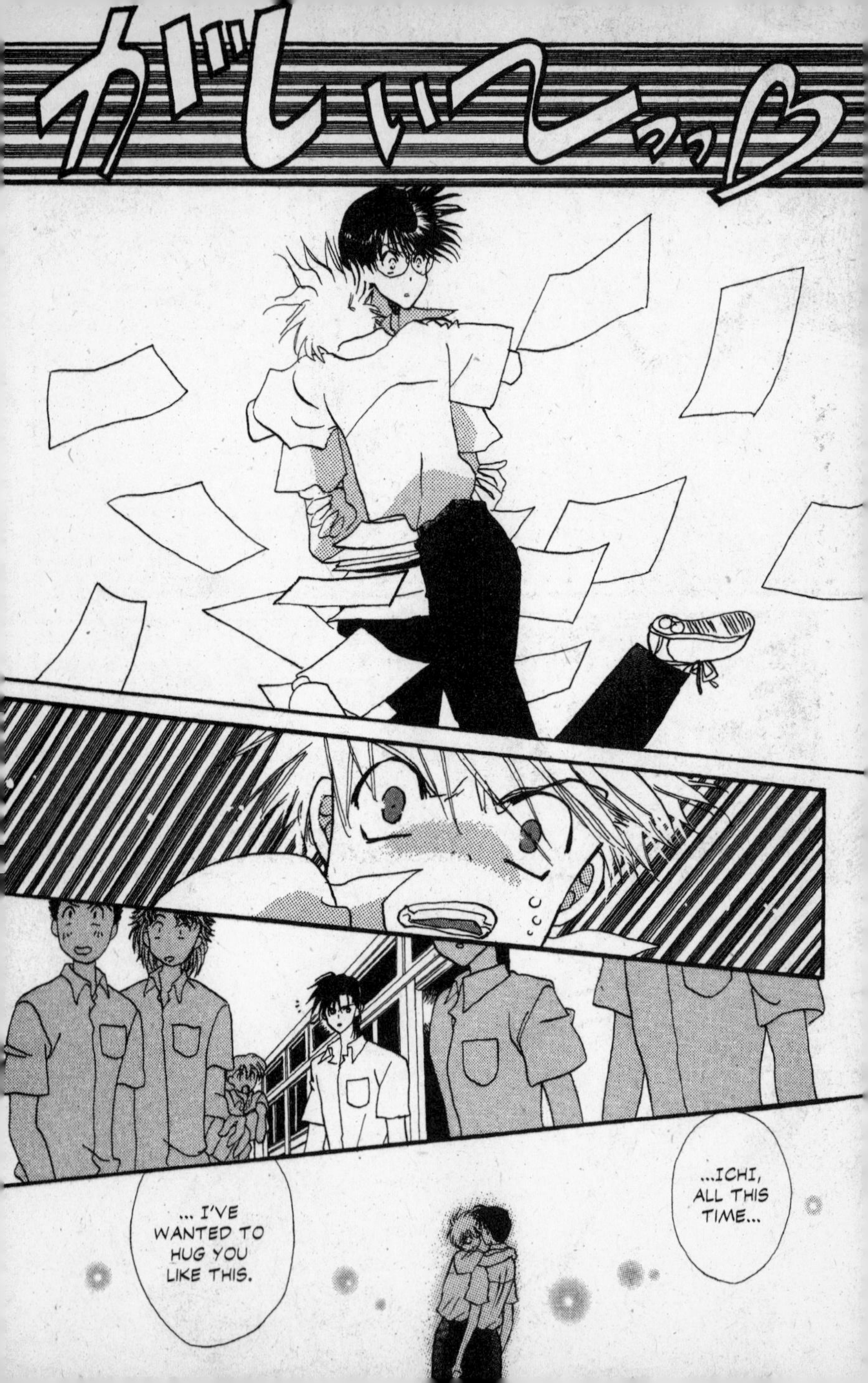
がしぃ〜っっ♡
...ICHI, ALL THIS TIME...
... I'VE WANTED TO HUG YOU LIKE THIS.

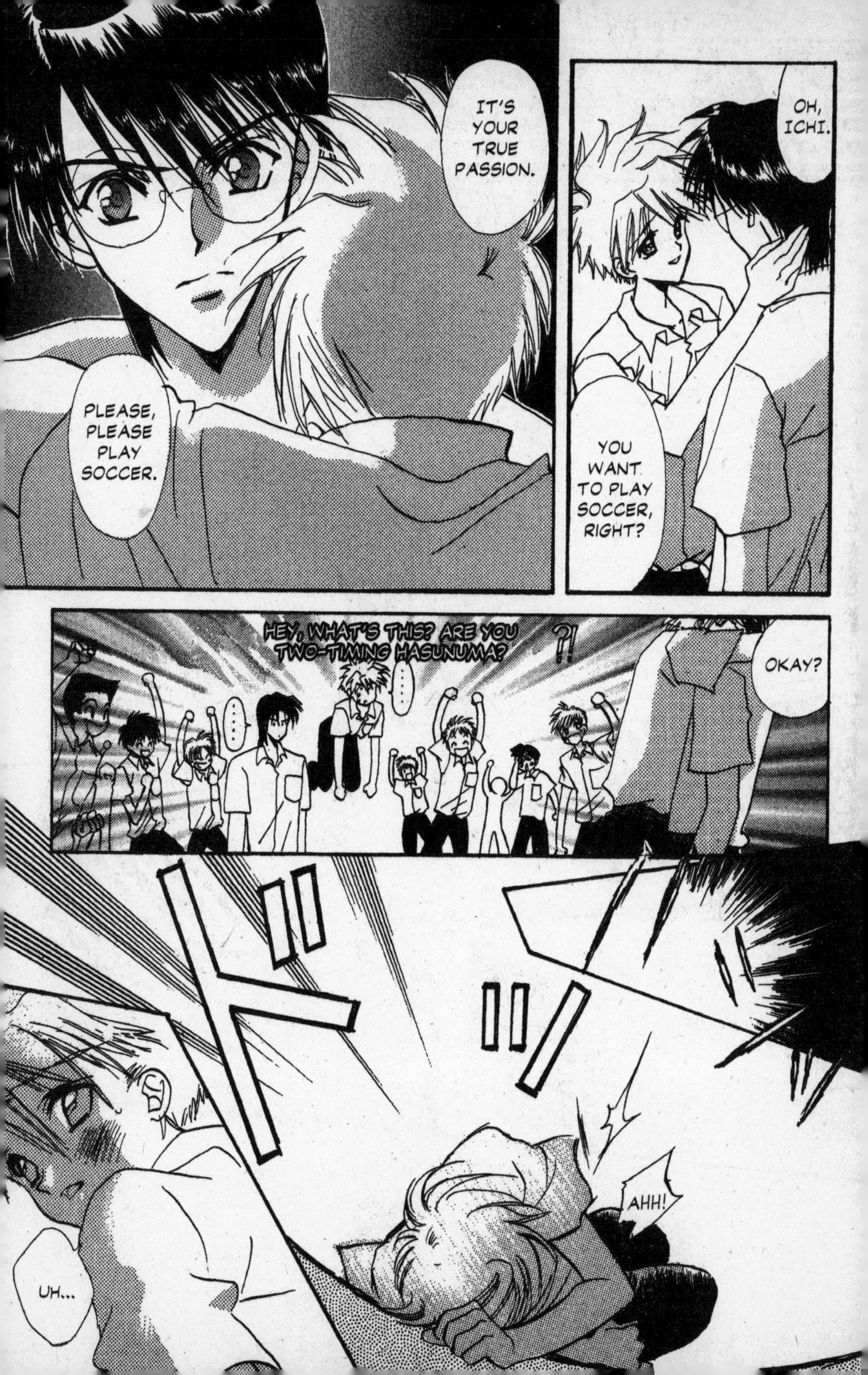
OH, ICHI.
YOU WANT TO PLAY SOCCER, RIGHT?
IT'S YOUR TRUE PASSION.
PLEASE, PLEASE PLAY SOCCER.
OKAY?
?!
HEY, WHAT'S THIS? ARE YOU TWO-TIMING HASUNUMA?
.....
.....
AHH!
UH...

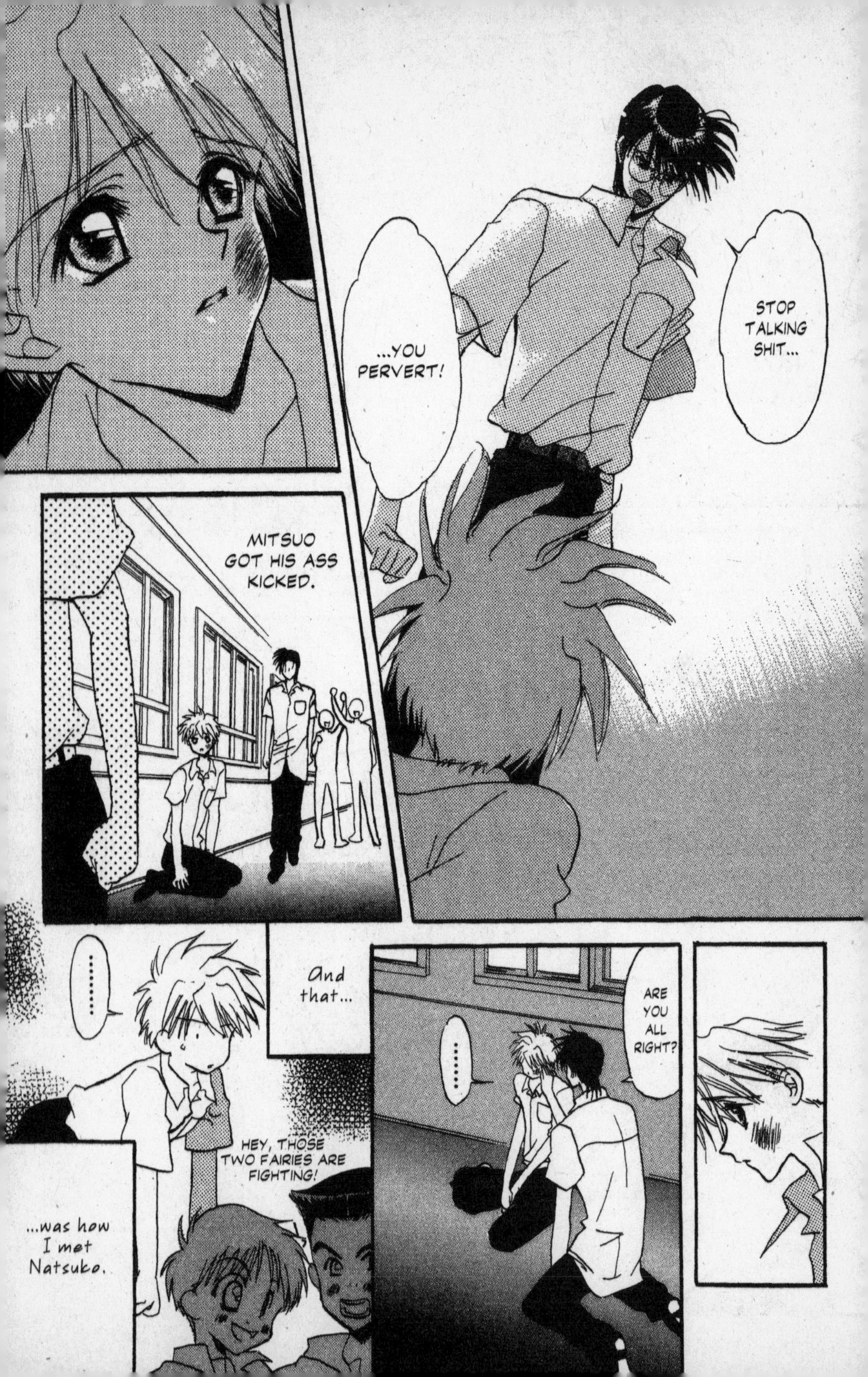
STOP TALKING SHIT...
...YOU PERVERT!
MITSUO GOT HIS ASS KICKED.
ARE YOU ALL RIGHT?
......
And that...
......
HEY, THOSE TWO FAIRIES ARE FIGHTING!
...was how I met Natsuko.

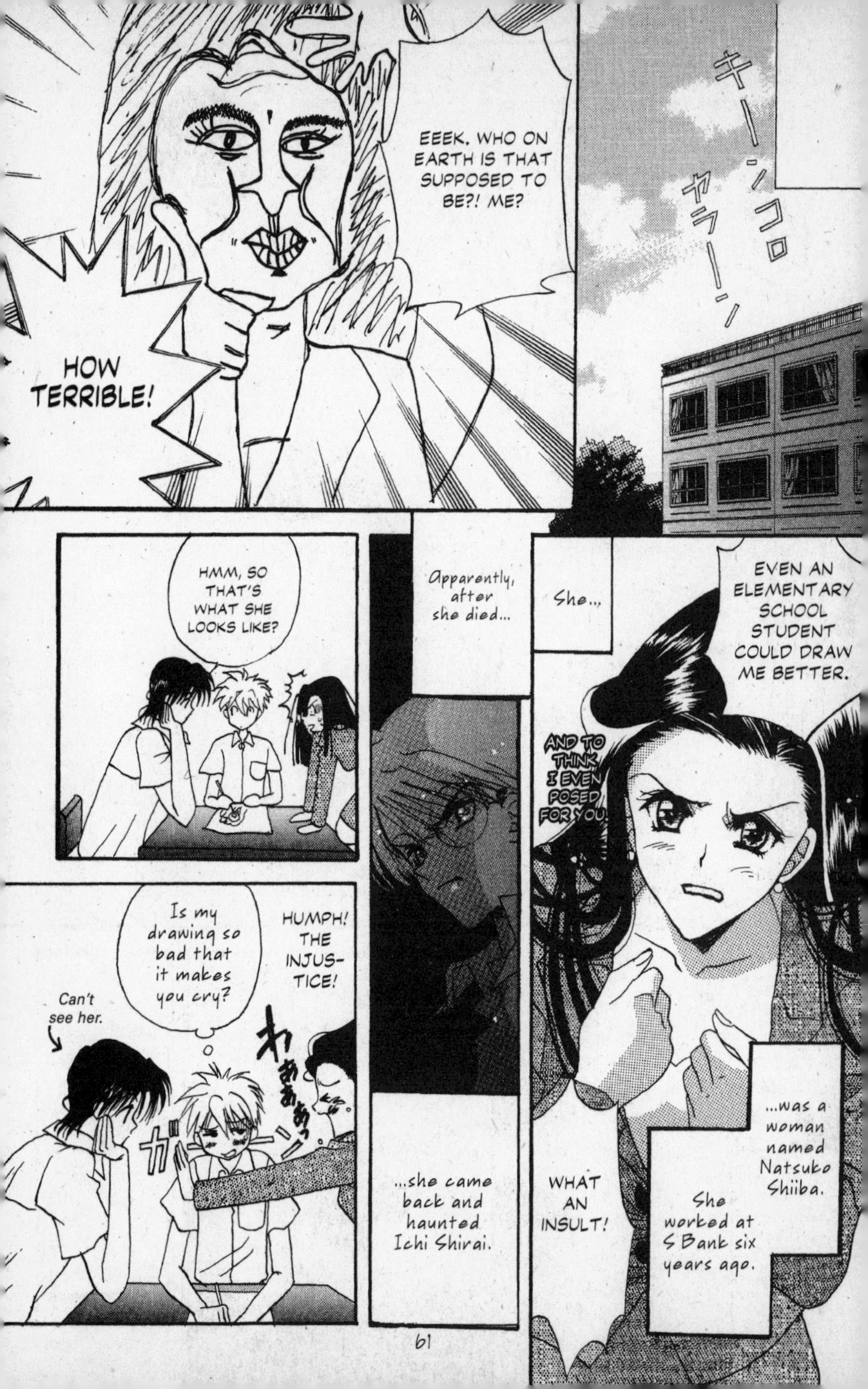
EEEK. WHO ON EARTH IS THAT SUPPOSED TO BE?! ME?
HOW TERRIBLE!
EVEN AN ELEMENTARY SCHOOL STUDENT COULD DRAW ME BETTER.
AND TO THINK I EVEN POSED FOR YOU.
She...
...was a woman named Natsuko Shiiba.
She worked at S Bank six years ago.
WHAT AN INSULT!
Apparently, after she died...
...she came back and haunted Ichi Shirai.
HMM, SO THAT'S WHAT SHE LOOKS LIKE?
Is my drawing so bad that it makes you cry?
HUMPH! THE INJUS-TICE!
Can't see her.

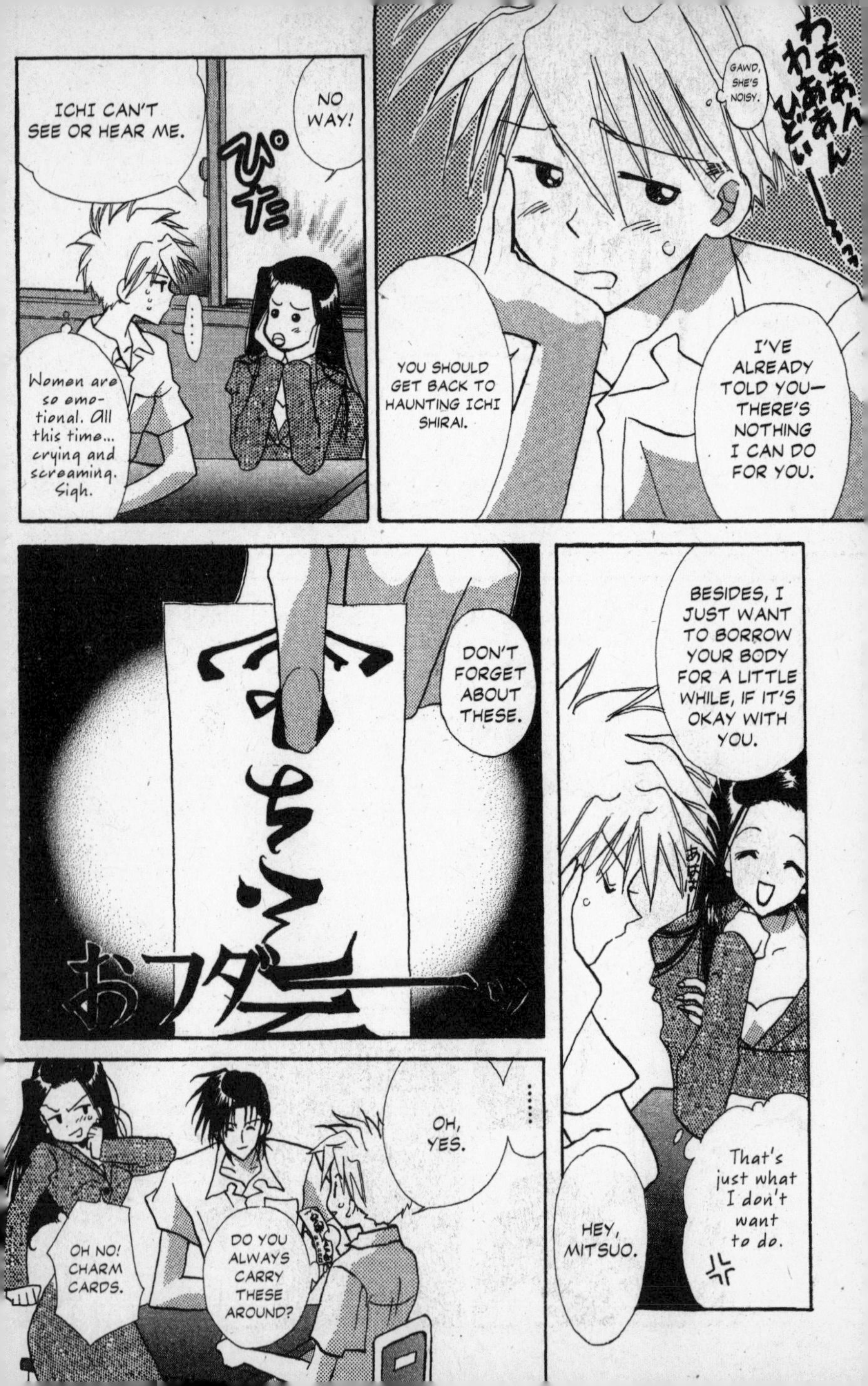

わあああん わあああん ひどい〜〜〜
GAWD, SHE'S NOISY.
I'VE ALREADY TOLD YOU—THERE'S NOTHING I CAN DO FOR YOU.
YOU SHOULD GET BACK TO HAUNTING ICHI SHIRAI.
NO WAY!
ぴたっ
ICHI CAN'T SEE OR HEAR ME.
......
Women are so emotional. All this time... crying and screaming. Sigh.
BESIDES, I JUST WANT TO BORROW YOUR BODY FOR A LITTLE WHILE, IF IT'S OKAY WITH YOU.
あはは
That's just what I don't want to do.
HEY, MITSUO.
DON'T FORGET ABOUT THESE.
おフダ〜〜っ
......
OH, YES.
DO YOU ALWAYS CARRY THESE AROUND?
OH NO! CHARM CARDS.

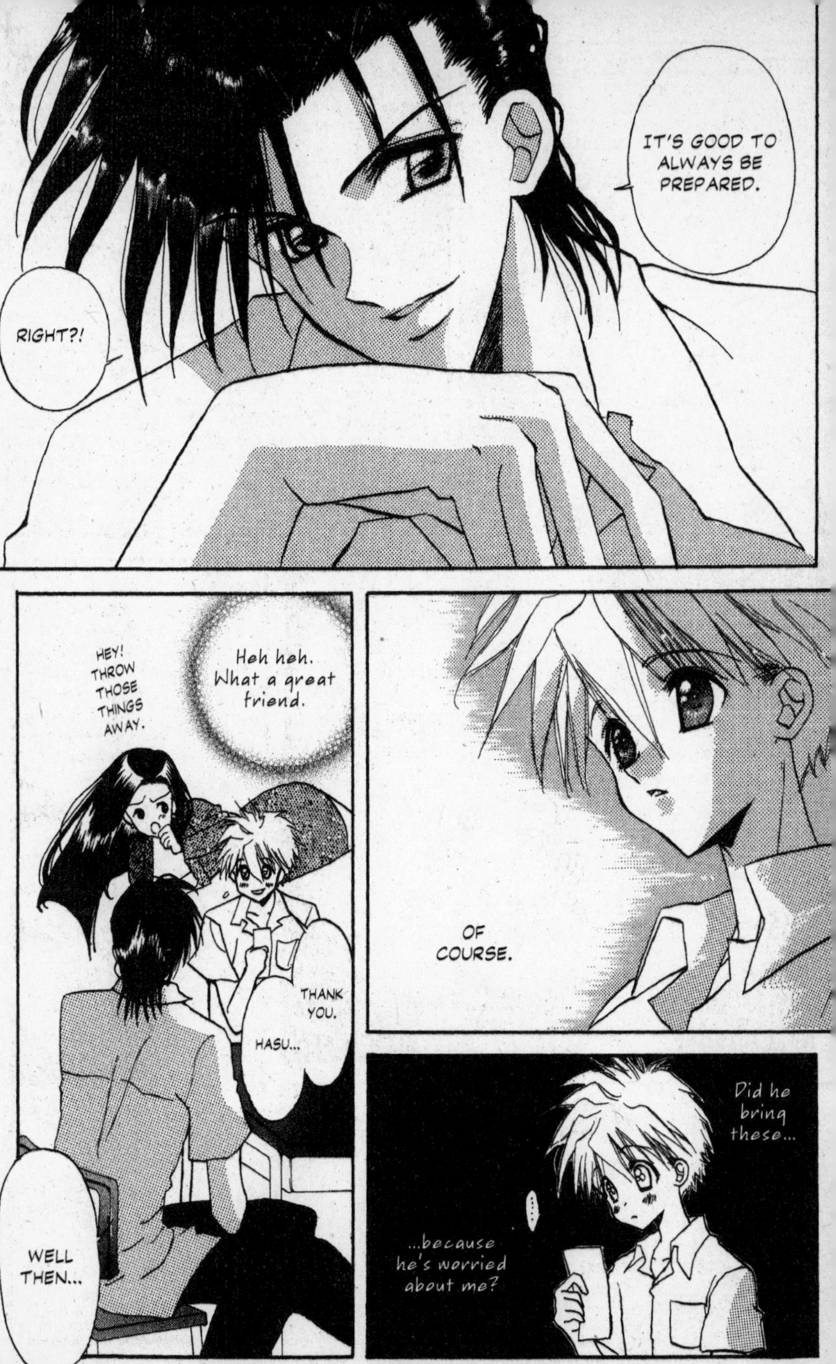
IT'S GOOD TO ALWAYS BE PREPARED.
RIGHT?!
OF COURSE.
Did he bring these...
.....
...because he's worried about me?
Heh heh. What a great friend.
HEY! THROW THOSE THINGS AWAY.
THANK YOU.
HASU...
WELL THEN...

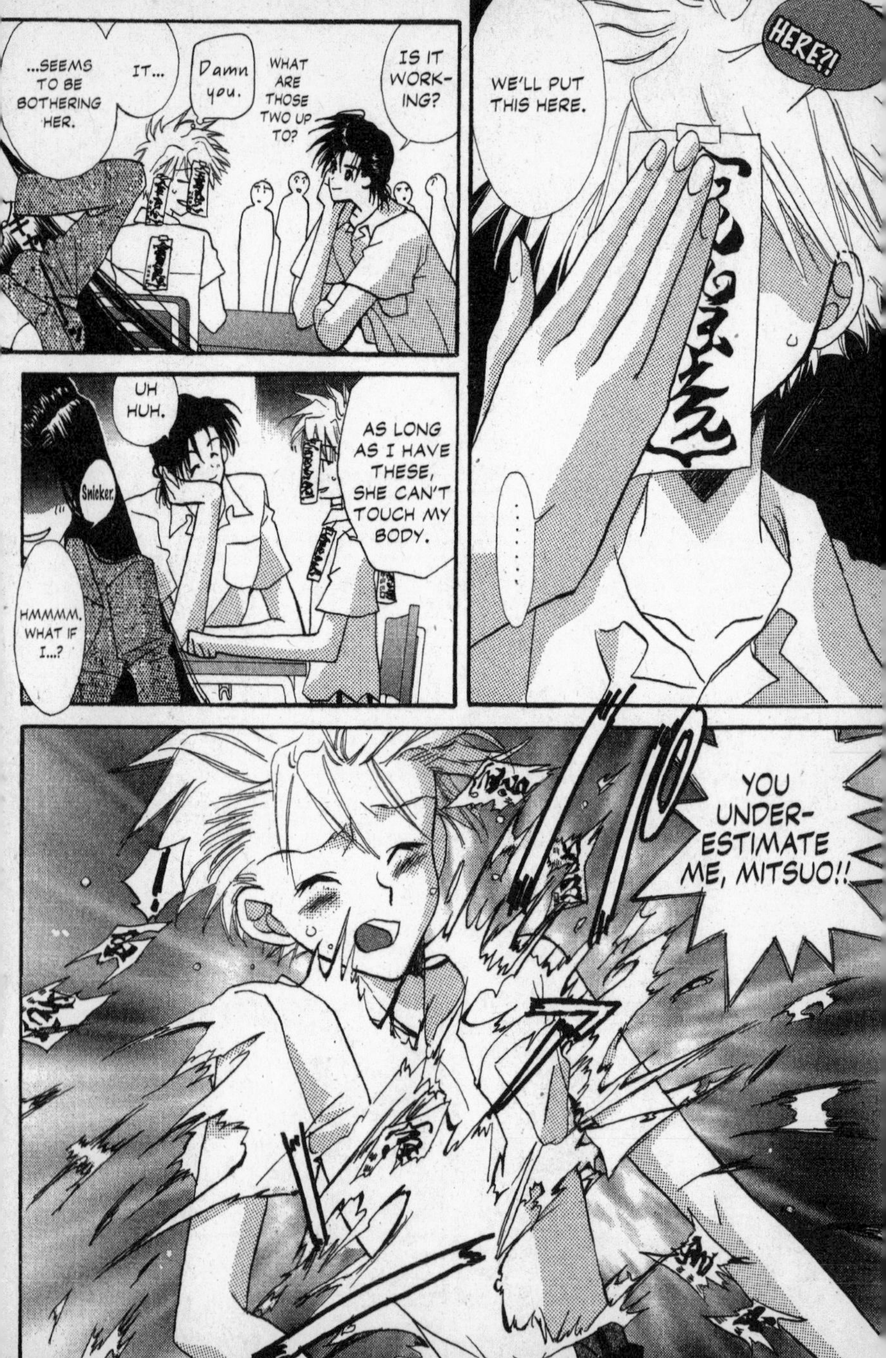
WE'LL PUT THIS HERE.
HERE?!
......
IS IT WORKING?
WHAT ARE THOSE TWO UP TO?
Damn you.
IT...
...SEEMS TO BE BOTHERING HER.
AS LONG AS I HAVE THESE, SHE CAN'T TOUCH MY BODY.
UH HUH.
Snicker.
HMMMM. WHAT IF I...?
YOU UNDER-ESTIMATE ME, MITSUO!!

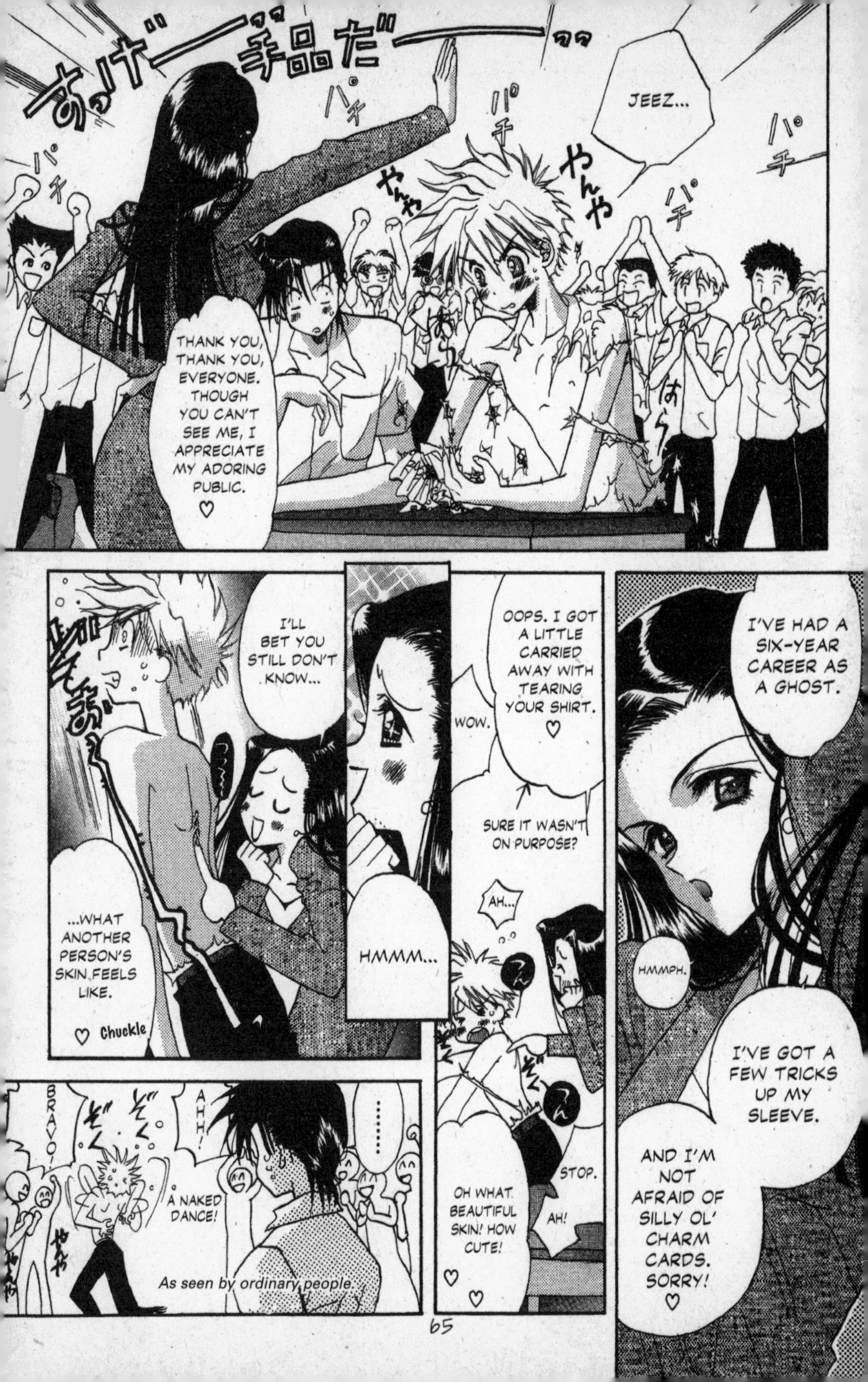
すっげー手品だーっっ
パチ パチ パチ パチ パチ
やんや やんや
JEEZ...
THANK YOU, THANK YOU, EVERYONE. THOUGH YOU CAN'T SEE ME, I APPRECIATE MY ADORING PUBLIC. ♡
I'VE HAD A SIX-YEAR CAREER AS A GHOST.
HMMPH.
I'VE GOT A FEW TRICKS UP MY SLEEVE.
AND I'M NOT AFRAID OF SILLY OL' CHARM CARDS. SORRY! ♡
OOPS. I GOT A LITTLE CARRIED AWAY WITH TEARING YOUR SHIRT. ♡
WOW.
SURE IT WASN'T ON PURPOSE?
AH...
STOP.
AH!
OH WHAT BEAUTIFUL SKIN! HOW CUTE! ♡ ♡
HMMM...
I'LL BET YOU STILL DON'T KNOW...
...WHAT ANOTHER PERSON'S SKIN FEELS LIKE.
♡ Chuckle
AHH!
......
BRAVO!
A NAKED DANCE!
As seen by ordinary people.

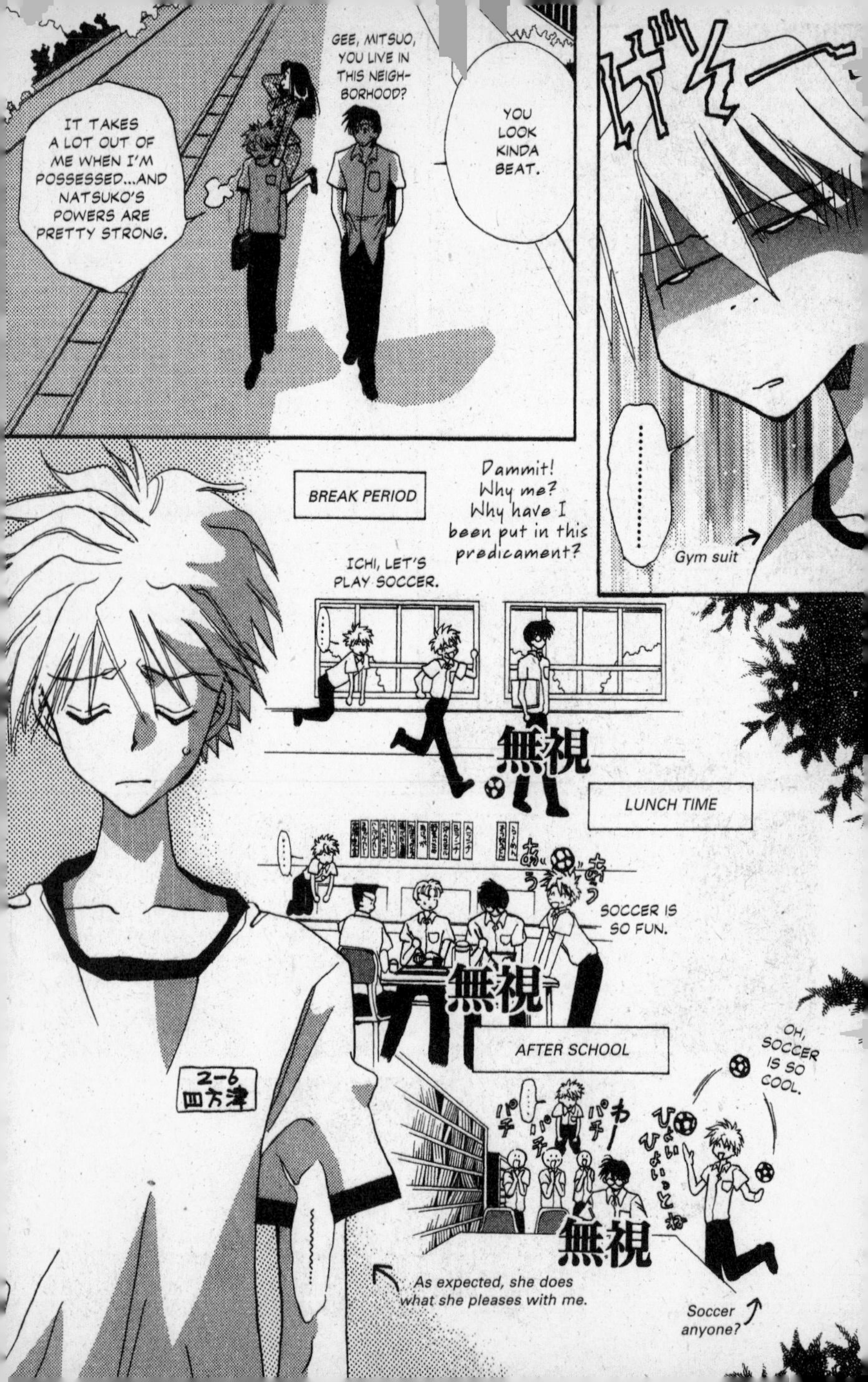

......
Gym suit
GEE, MITSUO, YOU LIVE IN THIS NEIGHBORHOOD?
YOU LOOK KINDA BEAT.
IT TAKES A LOT OUT OF ME WHEN I'M POSSESSED...AND NATSUKO'S POWERS ARE PRETTY STRONG.
Dammit! Why me? Why have I been put in this predicament?
BREAK PERIOD
ICHI, LET'S PLAY SOCCER.
無視
LUNCH TIME
SOCCER IS SO FUN.
無視
AFTER SCHOOL
OH, SOCCER IS SO COOL.
無視
Soccer anyone?
As expected, she does what she pleases with me.
2-6
四方津

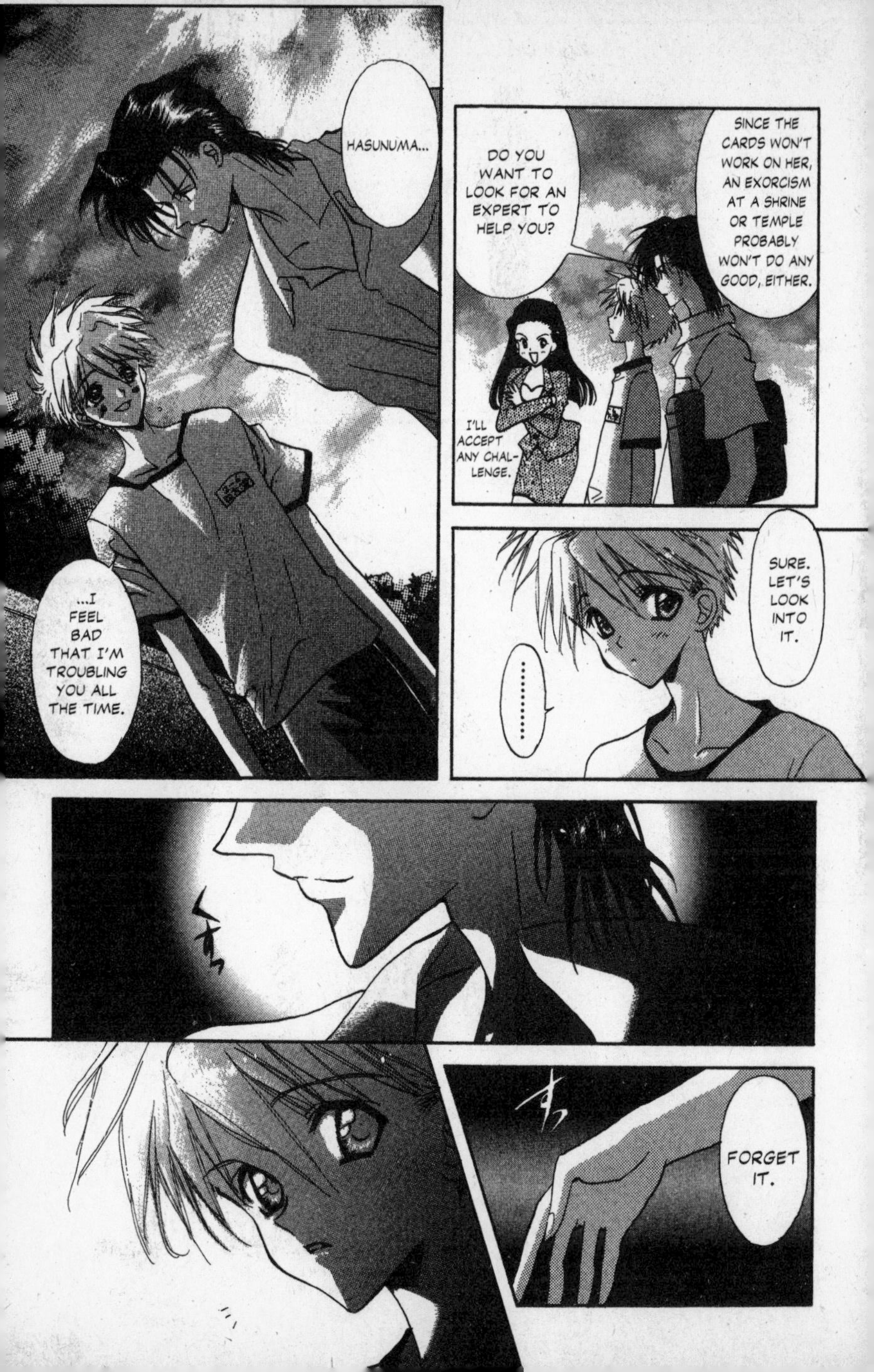
SINCE THE CARDS WON'T WORK ON HER, AN EXORCISM AT A SHRINE OR TEMPLE PROBABLY WON'T DO ANY GOOD, EITHER.
DO YOU WANT TO LOOK FOR AN EXPERT TO HELP YOU?
I'LL ACCEPT ANY CHAL-LENGE.
SURE. LET'S LOOK INTO IT.
....
HASUNUMA...
...I FEEL BAD THAT I'M TROUBLING YOU ALL THE TIME.
FORGET IT.

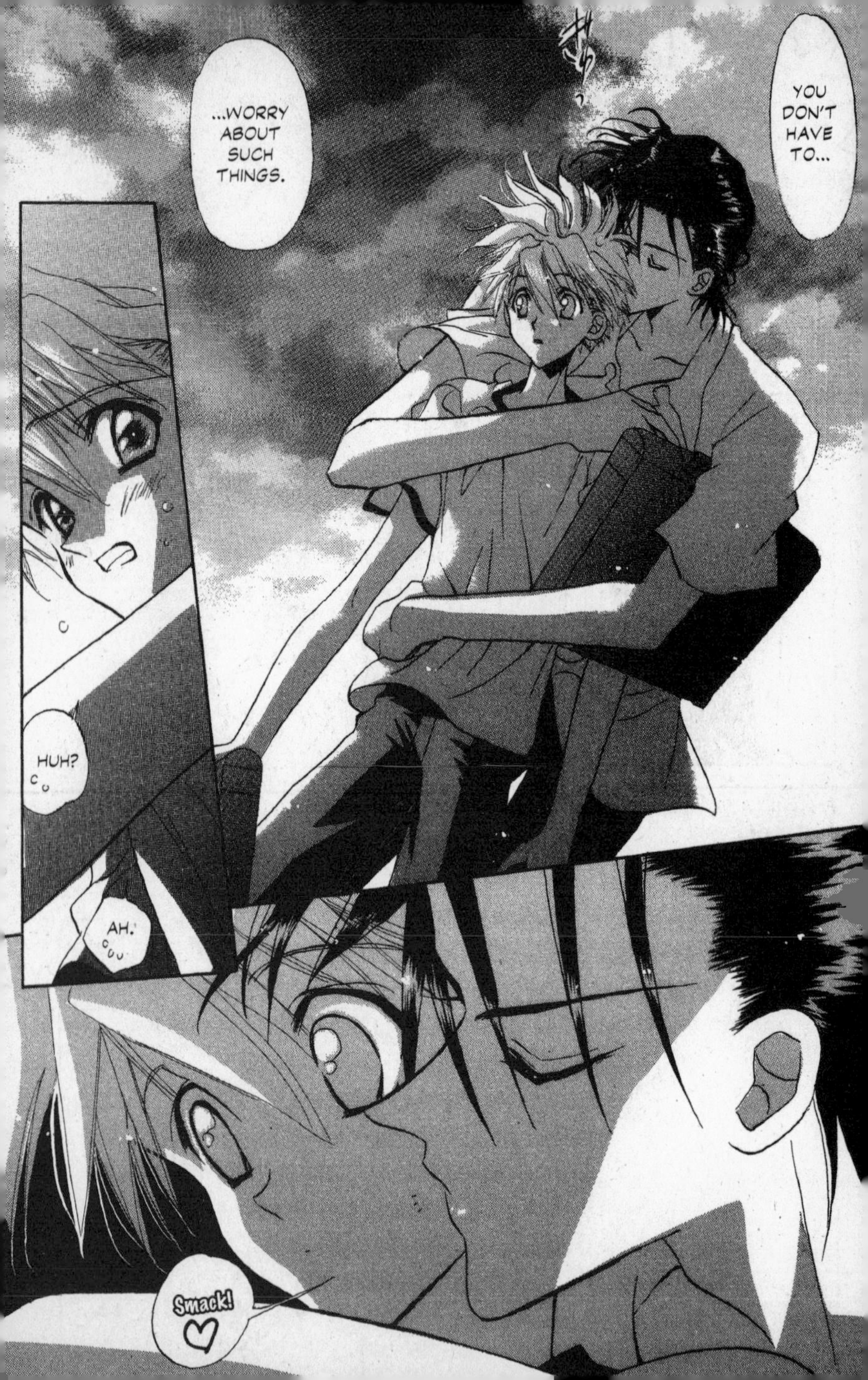
YOU DON'T HAVE TO...
...WORRY ABOUT SUCH THINGS.
HUH?
AH.
Smack!

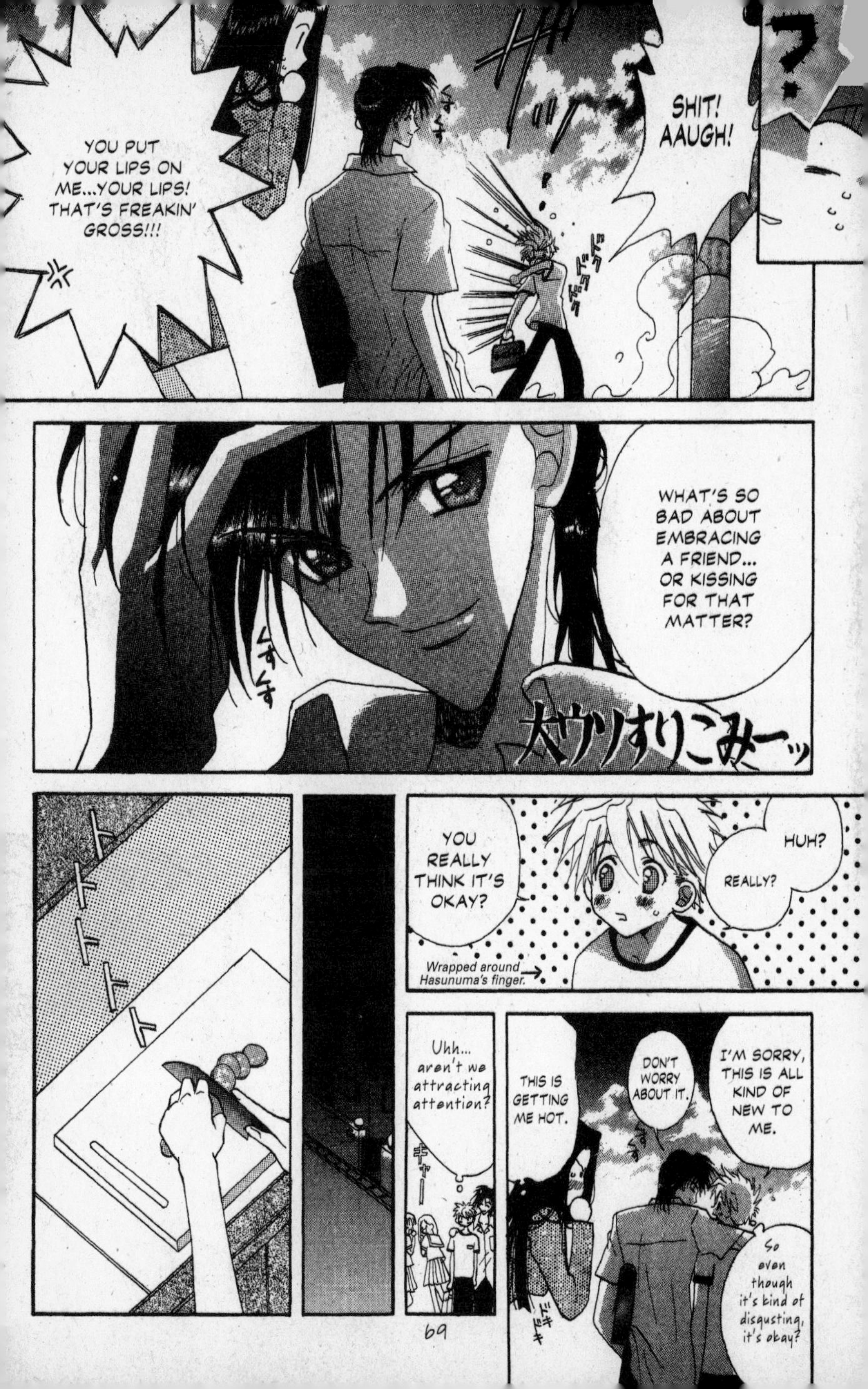
?
SHIT! AAUGH!
YOU PUT YOUR LIPS ON ME...YOUR LIPS! THAT'S FREAKIN' GROSS!!!
WHAT'S SO BAD ABOUT EMBRACING A FRIEND... OR KISSING FOR THAT MATTER?
くすくす
HUH?
REALLY?
YOU REALLY THINK IT'S OKAY?
Wrapped around Hasunuma's finger.
I'M SORRY, THIS IS ALL KIND OF NEW TO ME.
DON'T WORRY ABOUT IT.
THIS IS GETTING ME HOT.
So even though it's kind of disgusting, it's okay?
Uhh... aren't we attracting attention?
キャー

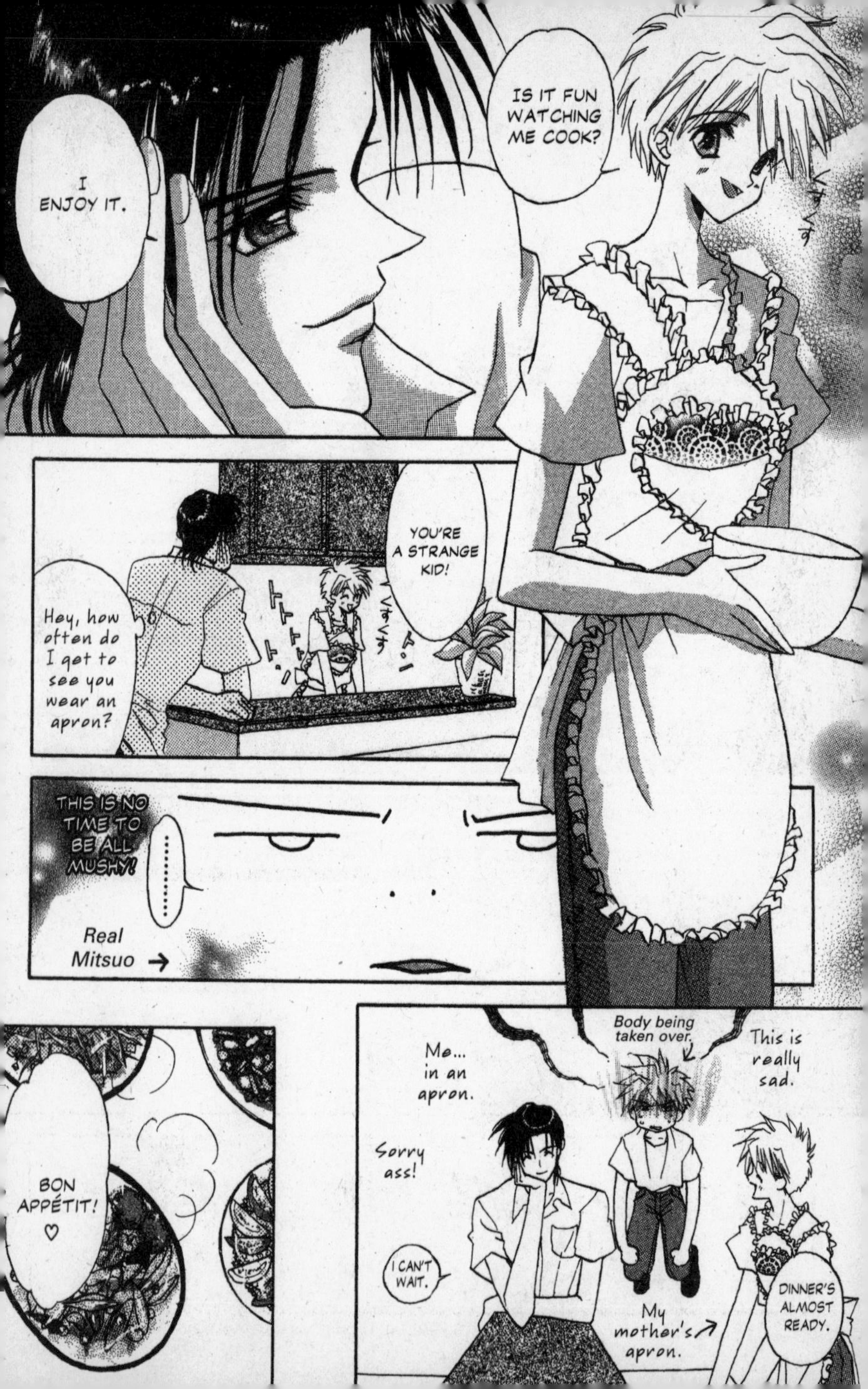
IS IT FUN WATCHING ME COOK?
I ENJOY IT.
YOU'RE A STRANGE KID!
Hey, how often do I get to see you wear an apron?
THIS IS NO TIME TO BE ALL MUSHY!
......
Real Mitsuo →
This is really sad.
Body being taken over.
Me... in an apron.
Sorry ass!
DINNER'S ALMOST READY.
My mother's apron.
I CAN'T WAIT.
BON APPÉTIT! ♡

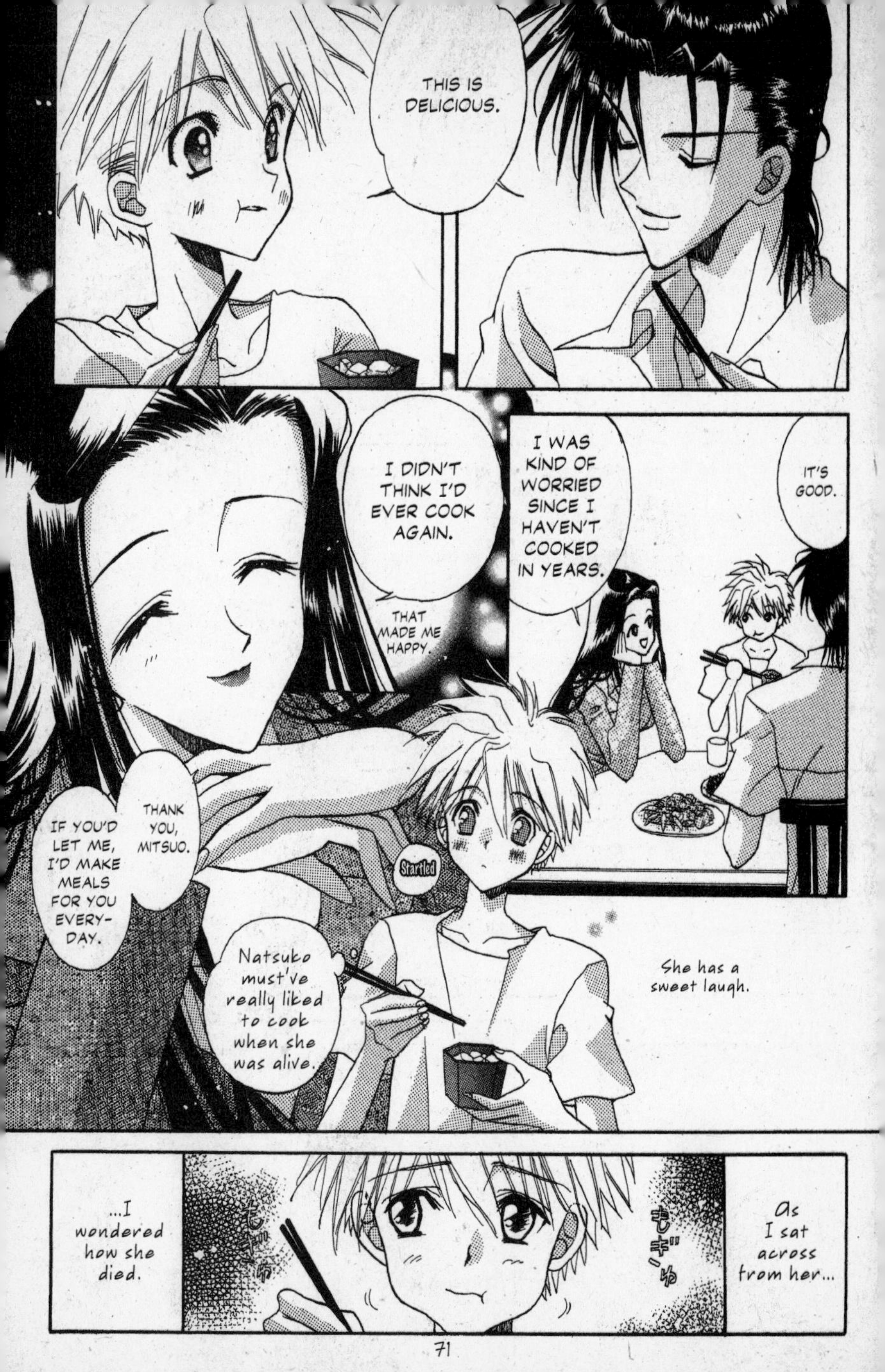
THIS IS DELICIOUS.
IT'S GOOD.
I WAS KIND OF WORRIED SINCE I HAVEN'T COOKED IN YEARS.
I DIDN'T THINK I'D EVER COOK AGAIN.
THAT MADE ME HAPPY.
THANK YOU, MITSUO.
IF YOU'D LET ME, I'D MAKE MEALS FOR YOU EVERY-DAY.
Startled
She has a sweet laugh.
Natsuko must've really liked to cook when she was alive.
As I sat across from her...
もぎゅ
もぎゅ
...I wondered how she died.

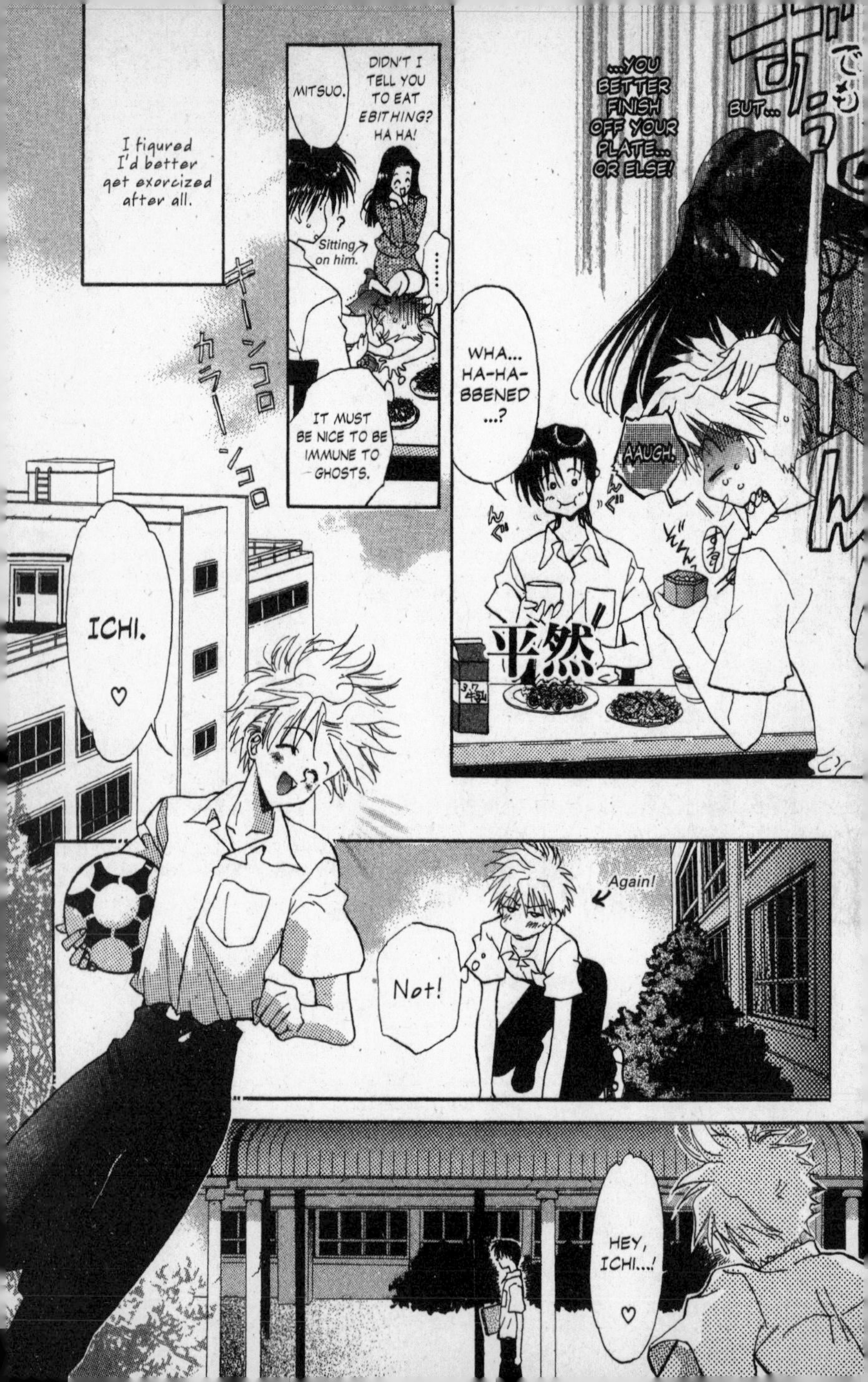

BUT...
...YOU BETTER FINISH OFF YOUR PLATE... OR ELSE!
AAUGH.
WHA... HA-HA-BBENED ...?
平然
DIDN'T I TELL YOU TO EAT EBITHING? HA HA!
MITSUO.
......
Sitting on him.
?
IT MUST BE NICE TO BE IMMUNE TO GHOSTS.
I figured I'd better get exorcized after all.
ICHI. ♡
Again!
Not!
HEY, ICHI...! ♡

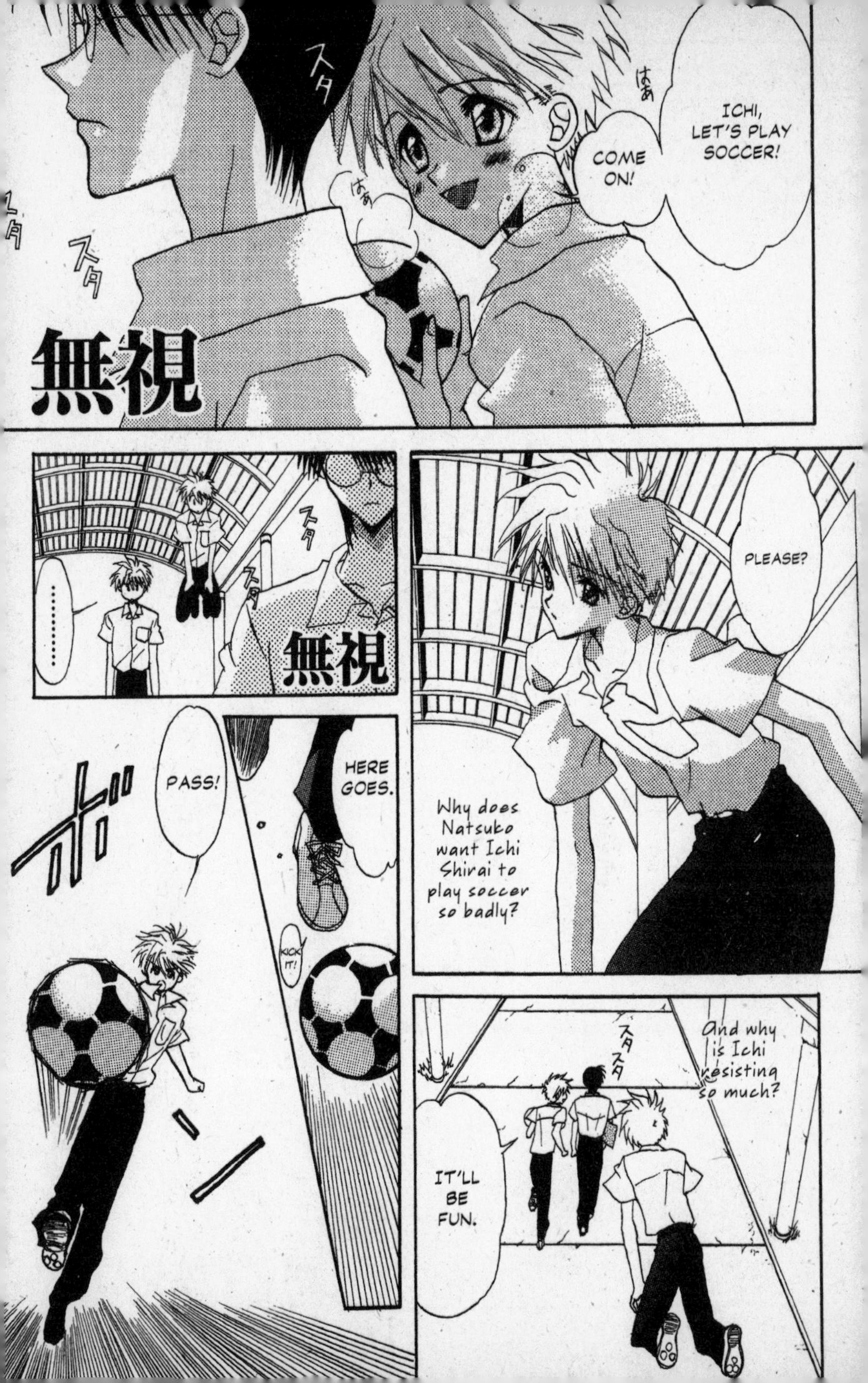
ICHI, LET'S PLAY SOCCER!
COME ON!
はぁ
スタ
はぁ
スタ
スタ
無視
PLEASE?
Why does Natsuko want Ichi Shirai to play soccer so badly?
スタ
スタ
無視
……
And why is Ichi resisting so much?
スタスタ
IT'LL BE FUN.
HERE GOES.
PASS!
KICK IT!
ボ

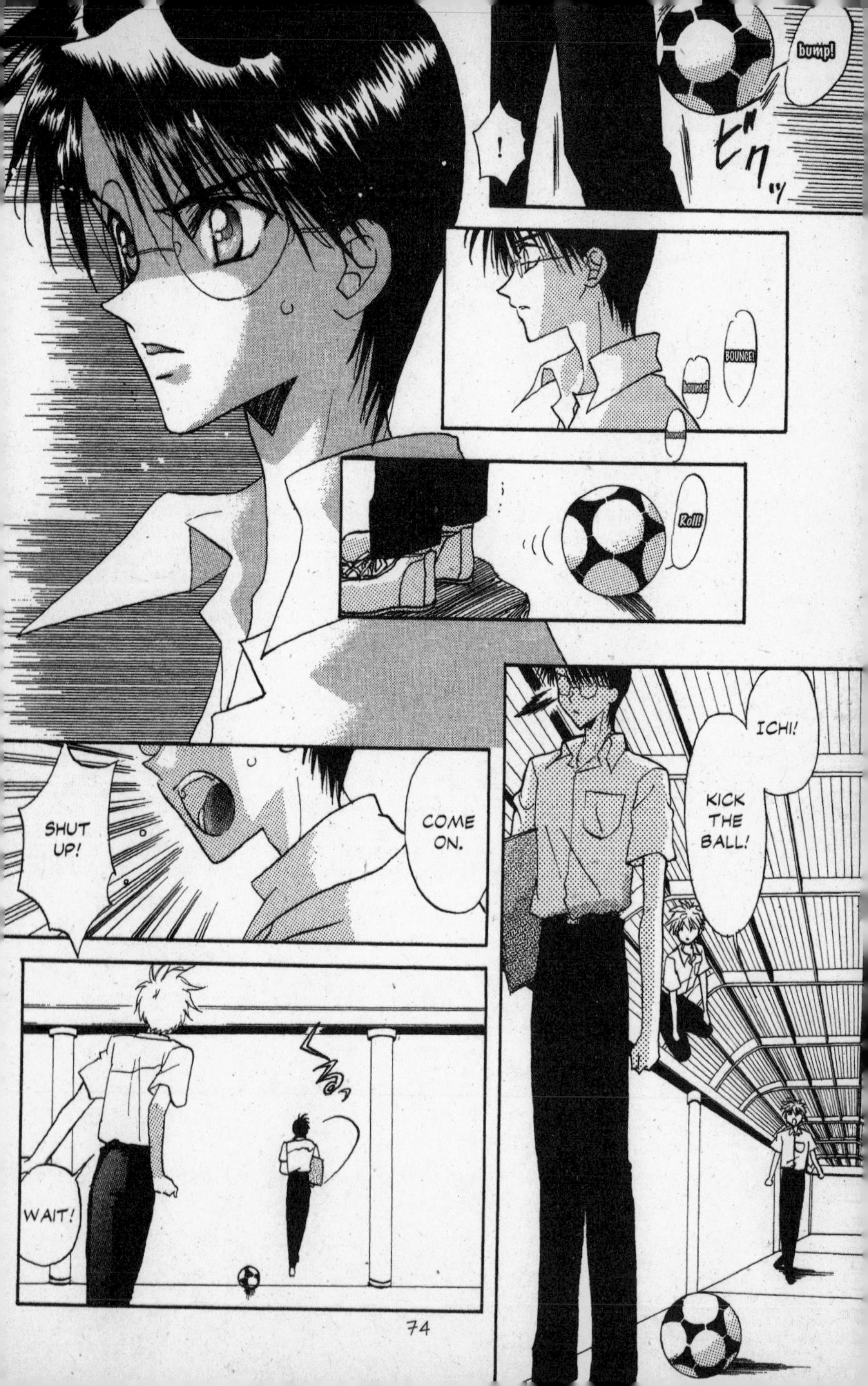
bump!
ビクッ
!
BOUNCE!
bounce!
bounce!
Roll!
ICHI!
KICK THE BALL!
COME ON.
SHUT UP!
WAIT!

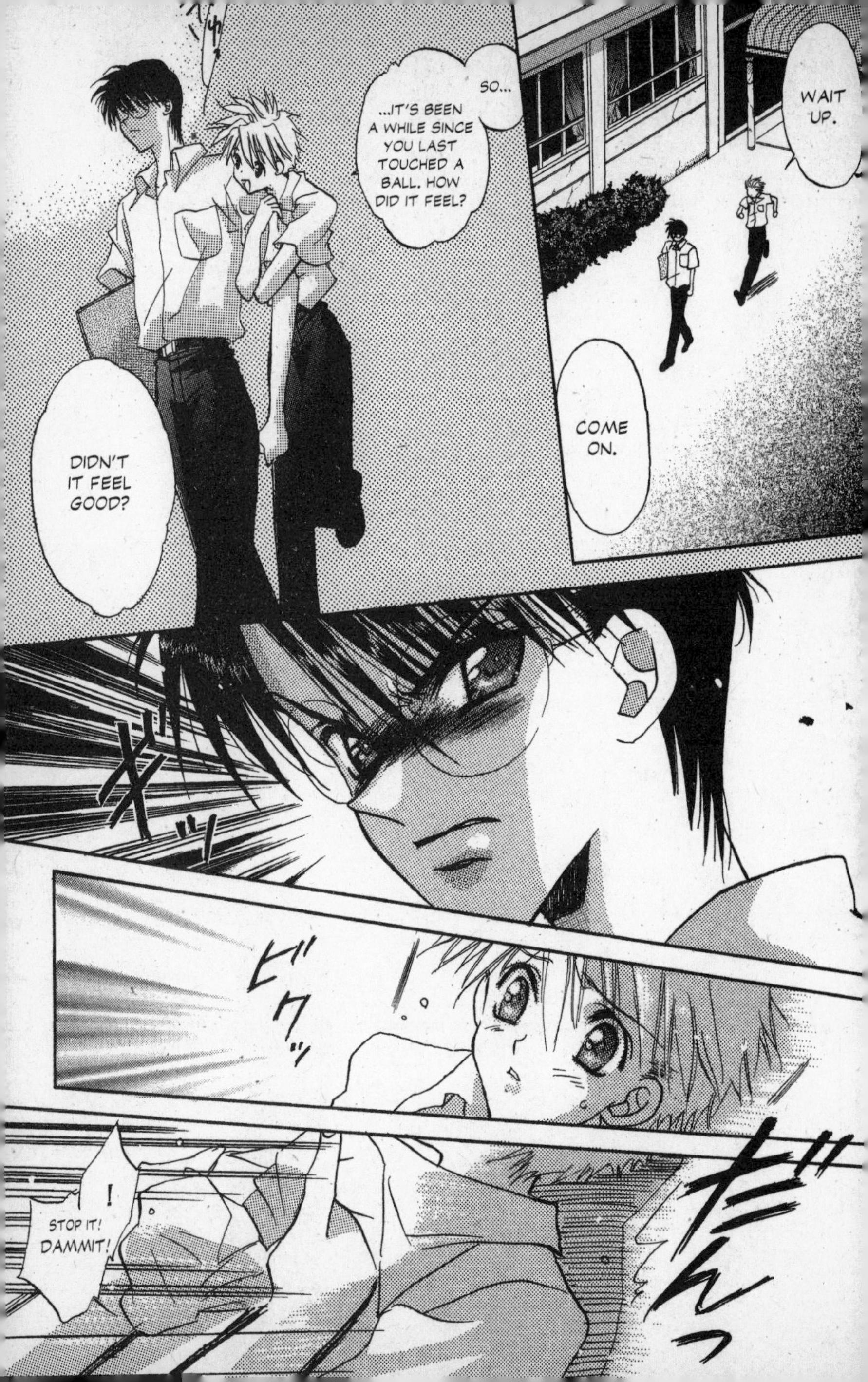
WAIT UP.
COME ON.
SO...
...IT'S BEEN A WHILE SINCE YOU LAST TOUCHED A BALL. HOW DID IT FEEL?
DIDN'T IT FEEL GOOD?
ビクッ
!
STOP IT! DAMMIT!
ダンッ

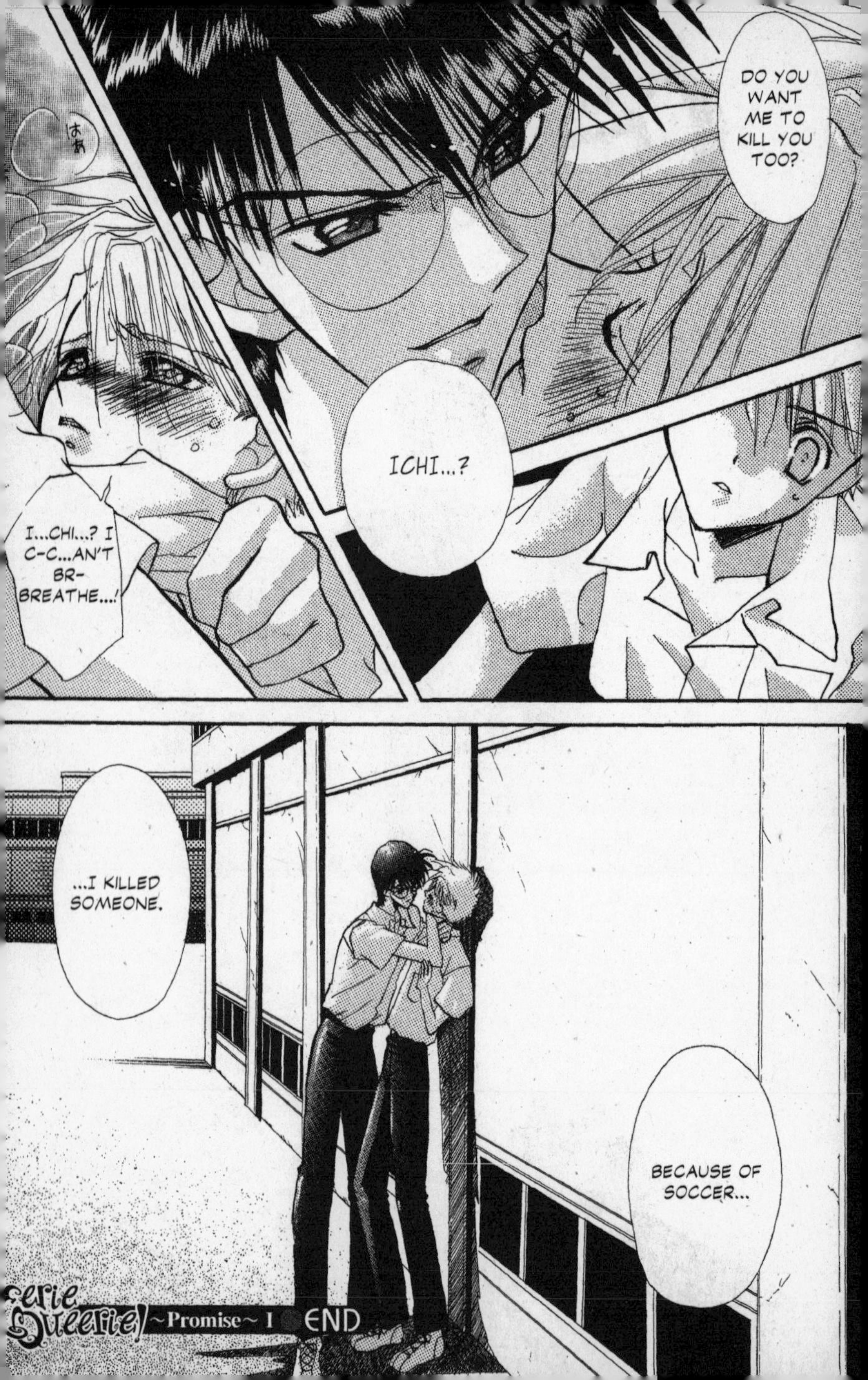

DO YOU WANT ME TO KILL YOU TOO?
ICHI...?
はぁ
I...CHI...? I C-C...AN'T BR-BREATHE...!
...I KILLED SOMEONE.
BECAUSE OF SOCCER...
Eerie Queerie! ~Promise~ I END

EERIE QUEERIE!

~Promise~ II

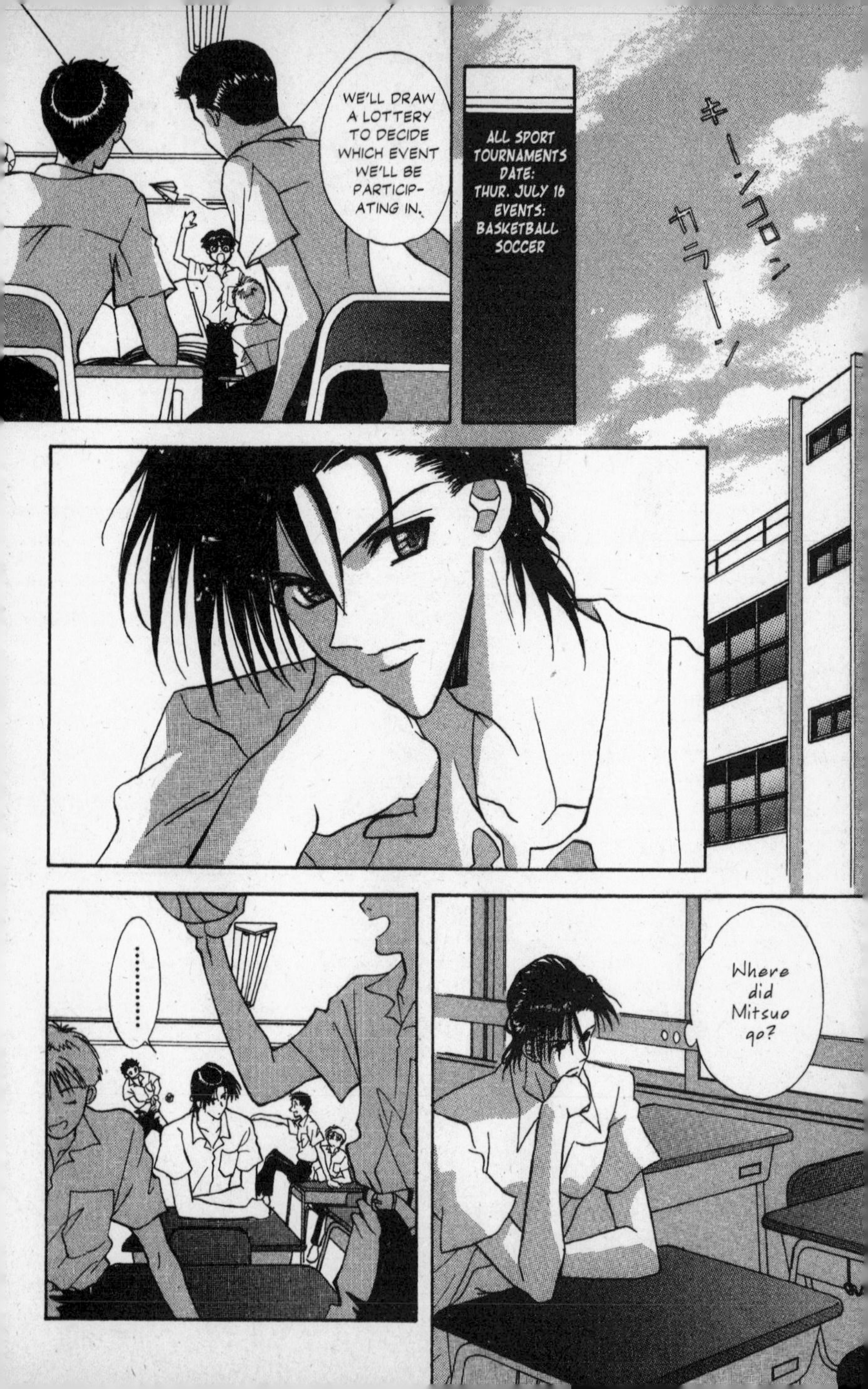
ALL SPORT TOURNAMENTS DATE: THUR. JULY 16 EVENTS: BASKETBALL SOCCER
キーンコロン
カラーン
WE'LL DRAW A LOTTERY TO DECIDE WHICH EVENT WE'LL BE PARTICIPATING IN.
Where did Mitsuo go?
....

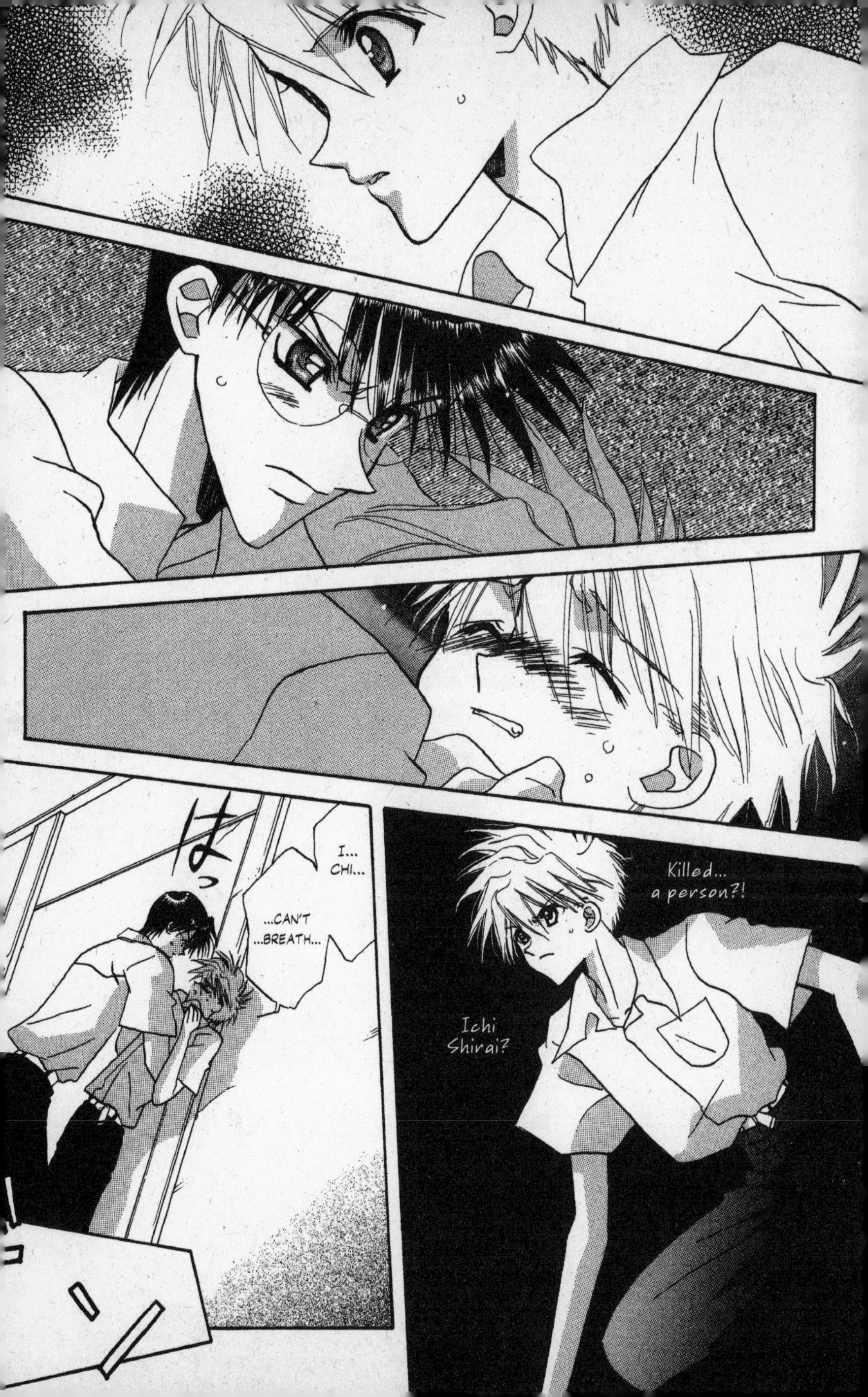
Killed... a person?!
Ichi Shirai?
はっ
I... CHI...
...CAN'T ...BREATH...

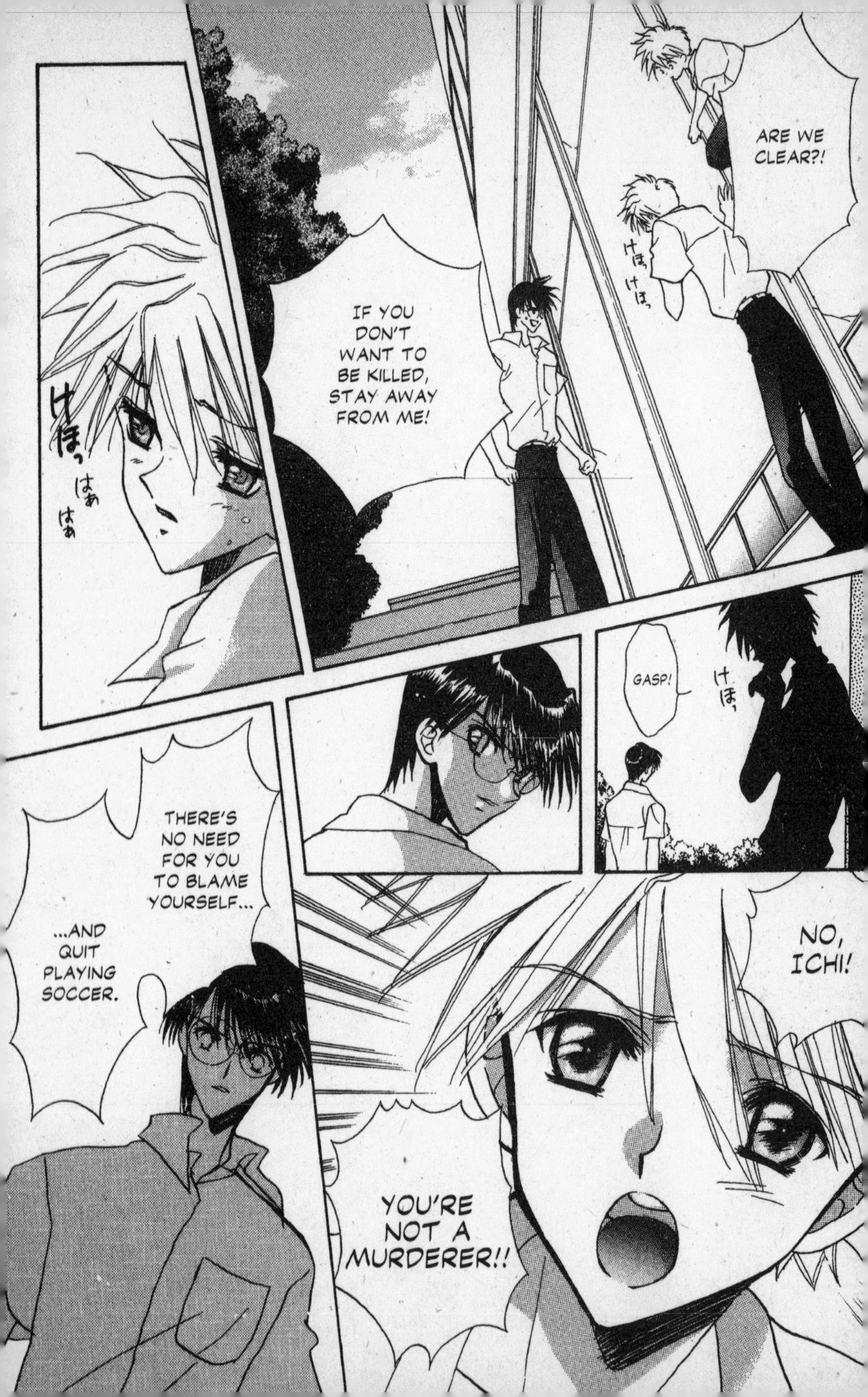
ARE WE CLEAR?!
けほっ けほっ
IF YOU DON'T WANT TO BE KILLED, STAY AWAY FROM ME!
GASP!
けほっ
けほっ
はぁ はぁ
NO, ICHI!
YOU'RE NOT A MURDERER!!
THERE'S NO NEED FOR YOU TO BLAME YOURSELF...
...AND QUIT PLAYING SOCCER.

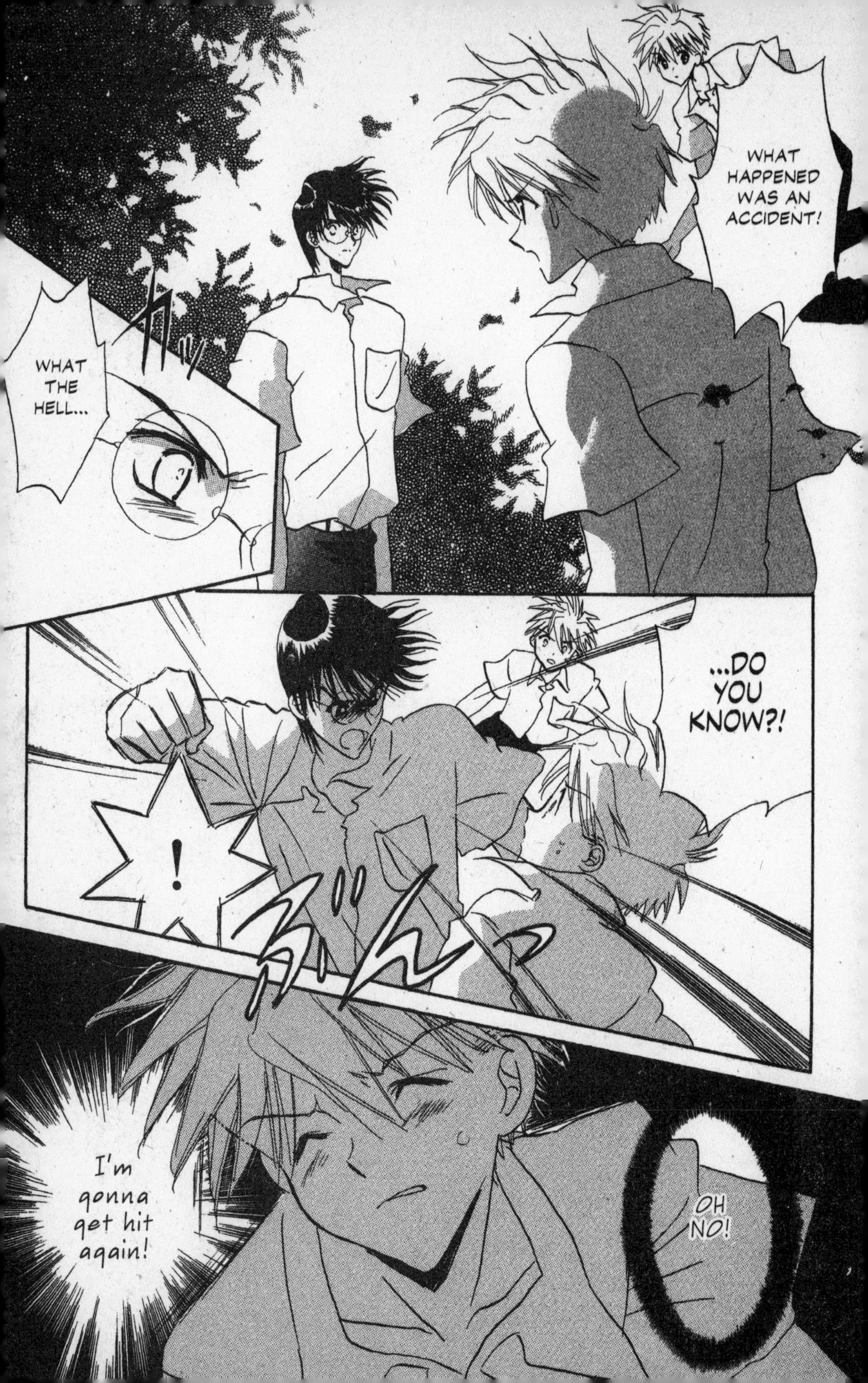
WHAT HAPPENED WAS AN ACCIDENT!
WHAT THE HELL...
...DO YOU KNOW?!
!
OH NO!
I'm gonna get hit again!

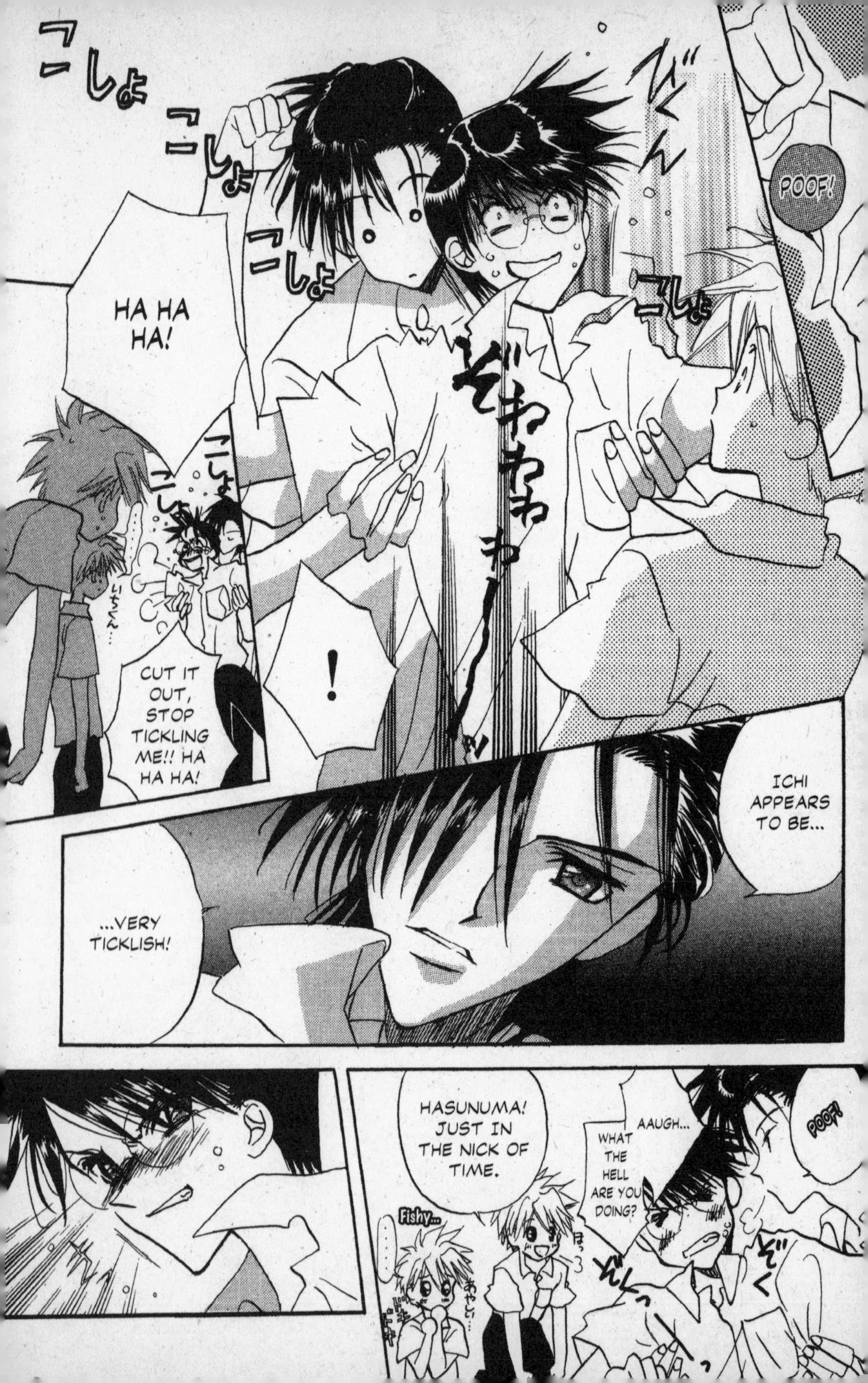
POOF!
びくん
こーしょ
こーしょ
こーしょ
こーしょ
HA HA HA!
ぞわわわ~
!
こしょ こしょ
CUT IT OUT, STOP TICKLING ME!! HA HA HA!
ICHI APPEARS TO BE...
...VERY TICKLISH!
POOF!
AAUGH...
WHAT THE HELL ARE YOU DOING?
HASUNUMA! JUST IN THE NICK OF TIME.
Fishy...

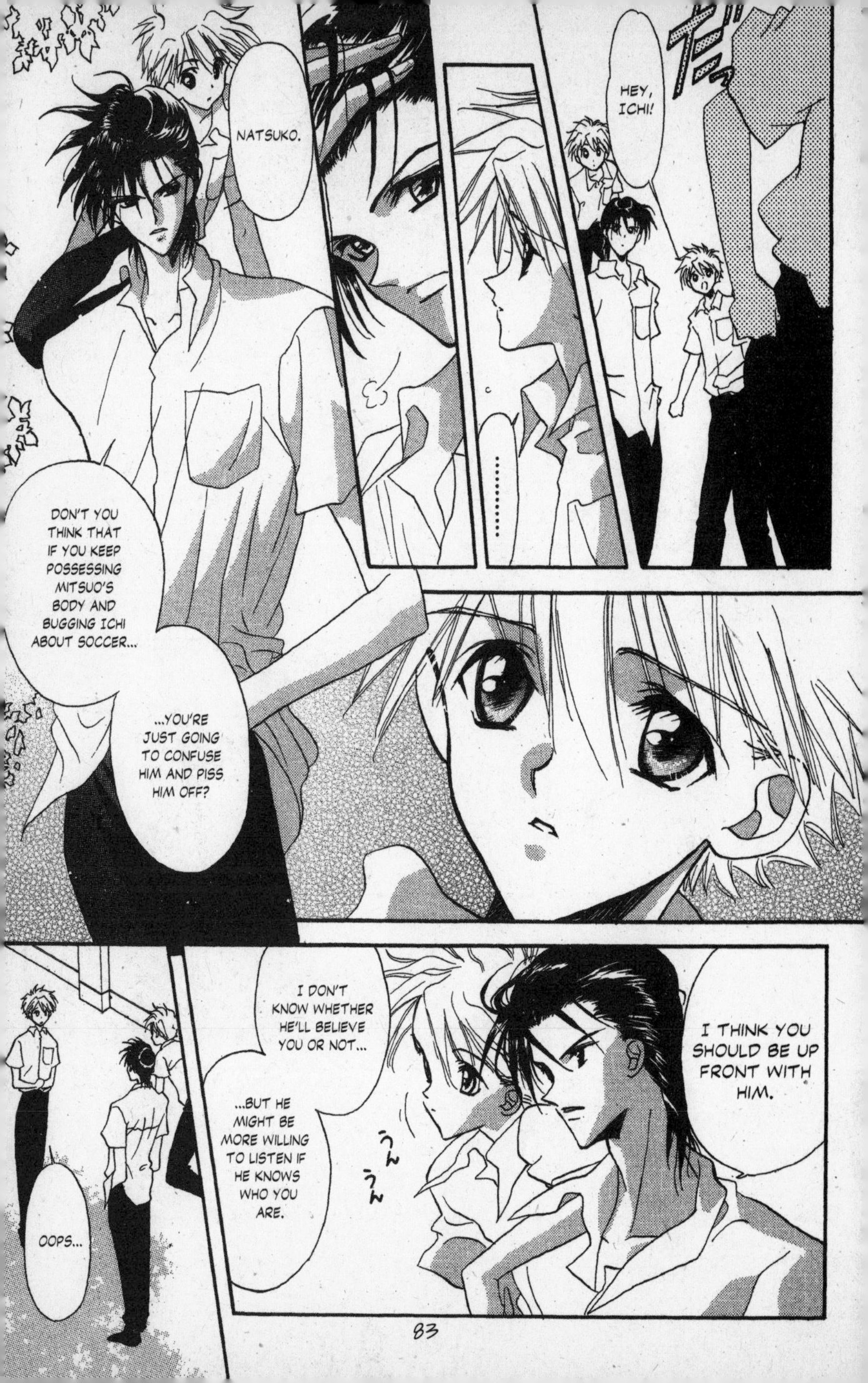
HEY, ICHI!
......
NATSUKO.
DON'T YOU THINK THAT IF YOU KEEP POSSESSING MITSUO'S BODY AND BUGGING ICHI ABOUT SOCCER...
...YOU'RE JUST GOING TO CONFUSE HIM AND PISS HIM OFF?
I THINK YOU SHOULD BE UP FRONT WITH HIM.
I DON'T KNOW WHETHER HE'LL BELIEVE YOU OR NOT...
...BUT HE MIGHT BE MORE WILLING TO LISTEN IF HE KNOWS WHO YOU ARE.
うん
うん
OOPS...

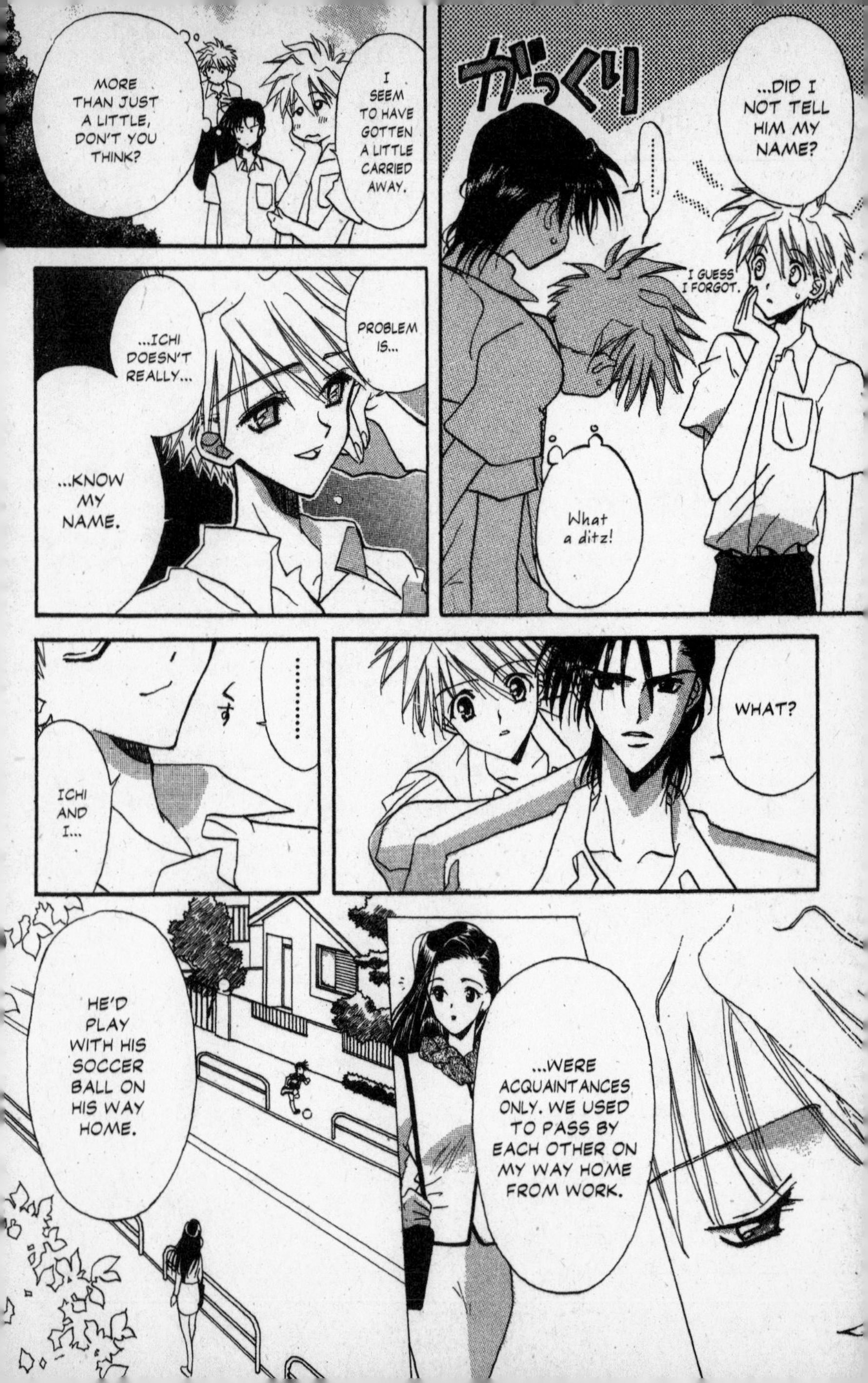
...DID I NOT TELL HIM MY NAME?
がっくり
I GUESS I FORGOT.
......
What a ditz!
I SEEM TO HAVE GOTTEN A LITTLE CARRIED AWAY.
MORE THAN JUST A LITTLE, DON'T YOU THINK?
PROBLEM IS...
...ICHI DOESN'T REALLY...
...KNOW MY NAME.
WHAT?
....
くす
ICHI AND I...
...WERE ACQUAINTANCES ONLY. WE USED TO PASS BY EACH OTHER ON MY WAY HOME FROM WORK.
HE'D PLAY WITH HIS SOCCER BALL ON HIS WAY HOME.

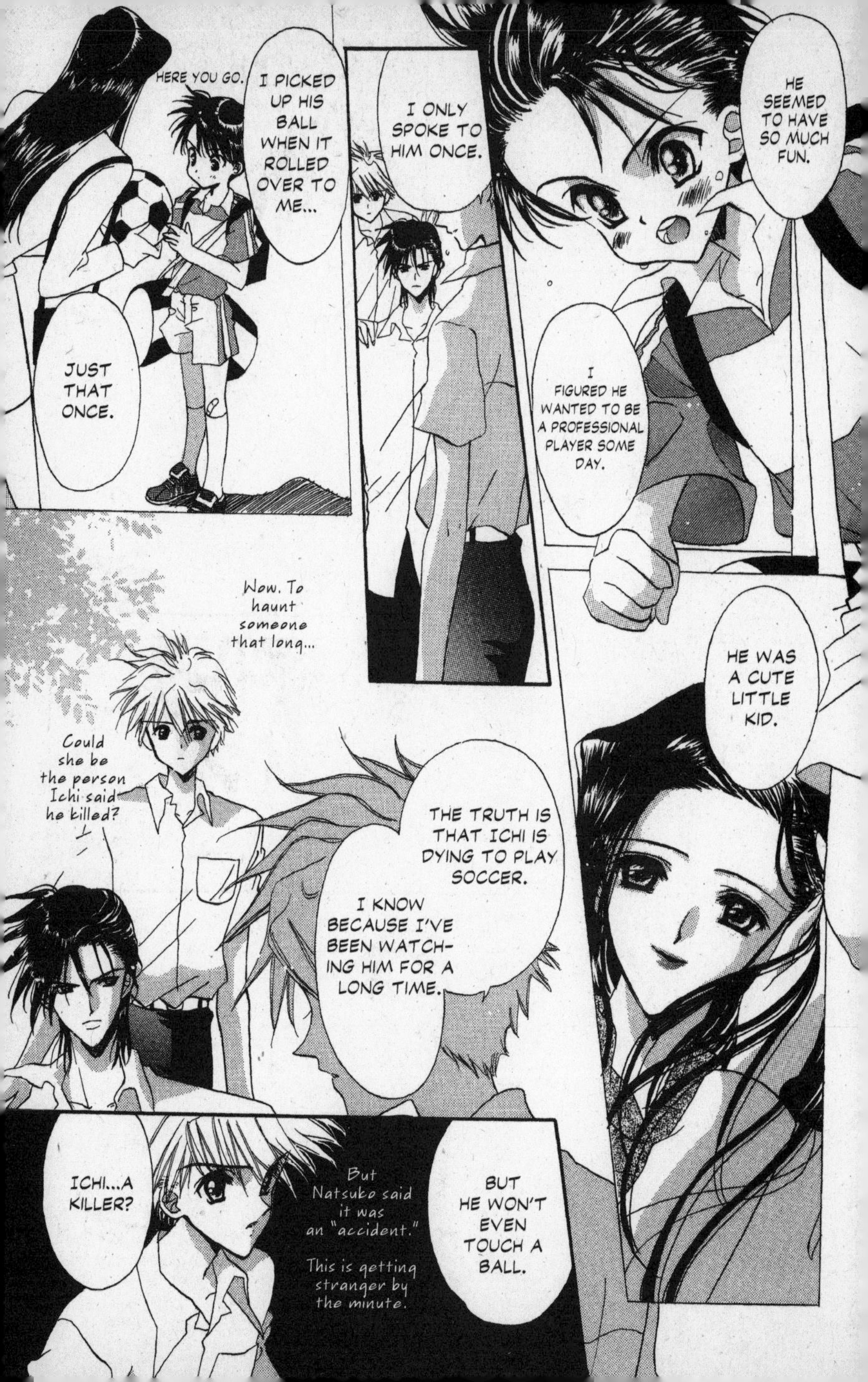
HE SEEMED TO HAVE SO MUCH FUN.
I FIGURED HE WANTED TO BE A PROFESSIONAL PLAYER SOME DAY.
I ONLY SPOKE TO HIM ONCE.
I PICKED UP HIS BALL WHEN IT ROLLED OVER TO ME...
HERE YOU GO.
JUST THAT ONCE.
HE WAS A CUTE LITTLE KID.
THE TRUTH IS THAT ICHI IS DYING TO PLAY SOCCER.
I KNOW BECAUSE I'VE BEEN WATCHING HIM FOR A LONG TIME.
Wow. To haunt someone that long...
Could she be the person Ichi said he killed?
BUT HE WON'T EVEN TOUCH A BALL.
But Natsuko said it was an "accident."
This is getting stranger by the minute.
ICHI...A KILLER?

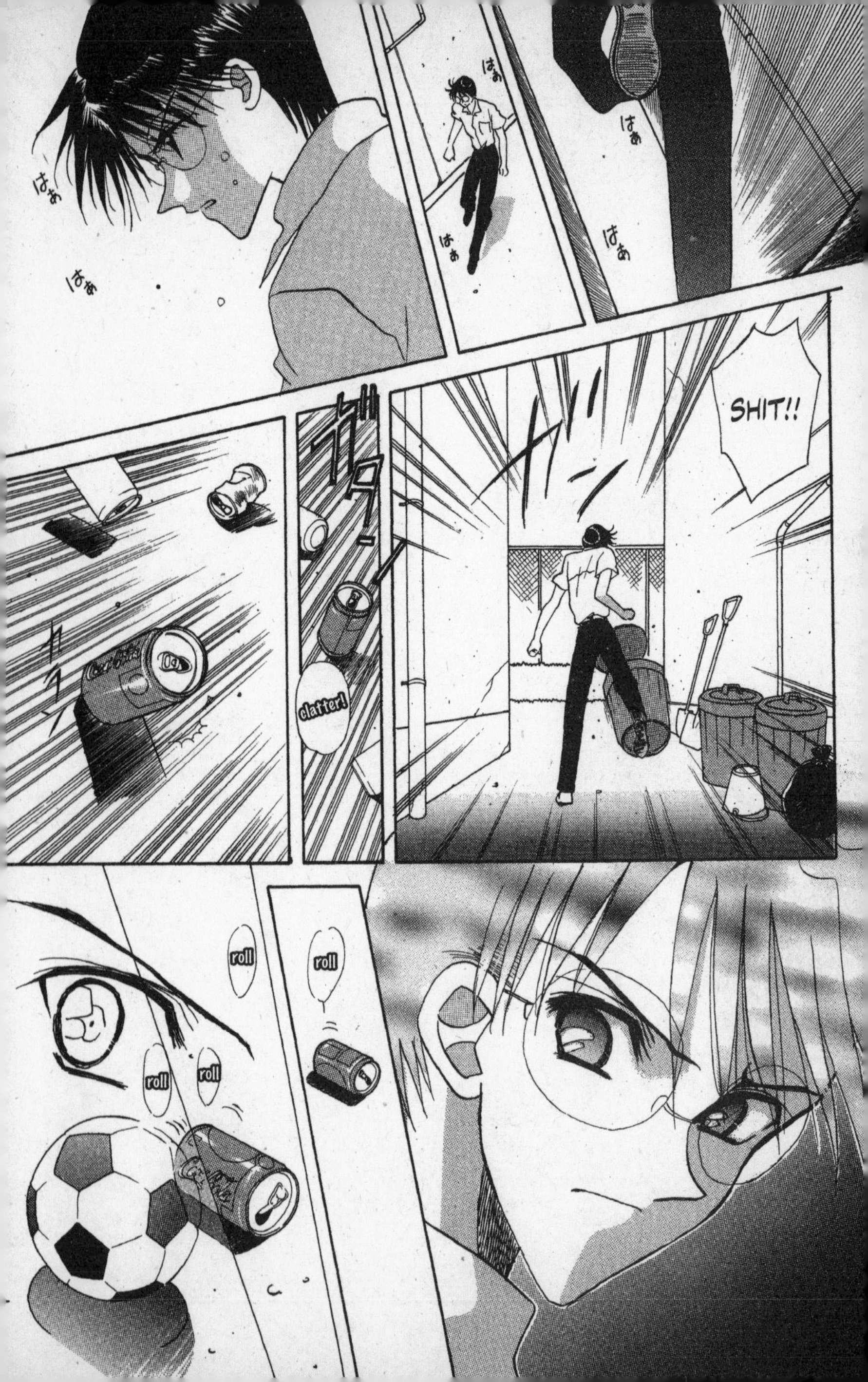
はぁ
はぁ
はぁ
はぁ
はぁ
はぁ
SHIT!!
clatter!
roll
roll
roll
roll

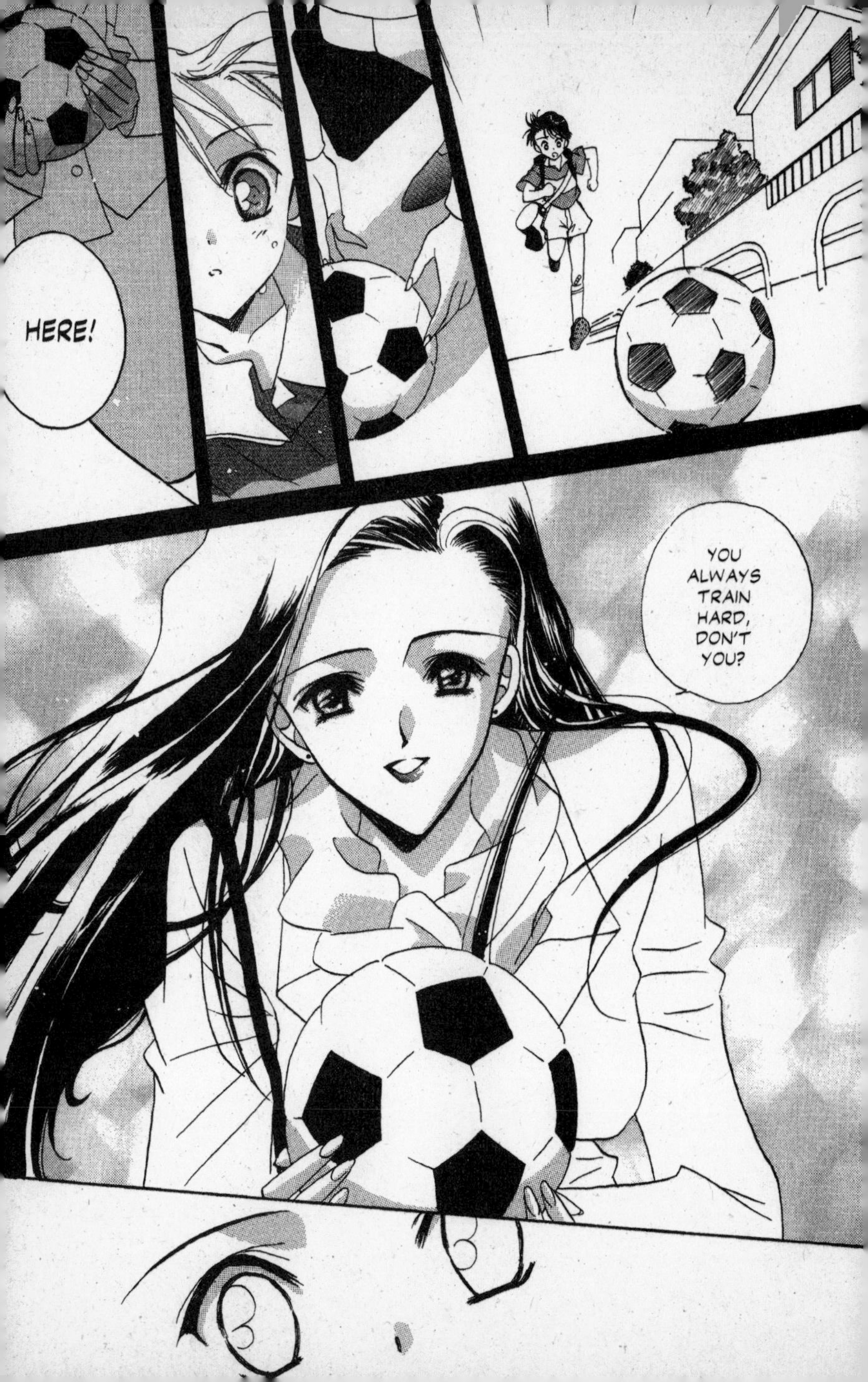
HERE!
YOU ALWAYS TRAIN HARD, DON'T YOU?

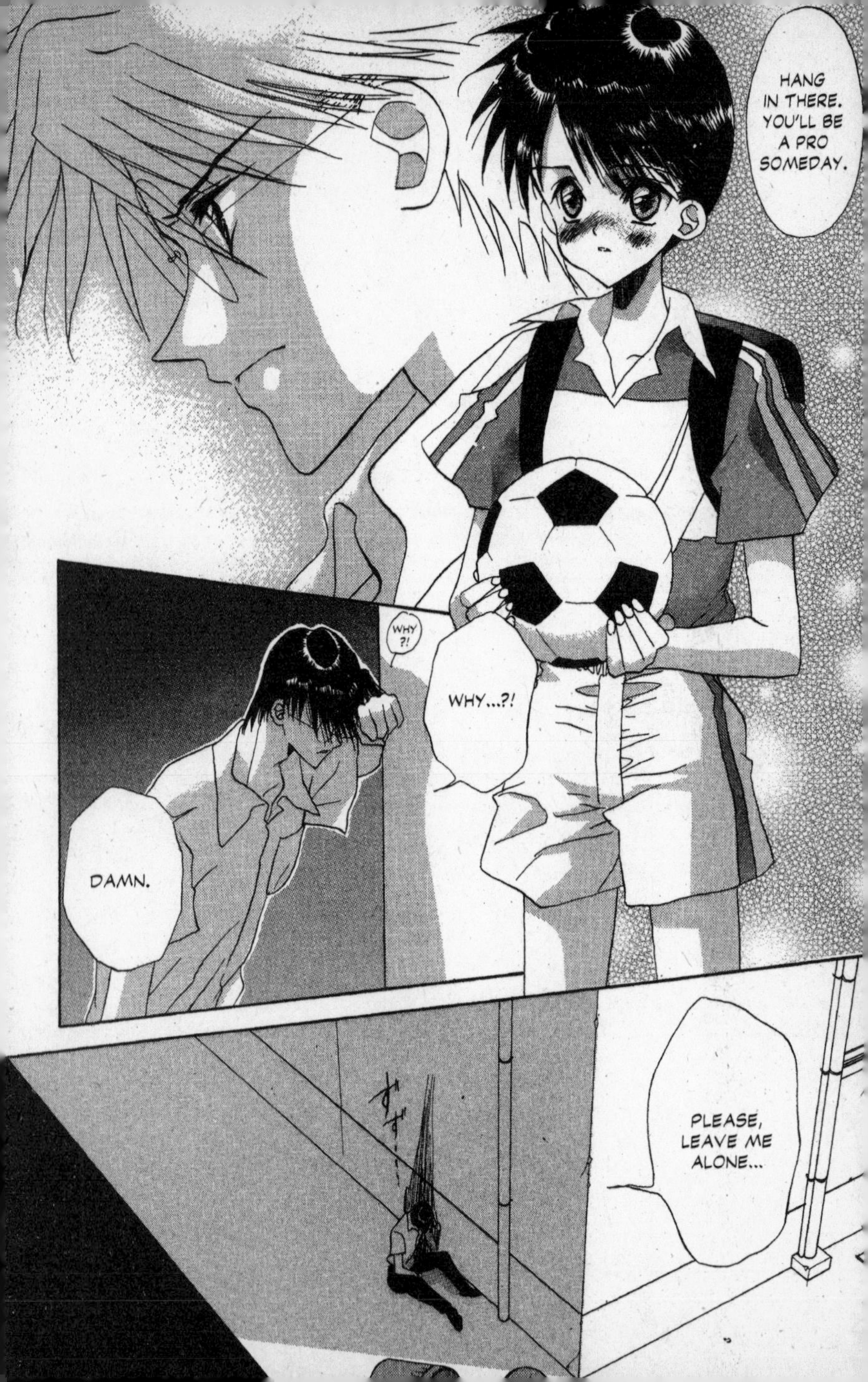
HANG IN THERE. YOU'LL BE A PRO SOMEDAY.
WHY ?!
WHY...?!
DAMN.
ずず
PLEASE, LEAVE ME ALONE...

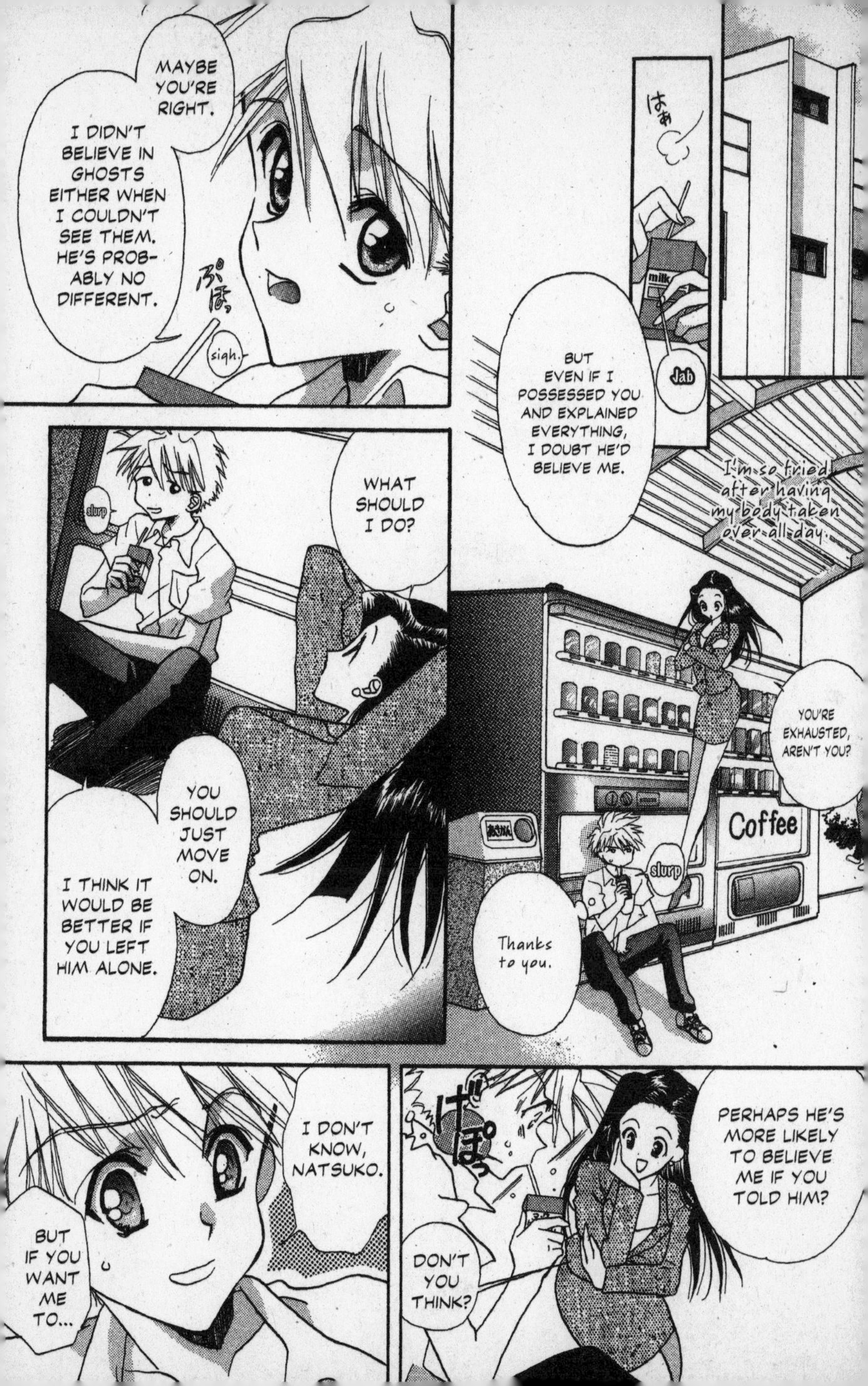
はぁ
Jab
BUT EVEN IF I POSSESSED YOU AND EXPLAINED EVERYTHING, I DOUBT HE'D BELIEVE ME.
I'm so tried after having my body taken over all day.
YOU'RE EXHAUSTED, AREN'T YOU?
slurp
Thanks to you.
MAYBE YOU'RE RIGHT.
I DIDN'T BELIEVE IN GHOSTS EITHER WHEN I COULDN'T SEE THEM. HE'S PROBABLY NO DIFFERENT.
ぷはっ
sigh.
WHAT SHOULD I DO?
slurp
YOU SHOULD JUST MOVE ON.
I THINK IT WOULD BE BETTER IF YOU LEFT HIM ALONE.
PERHAPS HE'S MORE LIKELY TO BELIEVE ME IF YOU TOLD HIM?
がぽっ
DON'T YOU THINK?
I DON'T KNOW, NATSUKO.
BUT IF YOU WANT ME TO...

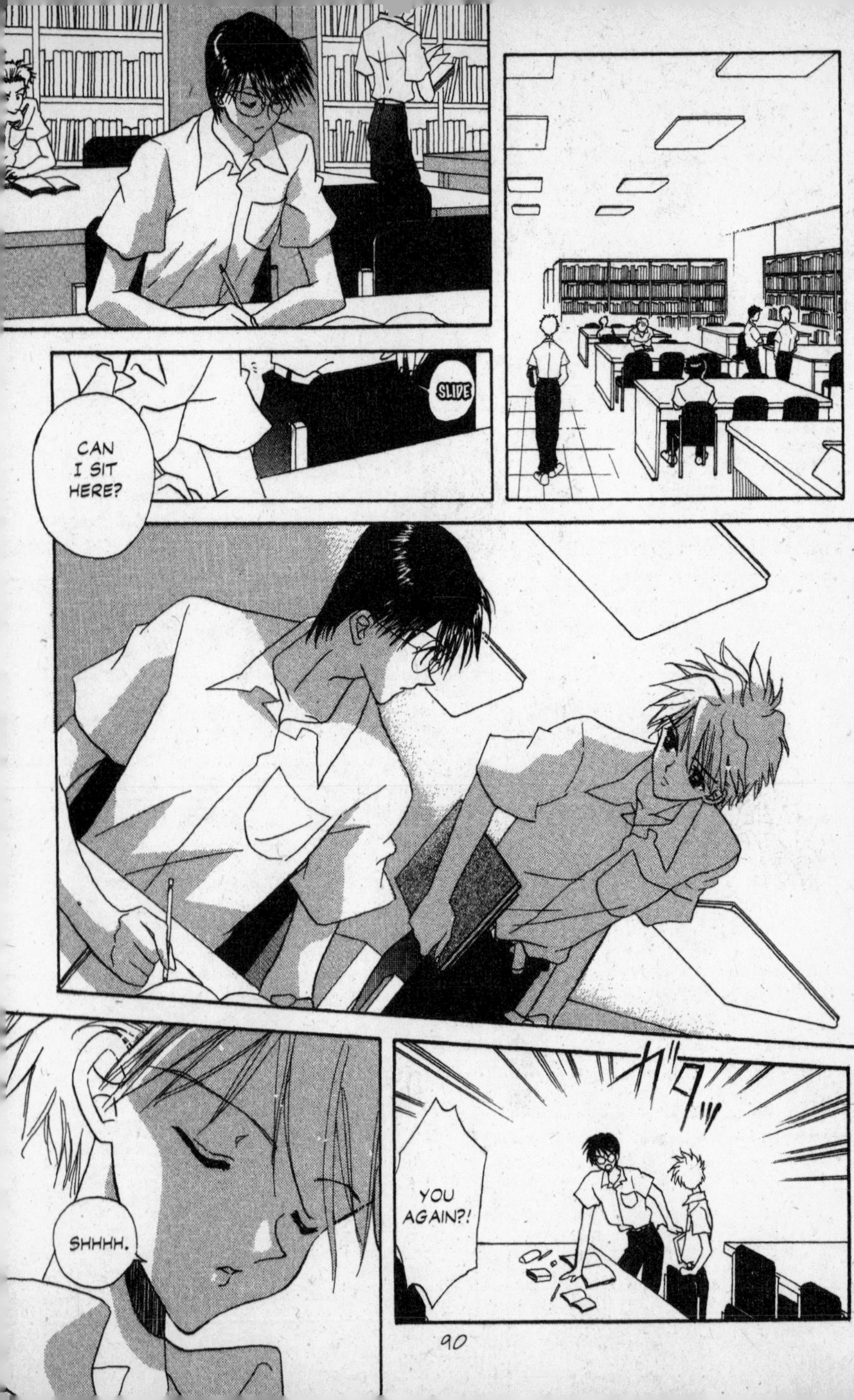
SLIDE
CAN I SIT HERE?
ガタッ
YOU AGAIN?!
SHHHH.

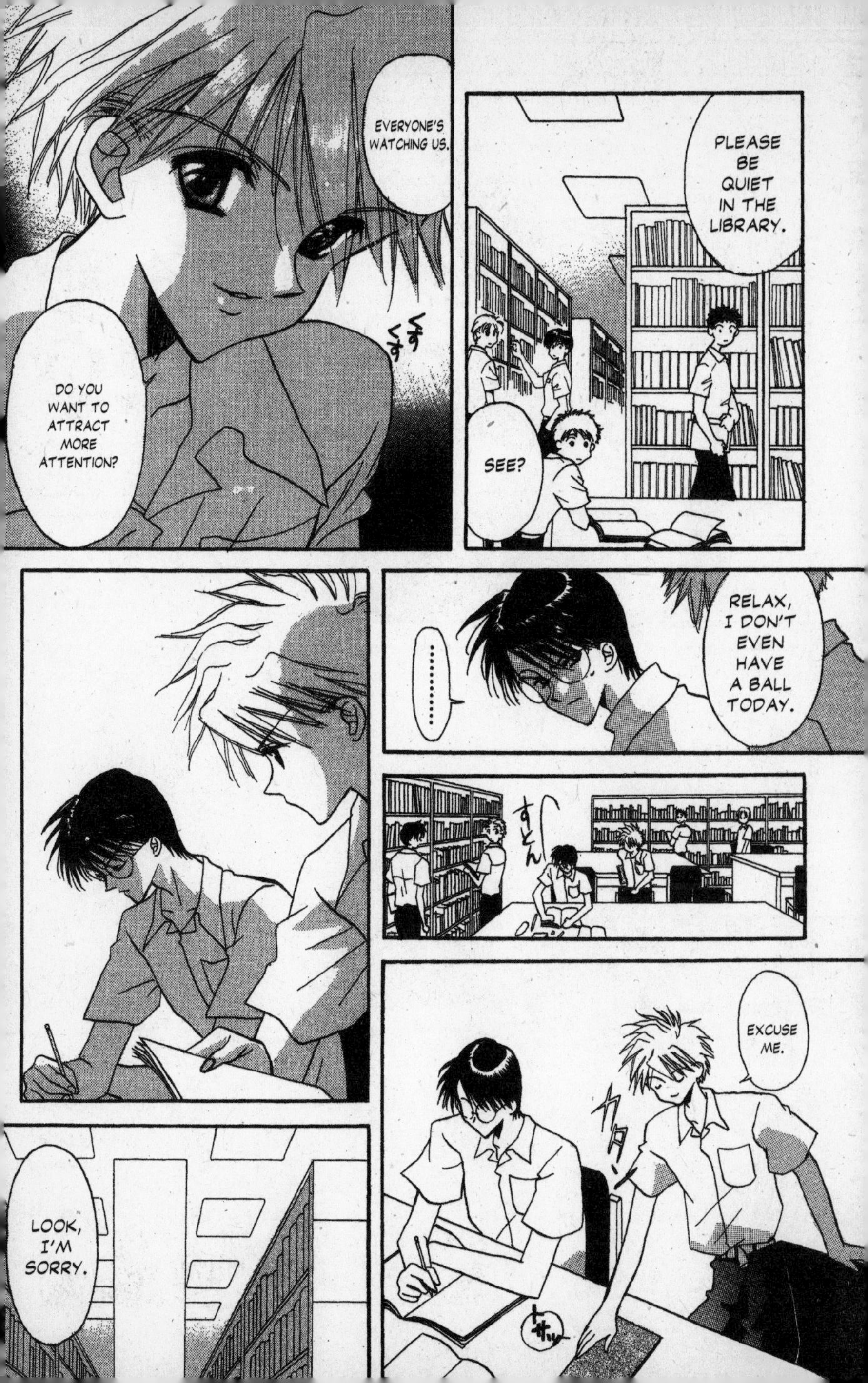

PLEASE BE QUIET IN THE LIBRARY.
SEE?
EVERYONE'S WATCHING US.
くすくす
DO YOU WANT TO ATTRACT MORE ATTENTION?
RELAX, I DON'T EVEN HAVE A BALL TODAY.
......
すとん
EXCUSE ME.
LOOK, I'M SORRY.

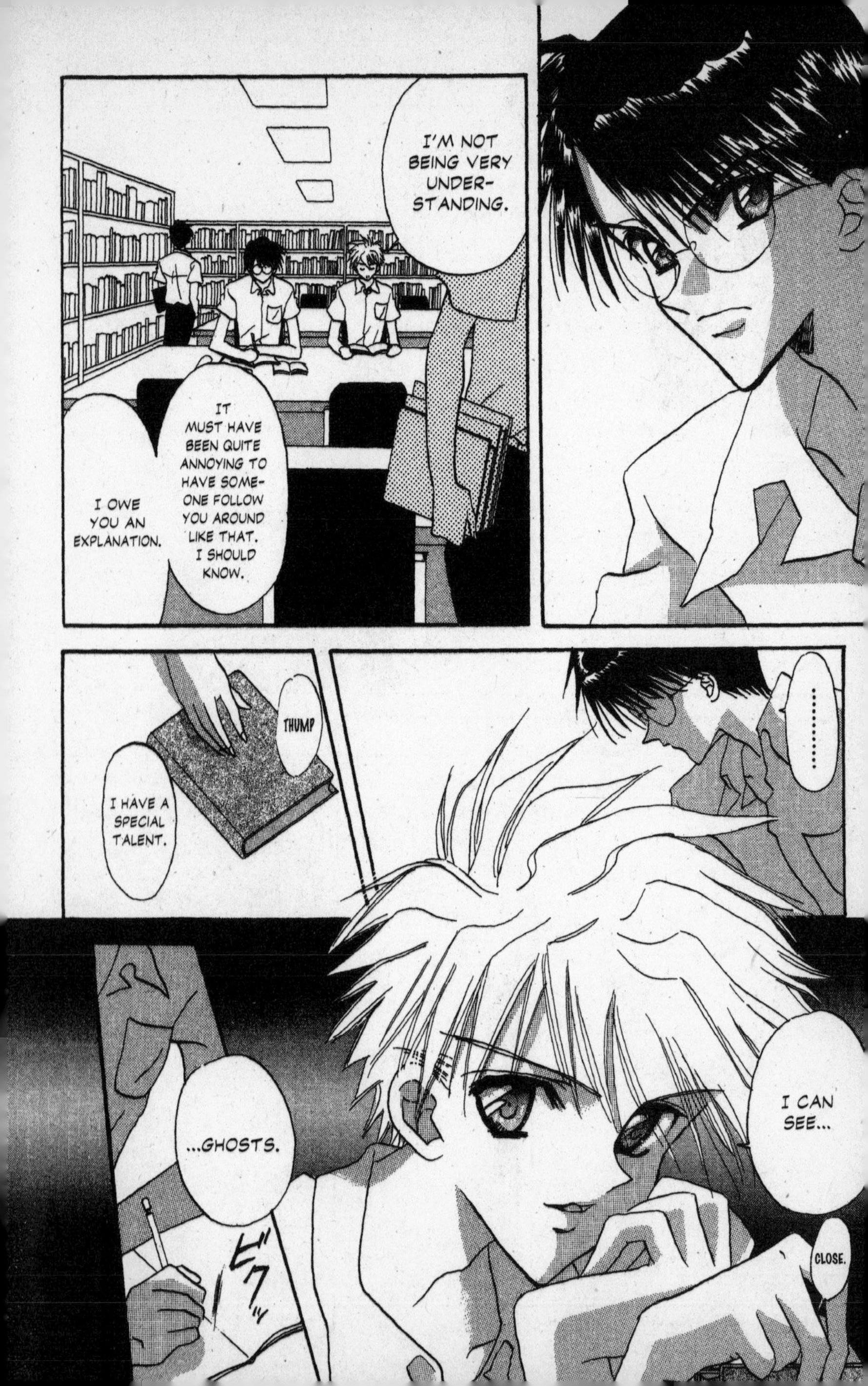
I'M NOT BEING VERY UNDER-STANDING.
IT MUST HAVE BEEN QUITE ANNOYING TO HAVE SOME-ONE FOLLOW YOU AROUND LIKE THAT. I SHOULD KNOW.
I OWE YOU AN EXPLANATION.
....
THUMP
I HAVE A SPECIAL TALENT.
I CAN SEE...
...GHOSTS.
CLOSE.
ビクッ

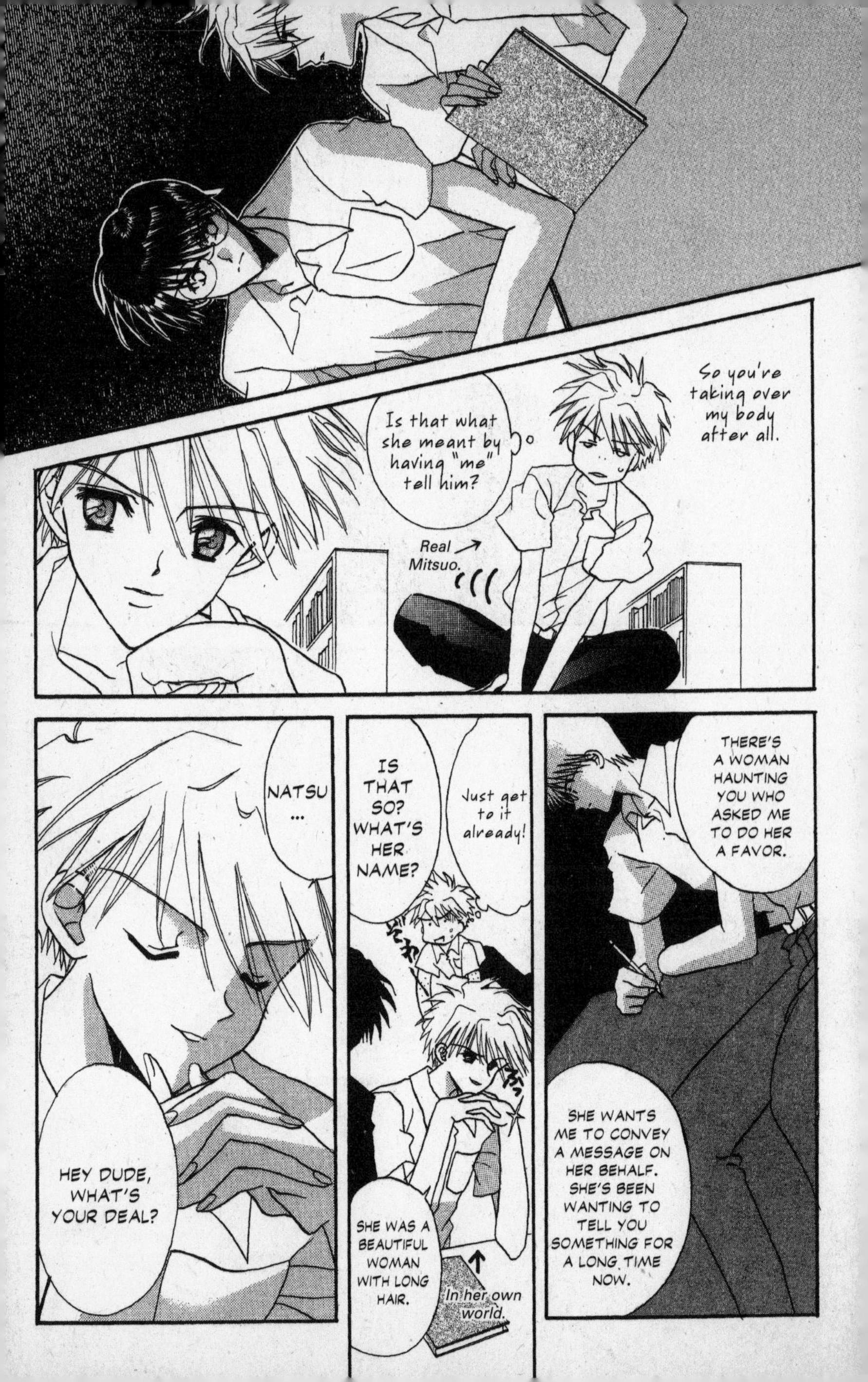
So you're taking over my body after all.
Is that what she meant by having "me" tell him?
Real Mitsuo.
THERE'S A WOMAN HAUNTING YOU WHO ASKED ME TO DO HER A FAVOR.
SHE WANTS ME TO CONVEY A MESSAGE ON HER BEHALF. SHE'S BEEN WANTING TO TELL YOU SOMETHING FOR A LONG TIME NOW.
Just get to it already!
IS THAT SO? WHAT'S HER NAME?
SHE WAS A BEAUTIFUL WOMAN WITH LONG HAIR.
In her own world.
NATSU ...
HEY DUDE, WHAT'S YOUR DEAL?

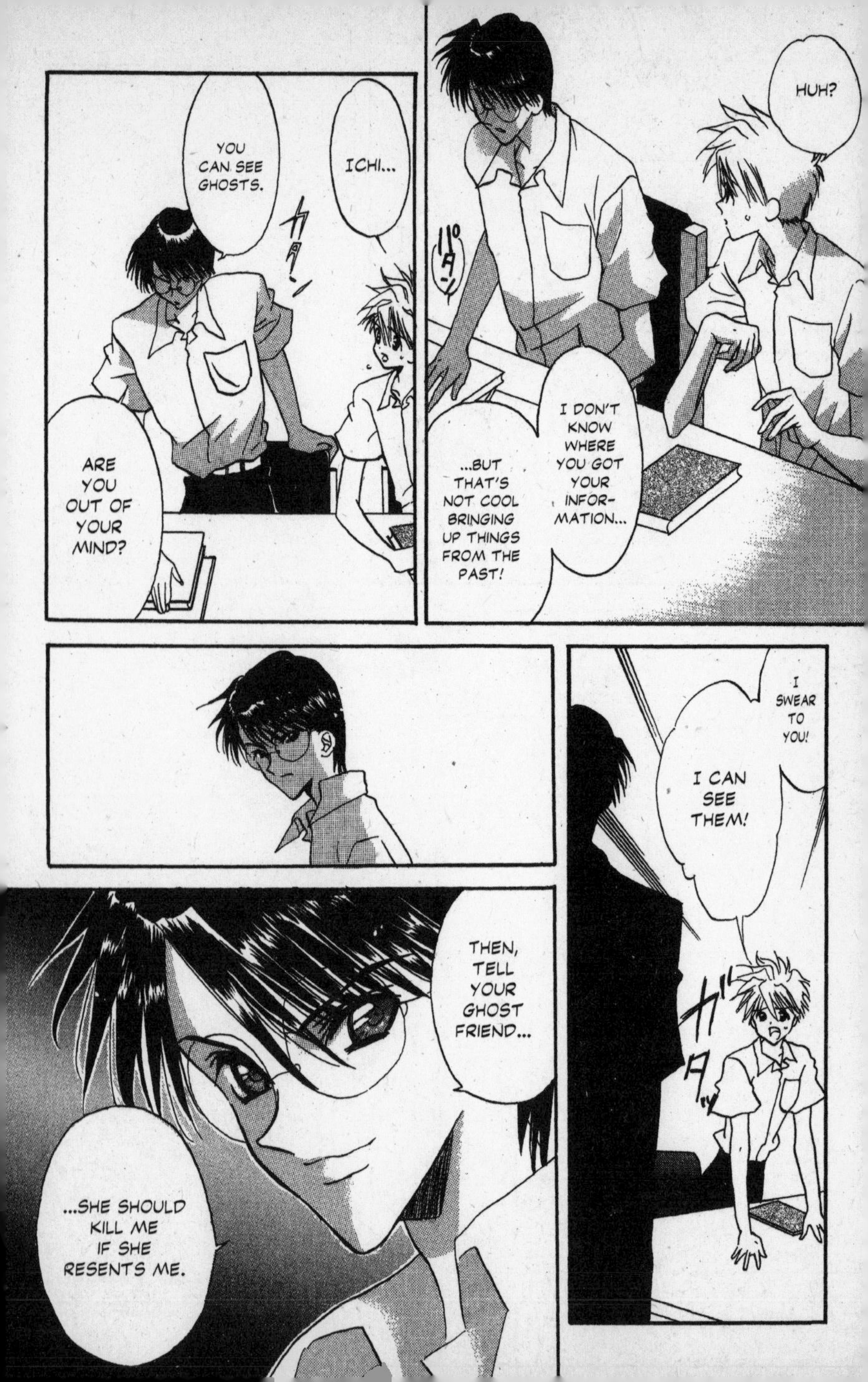
HUH?
I DON'T KNOW WHERE YOU GOT YOUR INFORMATION...
...BUT THAT'S NOT COOL BRINGING UP THINGS FROM THE PAST!
ICHI...
YOU CAN SEE GHOSTS.
ARE YOU OUT OF YOUR MIND?
I SWEAR TO YOU!
I CAN SEE THEM!
THEN, TELL YOUR GHOST FRIEND...
...SHE SHOULD KILL ME IF SHE RESENTS ME.

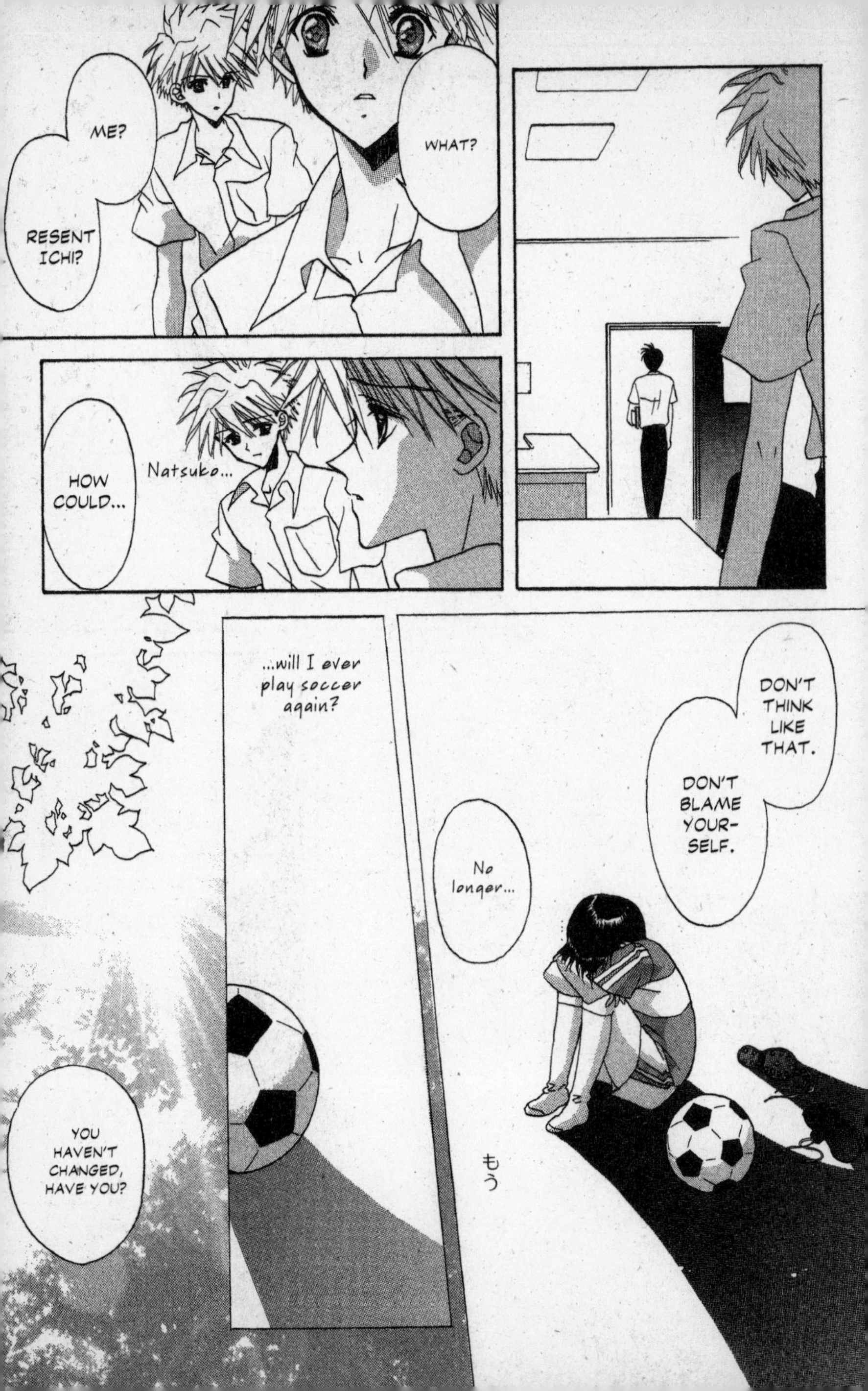
WHAT?
ME?
RESENT ICHI?
Natsuko...
HOW COULD...
DON'T THINK LIKE THAT.
DON'T BLAME YOUR-SELF.
No longer...
もう
...will I ever play soccer again?
YOU HAVEN'T CHANGED, HAVE YOU?

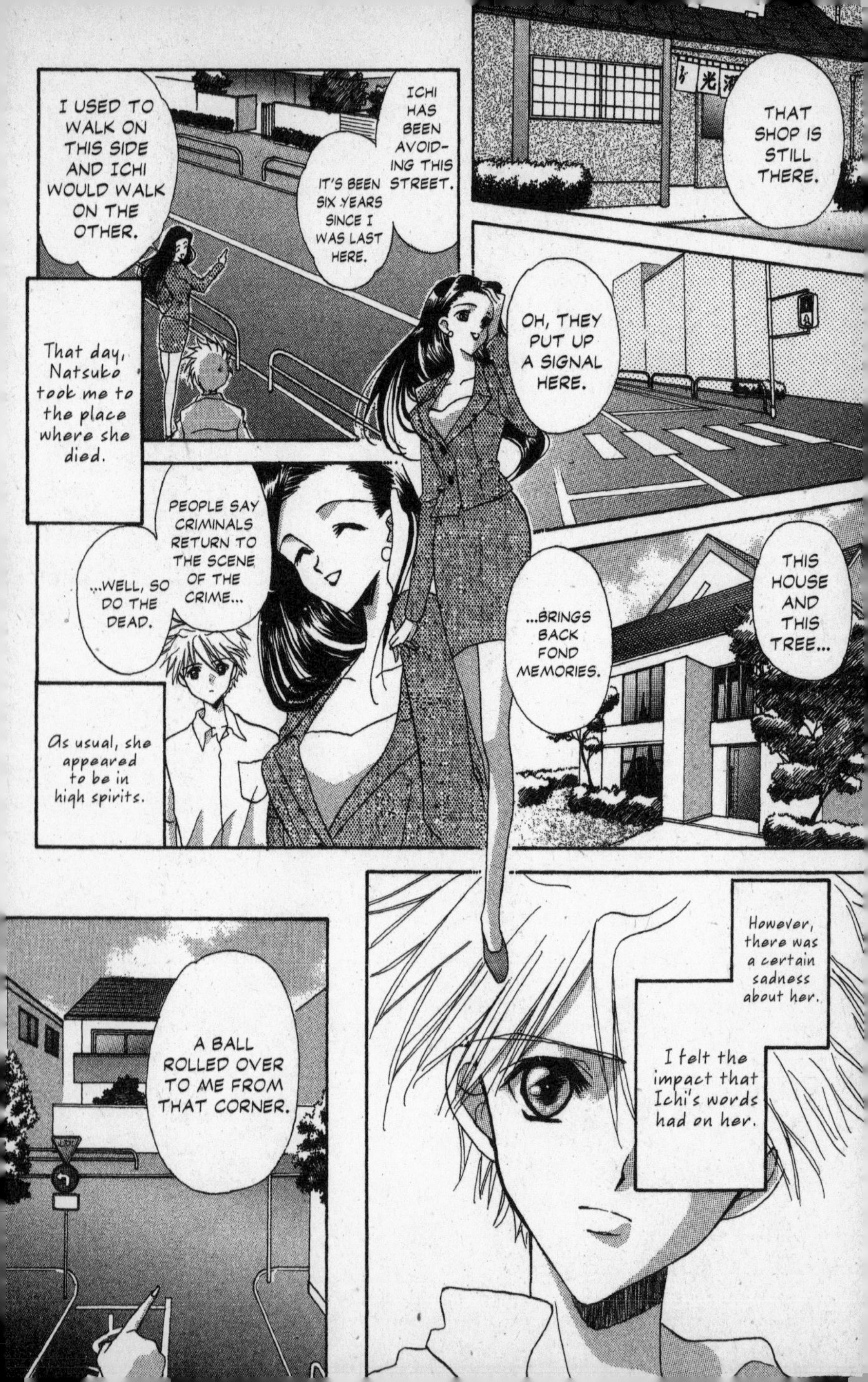
THAT SHOP IS STILL THERE.
OH, THEY PUT UP A SIGNAL HERE.
THIS HOUSE AND THIS TREE...
...BRINGS BACK FOND MEMORIES.
ICHI HAS BEEN AVOIDING THIS STREET.
IT'S BEEN SIX YEARS SINCE I WAS LAST HERE.
I USED TO WALK ON THIS SIDE AND ICHI WOULD WALK ON THE OTHER.
That day, Natsuko took me to the place where she died.
PEOPLE SAY CRIMINALS RETURN TO THE SCENE OF THE CRIME...
...WELL, SO DO THE DEAD.
As usual, she appeared to be in high spirits.
However, there was a certain sadness about her.
I felt the impact that Ichi's words had on her.
A BALL ROLLED OVER TO ME FROM THAT CORNER.

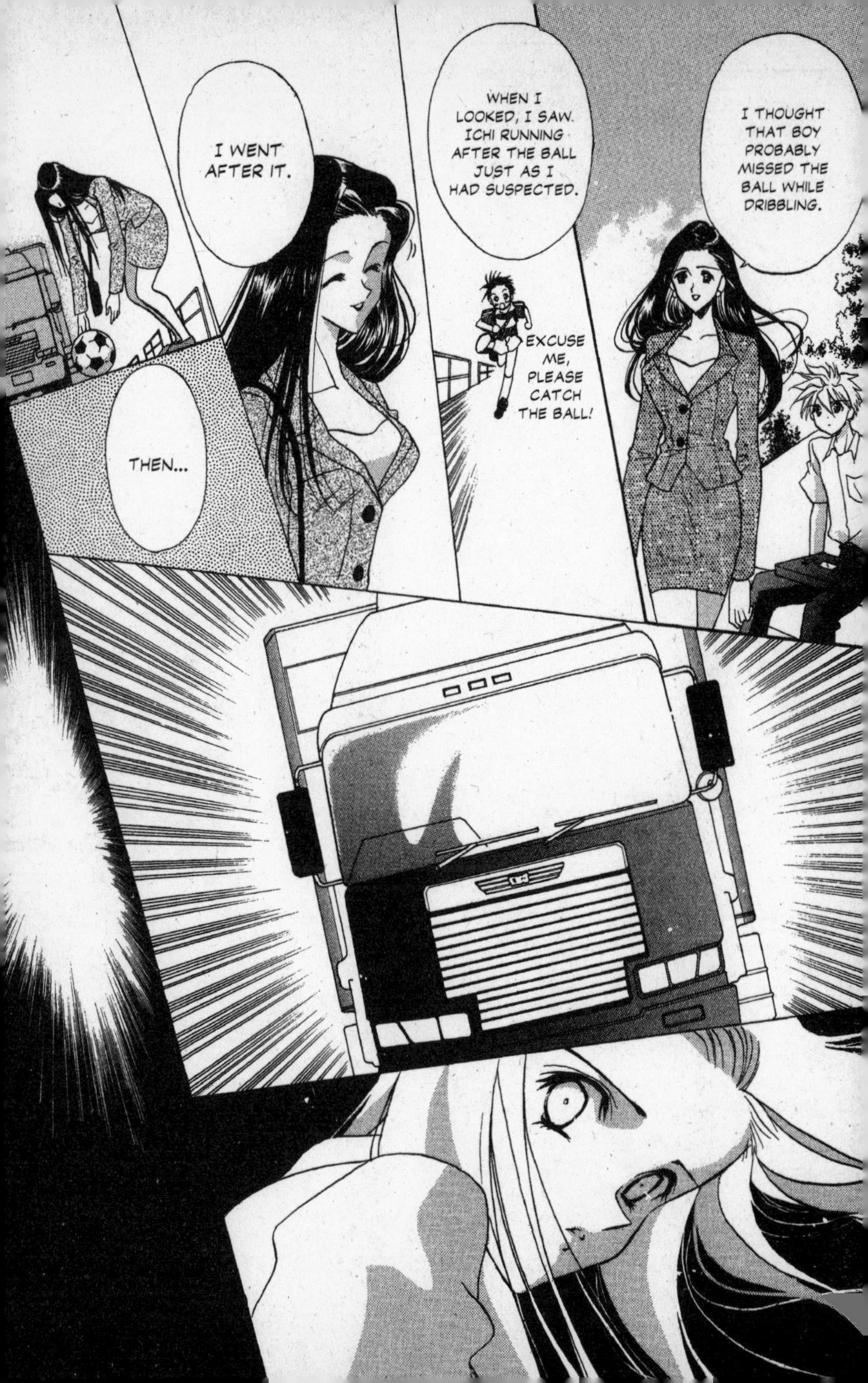
I THOUGHT THAT BOY PROBABLY MISSED THE BALL WHILE DRIBBLING.
WHEN I LOOKED, I SAW. ICHI RUNNING AFTER THE BALL JUST AS I HAD SUSPECTED.
EXCUSE ME, PLEASE CATCH THE BALL!
I WENT AFTER IT.
THEN...

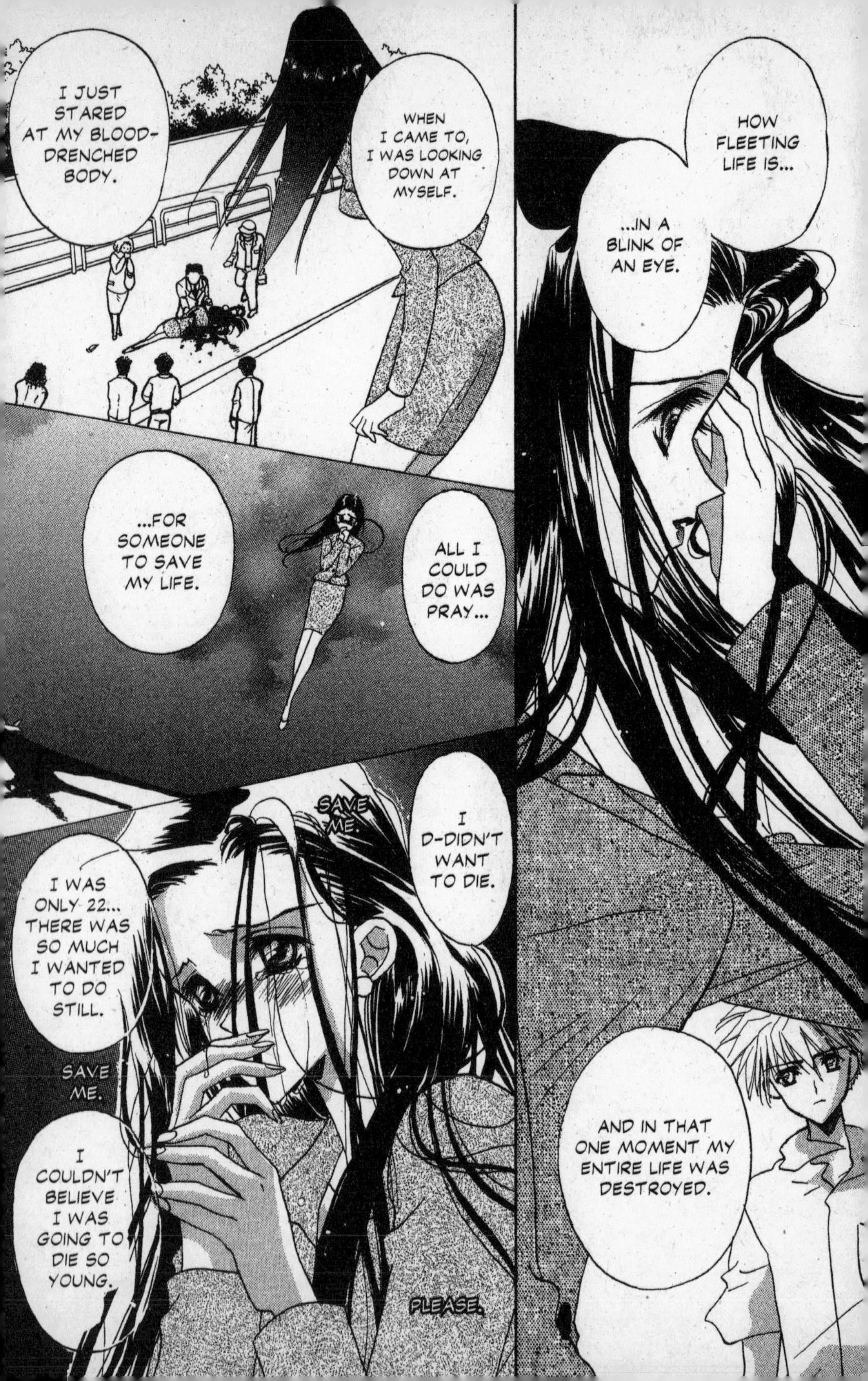
HOW FLEETING LIFE IS...
...IN A BLINK OF AN EYE.
AND IN THAT ONE MOMENT MY ENTIRE LIFE WAS DESTROYED.
WHEN I CAME TO, I WAS LOOKING DOWN AT MYSELF.
I JUST STARED AT MY BLOOD-DRENCHED BODY.
ALL I COULD DO WAS PRAY...
...FOR SOMEONE TO SAVE MY LIFE.
SAVE ME.
I D-DIDN'T WANT TO DIE.
I WAS ONLY 22... THERE WAS SO MUCH I WANTED TO DO STILL.
SAVE ME.
I COULDN'T BELIEVE I WAS GOING TO DIE SO YOUNG.
PLEASE.

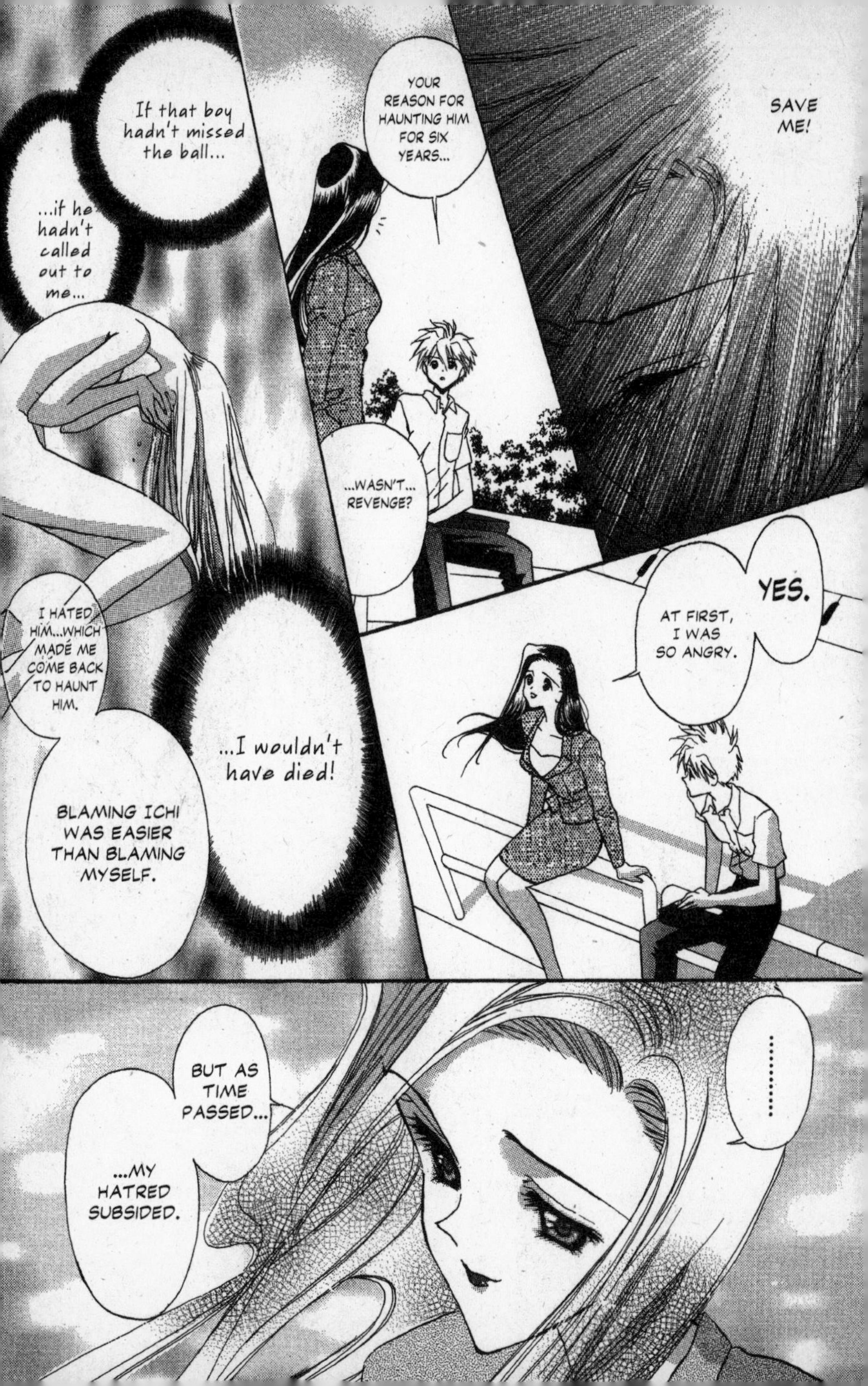

SAVE ME!
YOUR REASON FOR HAUNTING HIM FOR SIX YEARS...
...WASN'T... REVENGE?
YES.
AT FIRST, I WAS SO ANGRY.
If that boy hadn't missed the ball...
...if he hadn't called out to me...
...I wouldn't have died!
I HATED HIM...WHICH MADE ME COME BACK TO HAUNT HIM.
BLAMING ICHI WAS EASIER THAN BLAMING MYSELF.
......
BUT AS TIME PASSED...
...MY HATRED SUBSIDED.

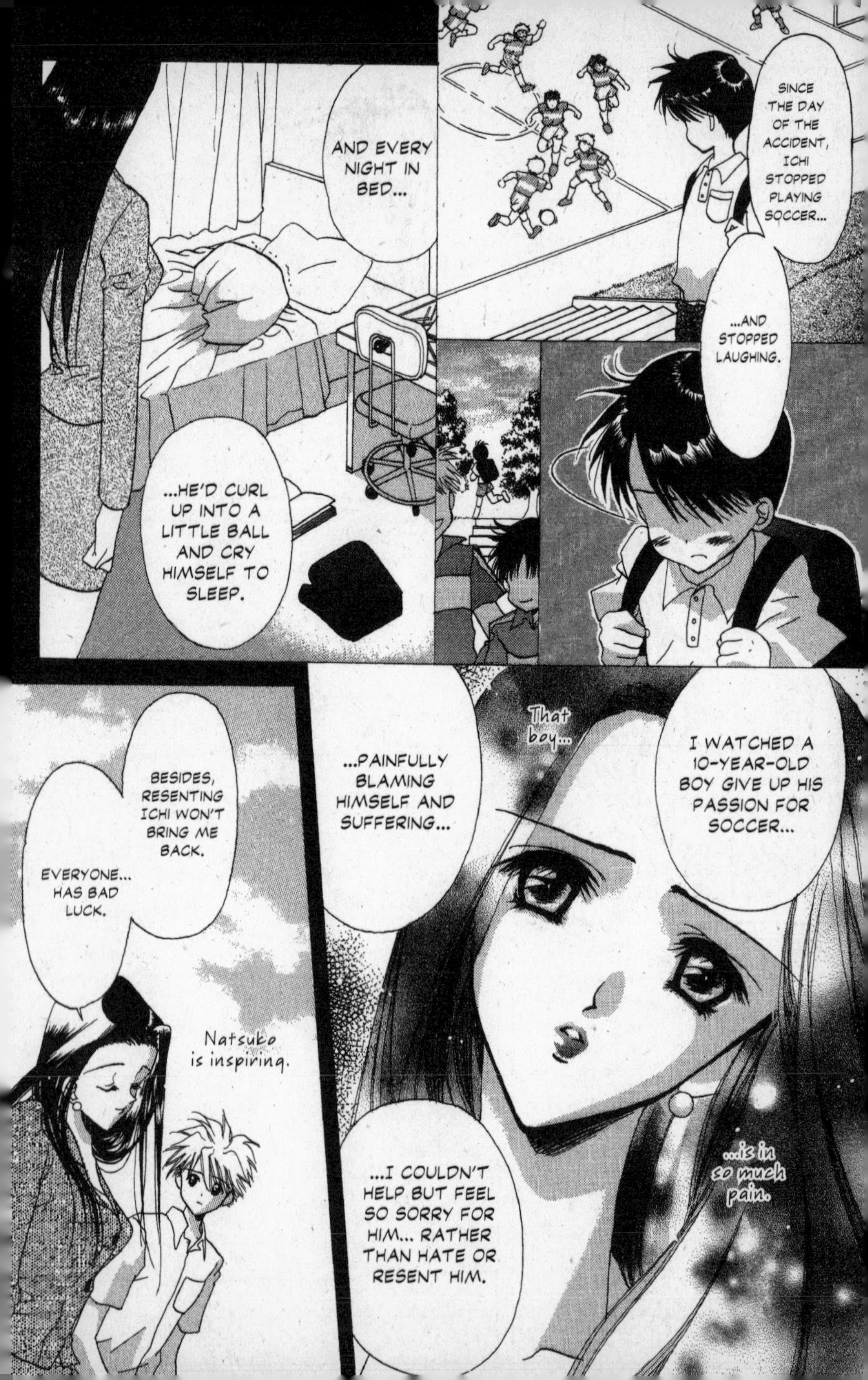
SINCE THE DAY OF THE ACCIDENT, ICHI STOPPED PLAYING SOCCER...
...AND STOPPED LAUGHING.
AND EVERY NIGHT IN BED...
...HE'D CURL UP INTO A LITTLE BALL AND CRY HIMSELF TO SLEEP.
I WATCHED A 10-YEAR-OLD BOY GIVE UP HIS PASSION FOR SOCCER...
...PAINFULLY BLAMING HIMSELF AND SUFFERING...
...I COULDN'T HELP BUT FEEL SO SORRY FOR HIM... RATHER THAN HATE OR RESENT HIM.
That boy...
...is in so much pain.
BESIDES, RESENTING ICHI WON'T BRING ME BACK.
EVERYONE... HAS BAD LUCK.
Natsuko is inspiring.

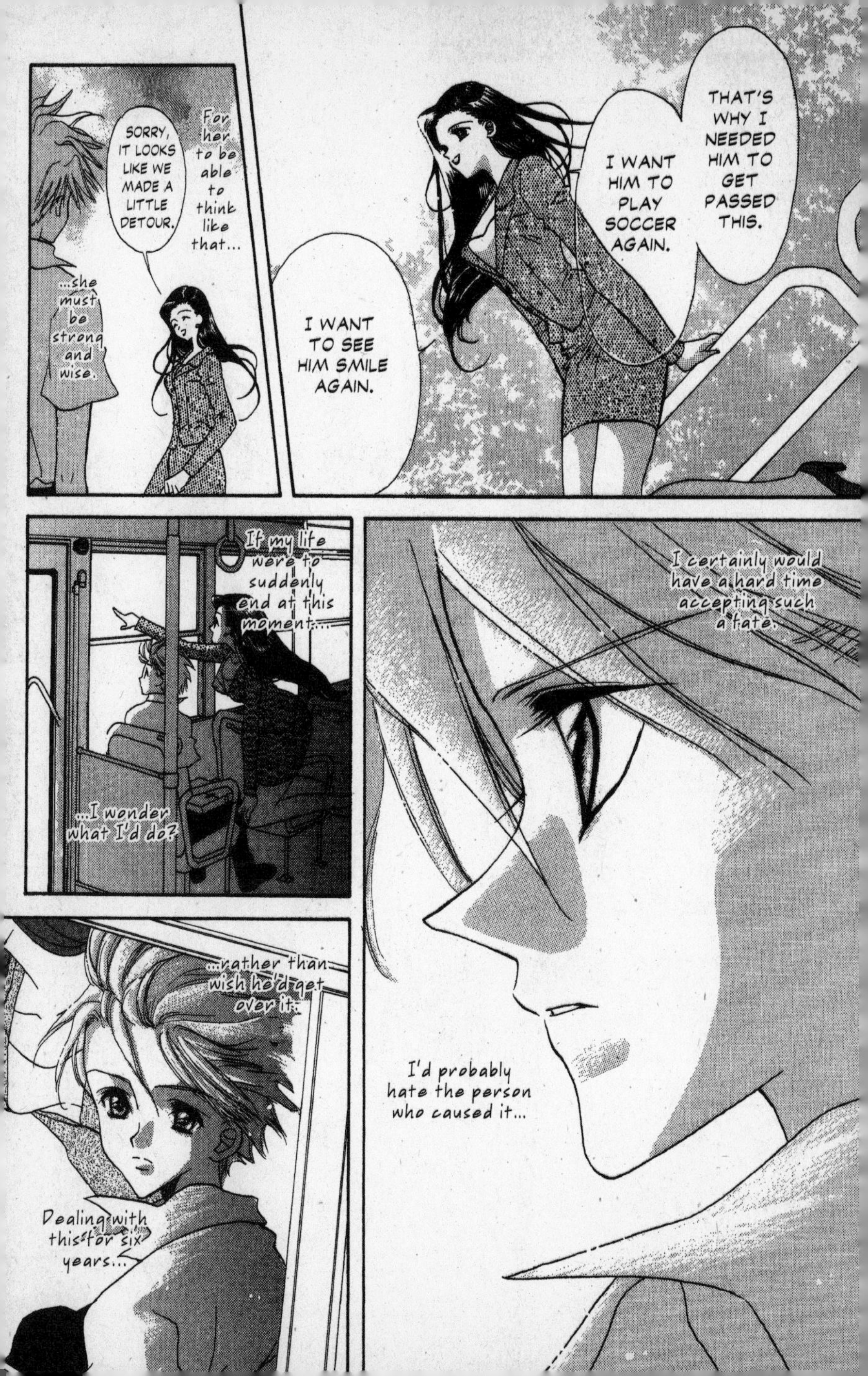
THAT'S WHY I NEEDED HIM TO GET PASSED THIS.
I WANT HIM TO PLAY SOCCER AGAIN.
I WANT TO SEE HIM SMILE AGAIN.
For her to be able to think like that...
SORRY, IT LOOKS LIKE WE MADE A LITTLE DETOUR.
...she must be strong and wise.
I certainly would have a hard time accepting such a fate.
I'd probably hate the person who caused it...
If my life were to suddenly end at this moment...
...I wonder what I'd do?
...rather than wish he'd get over it.
Dealing with this for six years...

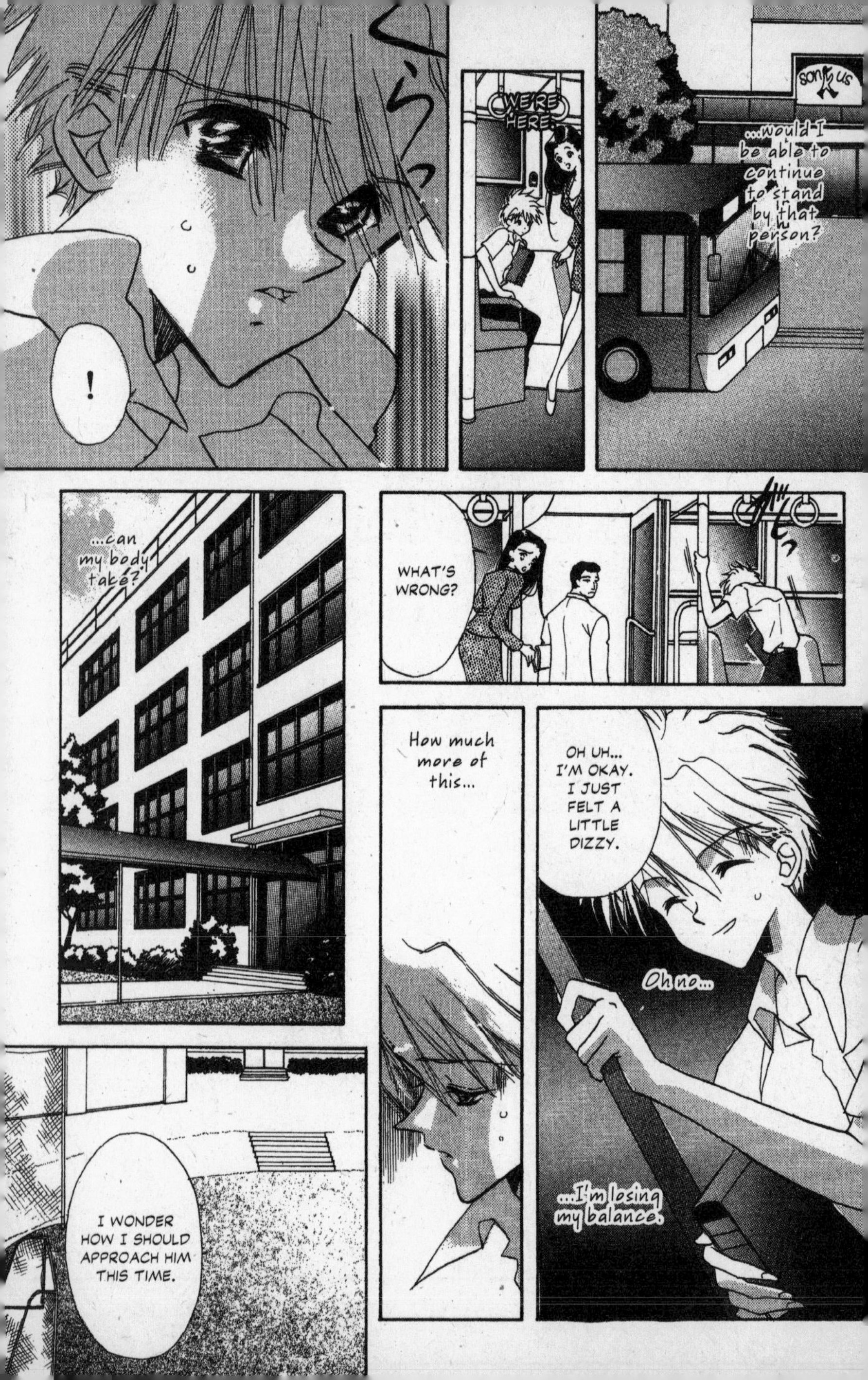
...would I be able to continue to stand by that person?
WE'RE HERE.
!
WHAT'S WRONG?
OH UH... I'M OKAY. I JUST FELT A LITTLE DIZZY.
Oh no...
...I'm losing my balance.
How much more of this...
...can my body take?
I WONDER HOW I SHOULD APPROACH HIM THIS TIME.

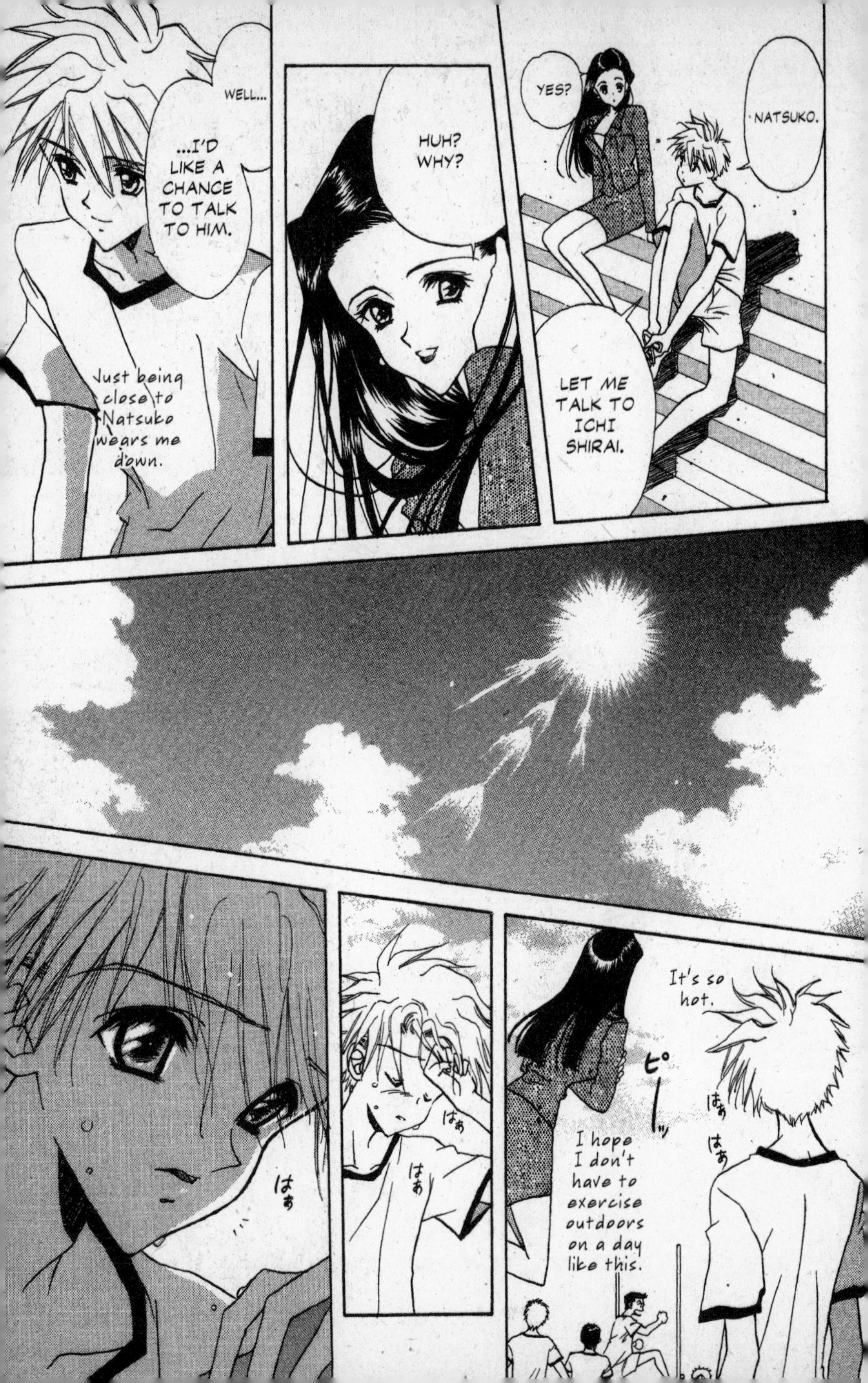
NATSUKO.
YES?
LET ME TALK TO ICHI SHIRAI.
HUH? WHY?
WELL...
...I'D LIKE A CHANCE TO TALK TO HIM.
Just being close to Natsuko wears me down.
It's so hot.
ピーッ
はぁ はぁ
I hope I don't have to exercise outdoors on a day like this.
はぁ はぁ
はぁ

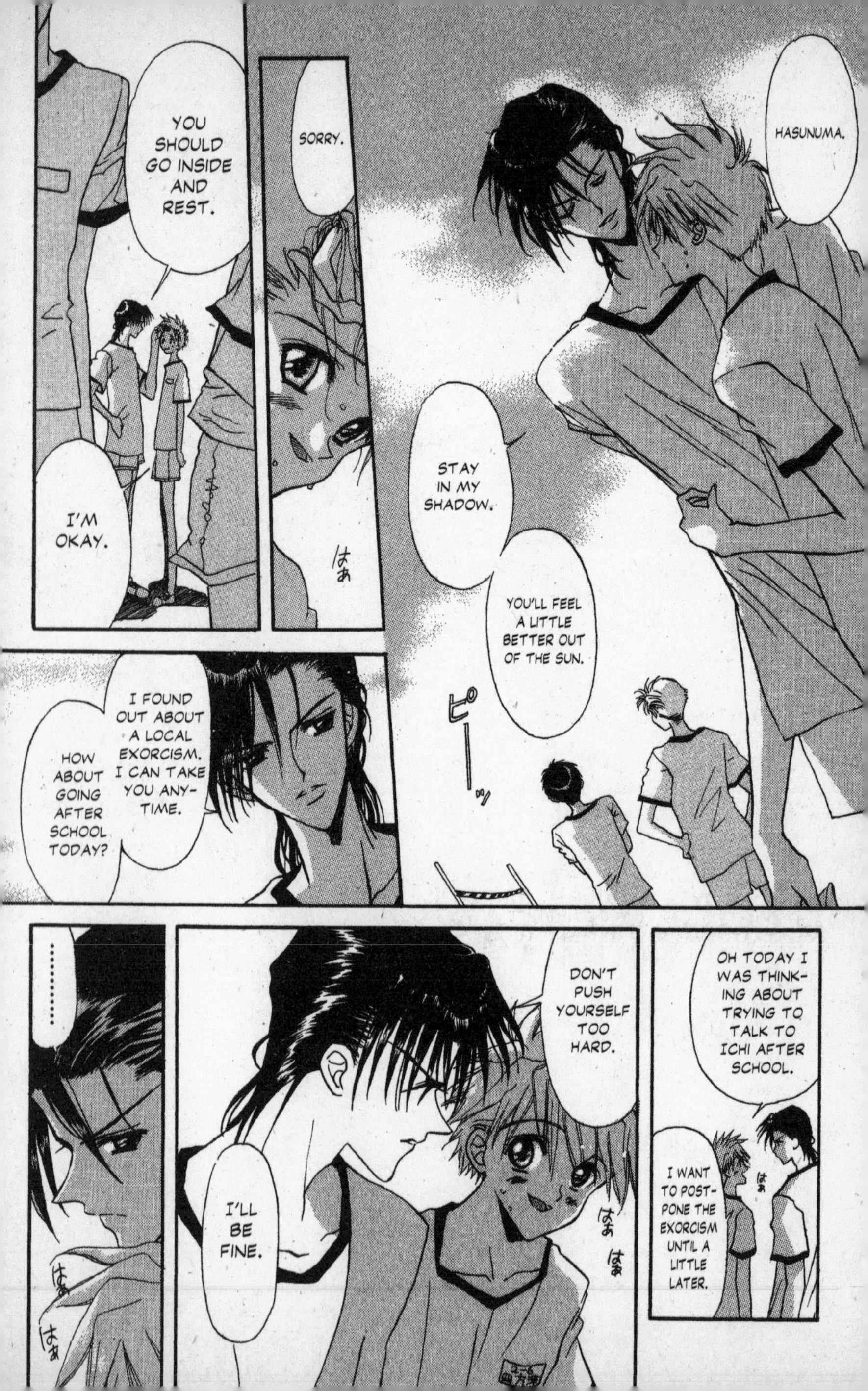
HASUNUMA.
STAY IN MY SHADOW.
YOU'LL FEEL A LITTLE BETTER OUT OF THE SUN.
ピーーッ
SORRY.
はぁ
YOU SHOULD GO INSIDE AND REST.
I'M OKAY.
I FOUND OUT ABOUT A LOCAL EXORCISM. I CAN TAKE YOU ANY-TIME.
HOW ABOUT GOING AFTER SCHOOL TODAY?
OH TODAY I WAS THINK-ING ABOUT TRYING TO TALK TO ICHI AFTER SCHOOL.
I WANT TO POST-PONE THE EXORCISM UNTIL A LITTLE LATER.
はぁ
DON'T PUSH YOURSELF TOO HARD.
I'LL BE FINE.
はぁ はぁ
....
はぁ はぁ

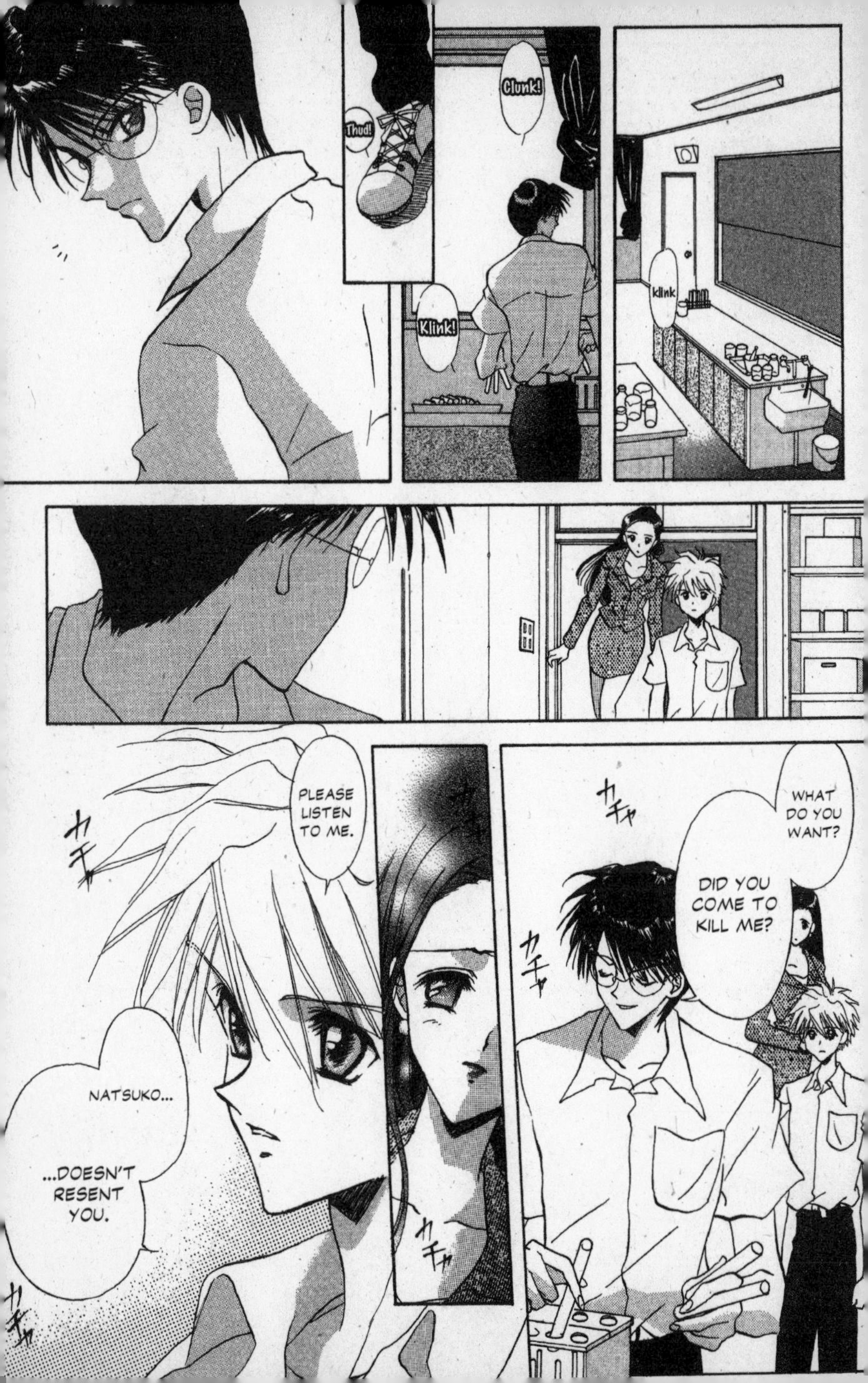
klink
Clunk!
Klink!
Thud!
カチャ
WHAT DO YOU WANT?
DID YOU COME TO KILL ME?
カチャ
カチャ
カチャ
PLEASE LISTEN TO ME.
NATSUKO...
...DOESN'T RESENT YOU.
カチャ

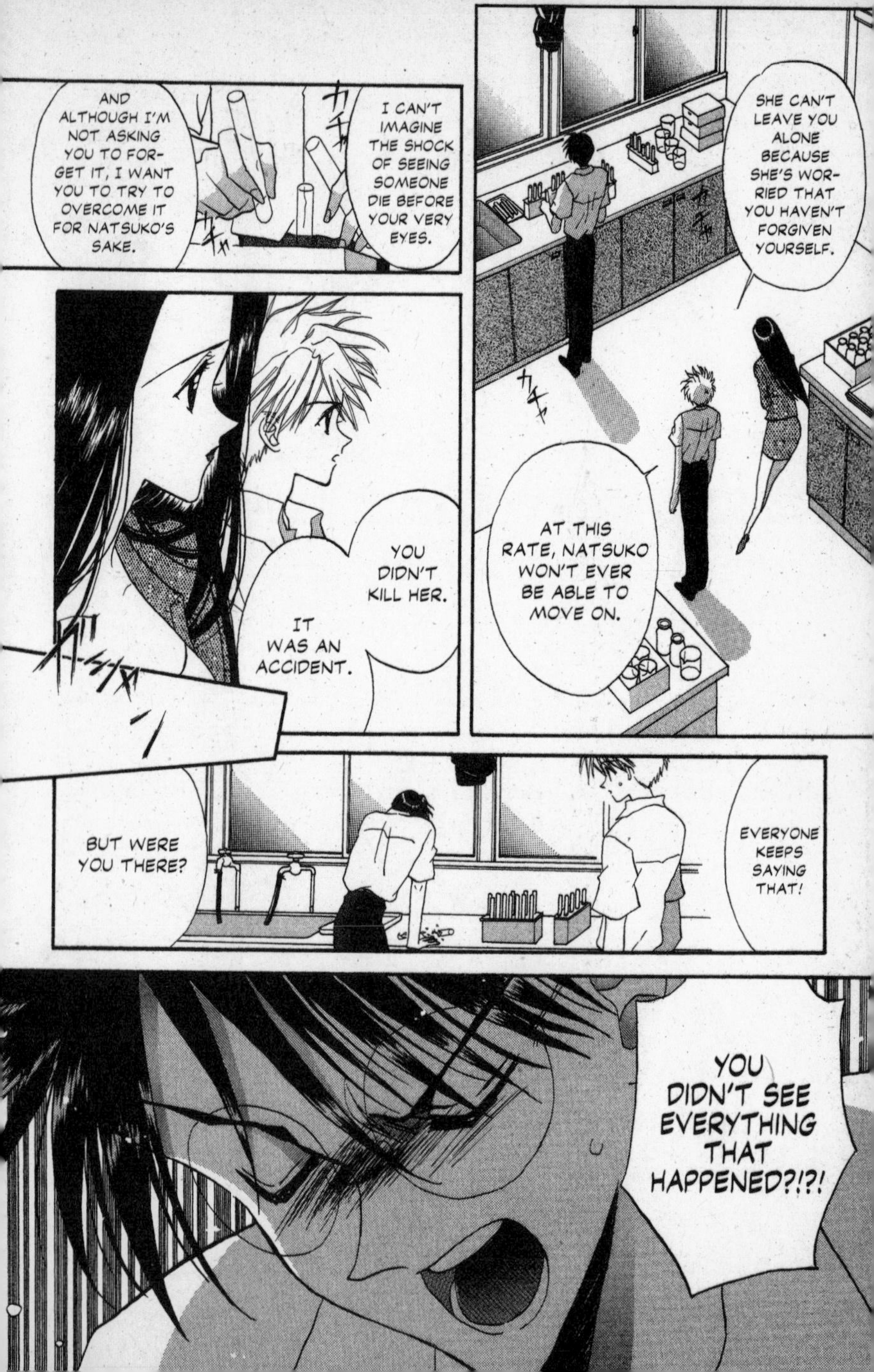
SHE CAN'T LEAVE YOU ALONE BECAUSE SHE'S WORRIED THAT YOU HAVEN'T FORGIVEN YOURSELF.
AT THIS RATE, NATSUKO WON'T EVER BE ABLE TO MOVE ON.
I CAN'T IMAGINE THE SHOCK OF SEEING SOMEONE DIE BEFORE YOUR VERY EYES.
AND ALTHOUGH I'M NOT ASKING YOU TO FORGET IT, I WANT YOU TO TRY TO OVERCOME IT FOR NATSUKO'S SAKE.
YOU DIDN'T KILL HER.
IT WAS AN ACCIDENT.
EVERYONE KEEPS SAYING THAT!
BUT WERE YOU THERE?
YOU DIDN'T SEE EVERYTHING THAT HAPPENED?!?!

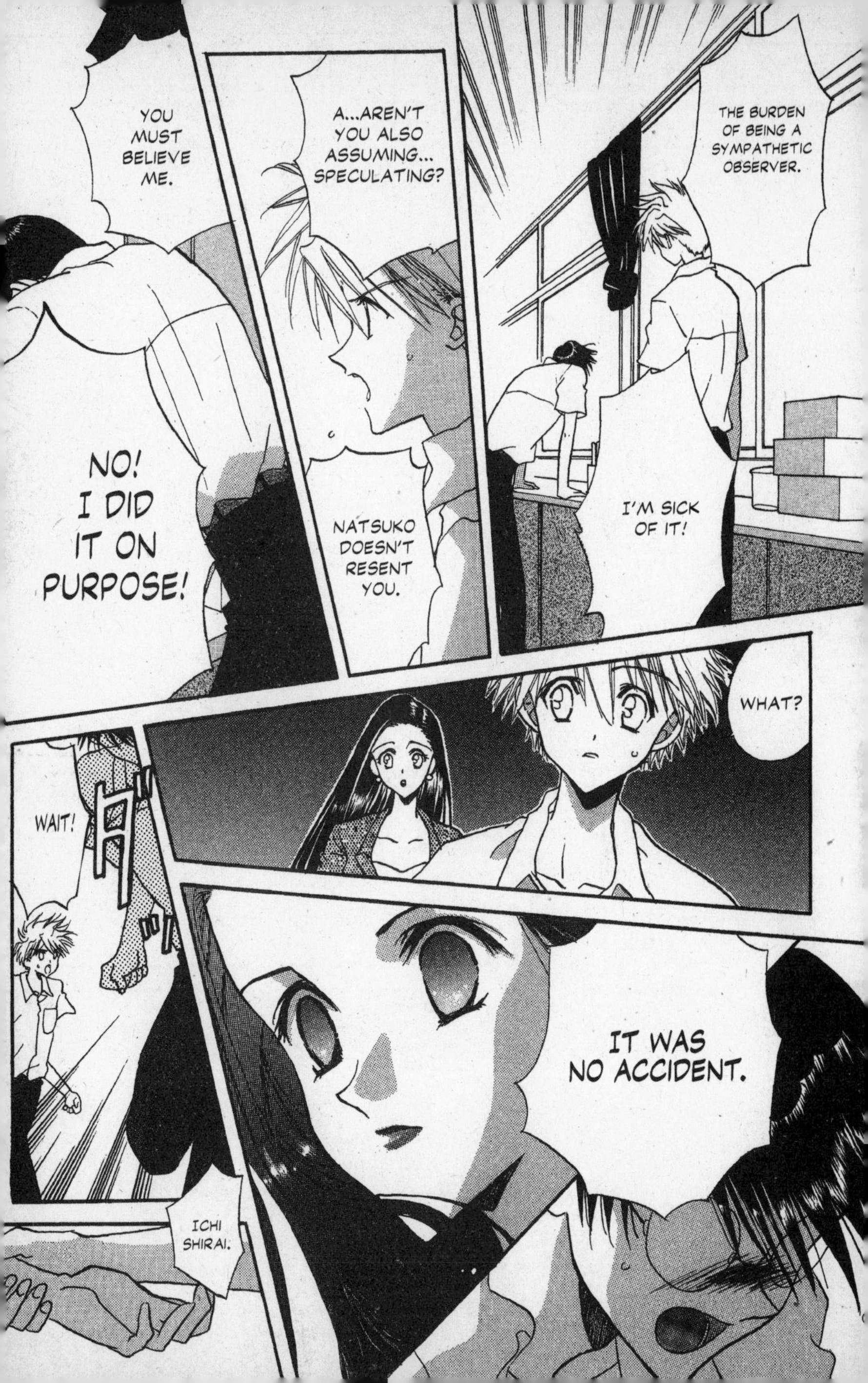
THE BURDEN OF BEING A SYMPATHETIC OBSERVER.
I'M SICK OF IT!
A...AREN'T YOU ALSO ASSUMING... SPECULATING?
NATSUKO DOESN'T RESENT YOU.
YOU MUST BELIEVE ME.
NO! I DID IT ON PURPOSE!
WHAT?
WAIT!
IT WAS NO ACCIDENT.
ICHI SHIRAI.

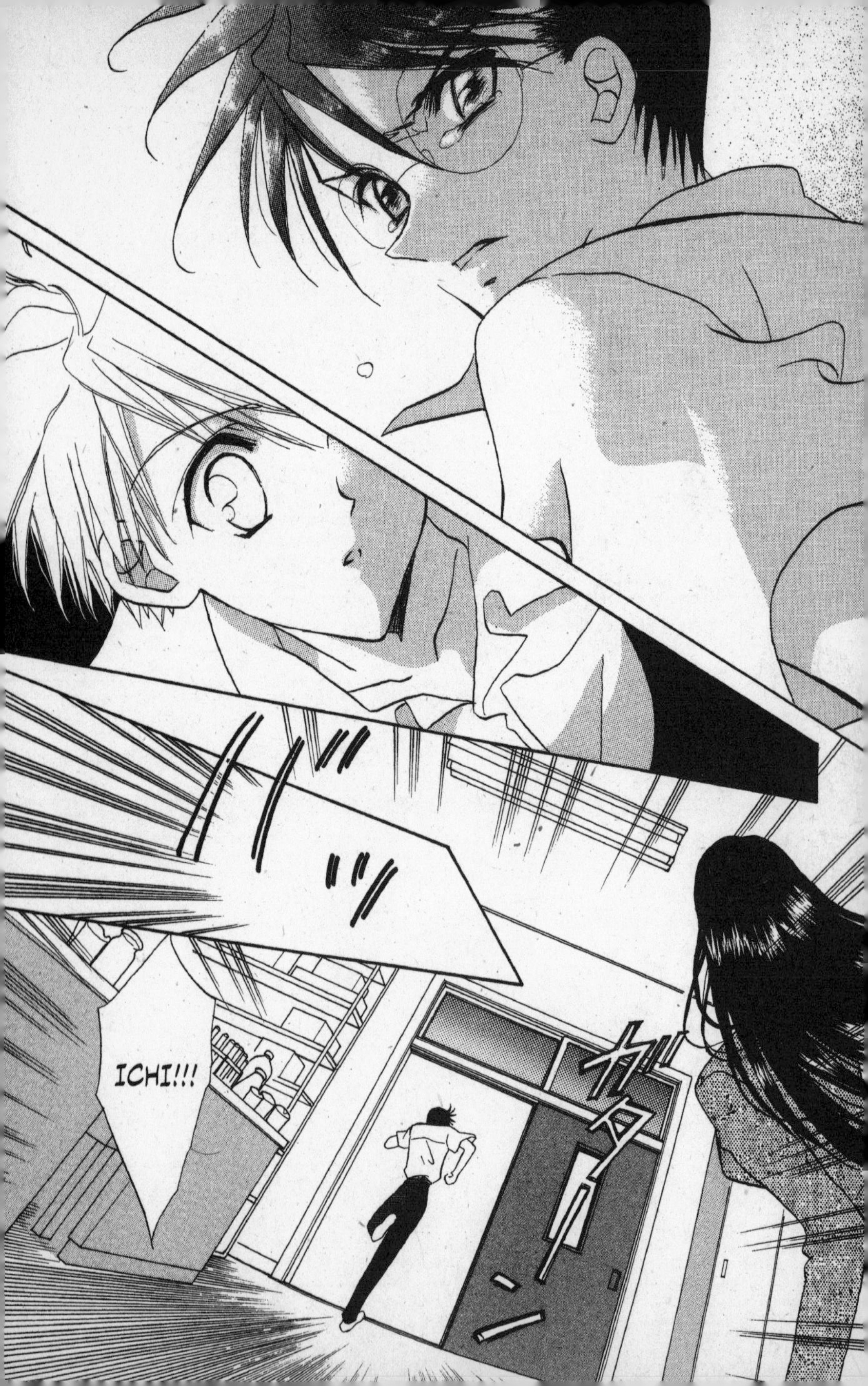
ICHI!!!

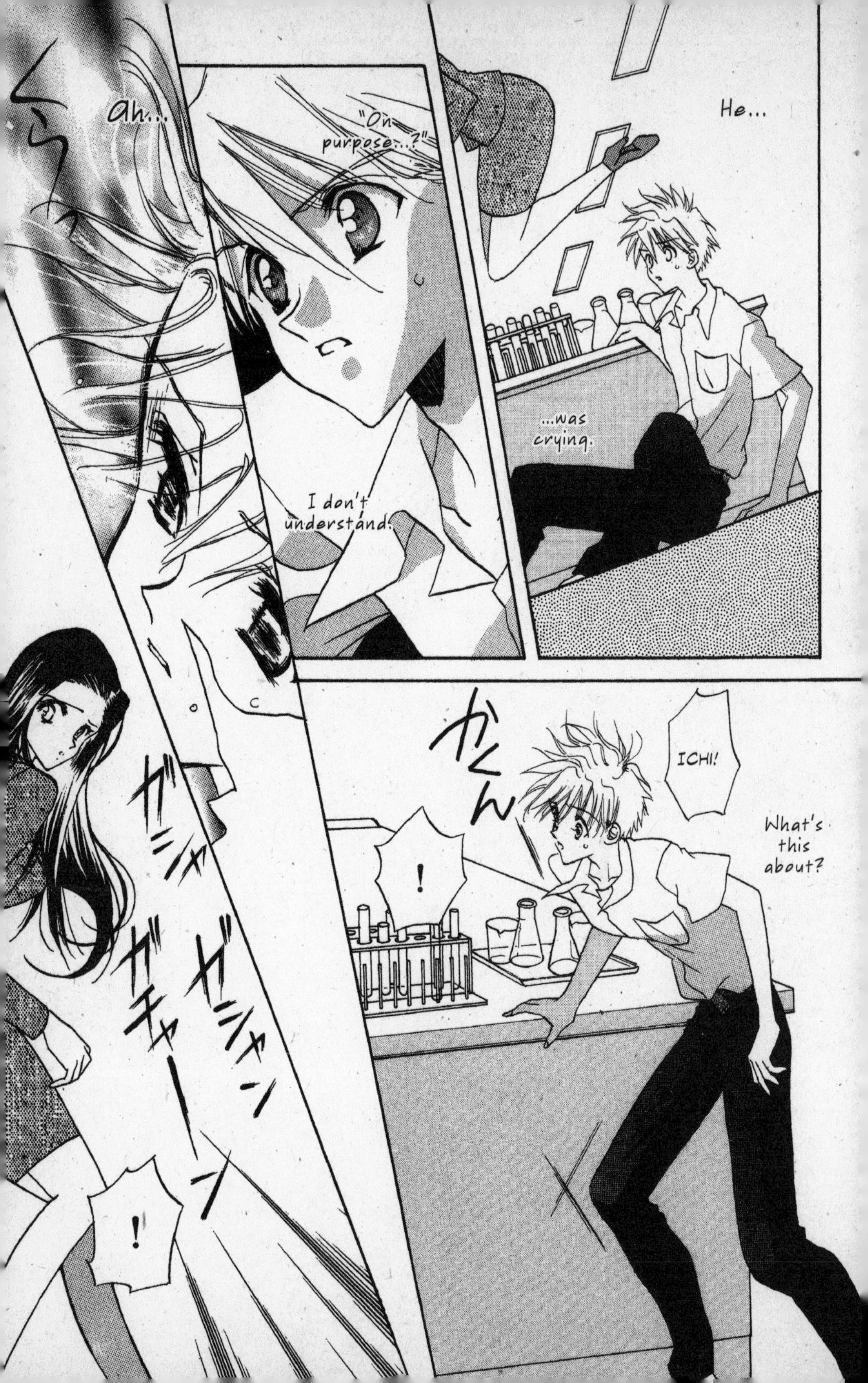
He...
...was crying.
"On purpose...?"
I don't understand.
ICHI!
What's this about?
かくん
!
ah...
ガシャ
ガシャン
ガチャーン
!

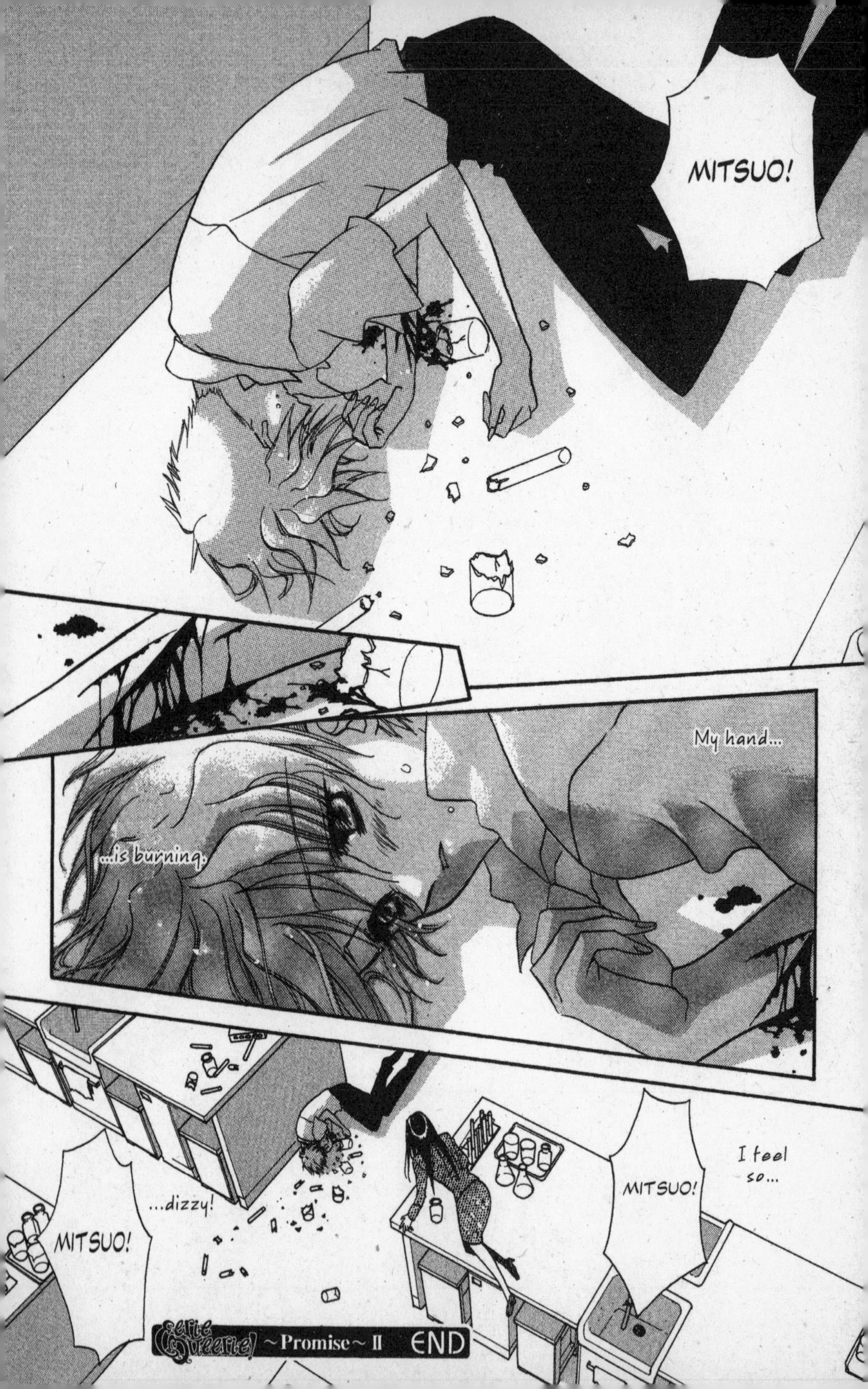
MITSUO!
My hand...
...is burning.
I feel so...
MITSUO!
...dizzy!
MITSUO!
~Promise~ II END

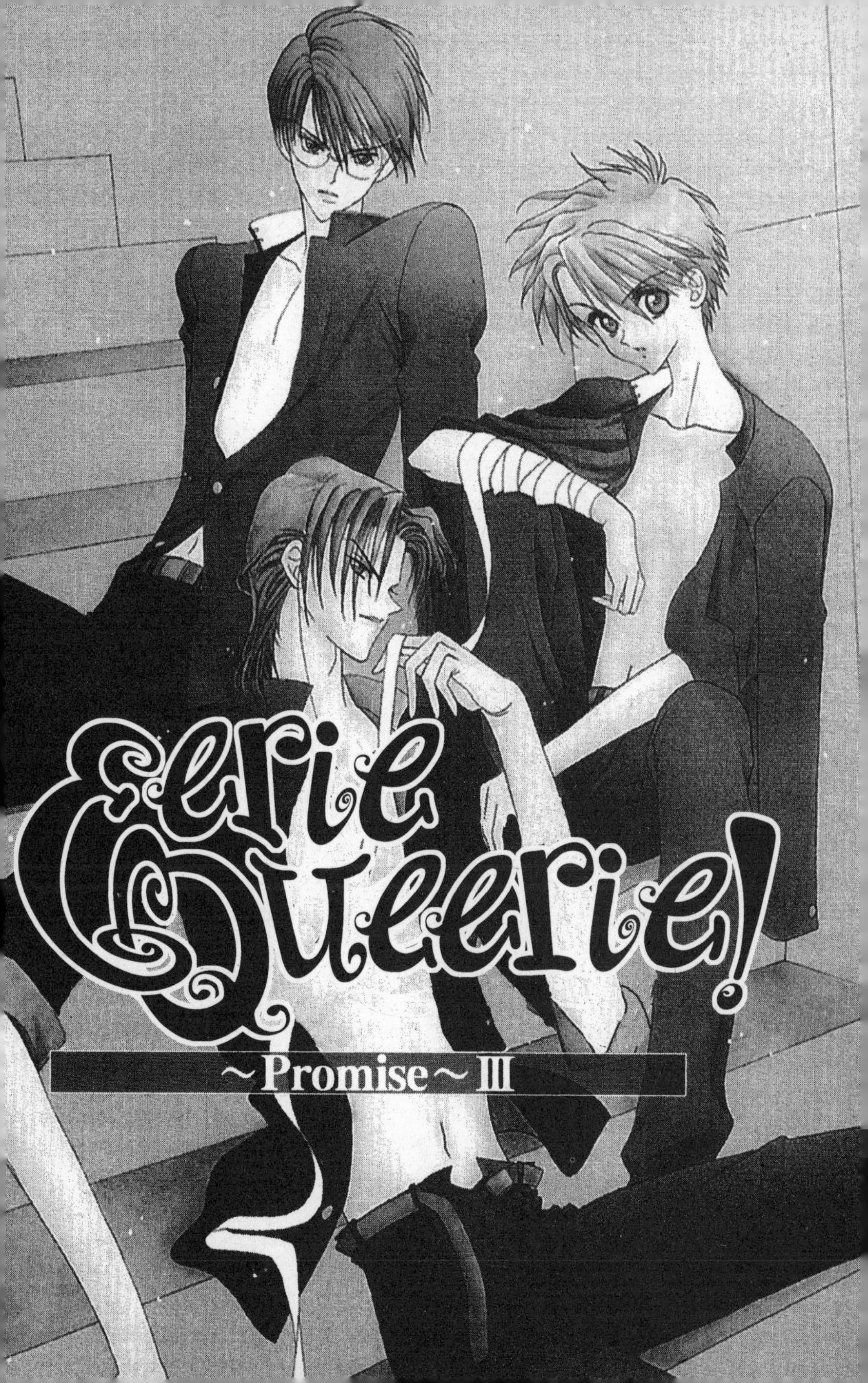
Eerie Queerie!
~Promise~ III

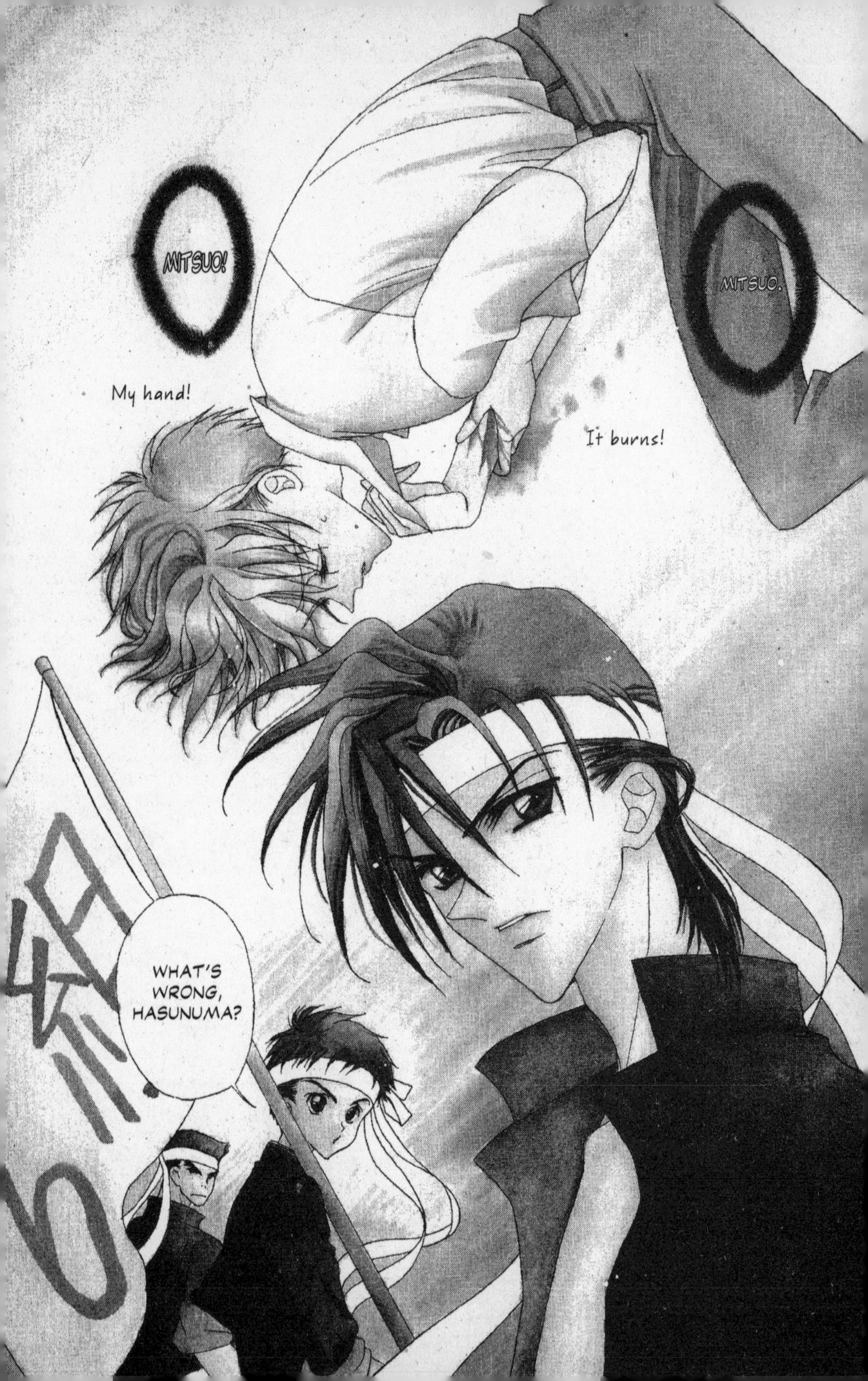
MITSUO.
MITSUO!
My hand!
It burns!
WHAT'S WRONG, HASUNUMA?

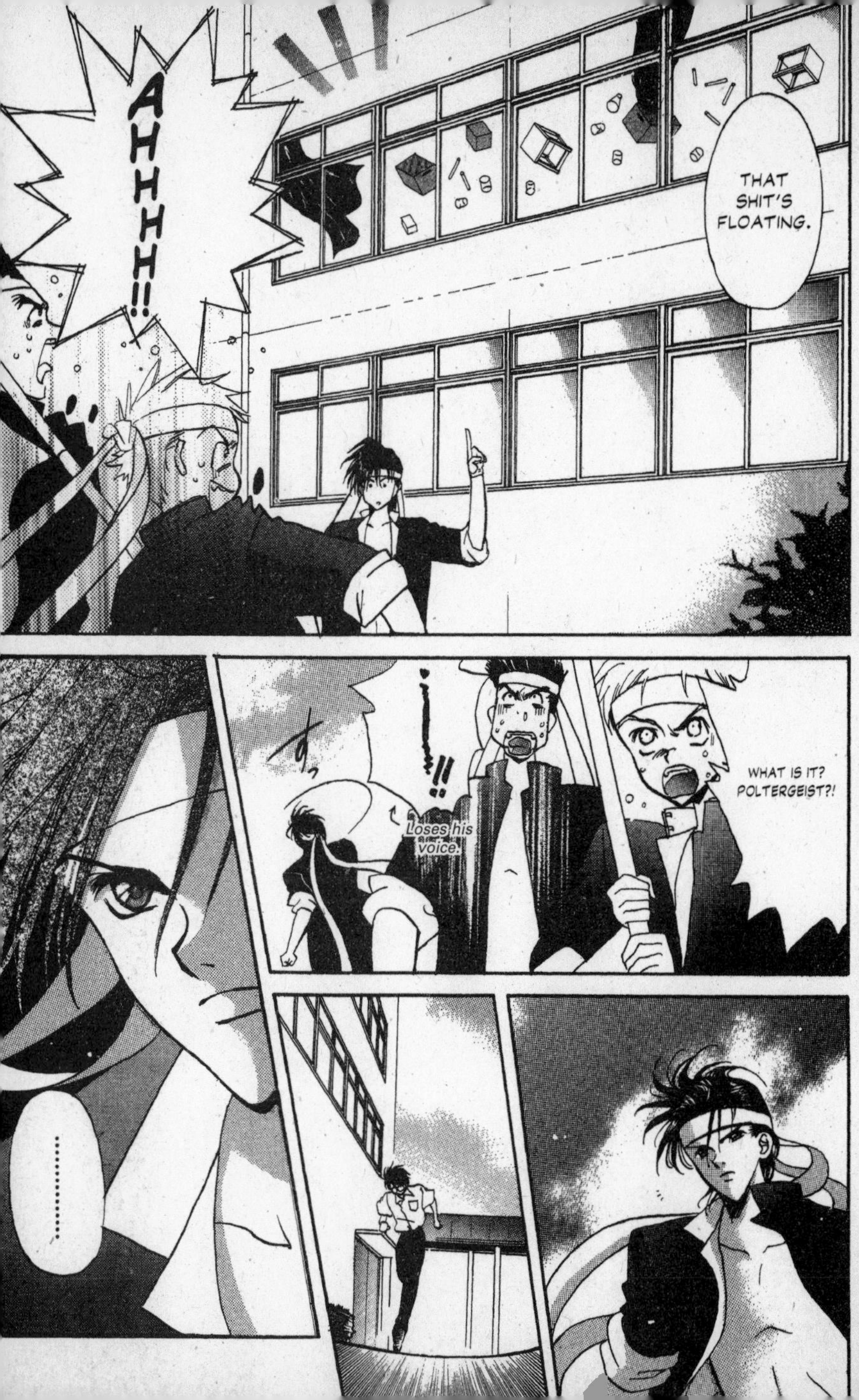
THAT SHIT'S FLOATING.
AHHHH!!
WHAT IS IT? POLTERGEIST?!
!!
Loses his voice.
......

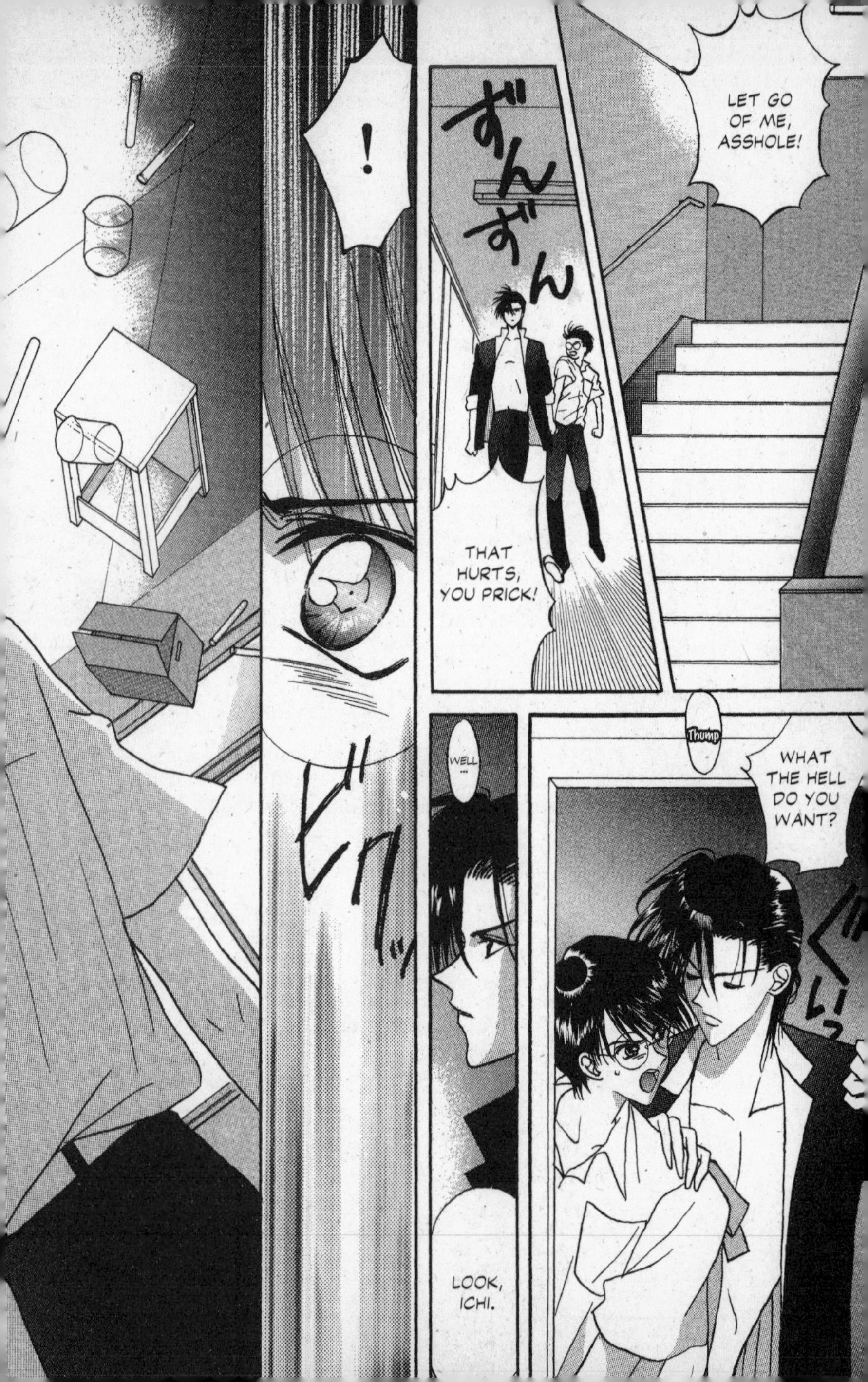
LET GO OF ME, ASSHOLE!
ずんずん
THAT HURTS, YOU PRICK!
Thump
WHAT THE HELL DO YOU WANT?
ぐいっ
WELL...
LOOK, ICHI.
!

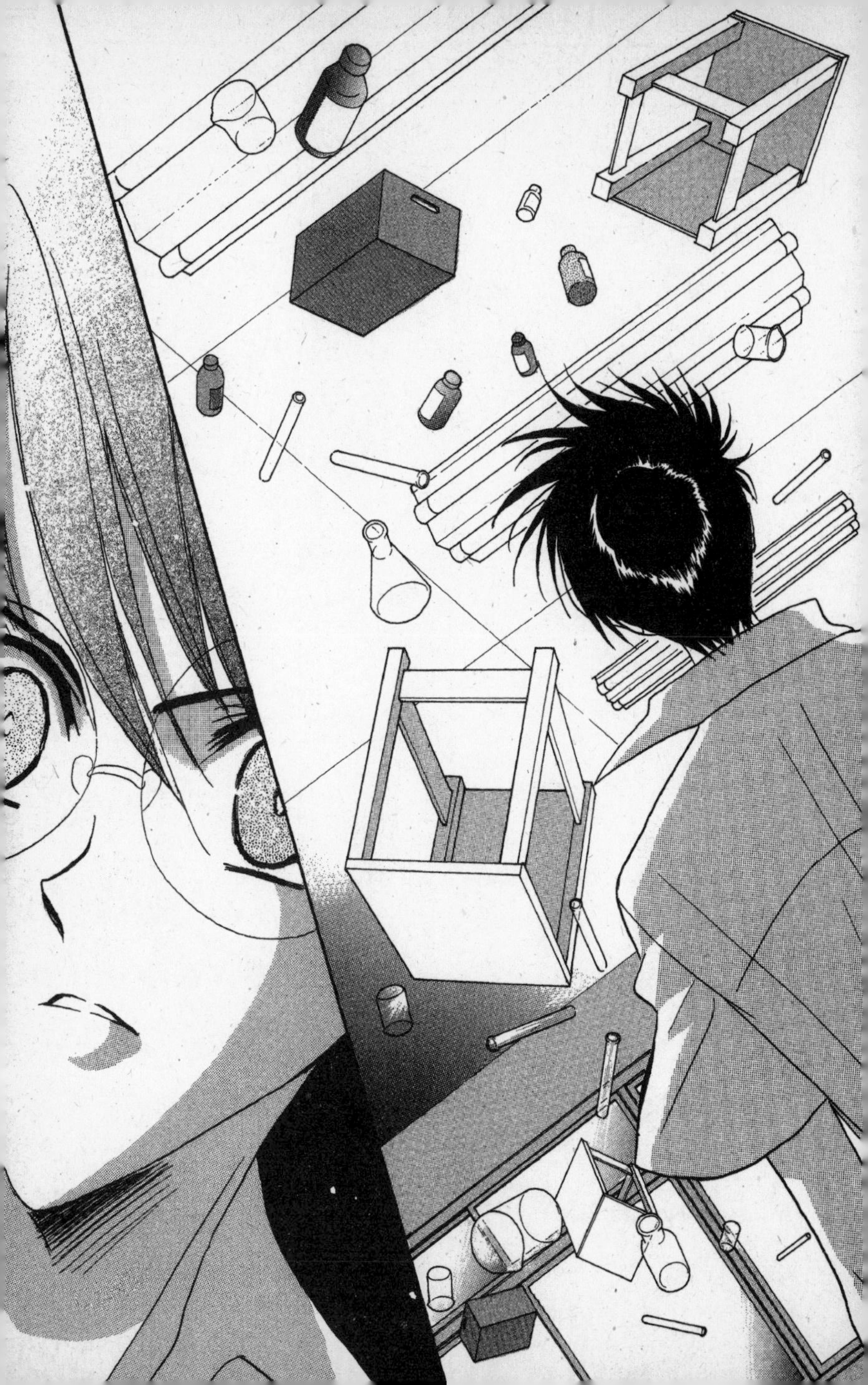

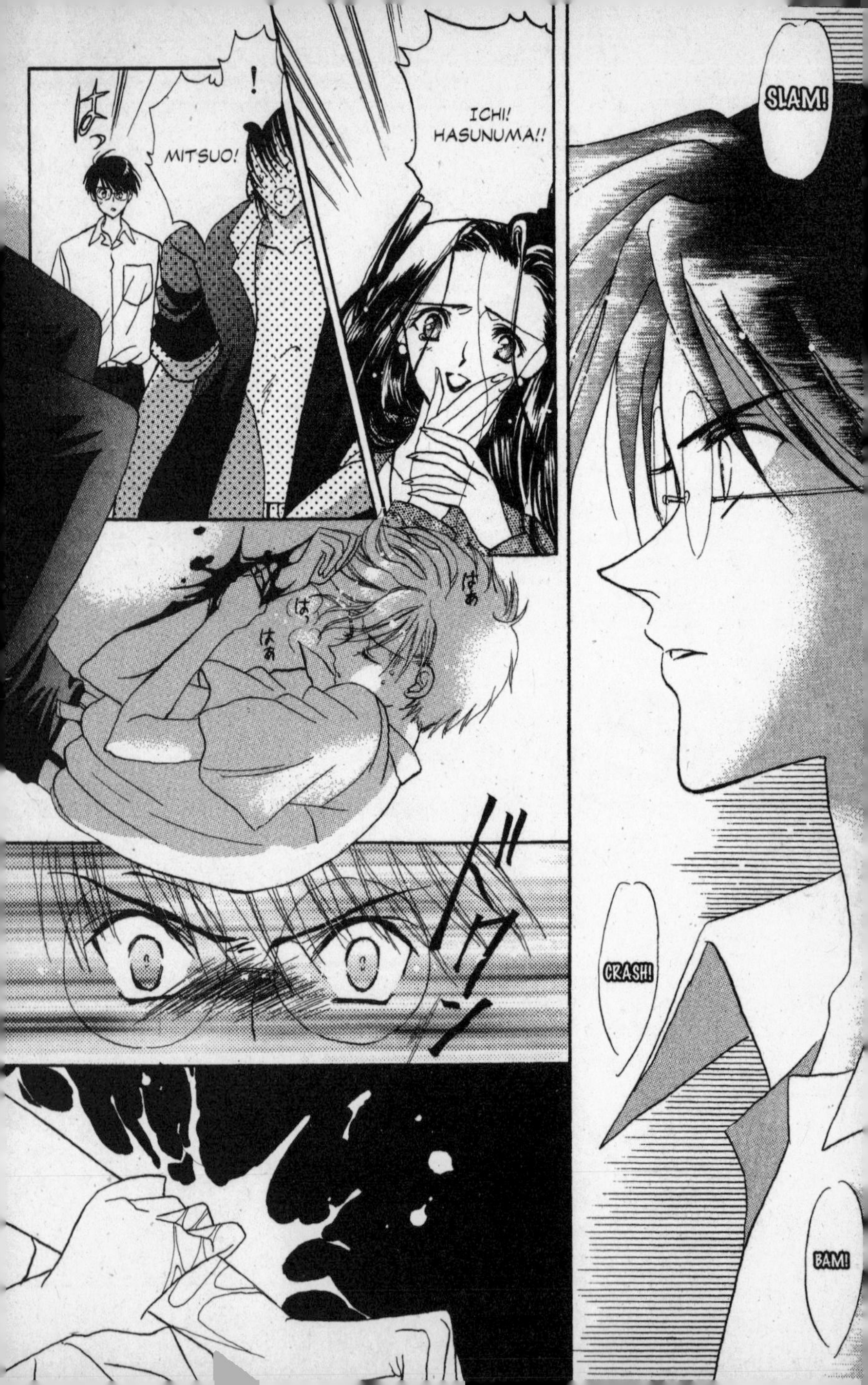
SLAM!
CRASH!
BAM!
ICHI! HASUNUMA!!
!
MITSUO!
はっ
はぁ
はっ
はぁ
ドタン

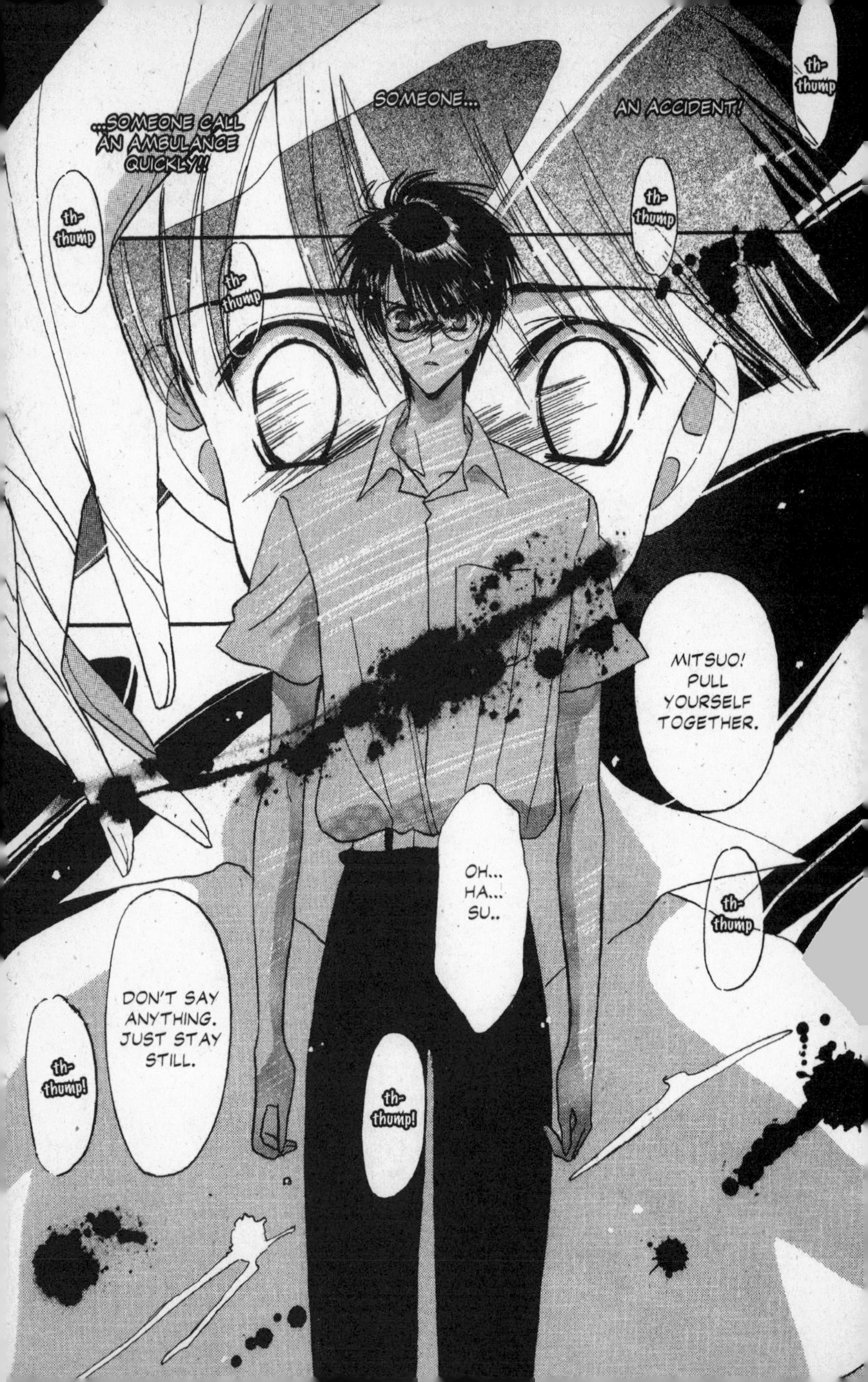

th-thump
AN ACCIDENT!
SOMEONE...
...SOMEONE CALL AN AMBULANCE QUICKLY!!
th-thump
th-thump
th-thump
MITSUO! PULL YOURSELF TOGETHER.
th-thump
OH... HA... SU..
DON'T SAY ANYTHING. JUST STAY STILL.
th-thump!
th-thump!

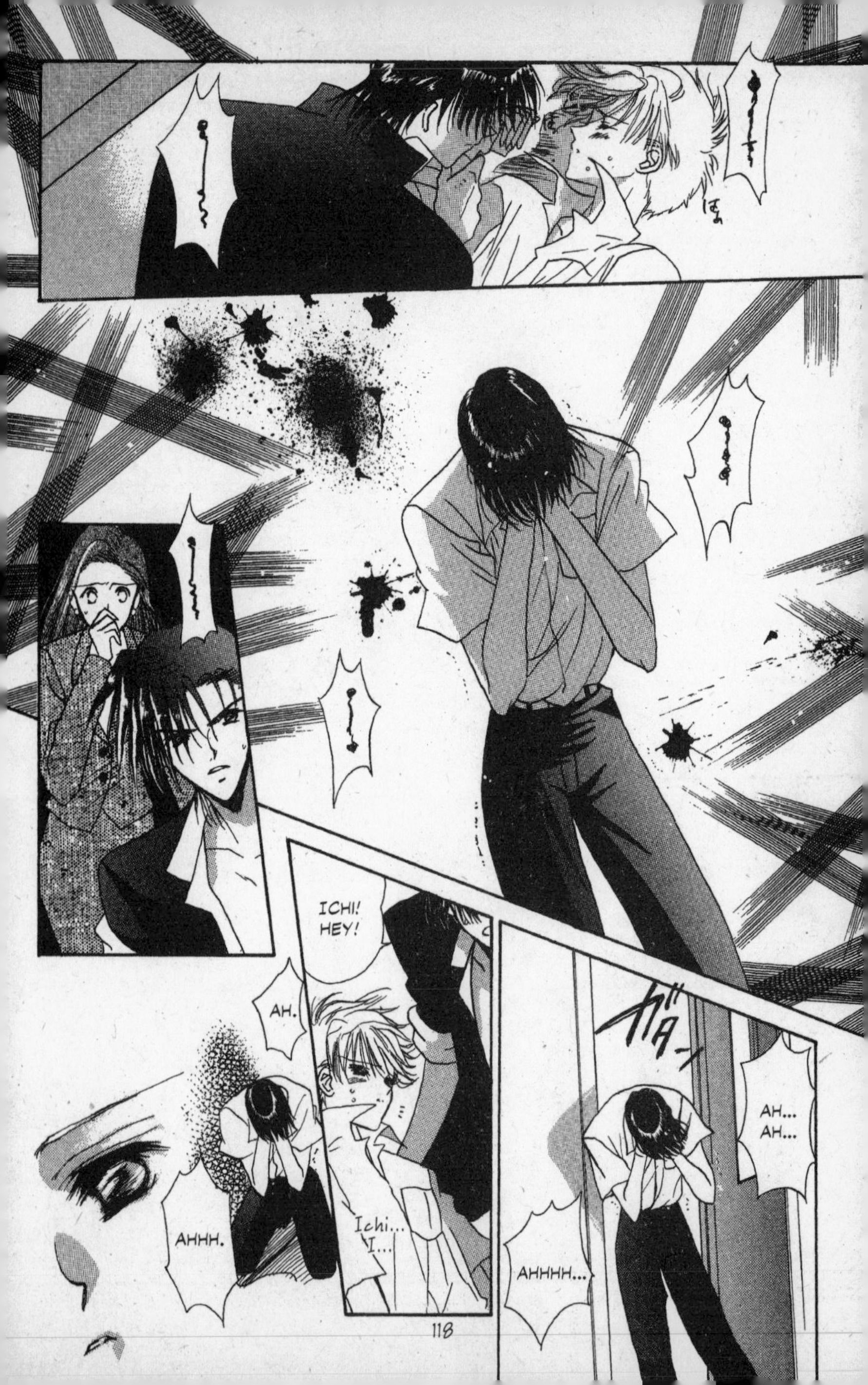
AH...
AH...
AHHHH...
ICHI!
HEY!
Ichi...
I...
AH.
AHHH.

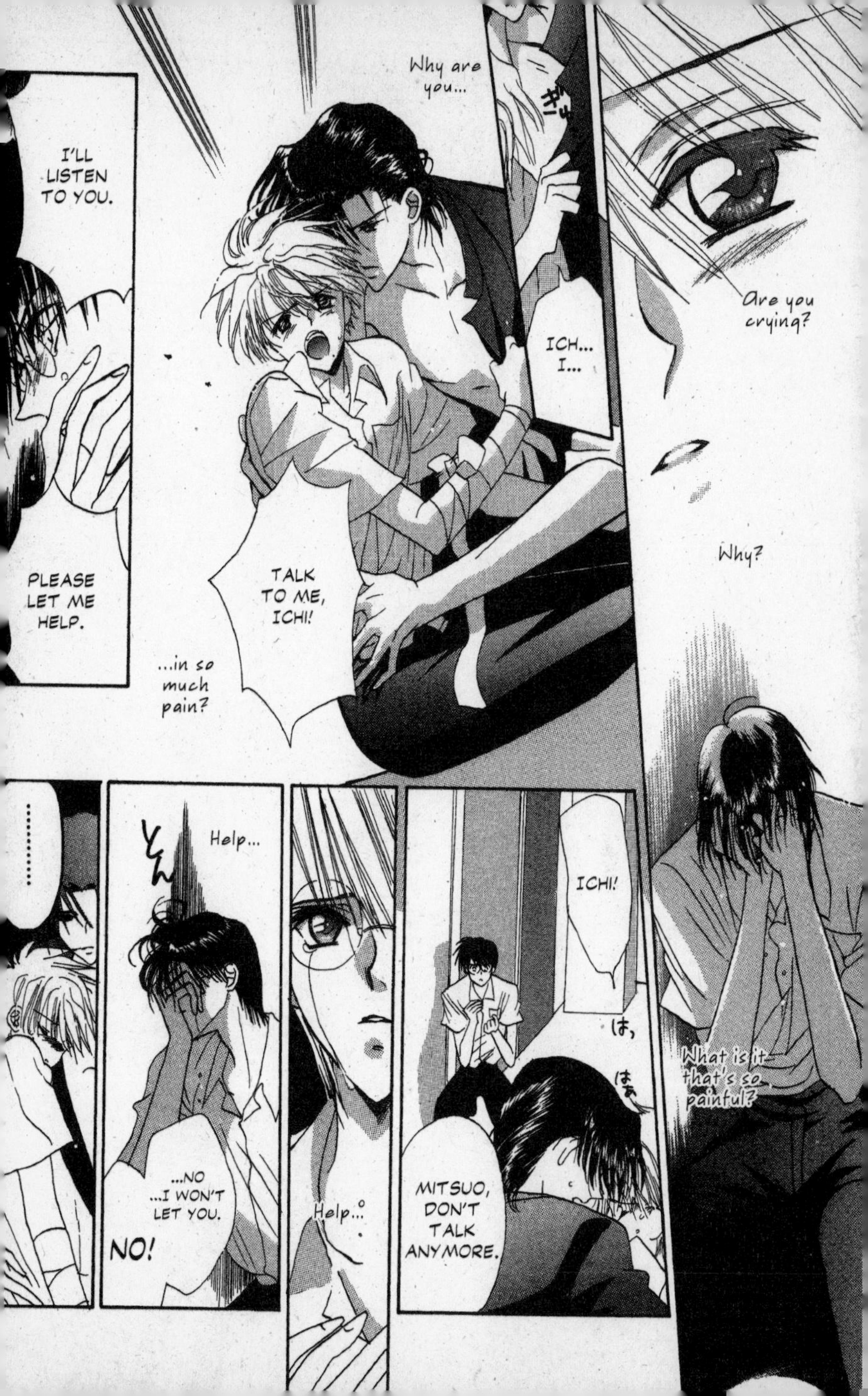
Are you crying?
Why?
ICH... I...
Why are you...
TALK TO ME, ICHI!
...in so much pain?
I'LL LISTEN TO YOU.
PLEASE LET ME HELP.
What is it that's so painful?
ICHI!
MITSUO, DON'T TALK ANYMORE.
Help...
Help...
...NO ...I WON'T LET YOU.
NO!
......

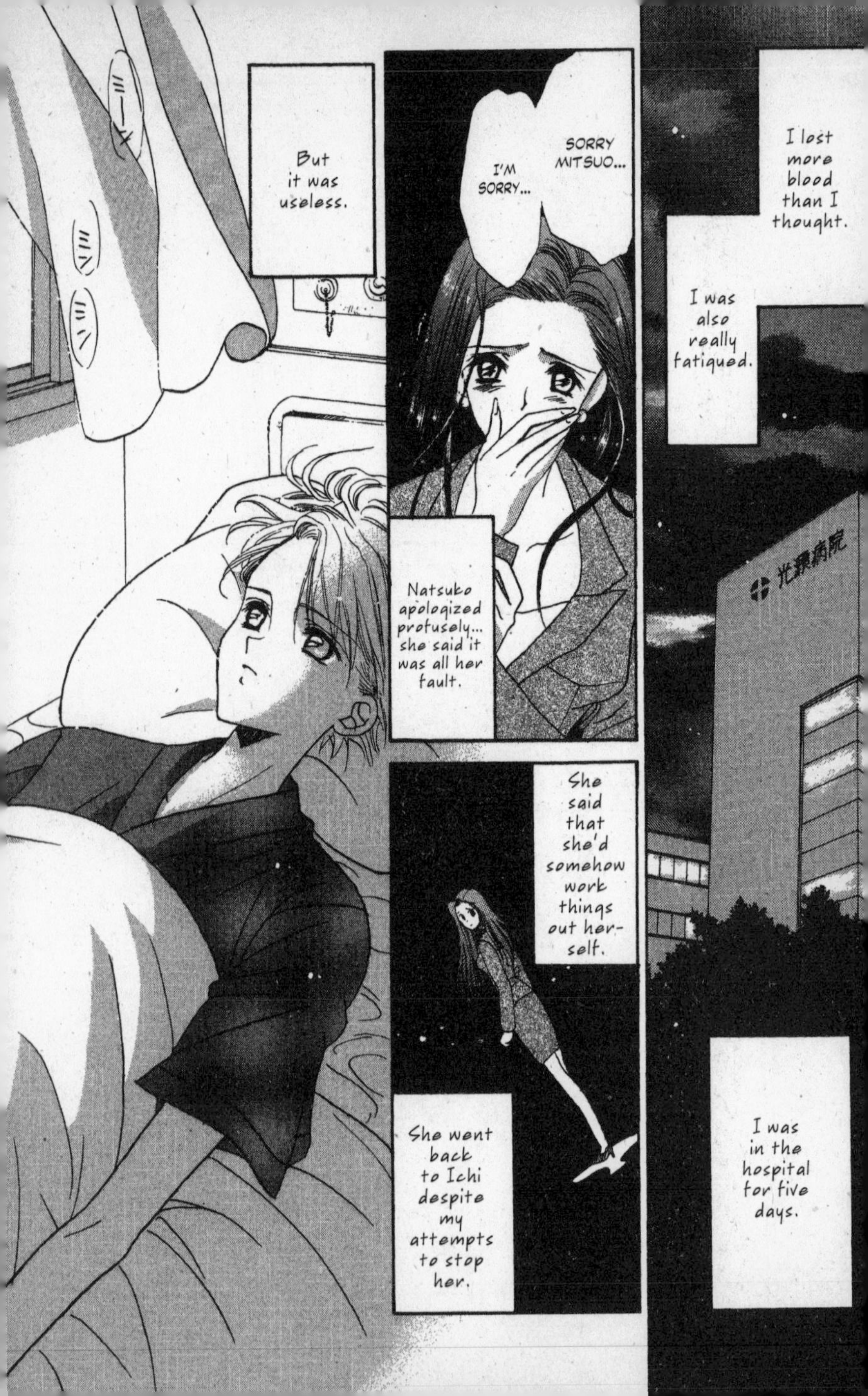
I lost more blood than I thought.
I was also really fatigued.
I was in the hospital for five days.
SORRY MITSUO...
I'M SORRY...
Natsuko apologized profusely... she said it was all her fault.
She said that she'd somehow work things out her-self.
She went back to Ichi despite my attempts to stop her.
But it was useless.

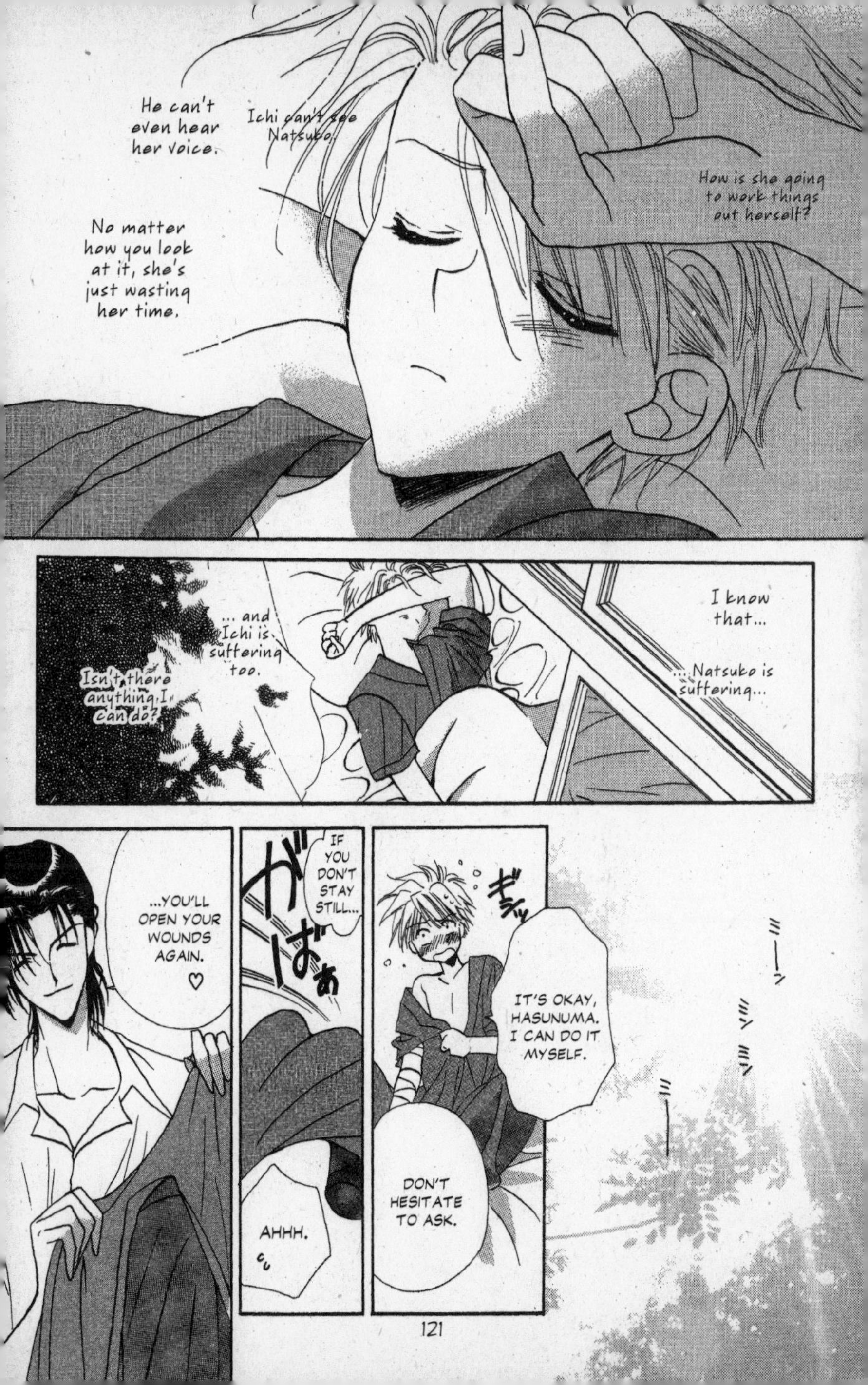
Ichi can't see Natsuko.
He can't even hear her voice.
How is she going to work things out herself?
No matter how you look at it, she's just wasting her time.
I know that...
...Natsuko is suffering...
... and Ichi is suffering too.
Isn't there anything I can do?
ミーン
ミン ミン
ミー
ギシッ
IT'S OKAY, HASUNUMA. I CAN DO IT MYSELF.
DON'T HESITATE TO ASK.
IF YOU DON'T STAY STILL...
がばぁ
AHHH.
...YOU'LL OPEN YOUR WOUNDS AGAIN. ♡

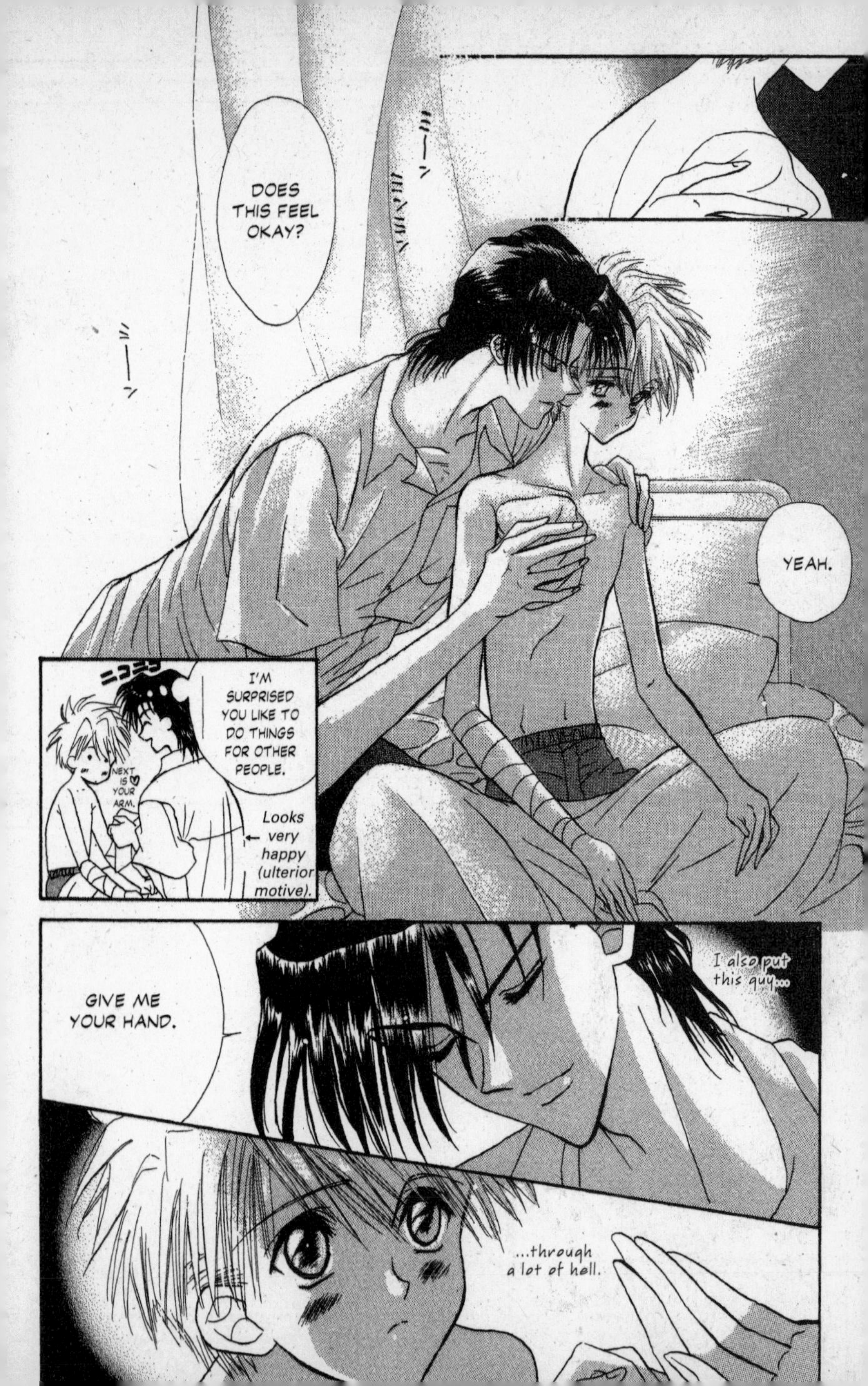
ミーン
DOES THIS FEEL OKAY?
ミーン
YEAH.
I'M SURPRISED YOU LIKE TO DO THINGS FOR OTHER PEOPLE.
ニコニコ
NEXT IS ♡ YOUR ARM.
Looks very happy (ulterior motive).
I also put this guy...
GIVE ME YOUR HAND.
...through a lot of hell.

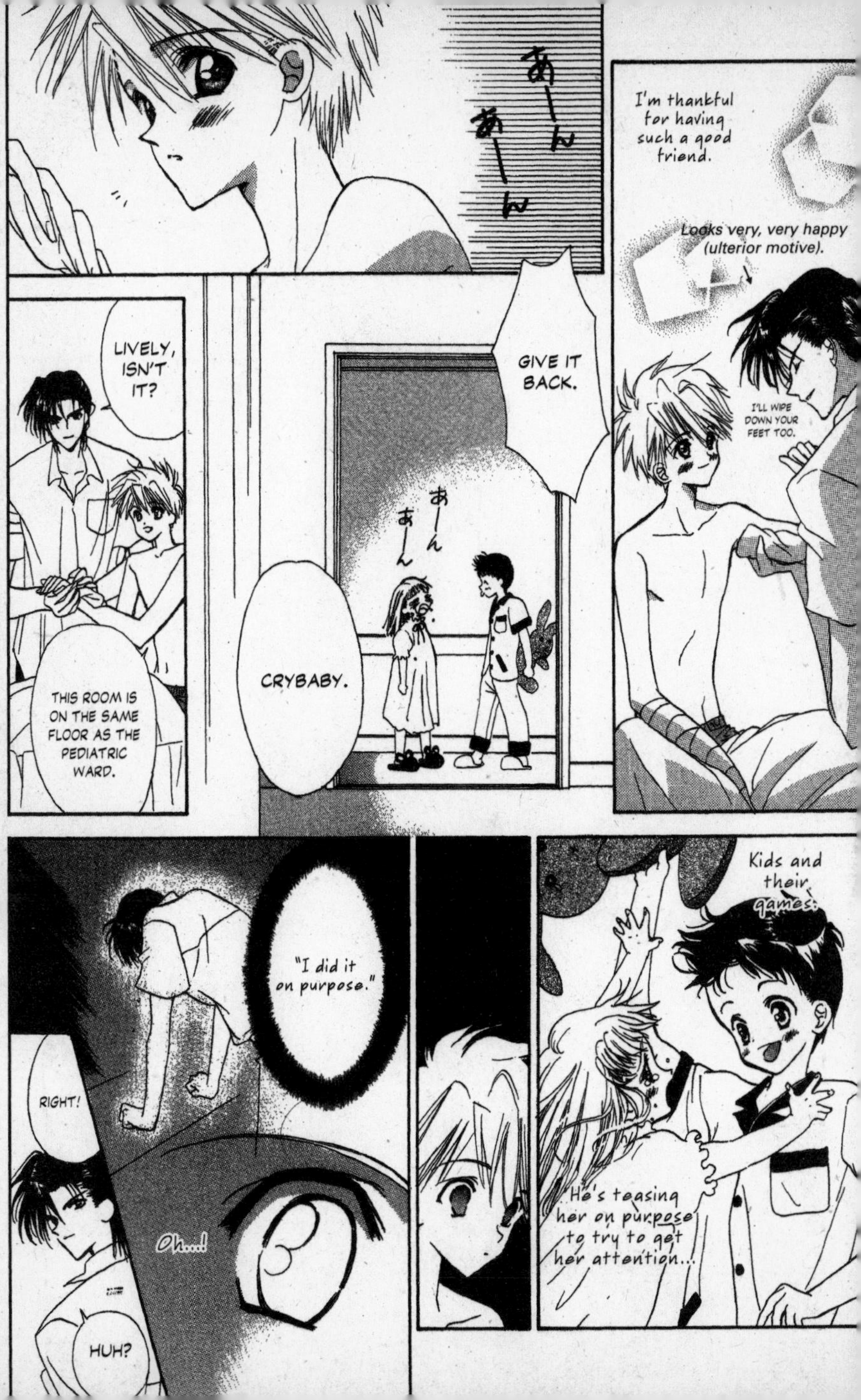
I'm thankful for having such a good friend.
Looks very, very happy (ulterior motive).
I'LL WIPE DOWN YOUR FEET TOO.
あーんあーん
GIVE IT BACK.
あーんあーん
CRYBABY.
LIVELY, ISN'T IT?
THIS ROOM IS ON THE SAME FLOOR AS THE PEDIATRIC WARD.
Kids and their games.
He's teasing her on purpose to try to get her attention...
"I did it on purpose."
RIGHT!
Oh...!
HUH?

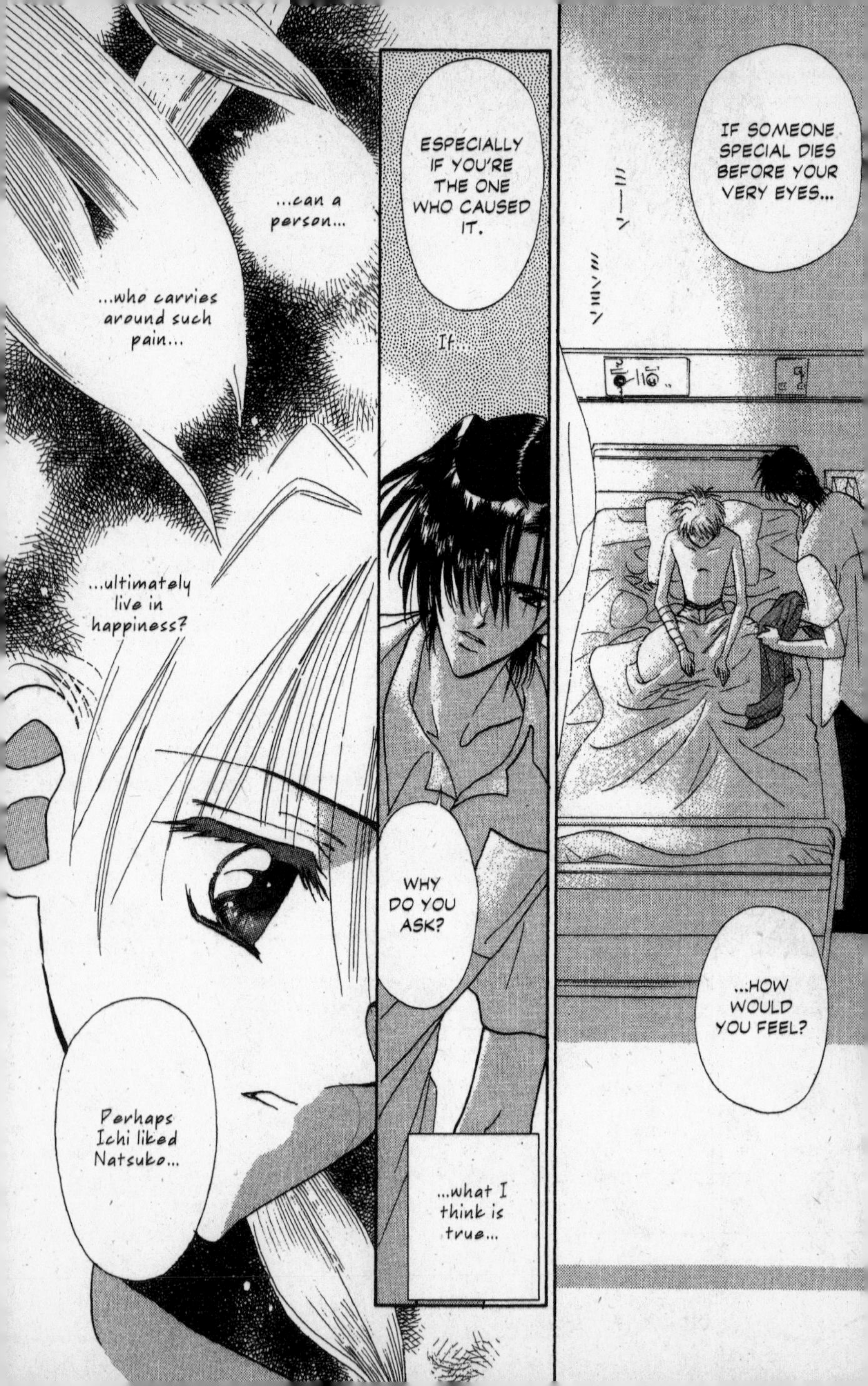
IF SOMEONE SPECIAL DIES BEFORE YOUR VERY EYES...
...HOW WOULD YOU FEEL?
ESPECIALLY IF YOU'RE THE ONE WHO CAUSED IT.
If...
WHY DO YOU ASK?
...what I think is true...
...can a person...
...who carries around such pain...
...ultimately live in happiness?
Perhaps Ichi liked Natsuko...

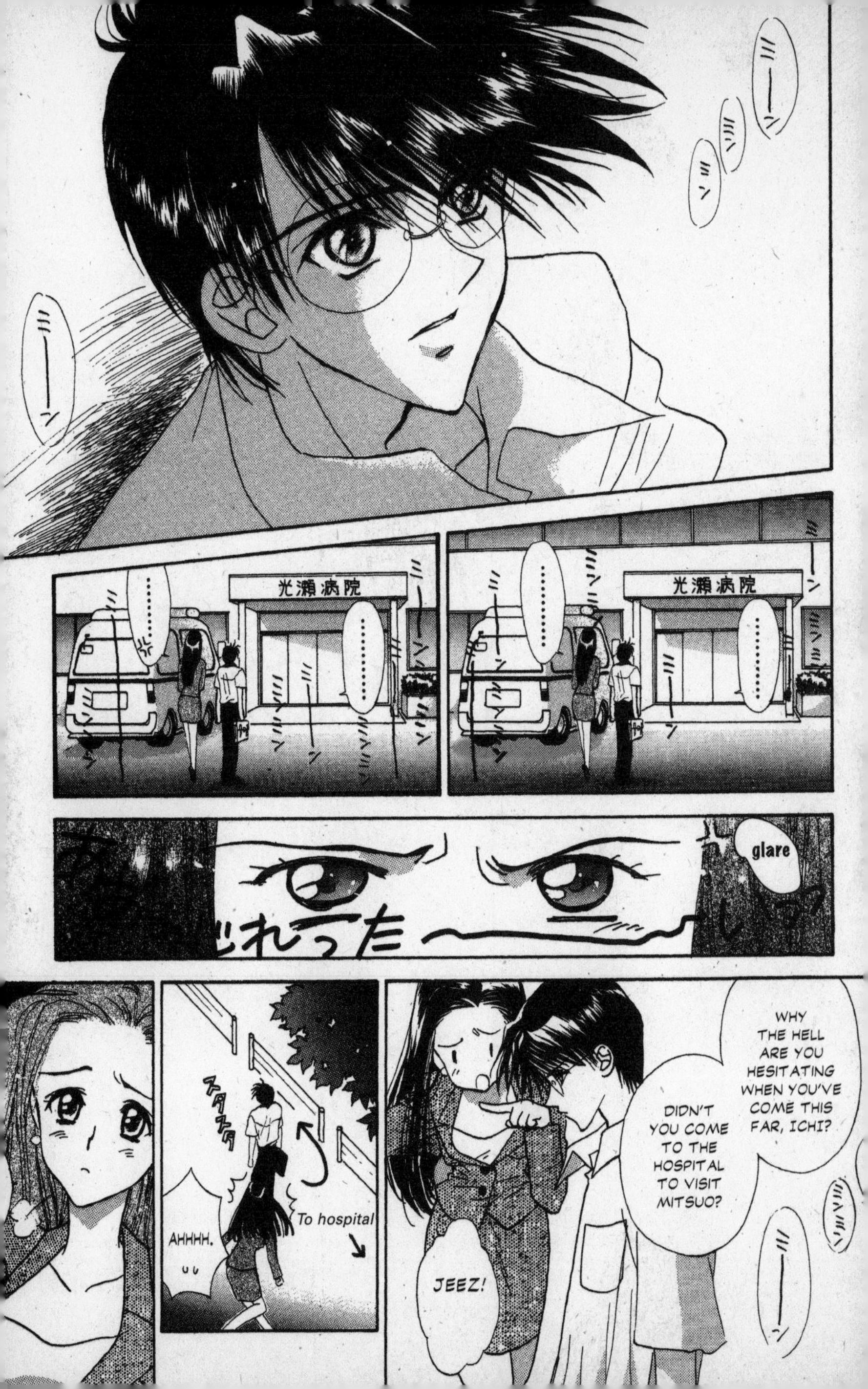
ミーーン
ミンミン
ミン
ミーーン
......
光瀬病院
......
......
光瀬病院
......
glare
WHY THE HELL ARE YOU HESITATING WHEN YOU'VE COME THIS FAR, ICHI?
DIDN'T YOU COME TO THE HOSPITAL TO VISIT MITSUO?
JEEZ!
To hospital
AHHHH.

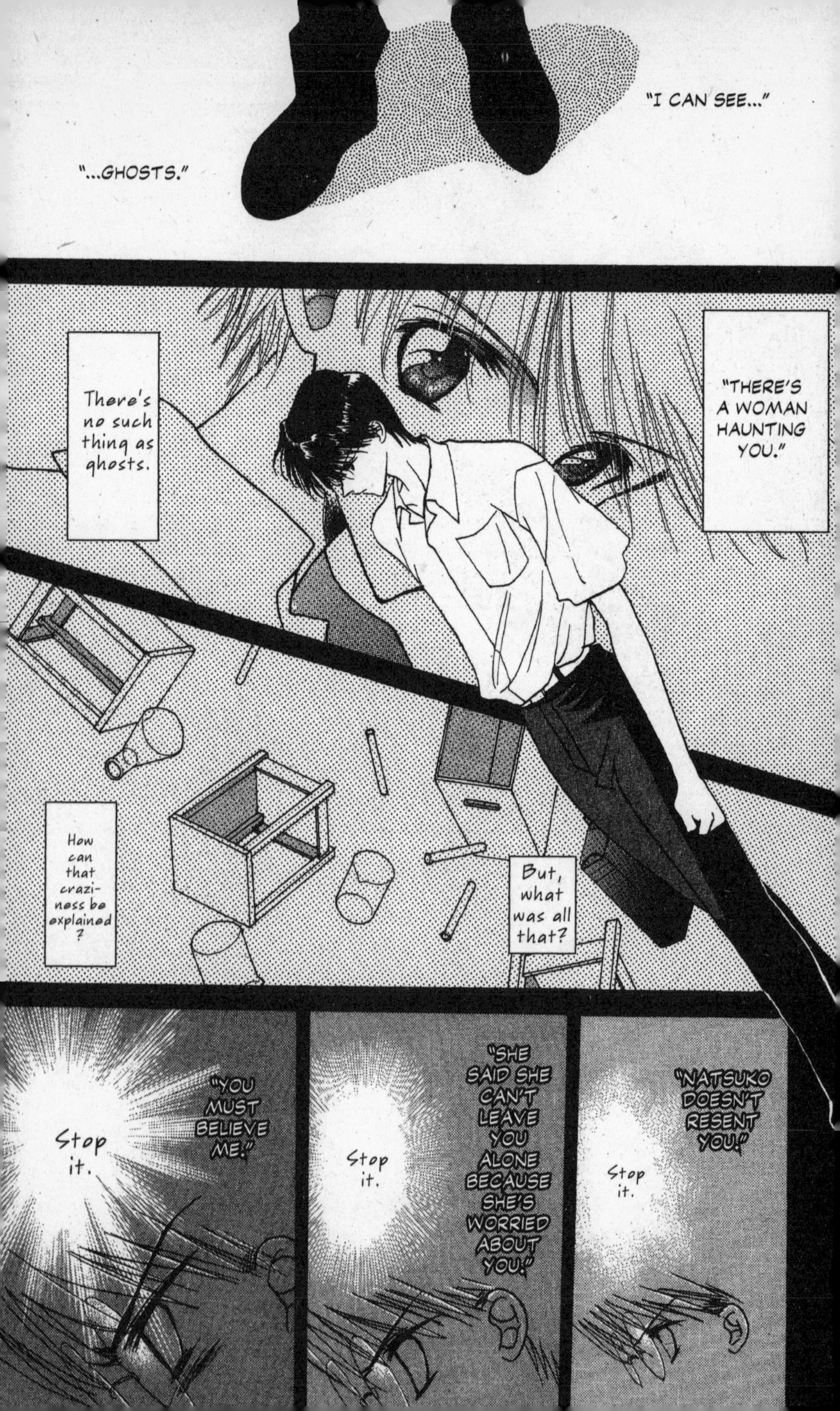
"I CAN SEE..."
"...GHOSTS."
"THERE'S A WOMAN HAUNTING YOU."
There's no such thing as ghosts.
But, what was all that?
How can that crazi-ness be explained?
"NATSUKO DOESN'T RESENT YOU."
Stop it.
"SHE SAID SHE CAN'T LEAVE YOU ALONE BECAUSE SHE'S WORRIED ABOUT YOU."
Stop it.
"YOU MUST BELIEVE ME."
Stop it.

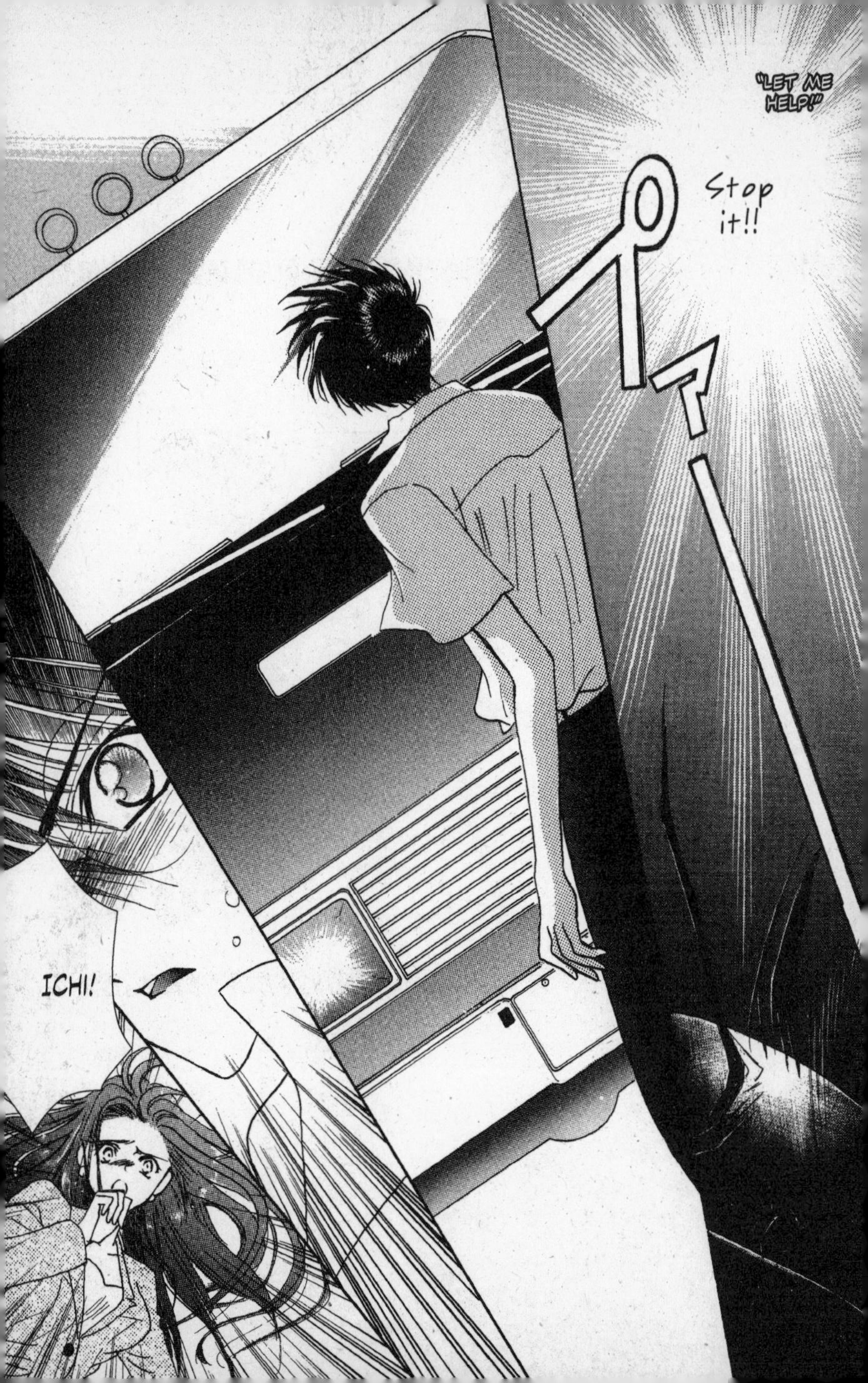
"LET ME HELP!"
Stop it!!
ICHI!

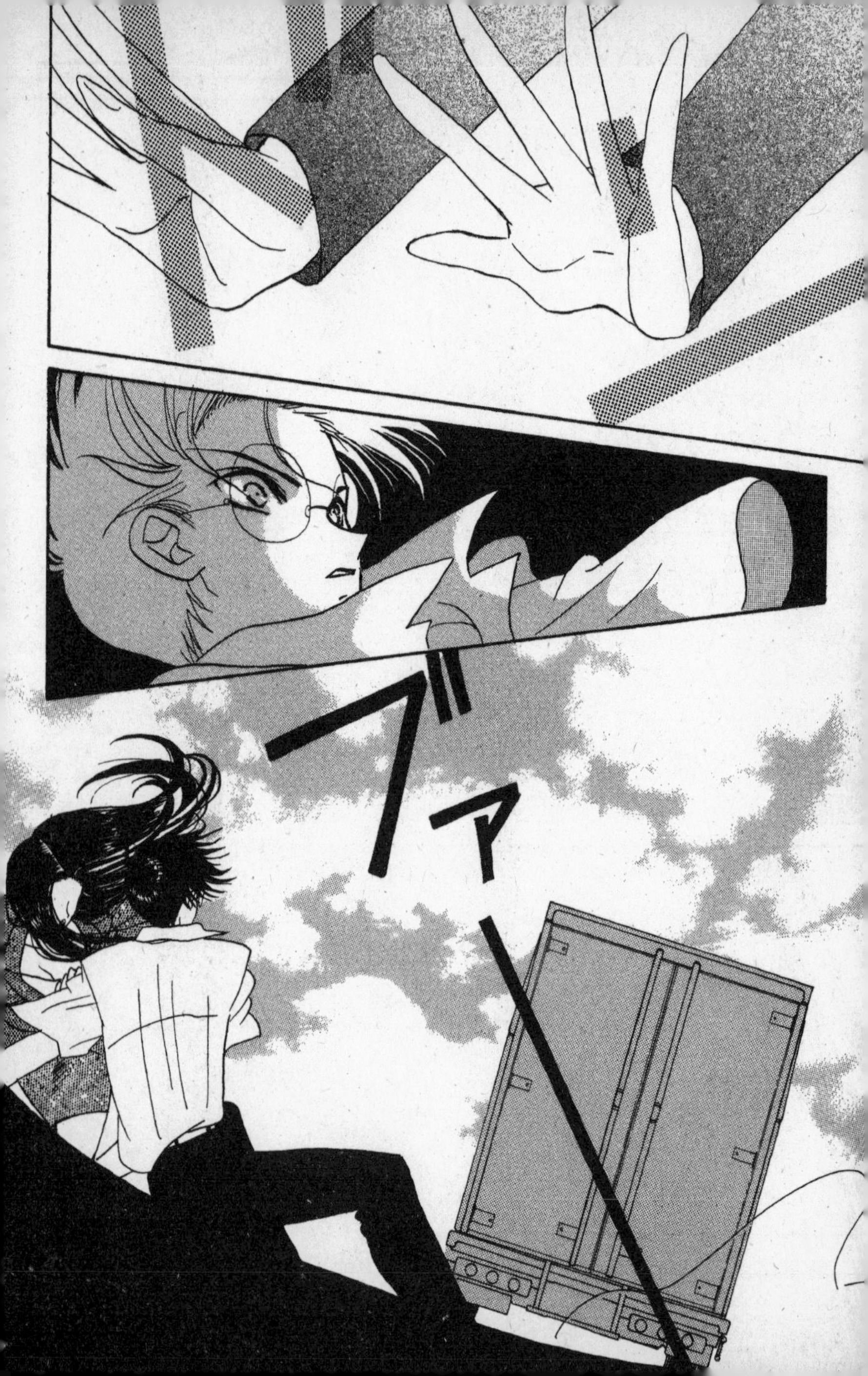
ブァー

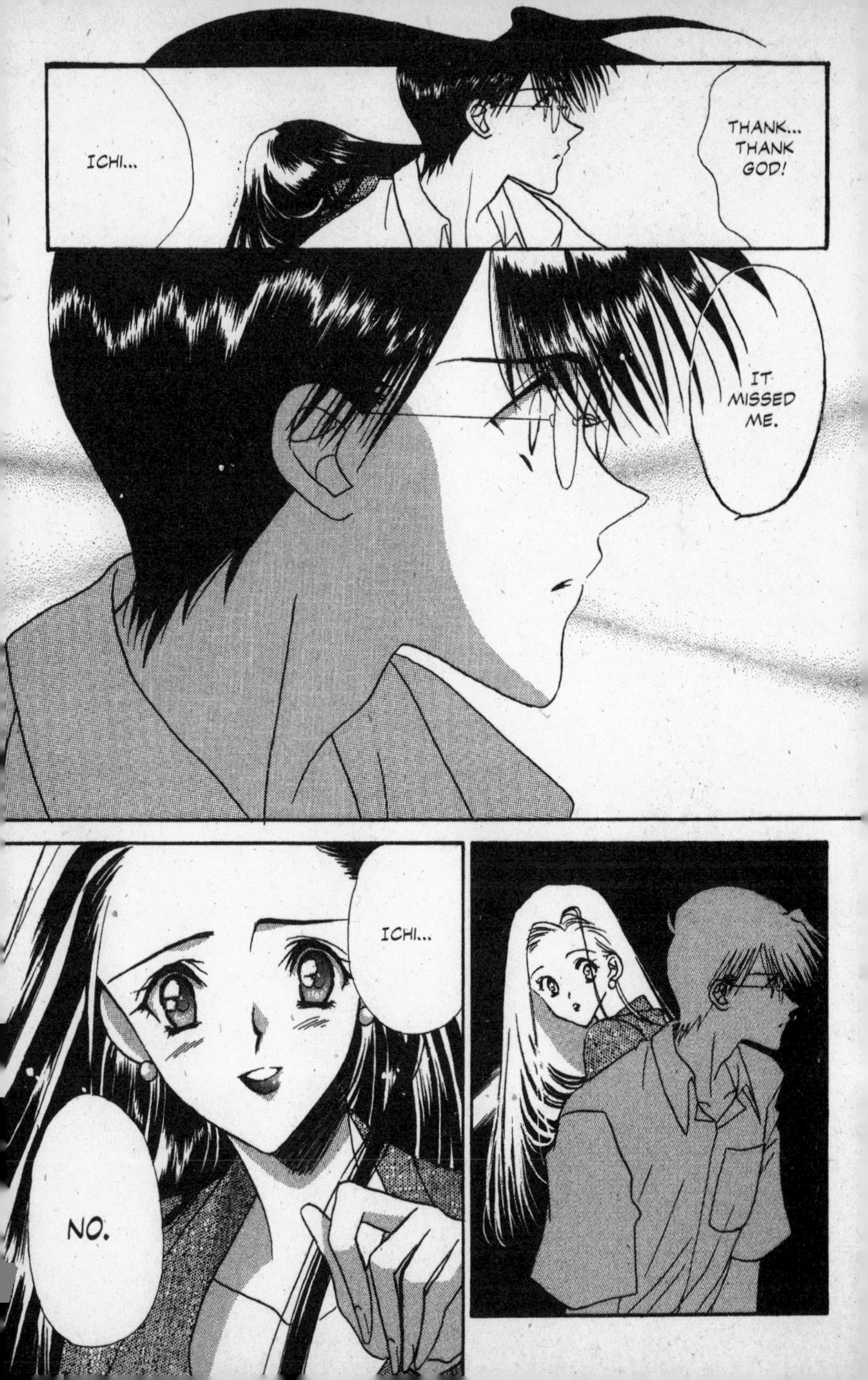
THANK... THANK GOD!
ICHI...
IT MISSED ME.
ICHI...
NO.

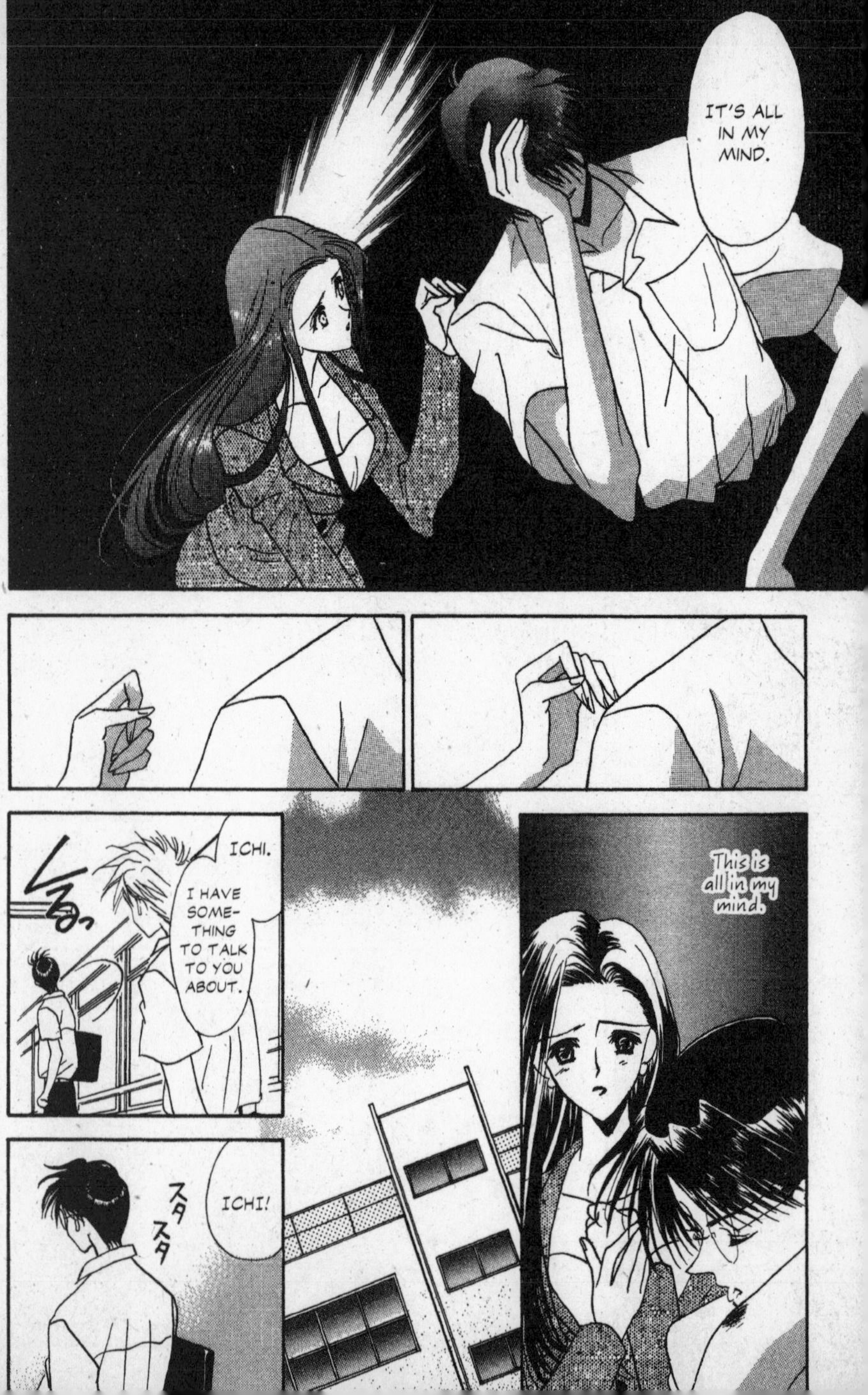
IT'S ALL IN MY MIND.
This is all in my mind.
ICHI.
I HAVE SOME-THING TO TALK TO YOU ABOUT.
ICHI!
スタ スタ

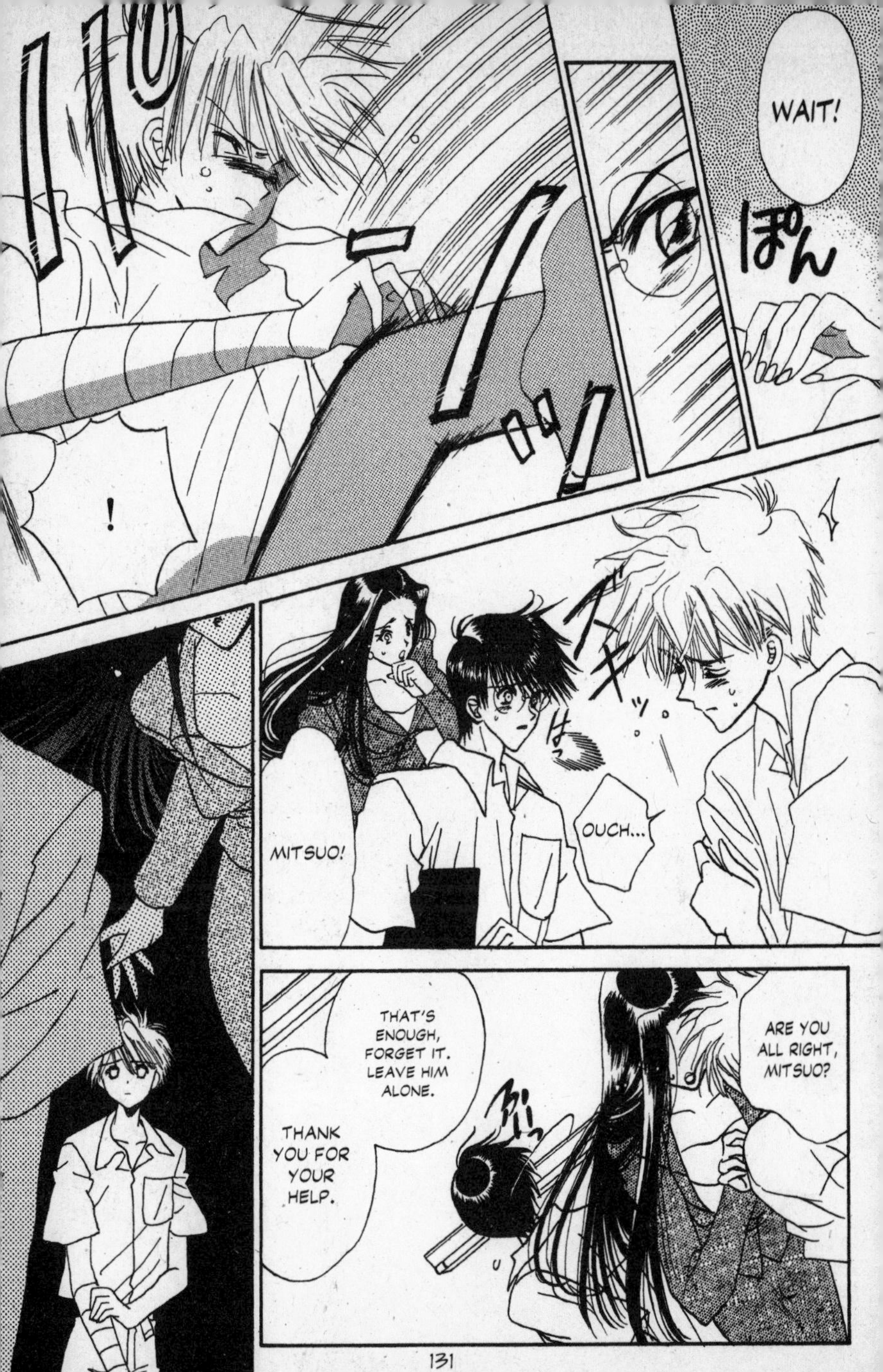
WAIT!
ぽん
!
OUCH...
MITSUO!
ARE YOU ALL RIGHT, MITSUO?
THAT'S ENOUGH, FORGET IT. LEAVE HIM ALONE.
THANK YOU FOR YOUR HELP.

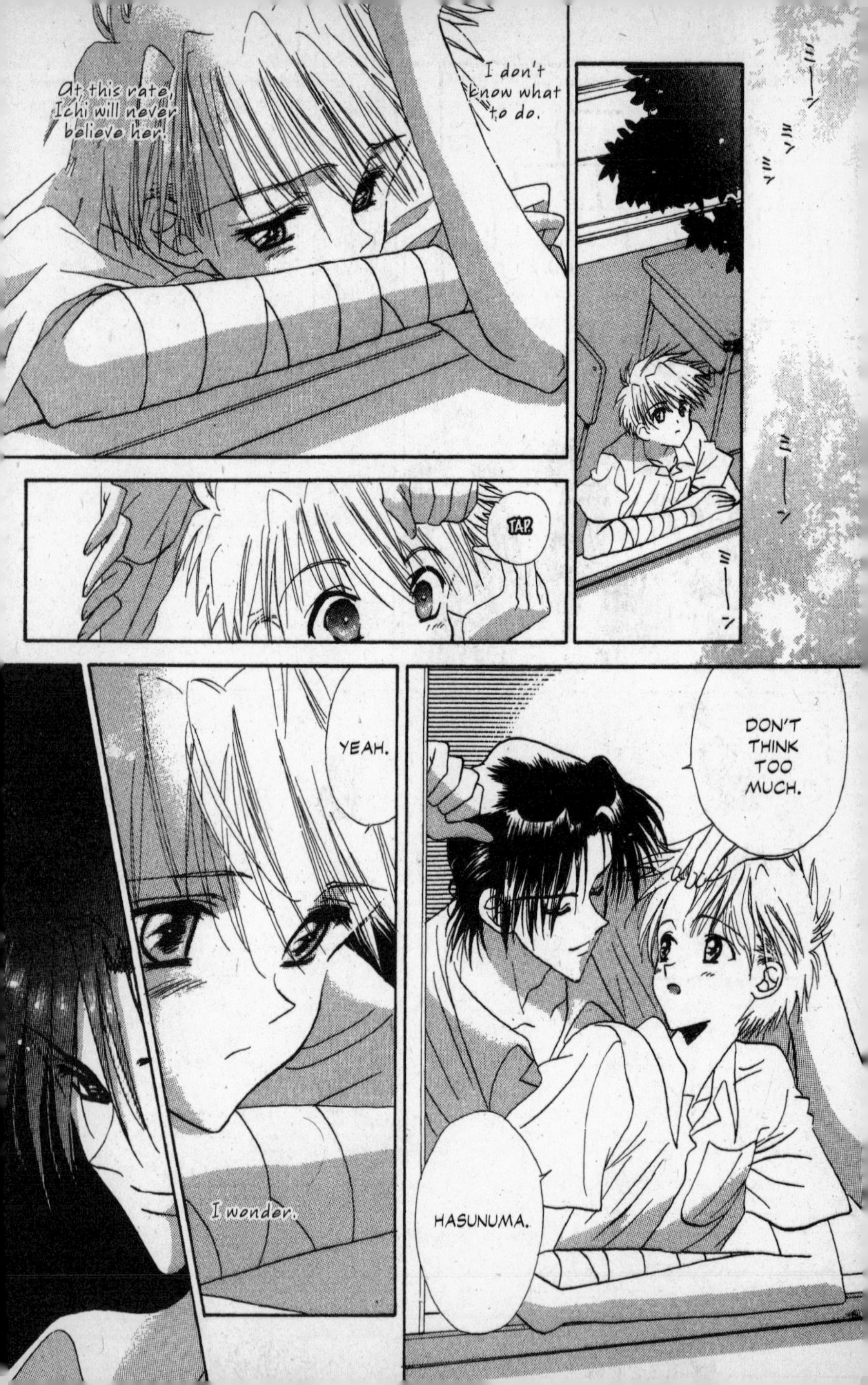

ミーン
ミン
ミン
ミーン
ミーン
I don't know what to do.
At this rate, Ichi will never believe her!
TAP
DON'T THINK TOO MUCH.
HASUNUMA.
YEAH.
I wonder.

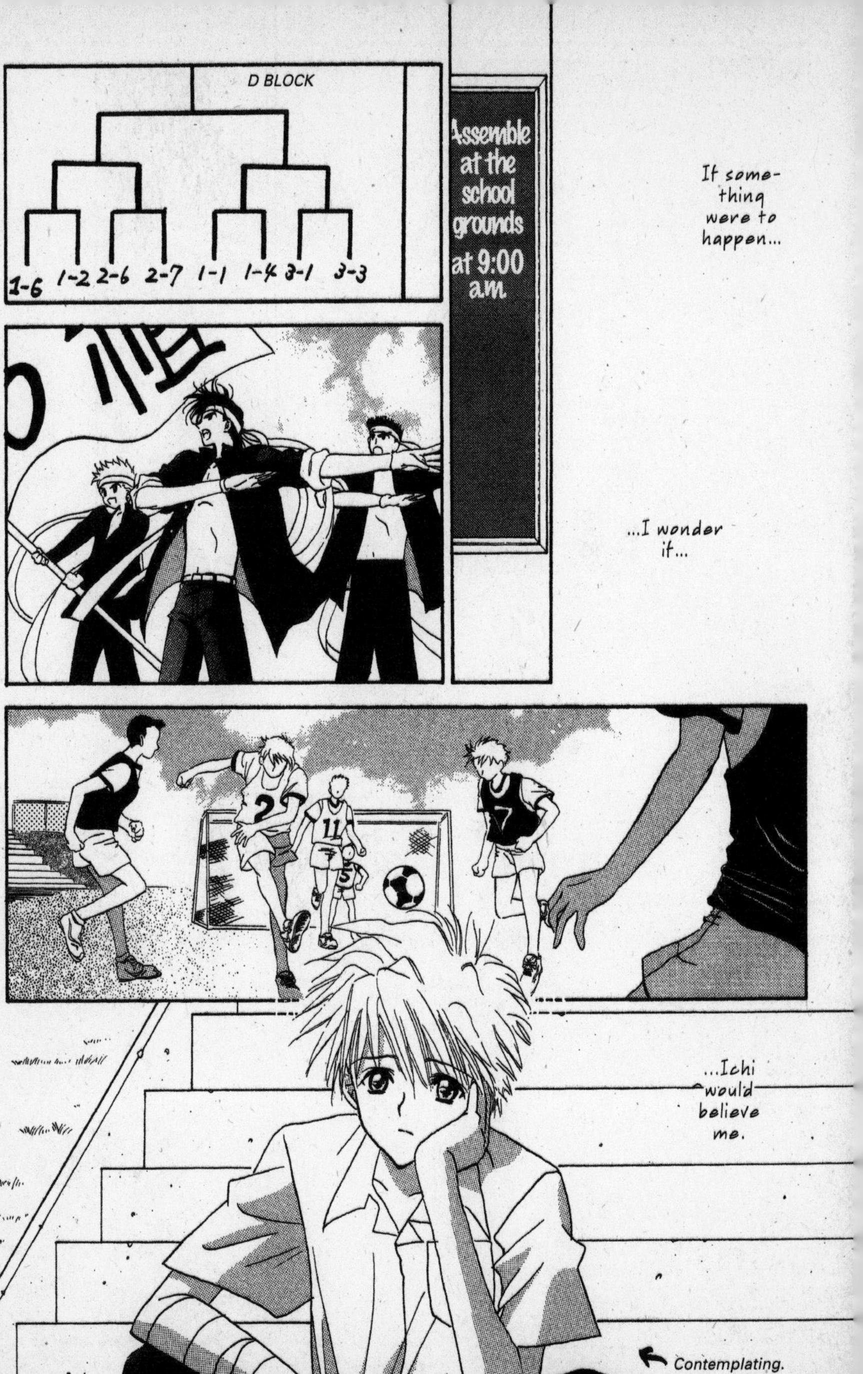
If something were to happen...
Assemble at the school grounds at 9:00 a.m.
D BLOCK
1-6 1-2 2-6 2-7 1-1 1-4 3-1 3-3
...I wonder if...
...Ichi would believe me.
Contemplating.

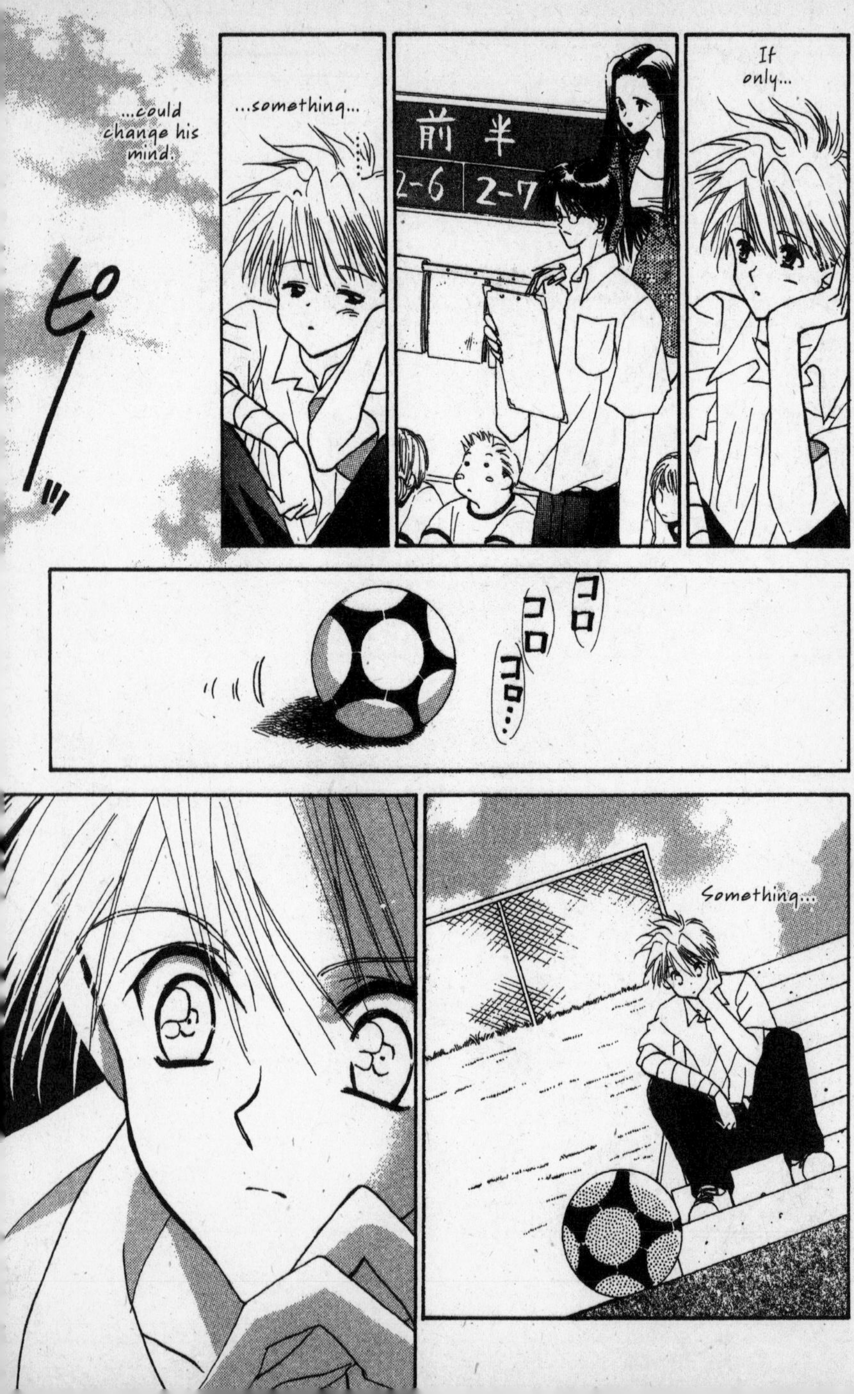
If only...
前半
2-6
2-7
...something...
...could change his mind.
ピーッ
コロ
コロ
コロ...
Something...

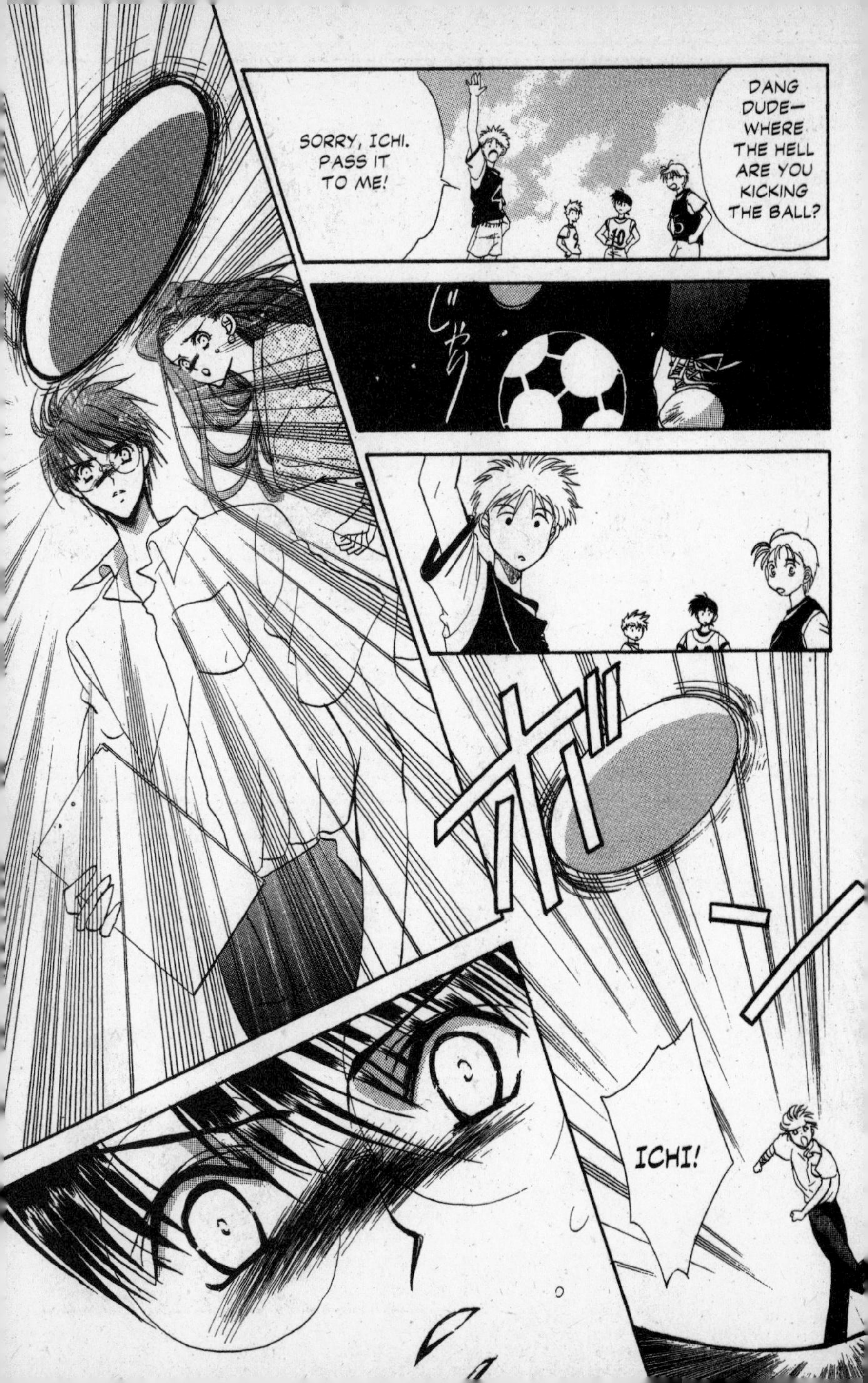
DANG DUDE— WHERE THE HELL ARE YOU KICKING THE BALL?
SORRY, ICHI. PASS IT TO ME!
ICHI!

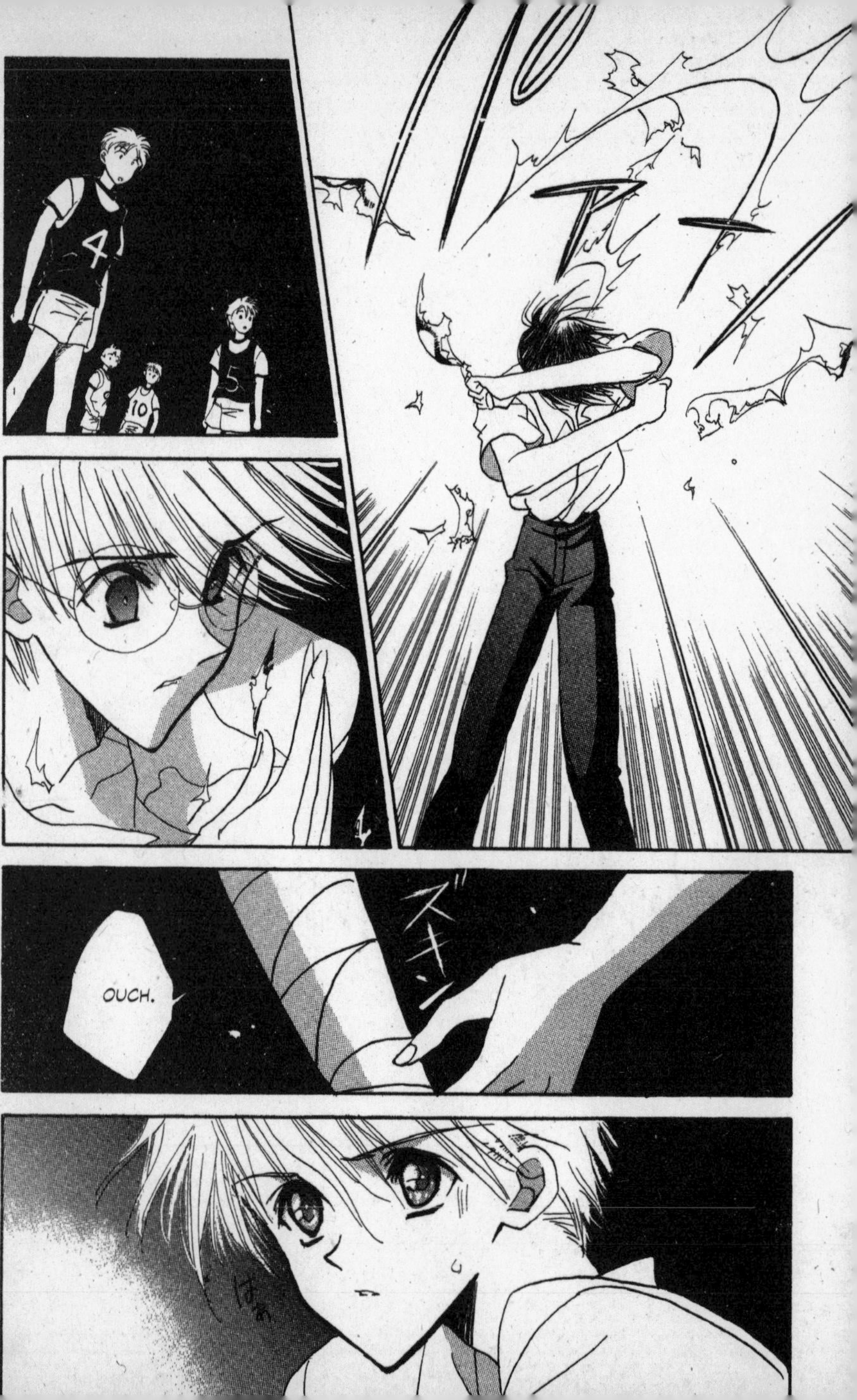
OUCH.

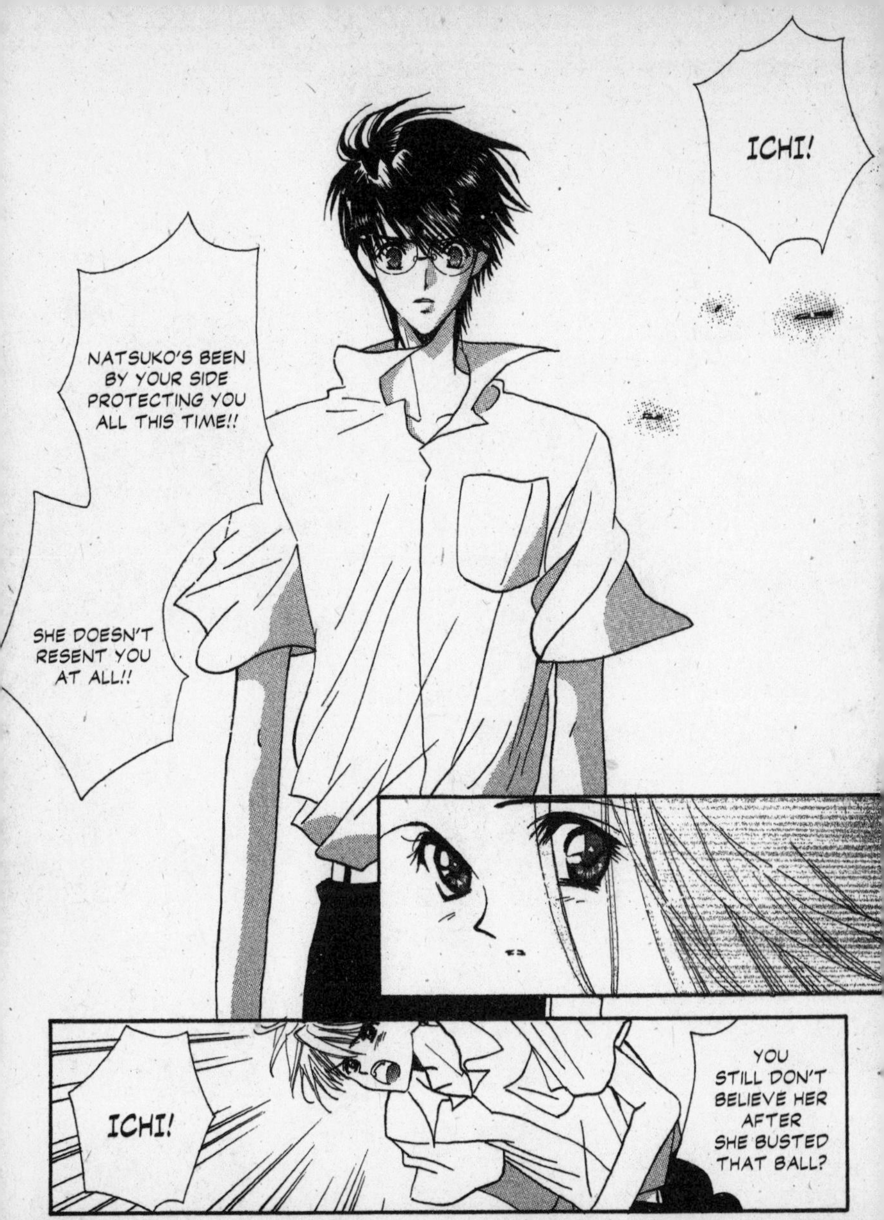
ICHI!
NATSUKO'S BEEN BY YOUR SIDE PROTECTING YOU ALL THIS TIME!!
SHE DOESN'T RESENT YOU AT ALL!!
YOU STILL DON'T BELIEVE HER AFTER SHE BUSTED THAT BALL?
ICHI!

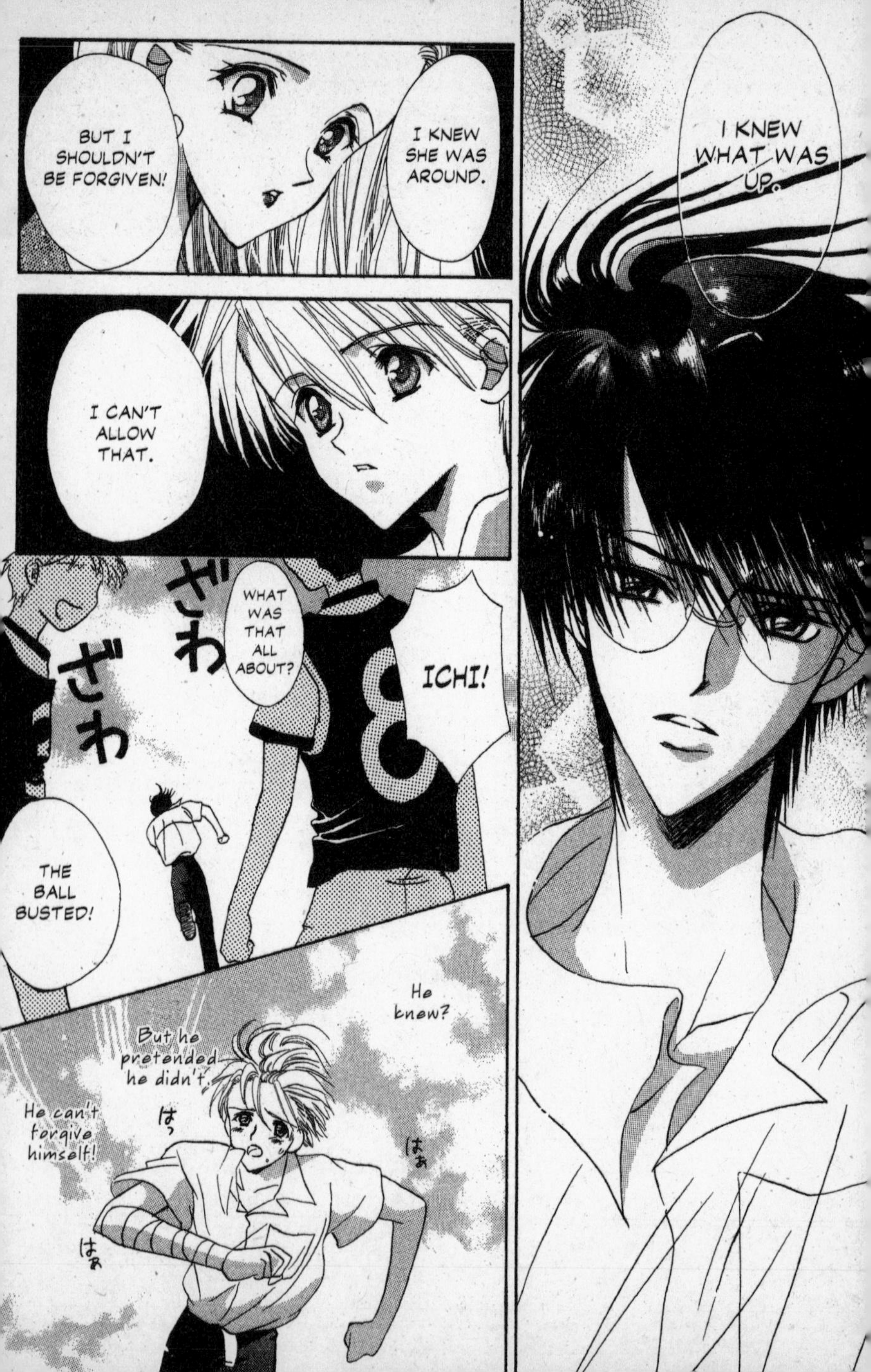
I KNEW WHAT WAS UP.
I KNEW SHE WAS AROUND.
BUT I SHOULDN'T BE FORGIVEN!
I CAN'T ALLOW THAT.
ICHI!
WHAT WAS THAT ALL ABOUT?
ざわ
ざわ
THE BALL BUSTED!
He knew?
But he pretended he didn't.
はっ
He can't forgive himself!
はぁ
はぁ

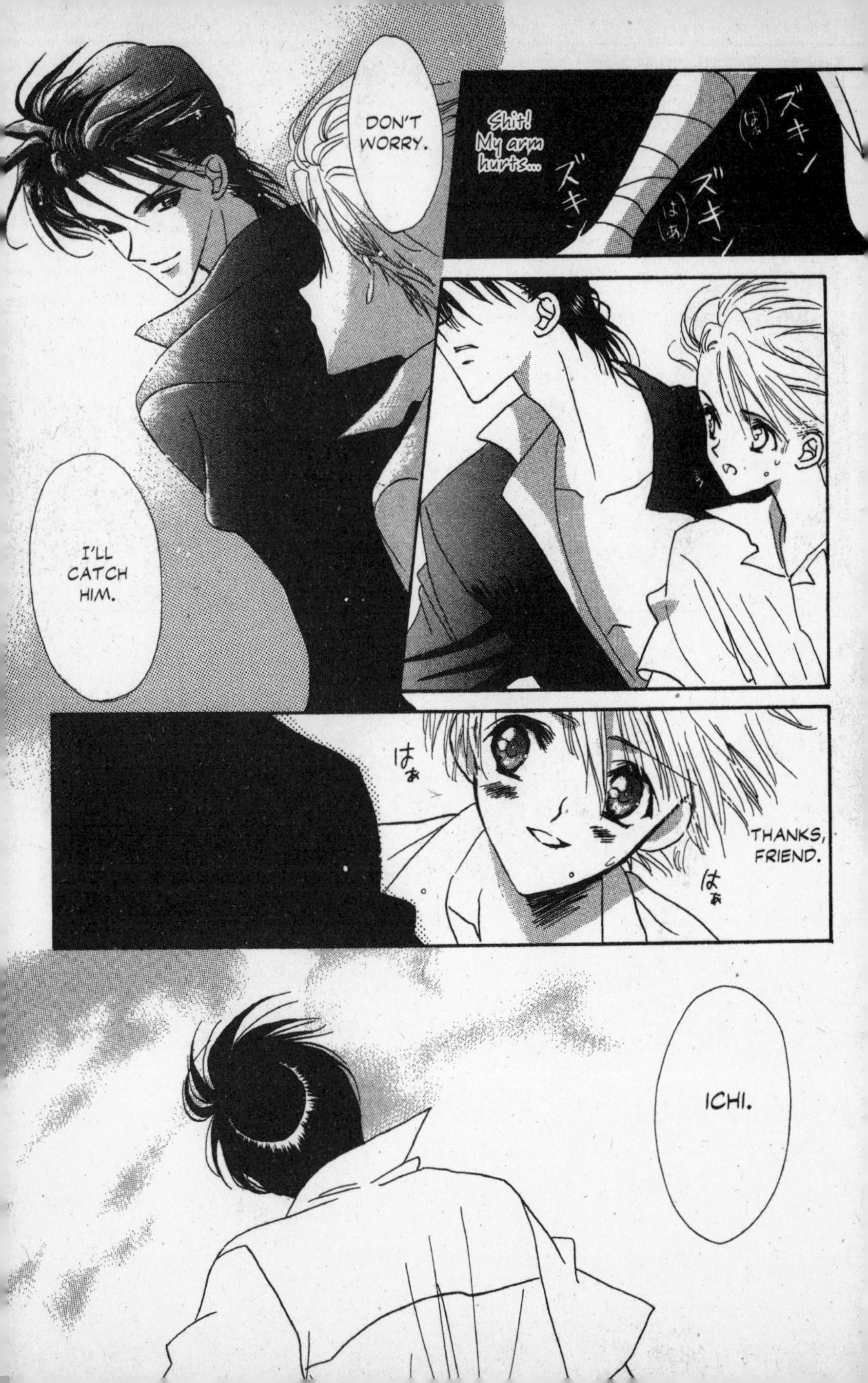
ズキン
はぁ
ズキン
はぁ
ズキン
Shit! My arm hurts...
DON'T WORRY.
I'LL CATCH HIM.
はぁ
THANKS, FRIEND.
はぁ
ICHI.

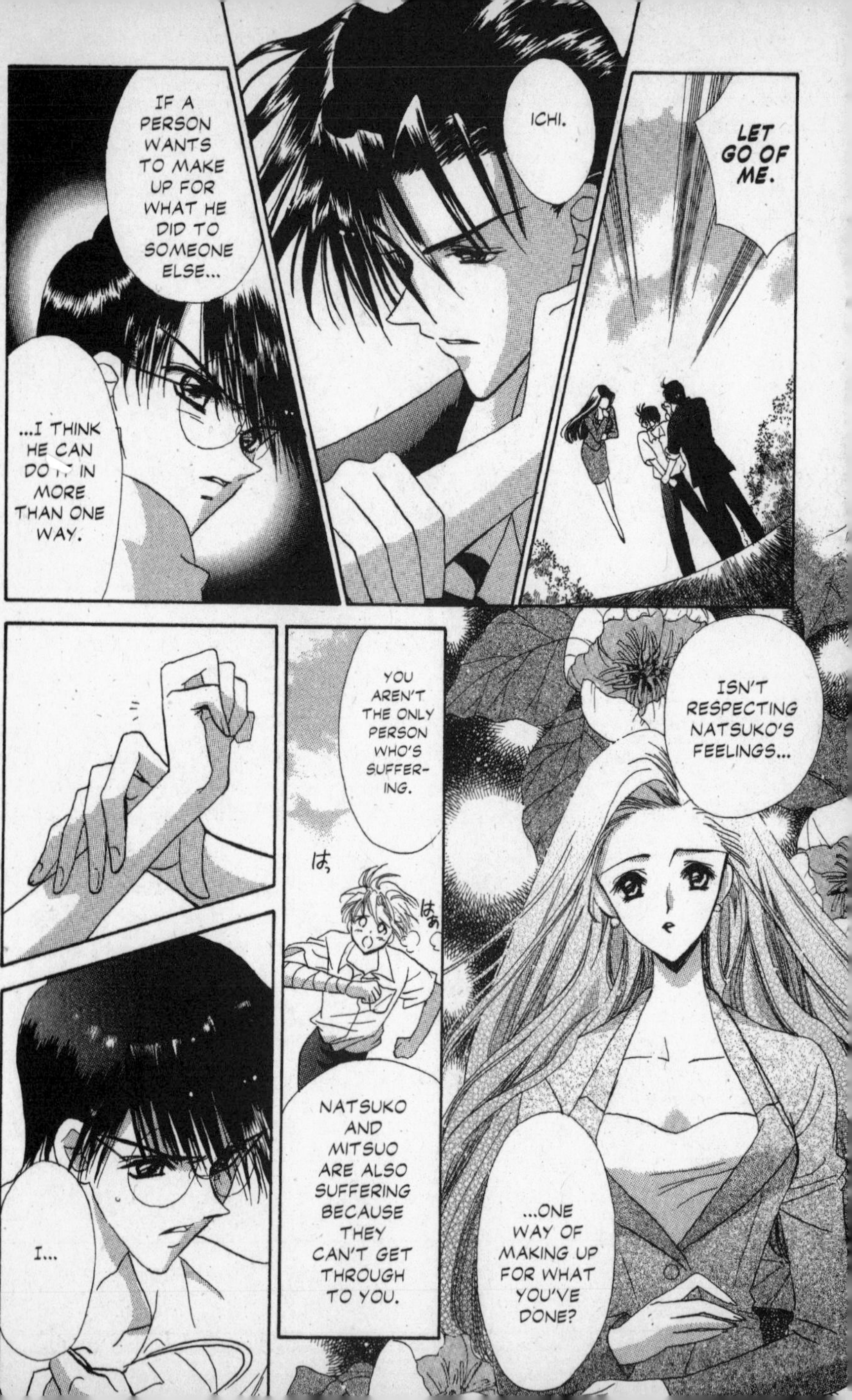
LET GO OF ME.
ICHI.
IF A PERSON WANTS TO MAKE UP FOR WHAT HE DID TO SOMEONE ELSE...
...I THINK HE CAN DO IT IN MORE THAN ONE WAY.
ISN'T RESPECTING NATSUKO'S FEELINGS...
...ONE WAY OF MAKING UP FOR WHAT YOU'VE DONE?
YOU AREN'T THE ONLY PERSON WHO'S SUFFER-ING.
は
はぁ
NATSUKO AND MITSUO ARE ALSO SUFFERING BECAUSE THEY CAN'T GET THROUGH TO YOU.
I...

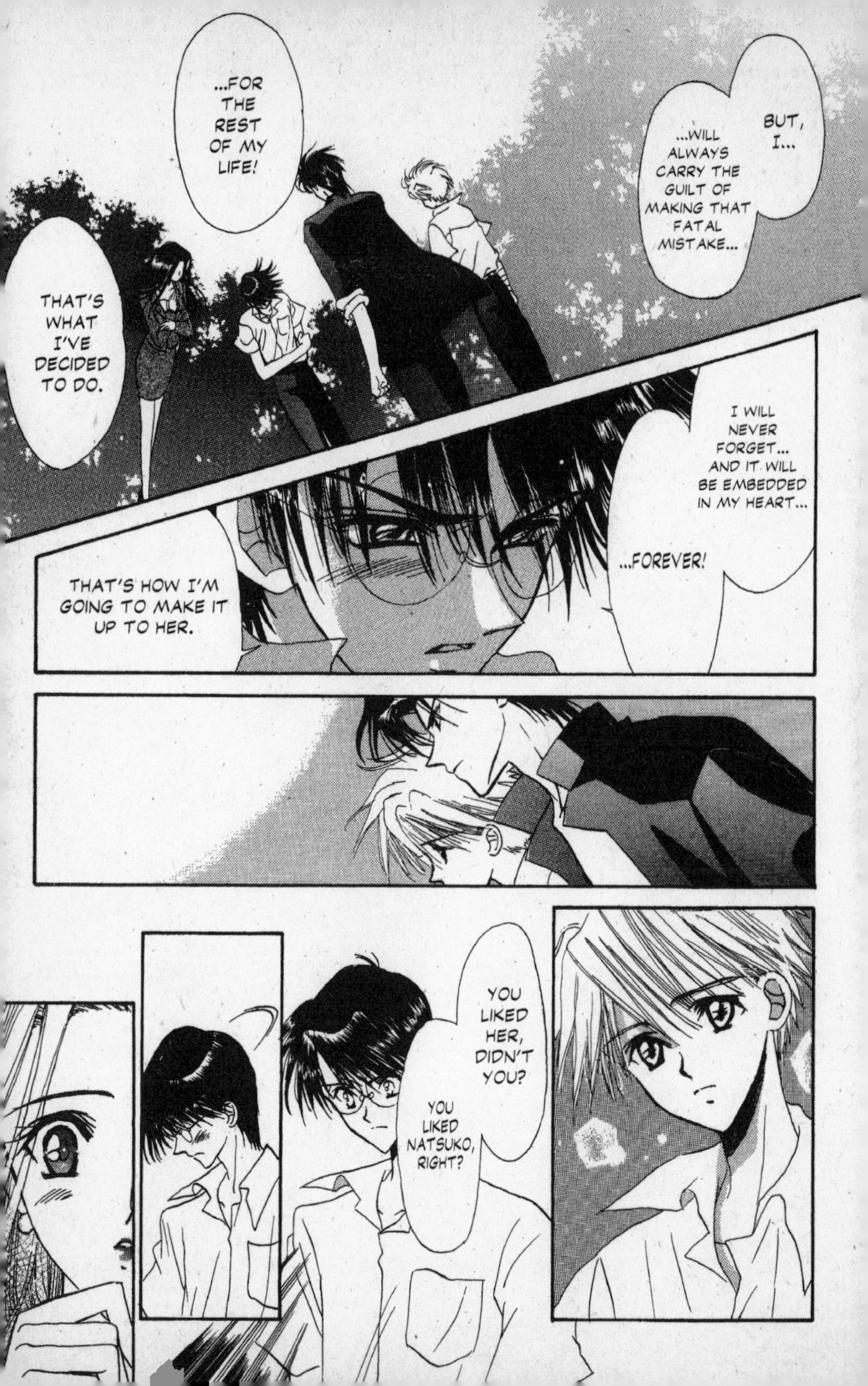
BUT, I...
...WILL ALWAYS CARRY THE GUILT OF MAKING THAT FATAL MISTAKE...
...FOR THE REST OF MY LIFE!
THAT'S WHAT I'VE DECIDED TO DO.
I WILL NEVER FORGET... AND IT WILL BE EMBEDDED IN MY HEART...
...FOREVER!
THAT'S HOW I'M GOING TO MAKE IT UP TO HER.
YOU LIKED HER, DIDN'T YOU?
YOU LIKED NATSUKO, RIGHT?

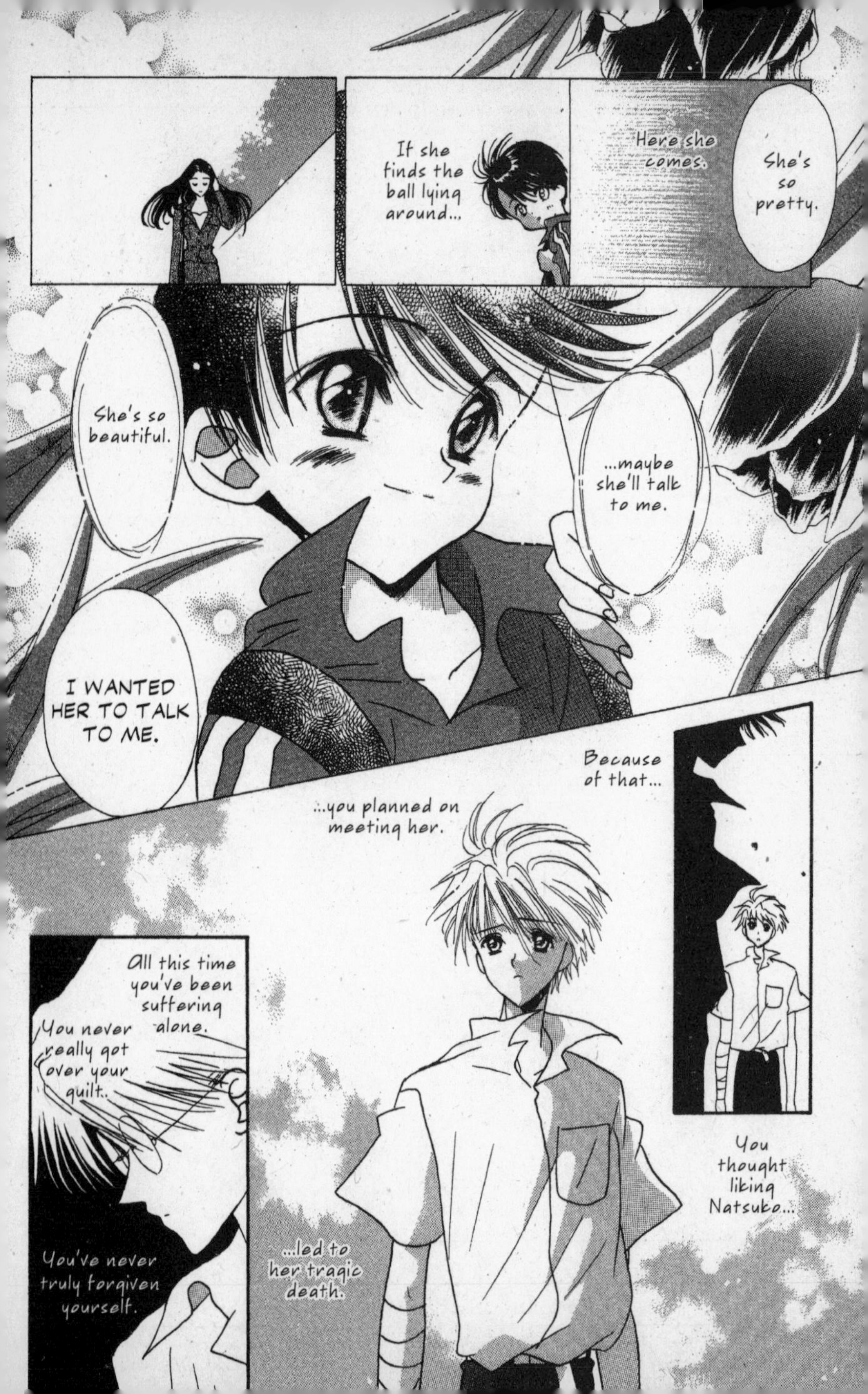
She's so pretty.
Here she comes.
If she finds the ball lying around...
...maybe she'll talk to me.
She's so beautiful.
I WANTED HER TO TALK TO ME.
Because of that...
...you planned on meeting her.
You thought liking Natsuko...
...led to her tragic death.
All this time you've been suffering alone.
You never really got over your guilt.
You've never truly forgiven yourself.

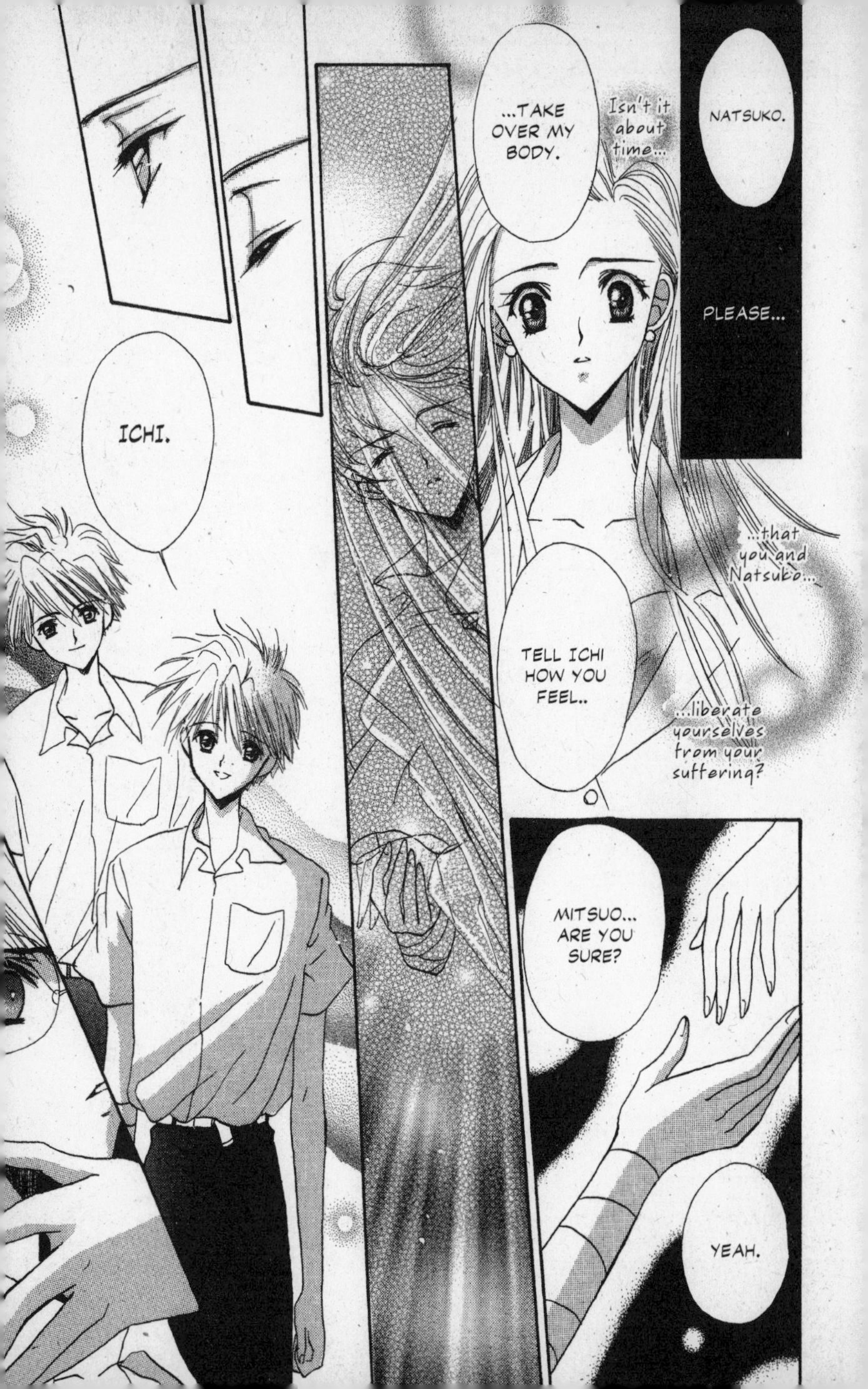
NATSUKO.
PLEASE...
...TAKE OVER MY BODY.
Isn't it about time...
...that you and Natsuko...
TELL ICHI HOW YOU FEEL..
...liberate yourselves from your suffering?
MITSUO... ARE YOU SURE?
YEAH.
ICHI.

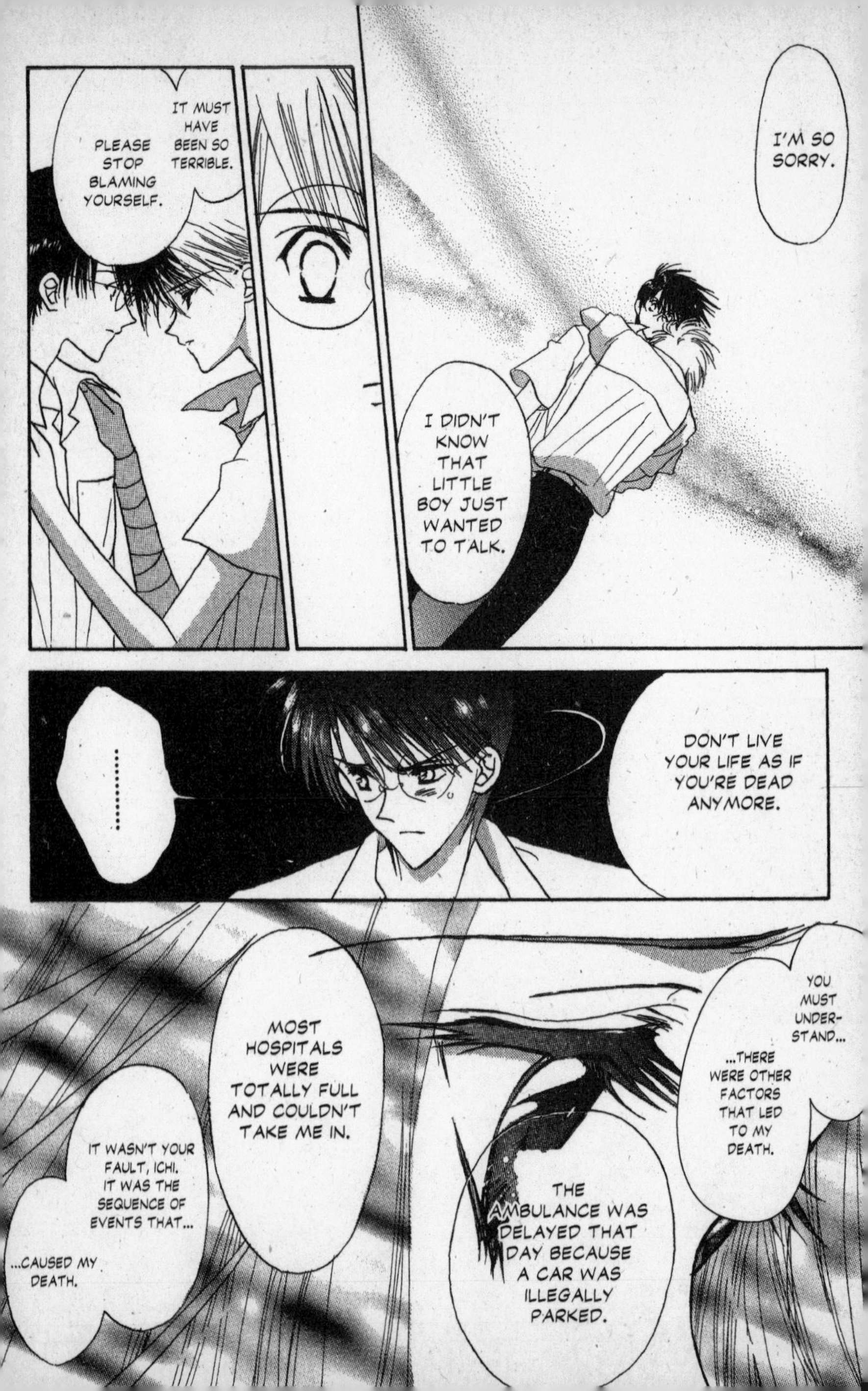
I'M SO SORRY.
I DIDN'T KNOW THAT LITTLE BOY JUST WANTED TO TALK.
IT MUST HAVE BEEN SO TERRIBLE.
PLEASE STOP BLAMING YOURSELF.
DON'T LIVE YOUR LIFE AS IF YOU'RE DEAD ANYMORE.
....
YOU MUST UNDER-STAND...
...THERE WERE OTHER FACTORS THAT LED TO MY DEATH.
THE AMBULANCE WAS DELAYED THAT DAY BECAUSE A CAR WAS ILLEGALLY PARKED.
MOST HOSPITALS WERE TOTALLY FULL AND COULDN'T TAKE ME IN.
IT WASN'T YOUR FAULT, ICHI. IT WAS THE SEQUENCE OF EVENTS THAT...
...CAUSED MY DEATH.

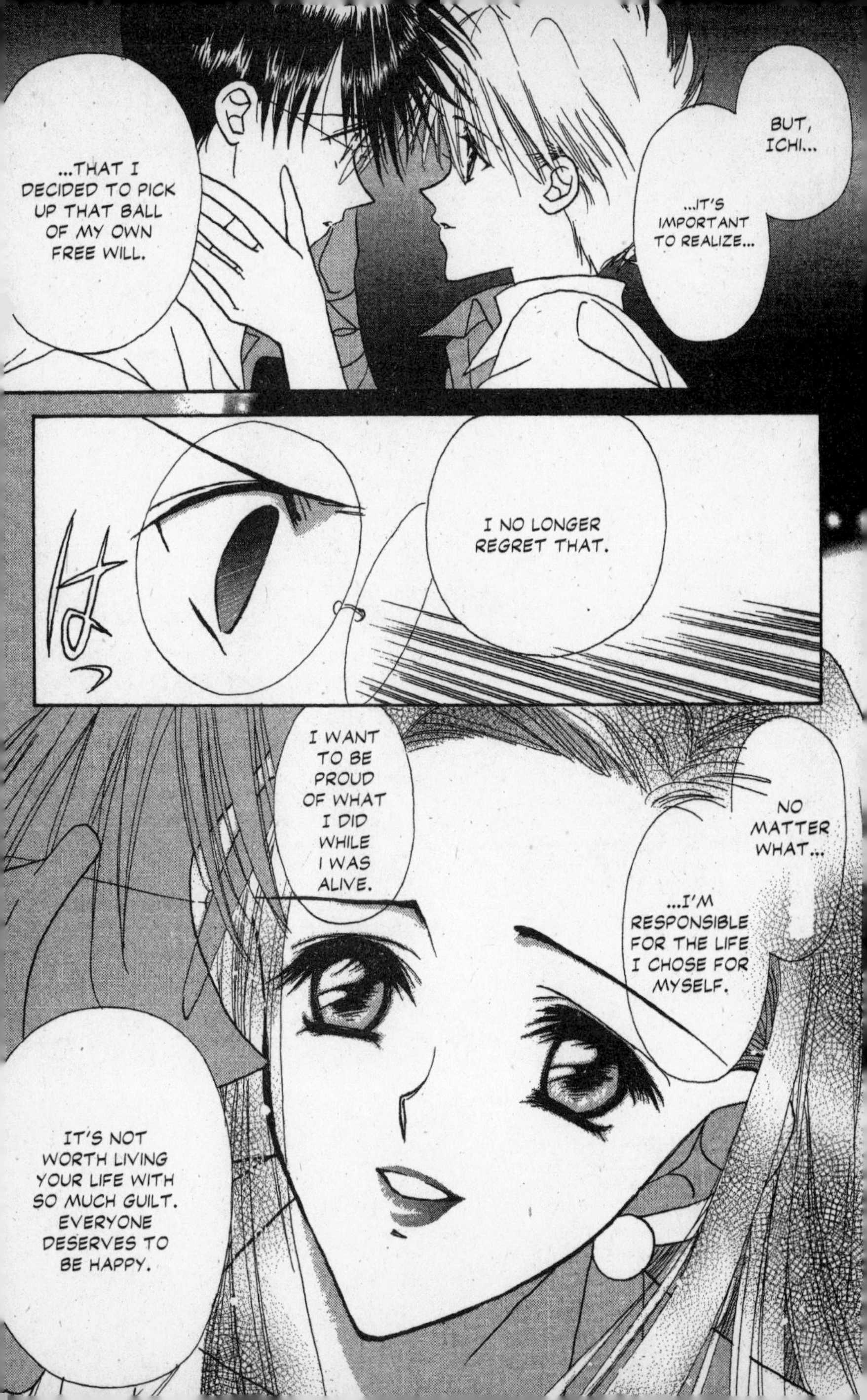
BUT, ICHI...
...IT'S IMPORTANT TO REALIZE...
...THAT I DECIDED TO PICK UP THAT BALL OF MY OWN FREE WILL.
I NO LONGER REGRET THAT.
はっ
NO MATTER WHAT...
...I'M RESPONSIBLE FOR THE LIFE I CHOSE FOR MYSELF.
I WANT TO BE PROUD OF WHAT I DID WHILE I WAS ALIVE.
IT'S NOT WORTH LIVING YOUR LIFE WITH SO MUCH GUILT. EVERYONE DESERVES TO BE HAPPY.

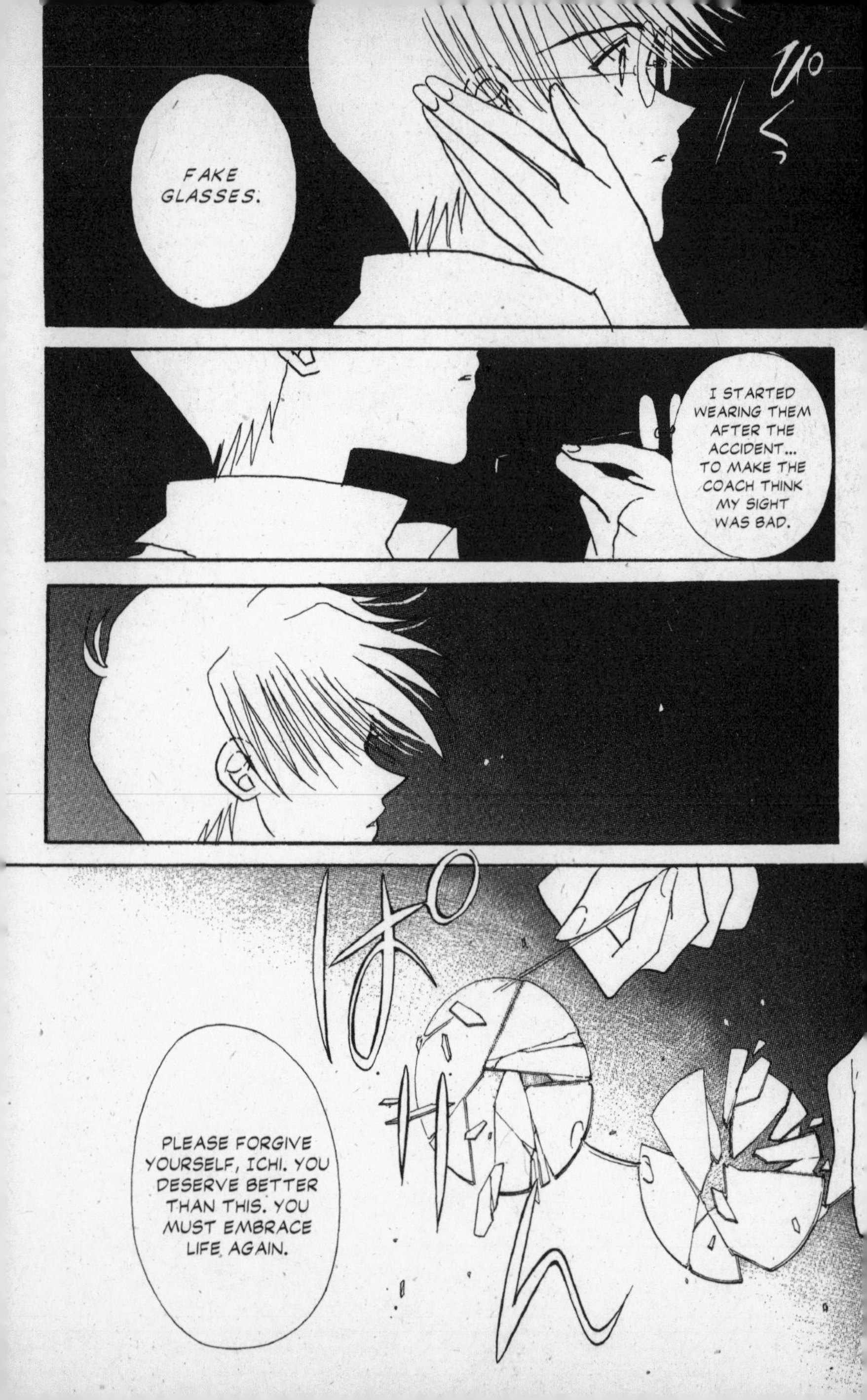
FAKE GLASSES.
I STARTED WEARING THEM AFTER THE ACCIDENT... TO MAKE THE COACH THINK MY SIGHT WAS BAD.
PLEASE FORGIVE YOURSELF, ICHI. YOU DESERVE BETTER THAN THIS. YOU MUST EMBRACE LIFE AGAIN.

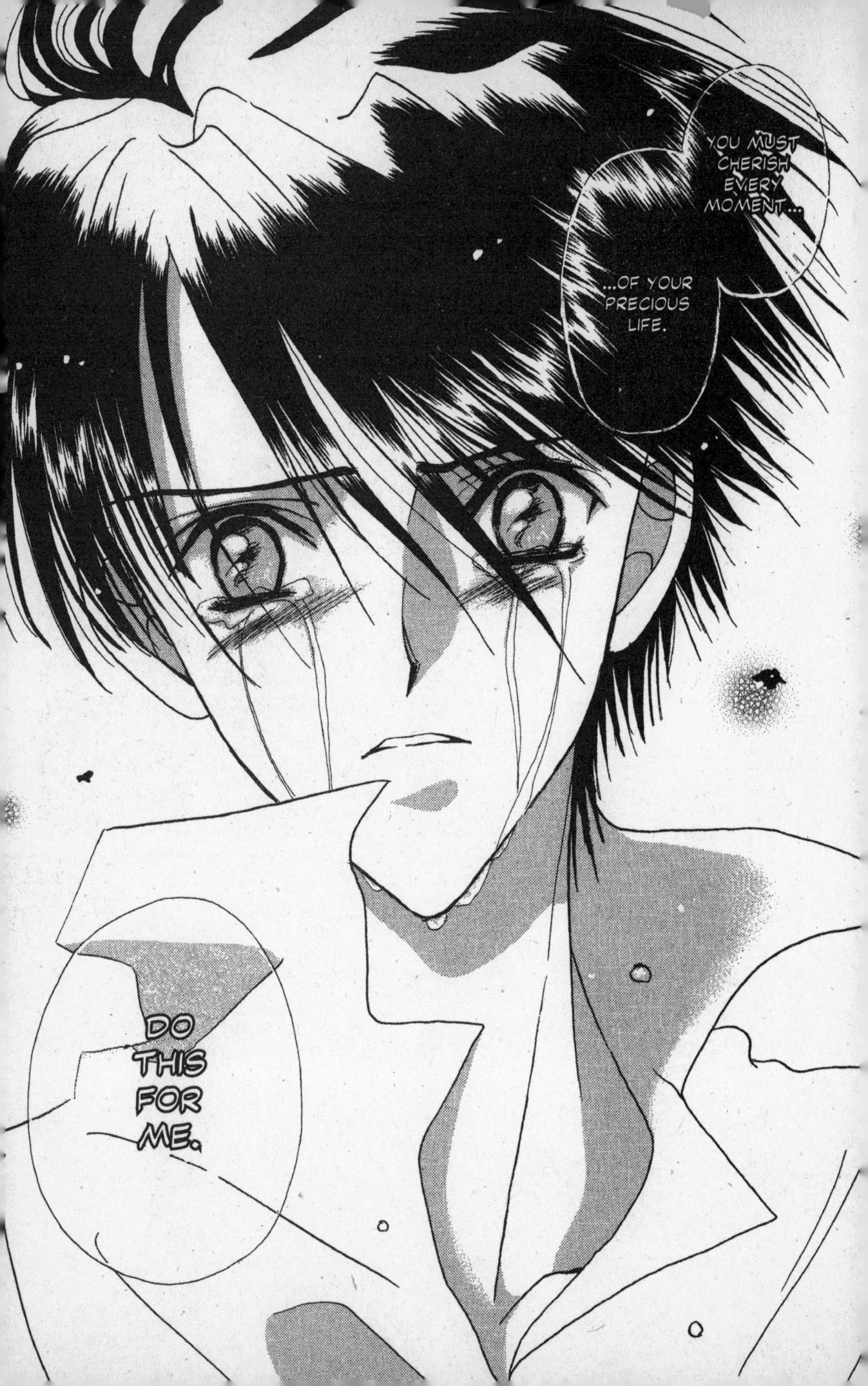
YOU MUST CHERISH EVERY MOMENT...
...OF YOUR PRECIOUS LIFE.
DO THIS FOR ME.

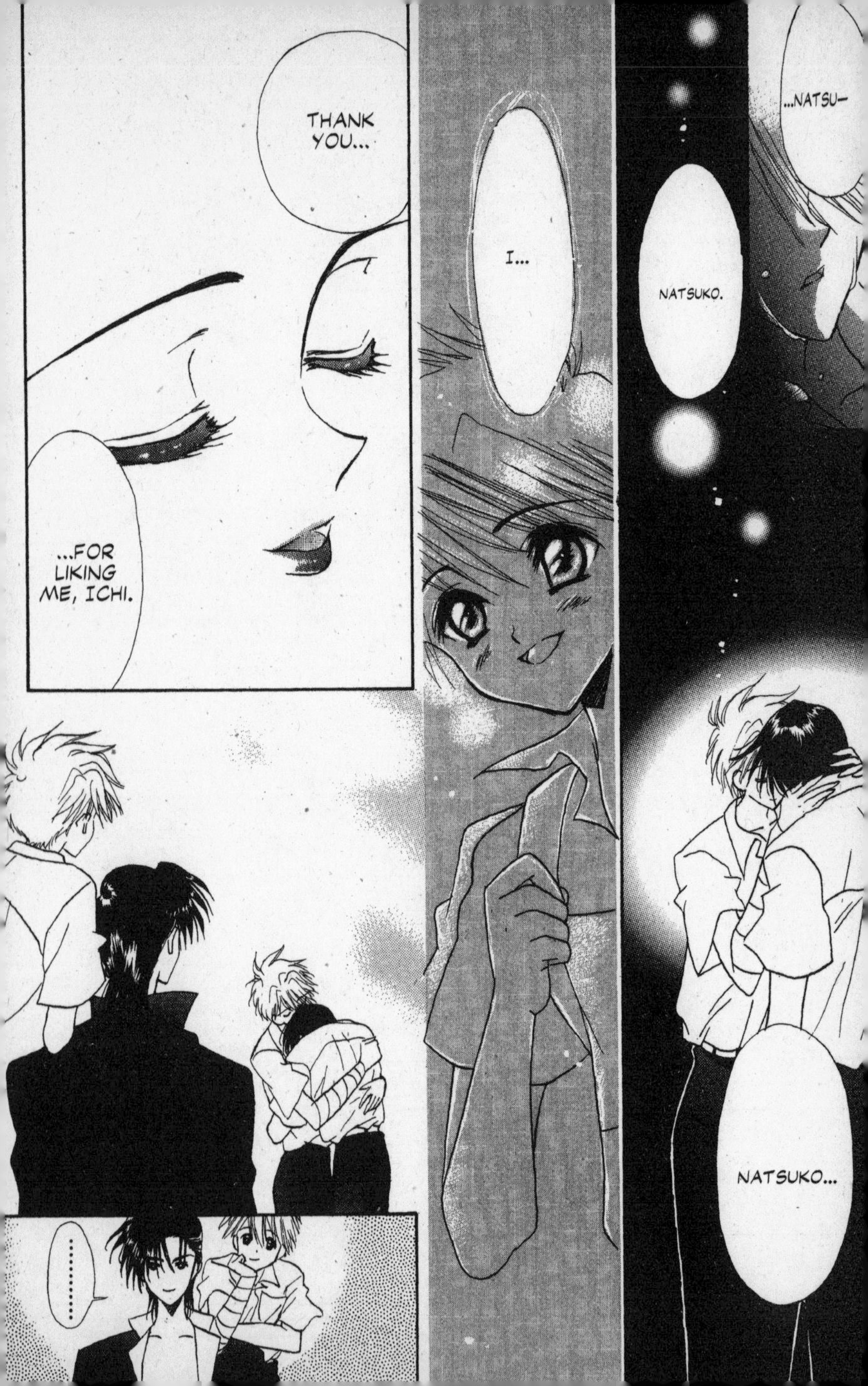
...NATSU-
NATSUKO.
NATSUKO...
I...
THANK YOU...
...FOR LIKING ME, ICHI.
......

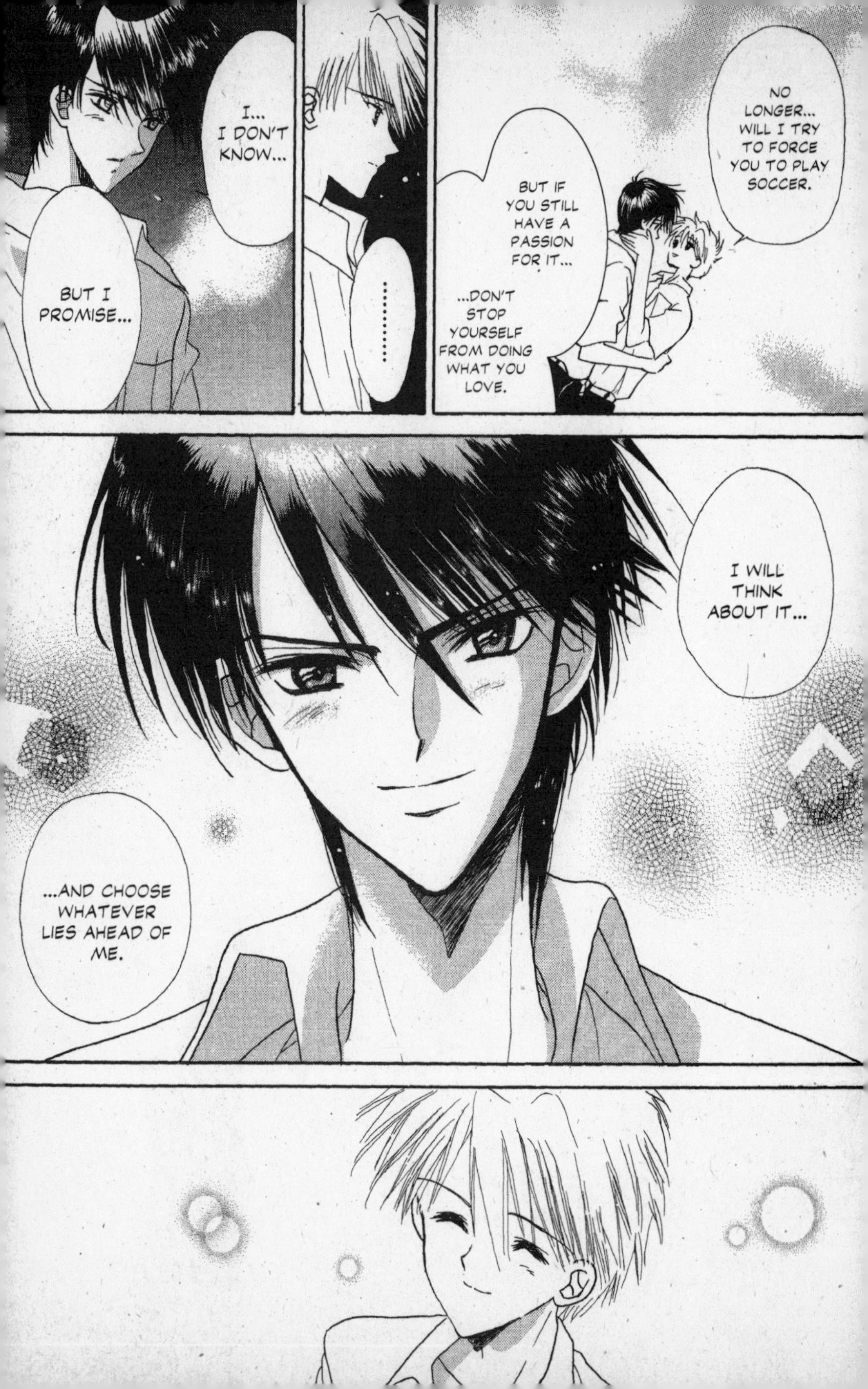
NO LONGER... WILL I TRY TO FORCE YOU TO PLAY SOCCER.
BUT IF YOU STILL HAVE A PASSION FOR IT...
...DON'T STOP YOURSELF FROM DOING WHAT YOU LOVE.
......
I... I DON'T KNOW...
BUT I PROMISE...
I WILL THINK ABOUT IT...
...AND CHOOSE WHATEVER LIES AHEAD OF ME.

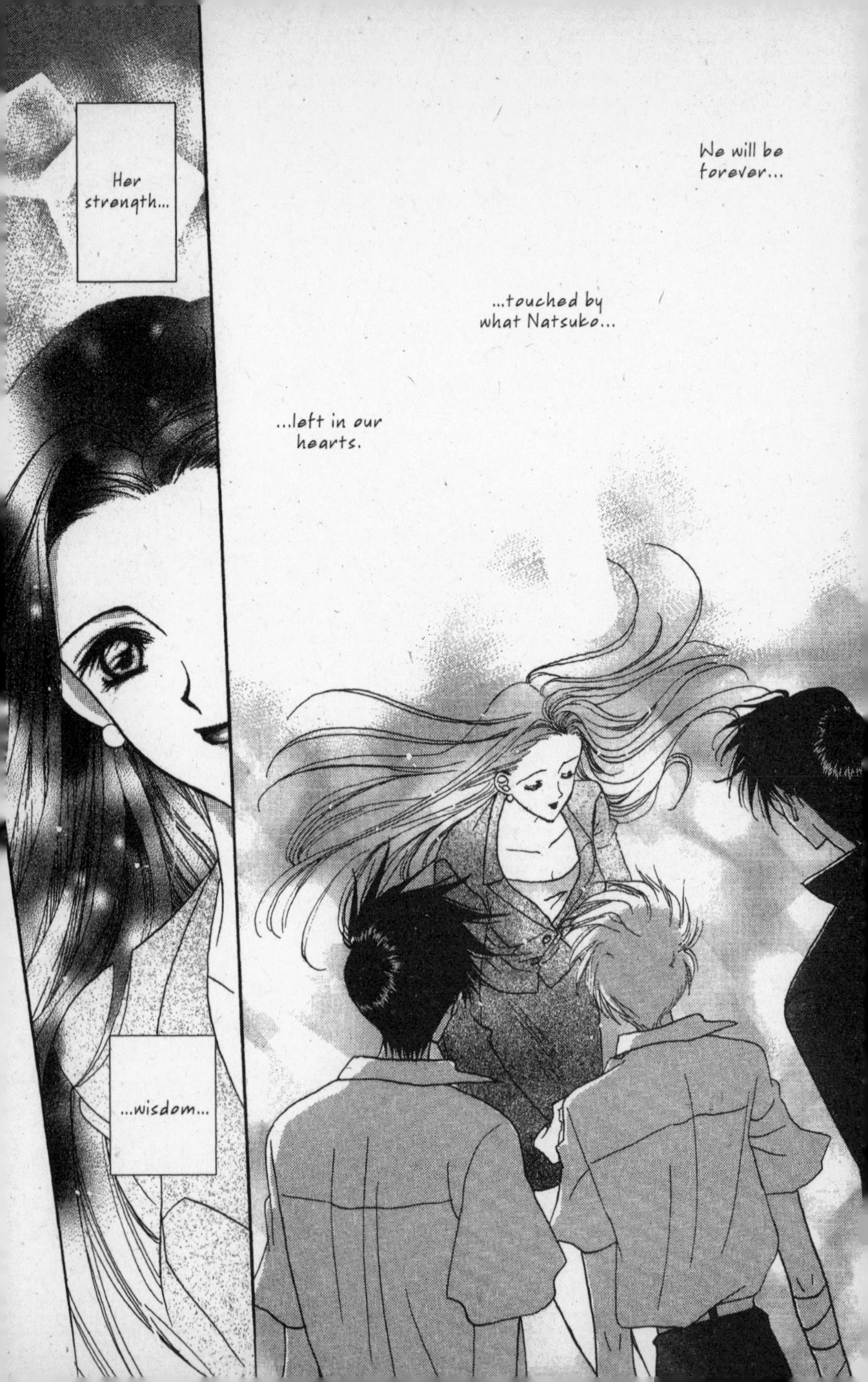
We will be forever...
...touched by what Natsuko...
...left in our hearts.
Her strength...
...wisdom...

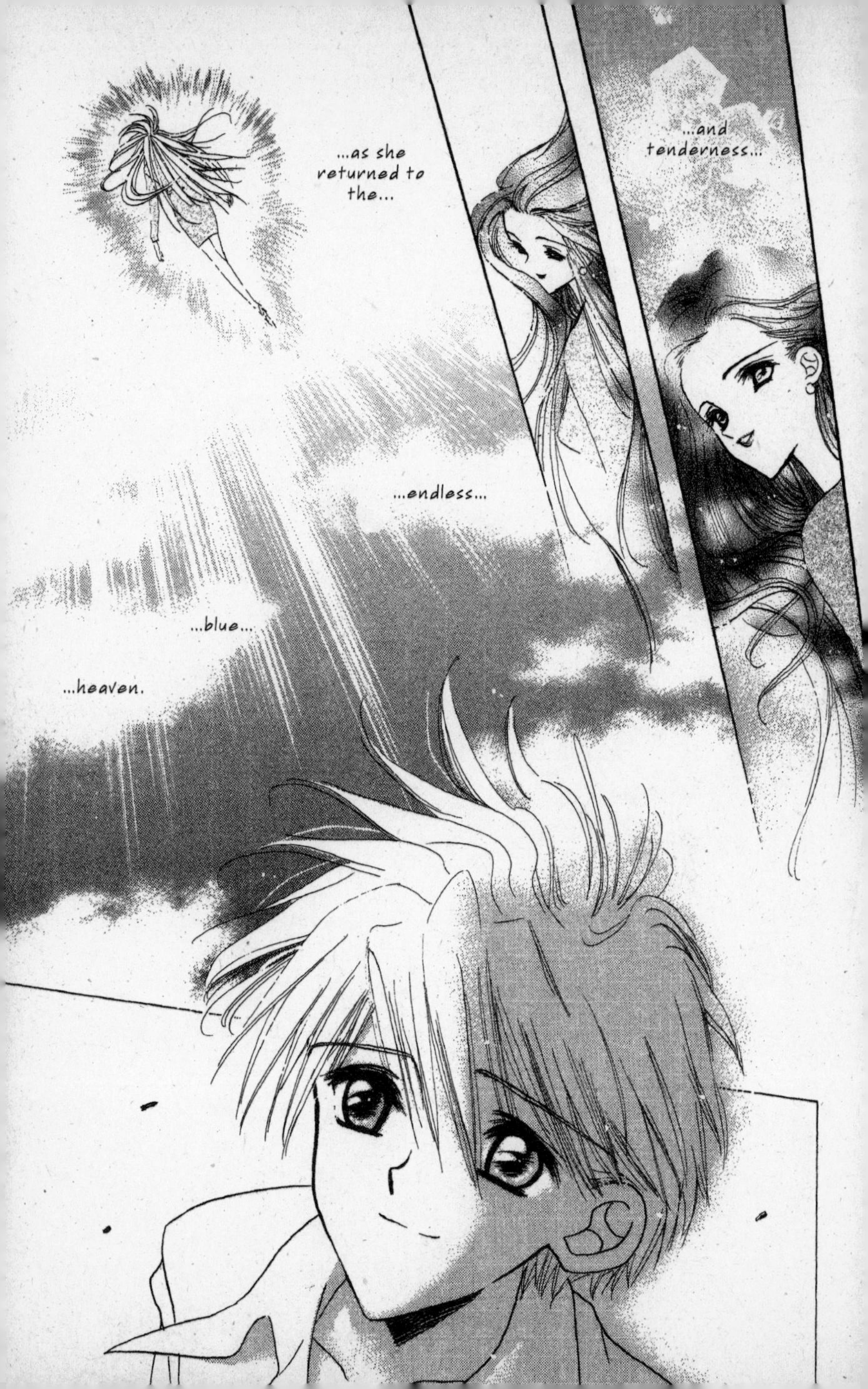
...and tenderness...
...as she returned to the...
...endless...
...blue...
...heaven.

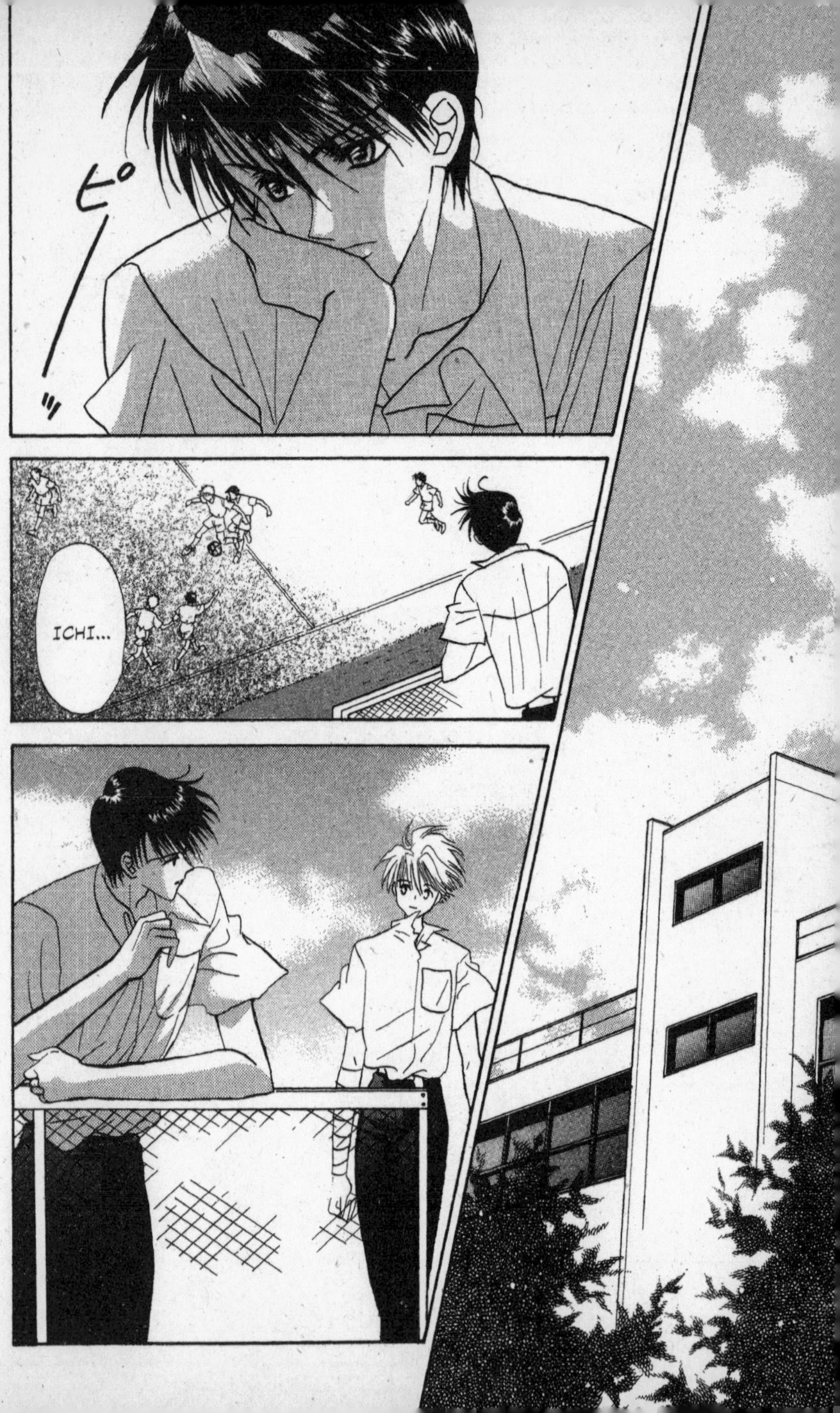
ピ
ッ
ICHI...

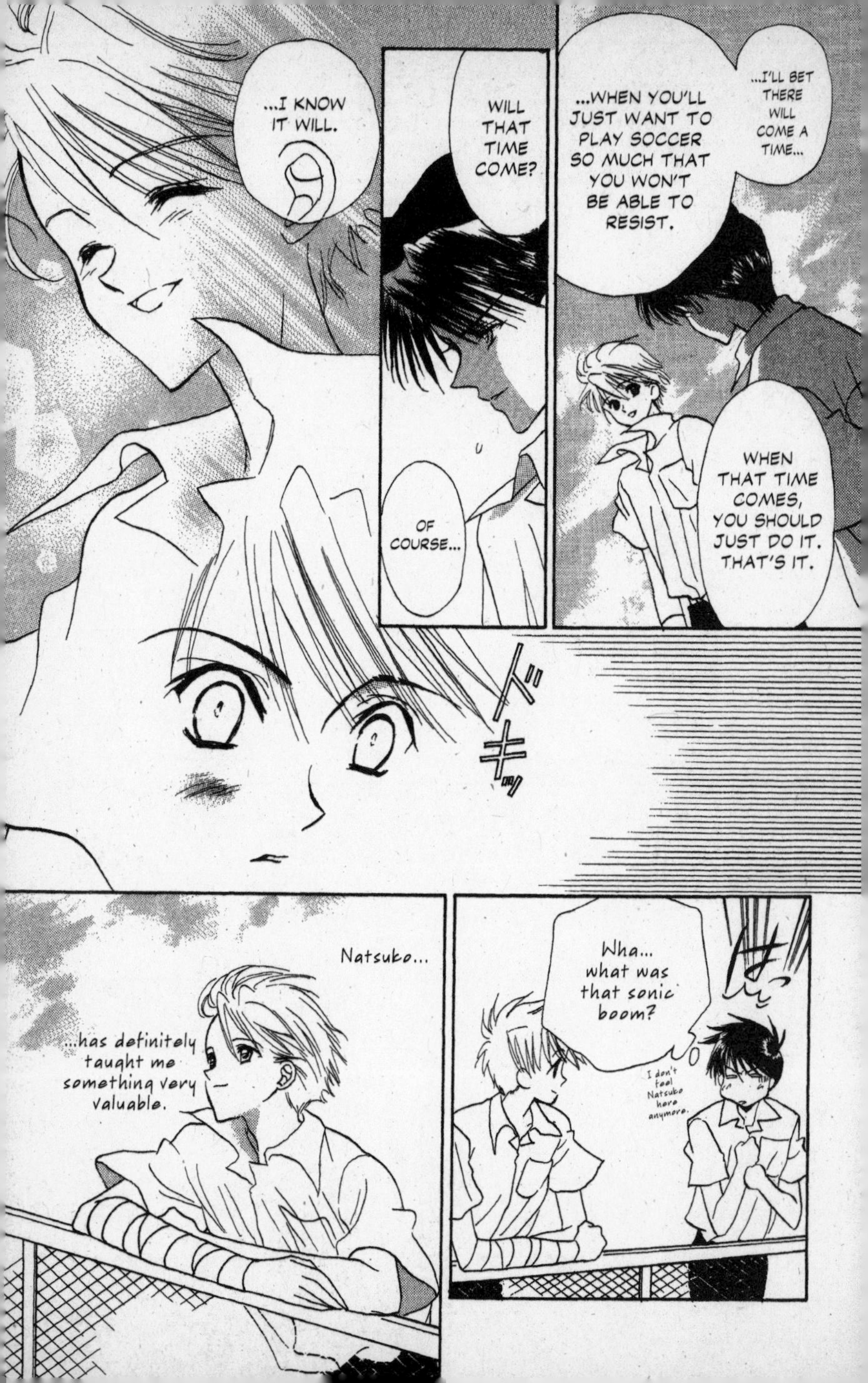
...I'LL BET THERE WILL COME A TIME...
...WHEN YOU'LL JUST WANT TO PLAY SOCCER SO MUCH THAT YOU WON'T BE ABLE TO RESIST.
WHEN THAT TIME COMES, YOU SHOULD JUST DO IT. THAT'S IT.
WILL THAT TIME COME?
OF COURSE...
...I KNOW IT WILL.
ドキッ
はっ
Wha... what was that sonic boom?
I don't feel Natsuko here anymore.
Natsuko...
...has definitely taught me something very valuable.

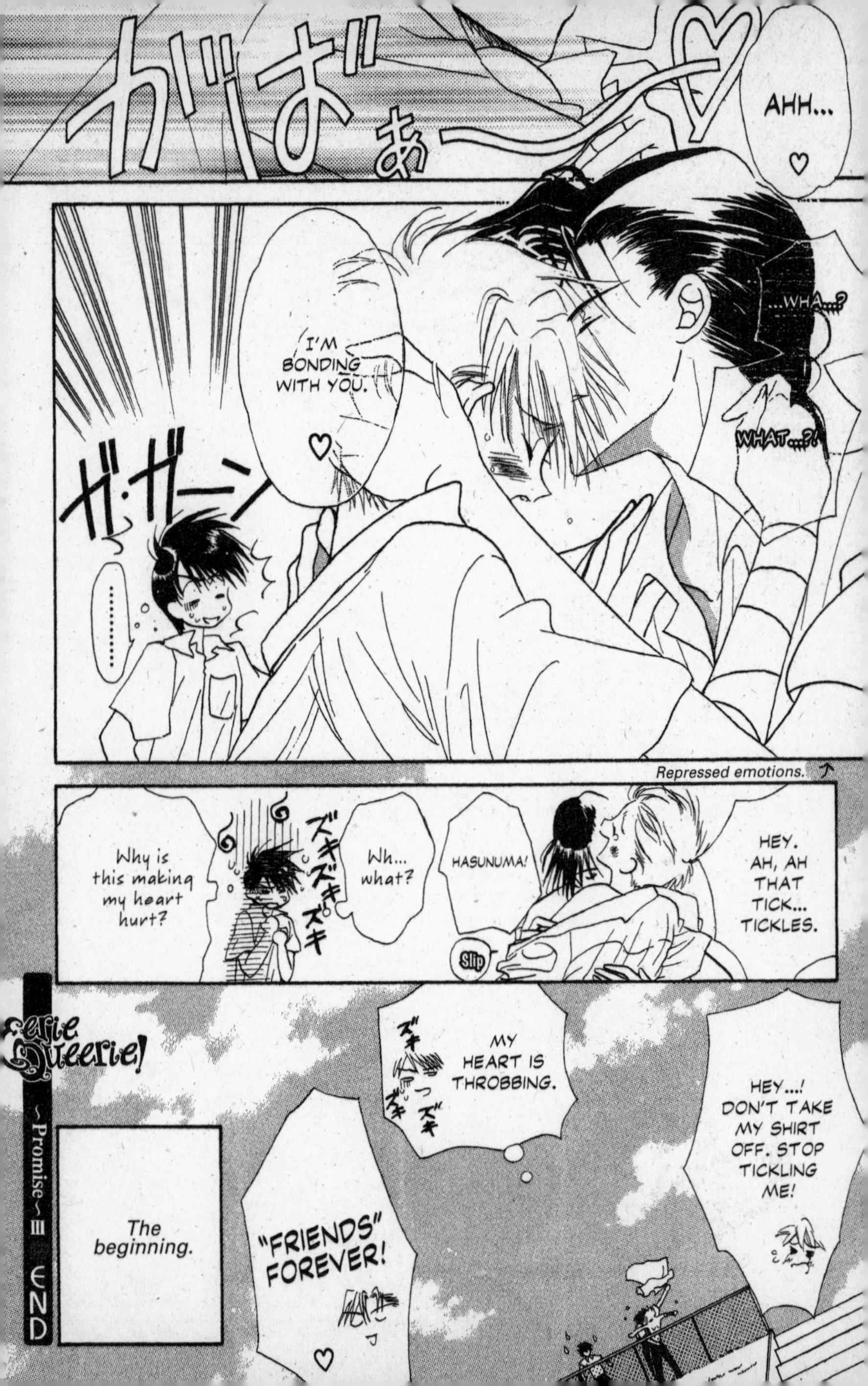
AHH... ♡
がばぁ〜♡
...WHA...?
WHAT...?!
I'M BONDING WITH YOU. ♡
ザ:ザーン
......
Repressed emotions.
HEY. AH, AH THAT TICK... TICKLES.
Slip
HASUNUMA!
Wh... what?
ズキズキズキ
Why is this making my heart hurt?
HEY...! DON'T TAKE MY SHIRT OFF. STOP TICKLING ME!
MY HEART IS THROBBING.
ズキズキズキズキ
"FRIENDS" FOREVER! ♡
The beginning.
Eerie Queerie!
~Promise~ III
END

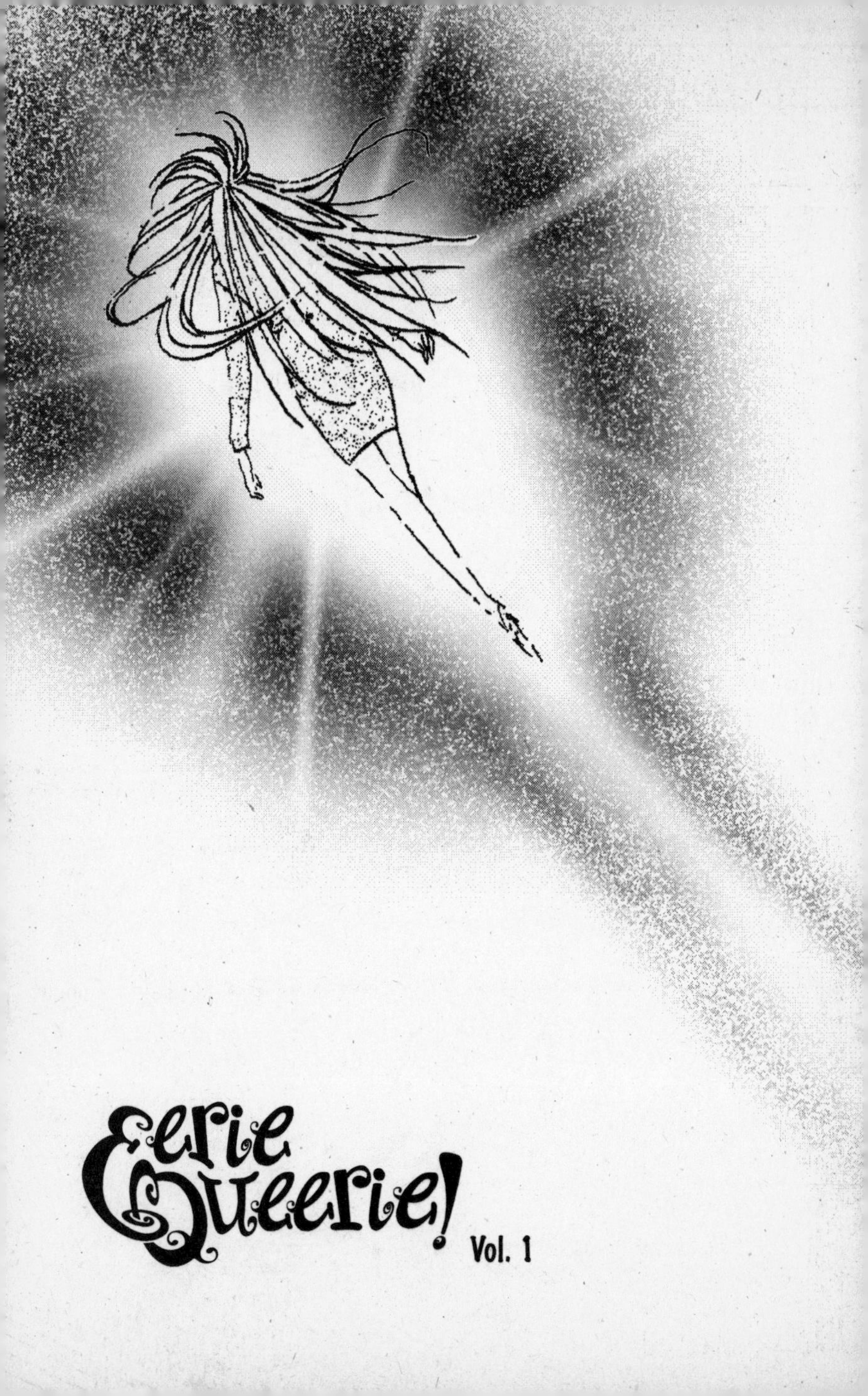
Eerie Queerie!
Vol. 1

> "To forgive is to set a prisoner free and discover the prisoner was YOU."
> -Unknown

Is there something you haven't forgiven yourself for? Write me and tell me about it:

Nora Wong, Editor
Eerie Queerie!
TOKYOPOP
5900 Wilshire Blvd., Suite 2000,
Los Angeles, CA 90036

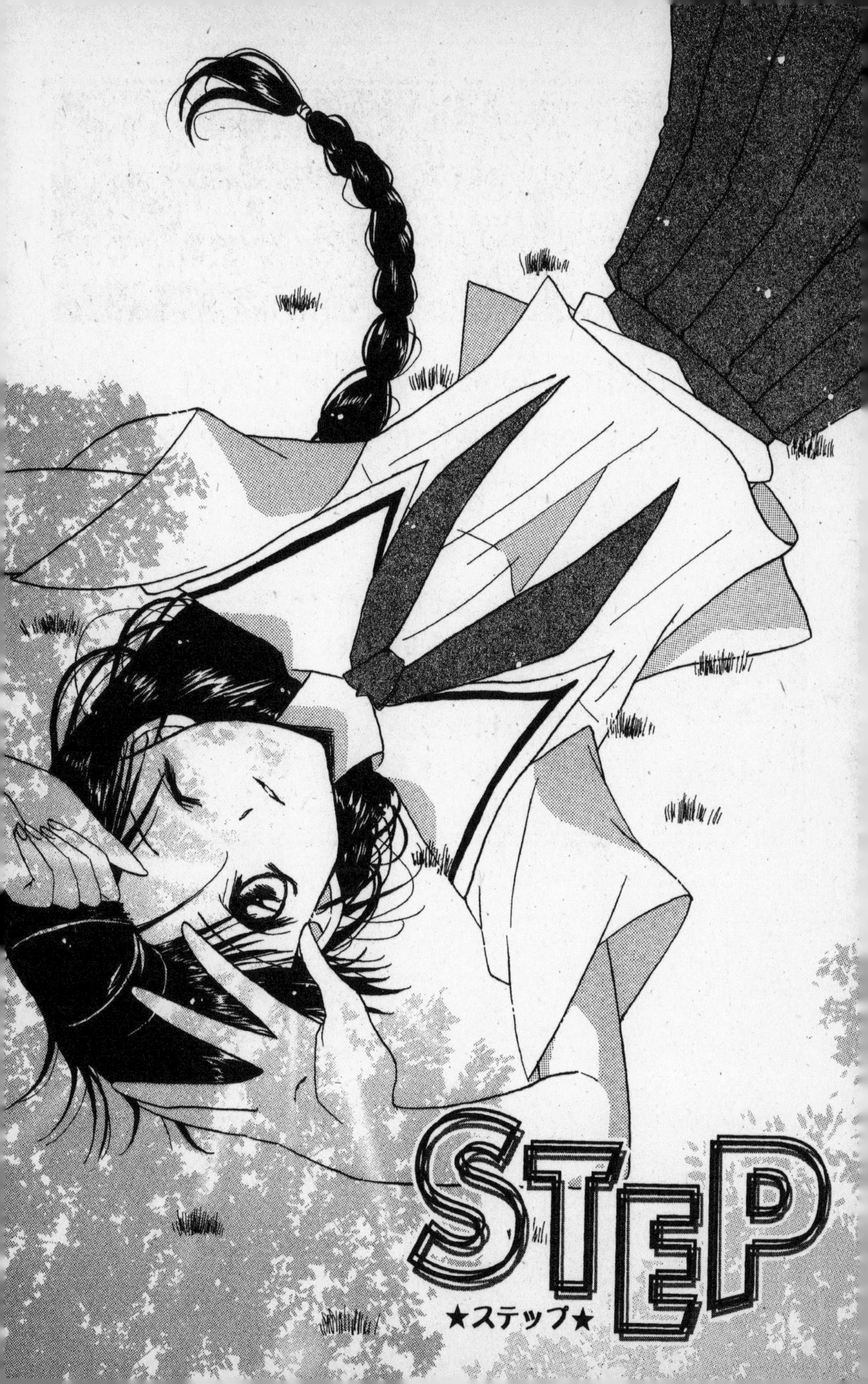
STEP
★ステップ★

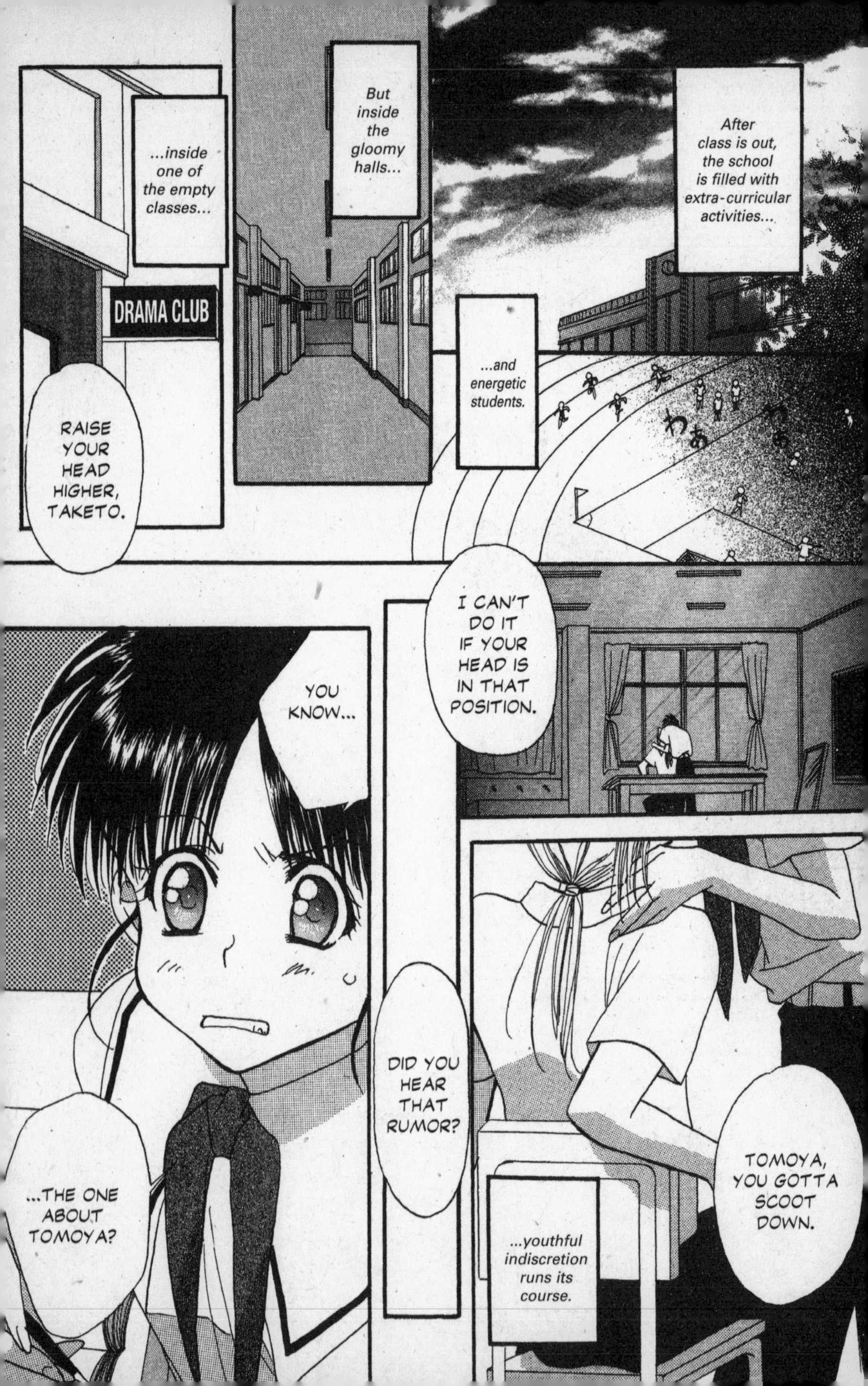
After class is out, the school is filled with extra-curricular activities...
わぁ
...and energetic students.
But inside the gloomy halls...
...inside one of the empty classes...
DRAMA CLUB
RAISE YOUR HEAD HIGHER, TAKETO.
I CAN'T DO IT IF YOUR HEAD IS IN THAT POSITION.
TOMOYA, YOU GOTTA SCOOT DOWN.
...youthful indiscretion runs its course.
YOU KNOW...
DID YOU HEAR THAT RUMOR?
...THE ONE ABOUT TOMOYA?

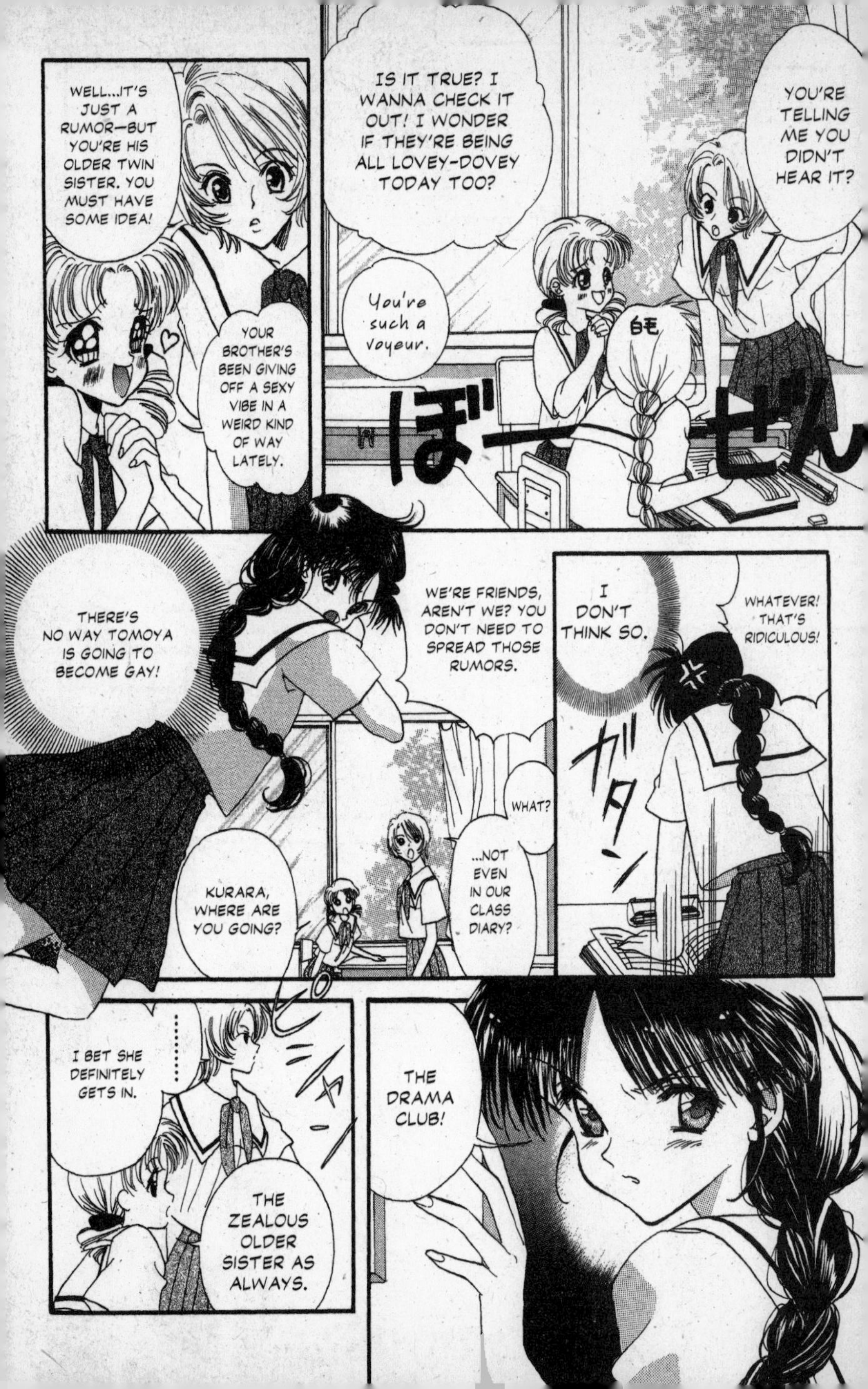
YOU'RE TELLING ME YOU DIDN'T HEAR IT?
IS IT TRUE? I WANNA CHECK IT OUT! I WONDER IF THEY'RE BEING ALL LOVEY-DOVEY TODAY TOO?
You're such a voyeur.
ぼーぜん
WELL...IT'S JUST A RUMOR—BUT YOU'RE HIS OLDER TWIN SISTER. YOU MUST HAVE SOME IDEA!
YOUR BROTHER'S BEEN GIVING OFF A SEXY VIBE IN A WEIRD KIND OF WAY LATELY.
I DON'T THINK SO.
WHATEVER! THAT'S RIDICULOUS!
ガタン
WE'RE FRIENDS, AREN'T WE? YOU DON'T NEED TO SPREAD THOSE RUMORS.
THERE'S NO WAY TOMOYA IS GOING TO BECOME GAY!
WHAT?
...NOT EVEN IN OUR CLASS DIARY?
KURARA, WHERE ARE YOU GOING?
THE DRAMA CLUB!
......
I BET SHE DEFINITELY GETS IN.
THE ZEALOUS OLDER SISTER AS ALWAYS.

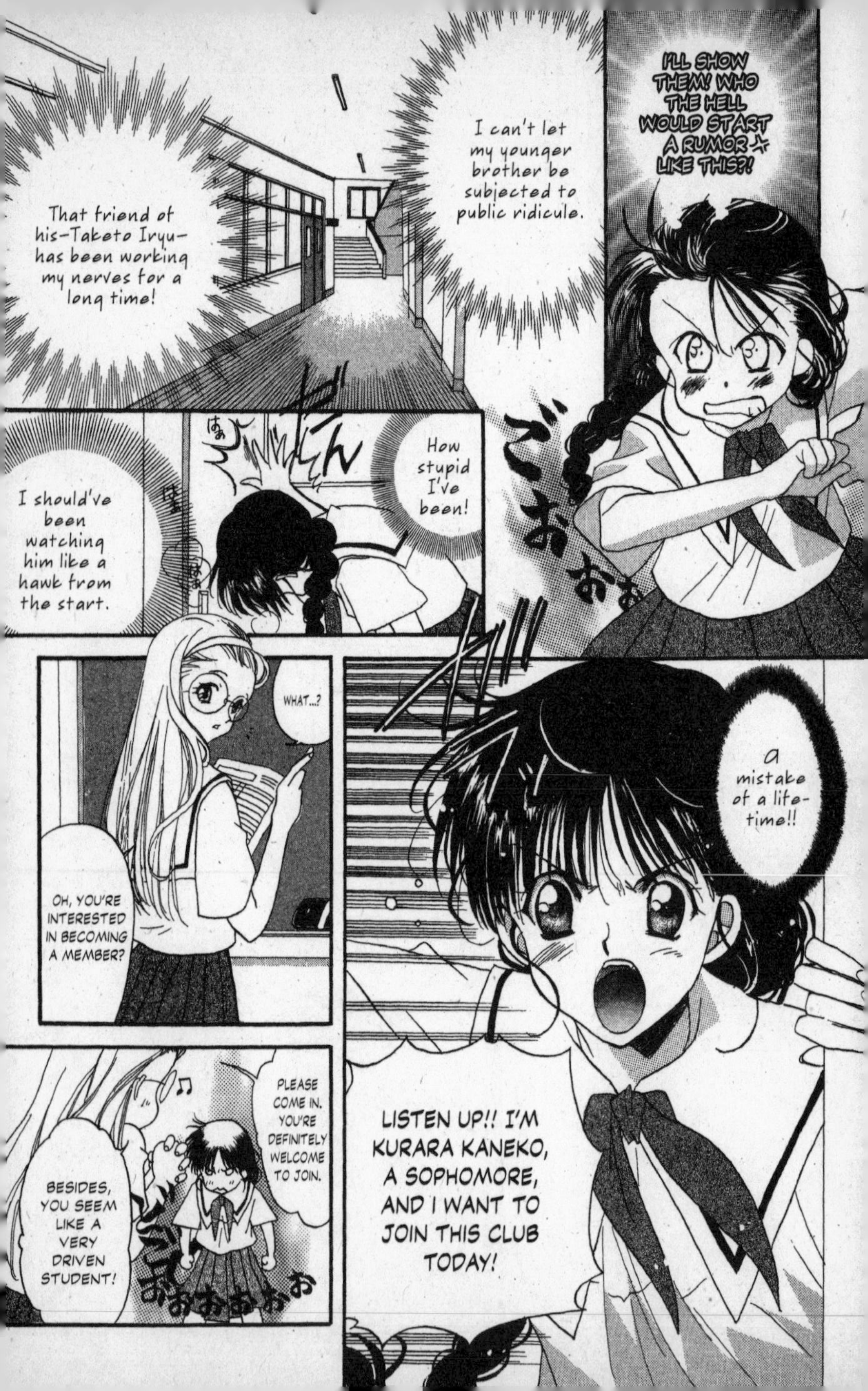
I'LL SHOW THEM! WHO THE HELL WOULD START A RUMOR LIKE THIS?!
I can't let my younger brother be subjected to public ridicule.
That friend of his—Taketo Iryu—has been working my nerves for a long time!
How stupid I've been!
I should've been watching him like a hawk from the start.
a mistake of a life-time!!
LISTEN UP!! I'M KURARA KANEKO, A SOPHOMORE, AND I WANT TO JOIN THIS CLUB TODAY!
WHAT...?
OH, YOU'RE INTERESTED IN BECOMING A MEMBER?
PLEASE COME IN. YOU'RE DEFINITELY WELCOME TO JOIN.
BESIDES, YOU SEEM LIKE A VERY DRIVEN STUDENT!

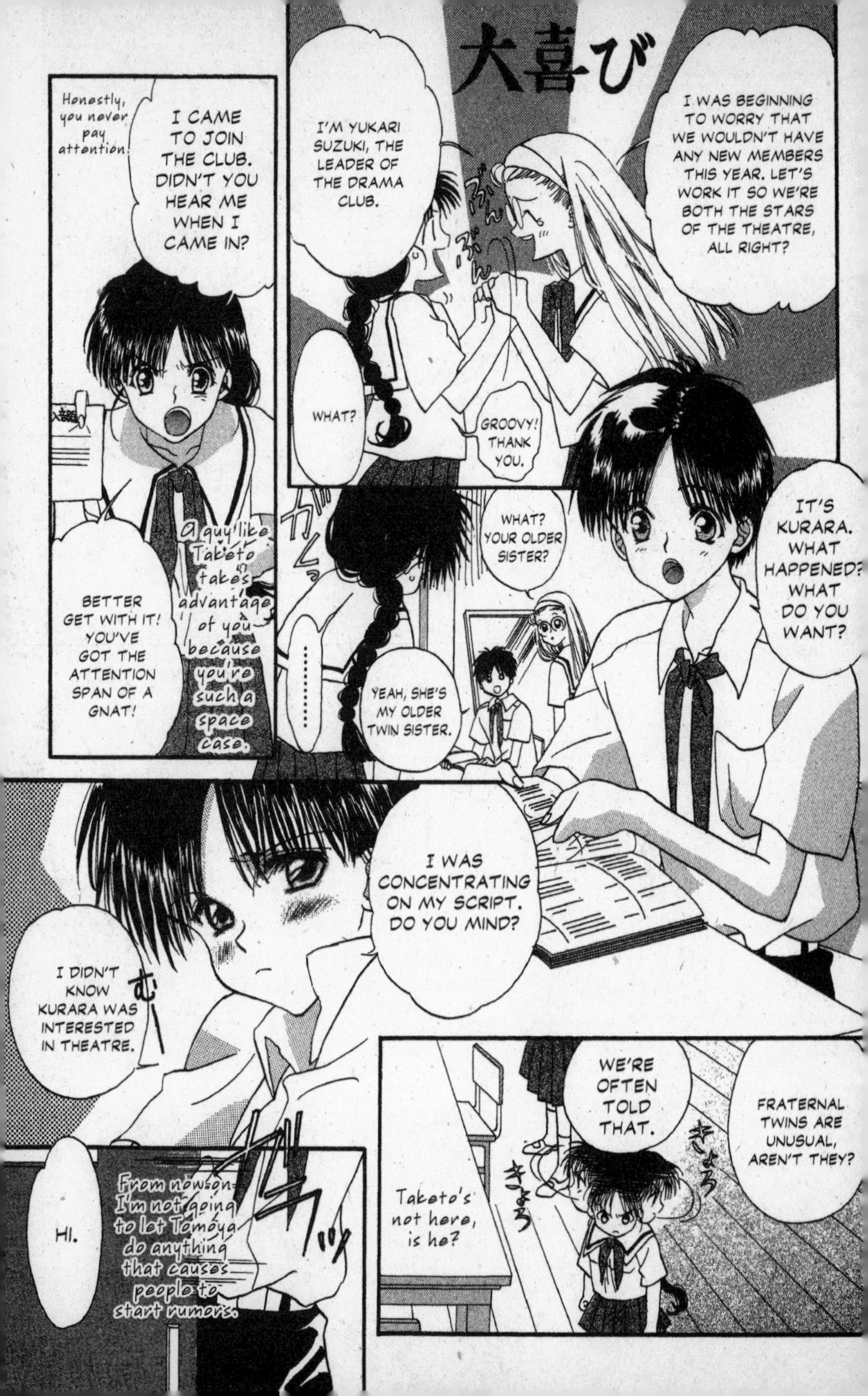

大喜び
I WAS BEGINNING TO WORRY THAT WE WOULDN'T HAVE ANY NEW MEMBERS THIS YEAR. LET'S WORK IT SO WE'RE BOTH THE STARS OF THE THEATRE, ALL RIGHT?
I'M YUKARI SUZUKI, THE LEADER OF THE DRAMA CLUB.
GROOVY! THANK YOU.
WHAT?
IT'S KURARA. WHAT HAPPENED? WHAT DO YOU WANT?
WHAT? YOUR OLDER SISTER?
YEAH, SHE'S MY OLDER TWIN SISTER.
......
I CAME TO JOIN THE CLUB. DIDN'T YOU HEAR ME WHEN I CAME IN?
Honestly, you never pay attention!
BETTER GET WITH IT! YOU'VE GOT THE ATTENTION SPAN OF A GNAT!
A guy like Taketo takes advantage of you because you're such a space case.
I WAS CONCENTRATING ON MY SCRIPT. DO YOU MIND?
I DIDN'T KNOW KURARA WAS INTERESTED IN THEATRE.
FRATERNAL TWINS ARE UNUSUAL, AREN'T THEY?
WE'RE OFTEN TOLD THAT.
Taketo's not here, is he?
From now on I'm not going to let Tomoya do anything that causes people to start rumors.
HI.

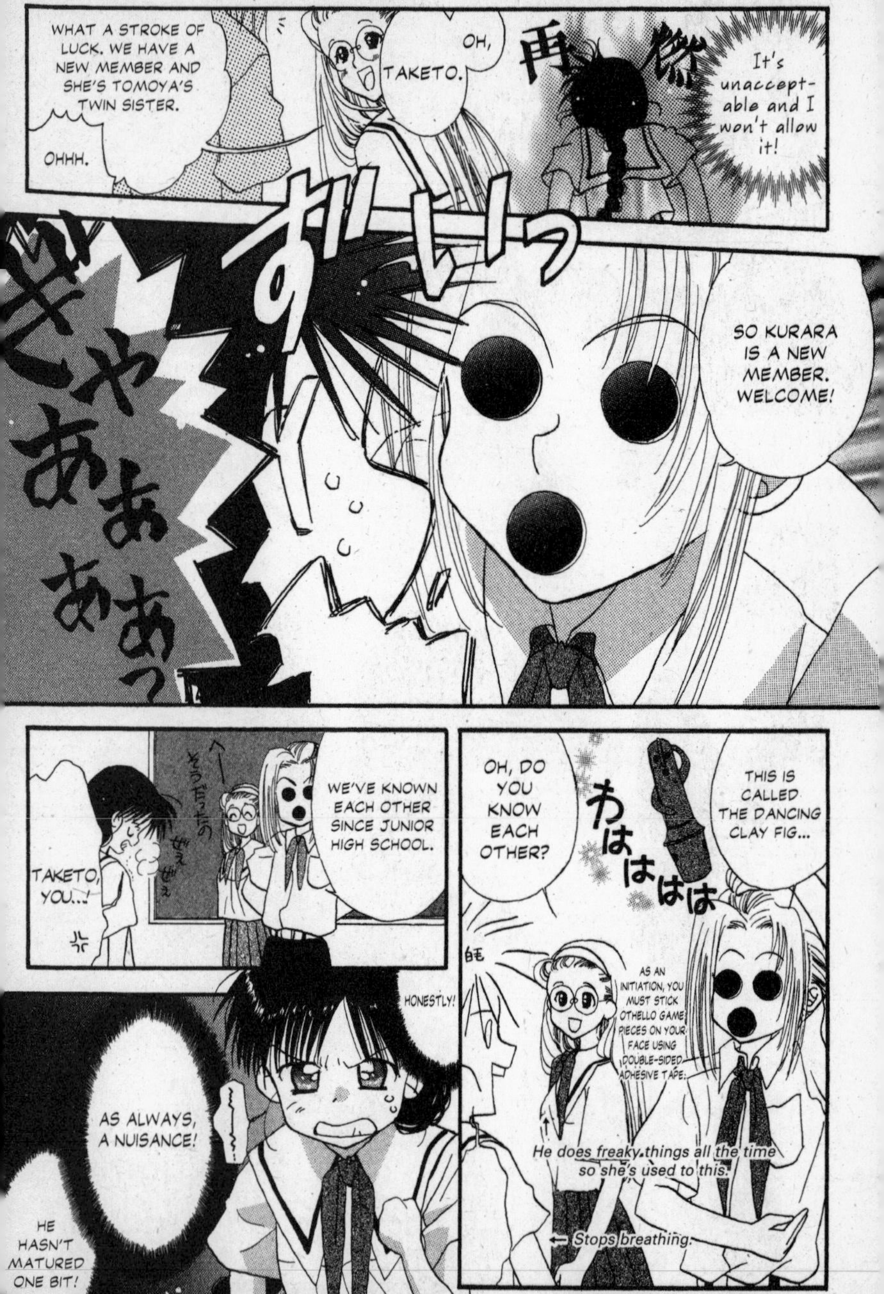
再燃
It's unacceptable and I won't allow it!
OH, TAKETO.
WHAT A STROKE OF LUCK. WE HAVE A NEW MEMBER AND SHE'S TOMOYA'S TWIN SISTER.
OHHH.
おいーっ
SO KURARA IS A NEW MEMBER. WELCOME!
ぎゃあああああっ
THIS IS CALLED THE DANCING CLAY FIG...
わはははは
OH, DO YOU KNOW EACH OTHER?
AS AN INITIATION, YOU MUST STICK OTHELLO GAME PIECES ON YOUR FACE USING DOUBLE-SIDED ADHESIVE TAPE.
He does freaky things all the time so she's used to this.
Stops breathing.
WE'VE KNOWN EACH OTHER SINCE JUNIOR HIGH SCHOOL.
へーそうだったの
ぜぇぜぇ
TAKETO, YOU...!
HONESTLY!
AS ALWAYS, A NUISANCE!
HE HASN'T MATURED ONE BIT!

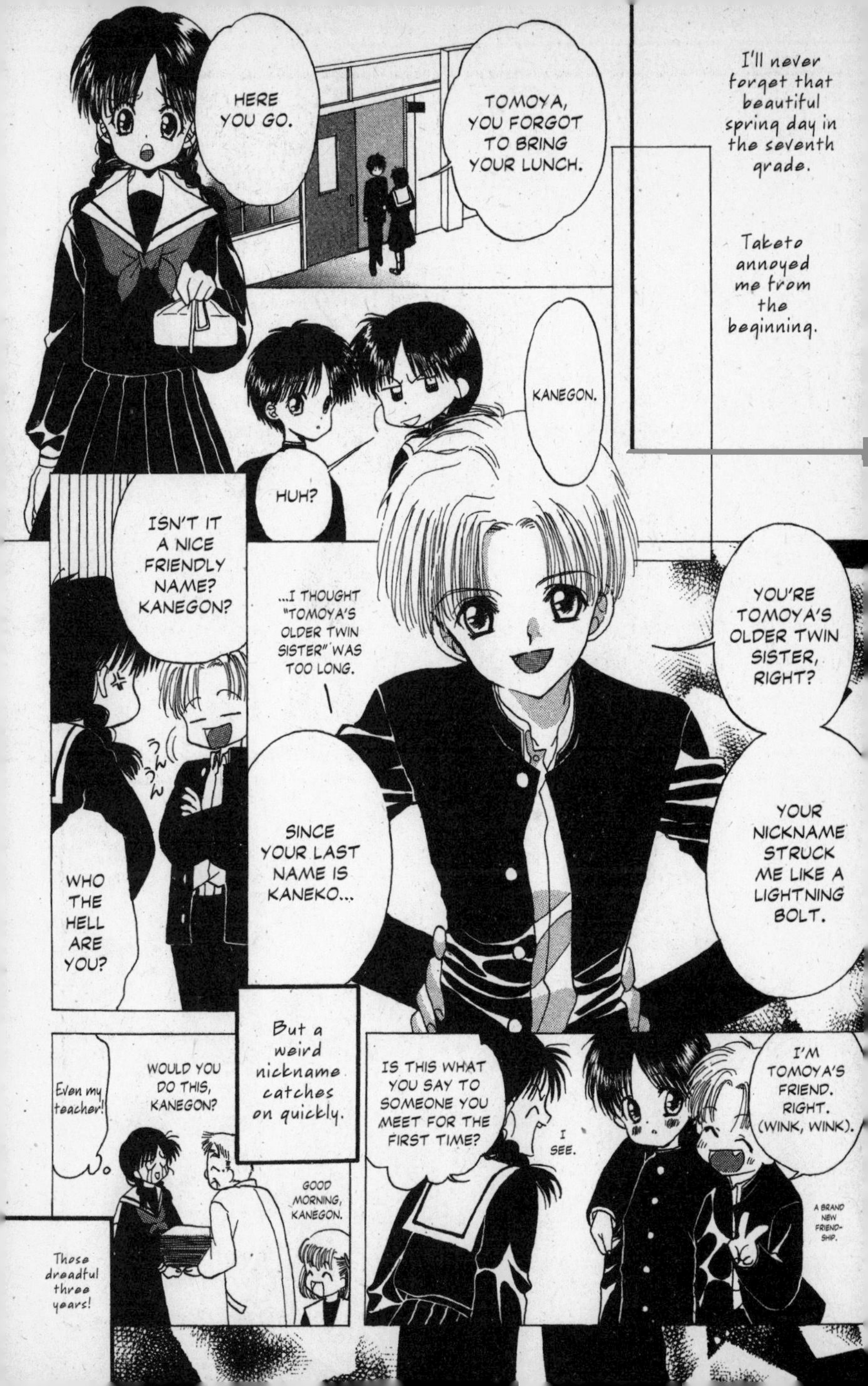
I'll never forget that beautiful spring day in the seventh grade.
Taketo annoyed me from the beginning.
TOMOYA, YOU FORGOT TO BRING YOUR LUNCH.
HERE YOU GO.
KANEGON.
HUH?
YOU'RE TOMOYA'S OLDER TWIN SISTER, RIGHT?
YOUR NICKNAME STRUCK ME LIKE A LIGHTNING BOLT.
SINCE YOUR LAST NAME IS KANEKO...
...I THOUGHT "TOMOYA'S OLDER TWIN SISTER" WAS TOO LONG.
ISN'T IT A NICE FRIENDLY NAME? KANEGON?
WHO THE HELL ARE YOU?
I'M TOMOYA'S FRIEND. RIGHT. (WINK, WINK).
A BRAND NEW FRIENDSHIP.
I SEE.
IS THIS WHAT YOU SAY TO SOMEONE YOU MEET FOR THE FIRST TIME?
But a weird nickname catches on quickly.
WOULD YOU DO THIS, KANEGON?
Even my teacher!
GOOD MORNING, KANEGON.
Those dreadful three years!

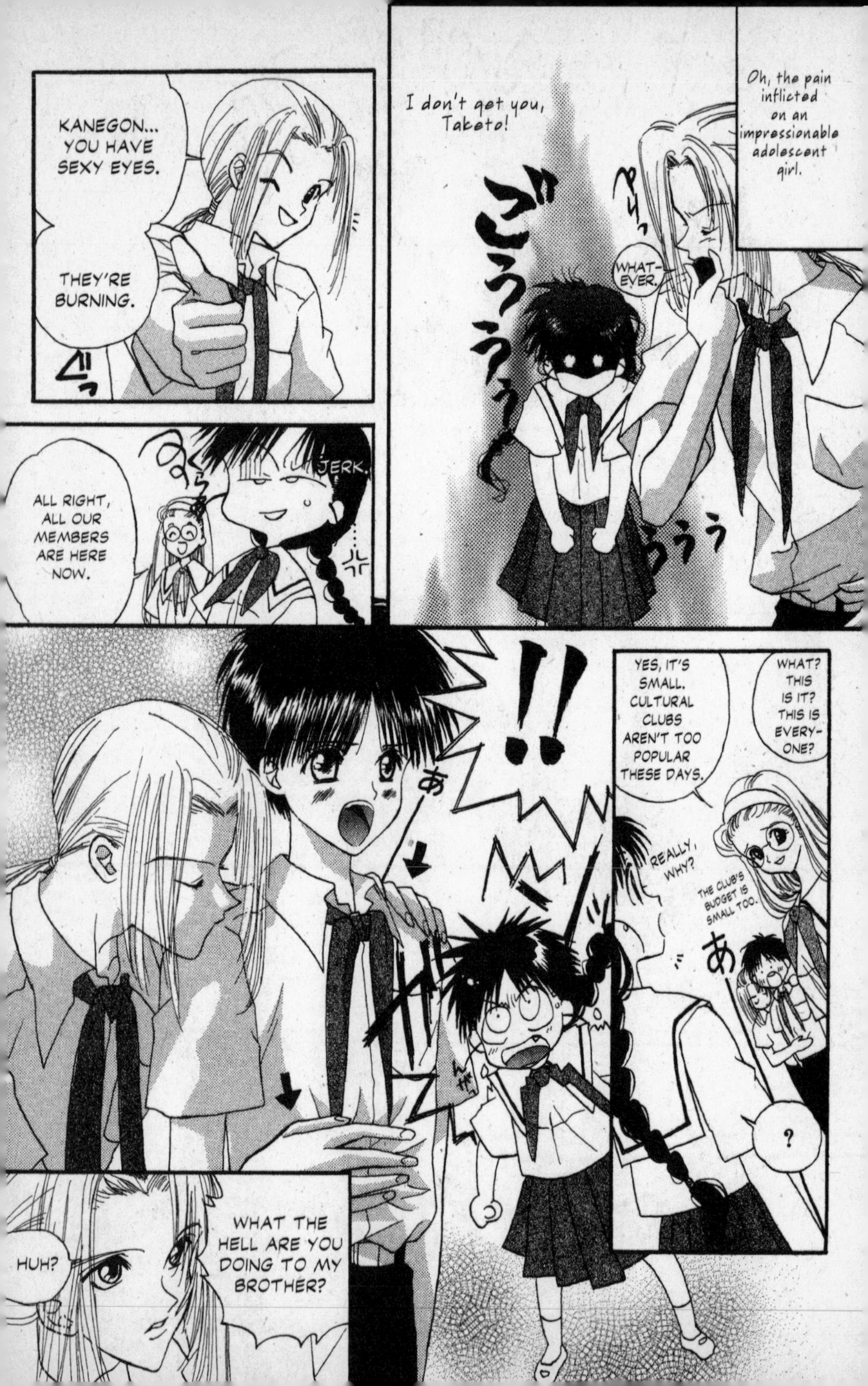
Oh, the pain inflicted on an impressionable adolescent girl.
WHAT-EVER.
I don't get you, Taketo!
KANEGON... YOU HAVE SEXY EYES.
THEY'RE BURNING.
JERK.
ALL RIGHT, ALL OUR MEMBERS ARE HERE NOW.
WHAT? THIS IS IT? THIS IS EVERY-ONE?
YES, IT'S SMALL. CULTURAL CLUBS AREN'T TOO POPULAR THESE DAYS.
REALLY, WHY?
THE CLUB'S BUDGET IS SMALL TOO.
あ
?
!!
あ
WHAT THE HELL ARE YOU DOING TO MY BROTHER?
HUH?

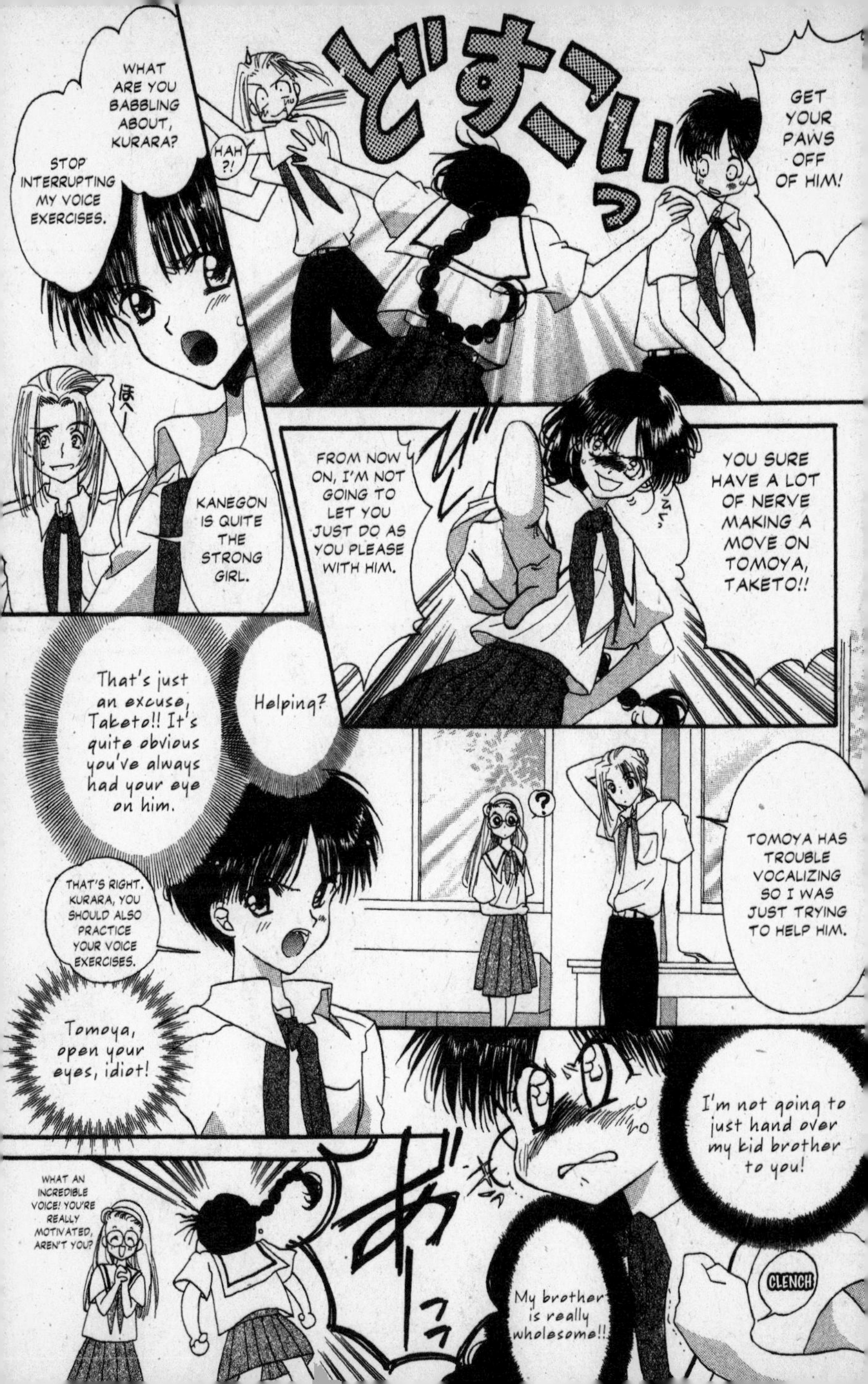
どすこいっ
GET YOUR PAWS OFF OF HIM!
HAH?!
WHAT ARE YOU BABBLING ABOUT, KURARA?
STOP INTERRUPTING MY VOICE EXERCISES.
YOU SURE HAVE A LOT OF NERVE MAKING A MOVE ON TOMOYA, TAKETO!!
FROM NOW ON, I'M NOT GOING TO LET YOU JUST DO AS YOU PLEASE WITH HIM.
ほー
KANEGON IS QUITE THE STRONG GIRL.
TOMOYA HAS TROUBLE VOCALIZING SO I WAS JUST TRYING TO HELP HIM.
?
Helping?
That's just an excuse, Taketo!! It's quite obvious you've always had your eye on him.
THAT'S RIGHT. KURARA, YOU SHOULD ALSO PRACTICE YOUR VOICE EXERCISES.
Tomoya, open your eyes, idiot!
I'm not going to just hand over my kid brother to you!
CLENCH
My brother is really wholesome!!
あーっ
WHAT AN INCREDIBLE VOICE! YOU'RE REALLY MOTIVATED, AREN'T YOU?

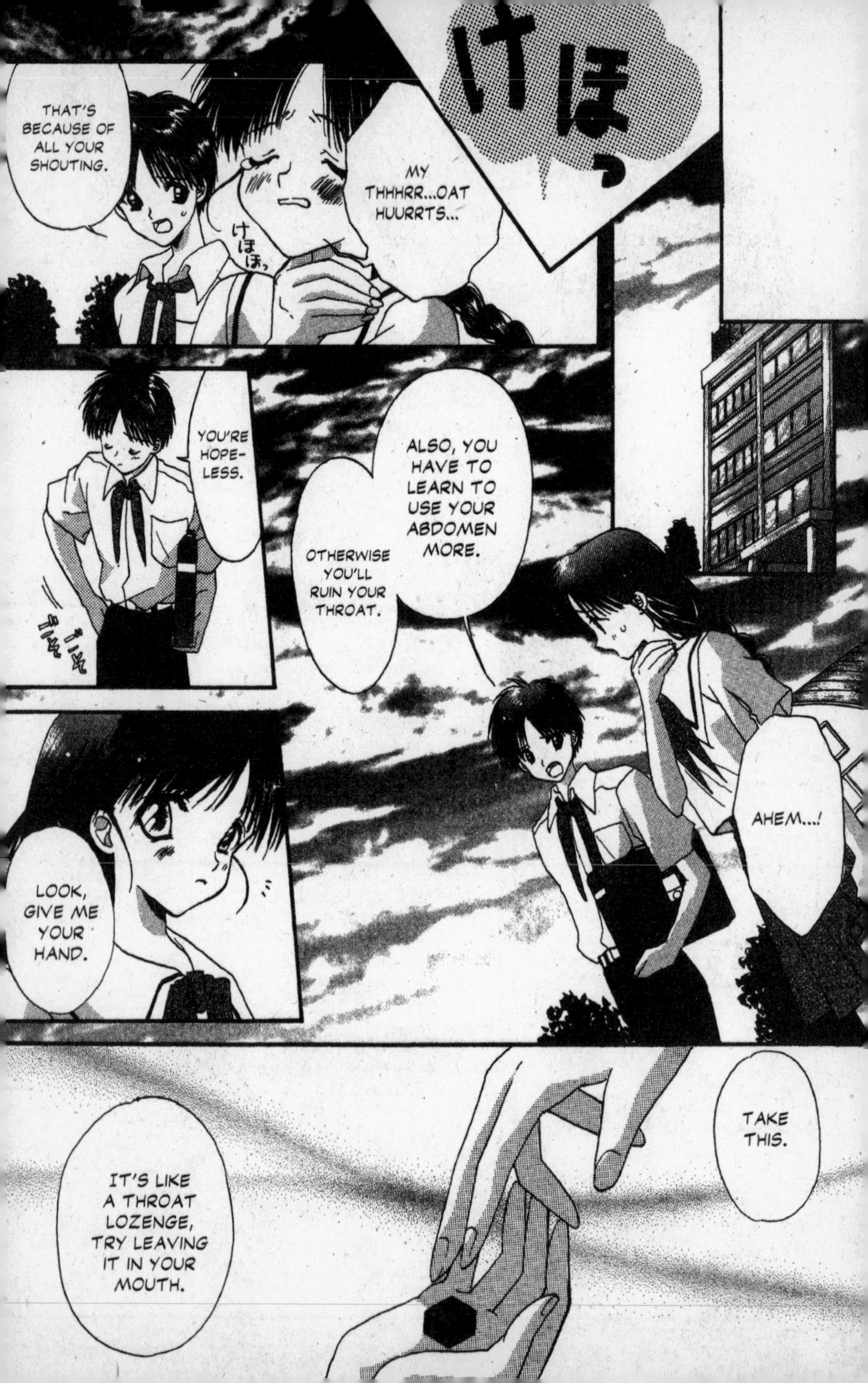
けほっ
MY THHHRR...OAT HUURRTS...
けほほっ
THAT'S BECAUSE OF ALL YOUR SHOUTING.
ALSO, YOU HAVE TO LEARN TO USE YOUR ABDOMEN MORE.
OTHERWISE YOU'LL RUIN YOUR THROAT.
AHEM...!
YOU'RE HOPE-LESS.
ごそごそ
LOOK, GIVE ME YOUR HAND.
TAKE THIS.
IT'S LIKE A THROAT LOZENGE, TRY LEAVING IT IN YOUR MOUTH.

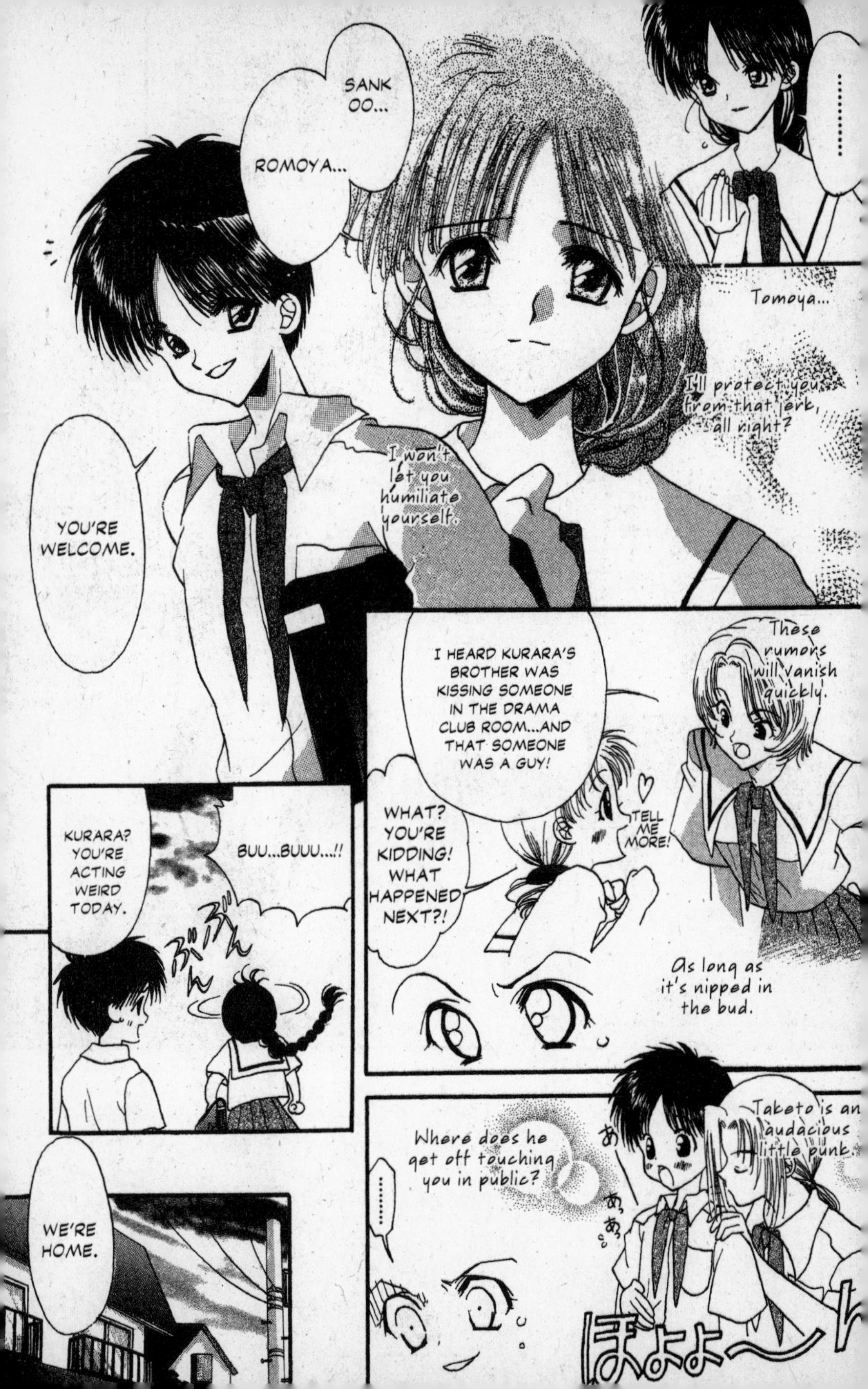
......
Tomoya...
I'll protect you from that jerk, all right?
SANK OO...
ROMOYA...
I won't let you humiliate yourself.
YOU'RE WELCOME.
These rumors will vanish quickly.
I HEARD KURARA'S BROTHER WAS KISSING SOMEONE IN THE DRAMA CLUB ROOM...AND THAT SOMEONE WAS A GUY!
TELL ME MORE!
WHAT? YOU'RE KIDDING! WHAT HAPPENED NEXT?!
As long as it's nipped in the bud.
BUU...BUUU...!!
KURARA? YOU'RE ACTING WEIRD TODAY.
ぶん ぶん
Taketo is an audacious little punk.
あ
あ あ
Where does he get off touching you in public?
......
ほよよ～
WE'RE HOME.

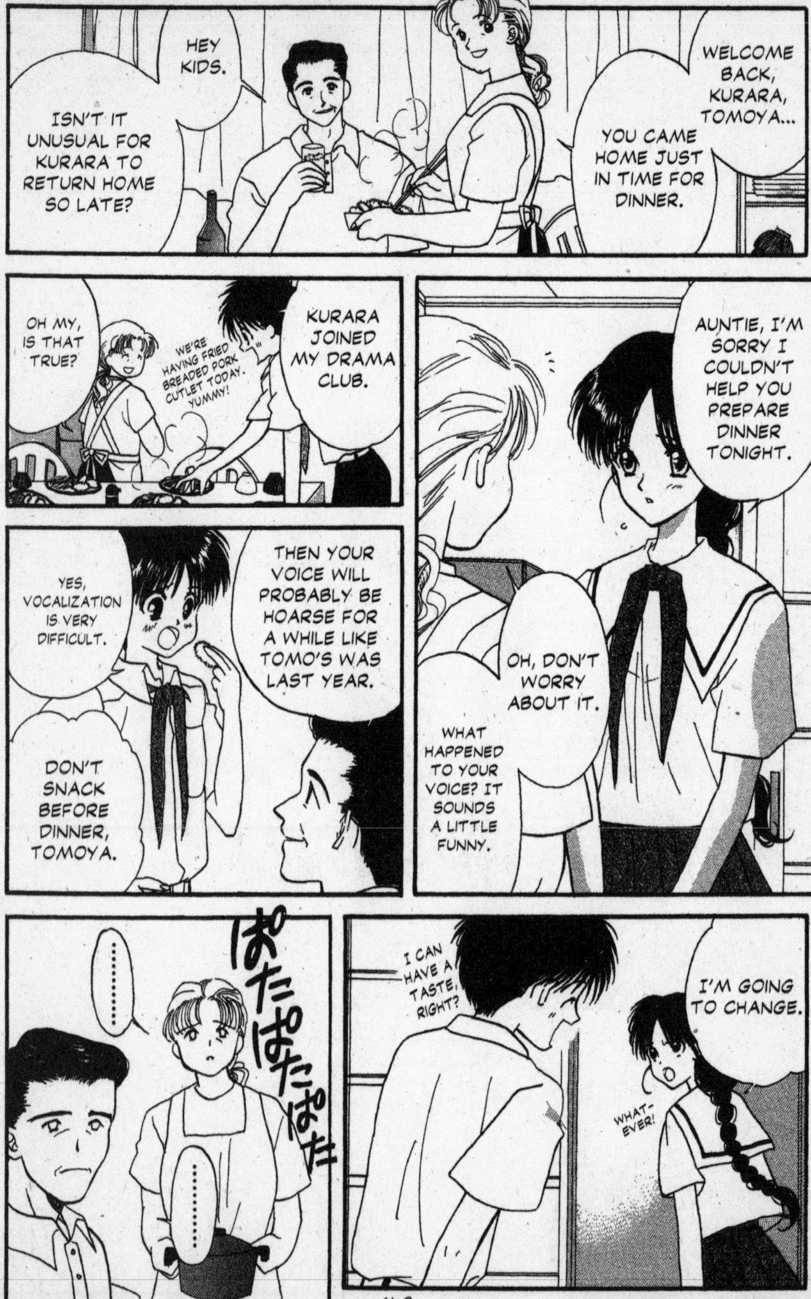
WELCOME BACK, KURARA, TOMOYA...
YOU CAME HOME JUST IN TIME FOR DINNER.
HEY KIDS.
ISN'T IT UNUSUAL FOR KURARA TO RETURN HOME SO LATE?
AUNTIE, I'M SORRY I COULDN'T HELP YOU PREPARE DINNER TONIGHT.
OH, DON'T WORRY ABOUT IT.
WHAT HAPPENED TO YOUR VOICE? IT SOUNDS A LITTLE FUNNY.
KURARA JOINED MY DRAMA CLUB.
WE'RE HAVING FRIED BREADED PORK CUTLET TODAY. YUMMY!
OH MY, IS THAT TRUE?
THEN YOUR VOICE WILL PROBABLY BE HOARSE FOR A WHILE LIKE TOMO'S WAS LAST YEAR.
YES, VOCALIZATION IS VERY DIFFICULT.
DON'T SNACK BEFORE DINNER, TOMOYA.
I'M GOING TO CHANGE.
I CAN HAVE A TASTE, RIGHT?
WHATEVER!
ぱたぱたぱた
......
......

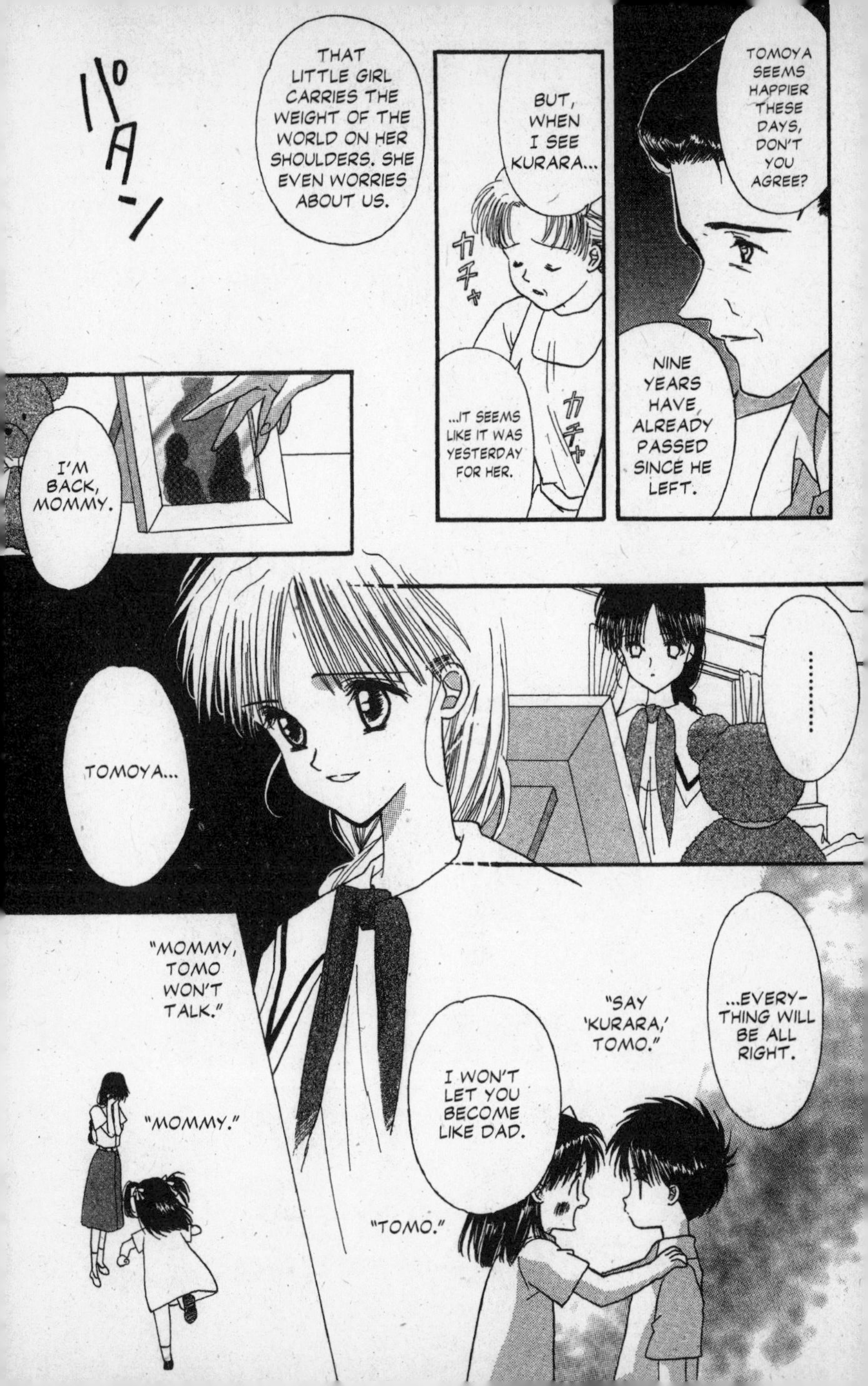
TOMOYA SEEMS HAPPIER THESE DAYS, DON'T YOU AGREE?
NINE YEARS HAVE ALREADY PASSED SINCE HE LEFT.
BUT, WHEN I SEE KURARA...
カチャ
カチャ
...IT SEEMS LIKE IT WAS YESTERDAY FOR HER.
THAT LITTLE GIRL CARRIES THE WEIGHT OF THE WORLD ON HER SHOULDERS. SHE EVEN WORRIES ABOUT US.
パァーン
......
I'M BACK, MOMMY.
TOMOYA...
...EVERY-THING WILL BE ALL RIGHT.
"SAY 'KURARA,' TOMO."
I WON'T LET YOU BECOME LIKE DAD.
"TOMO."
"MOMMY, TOMO WON'T TALK."
"MOMMY."

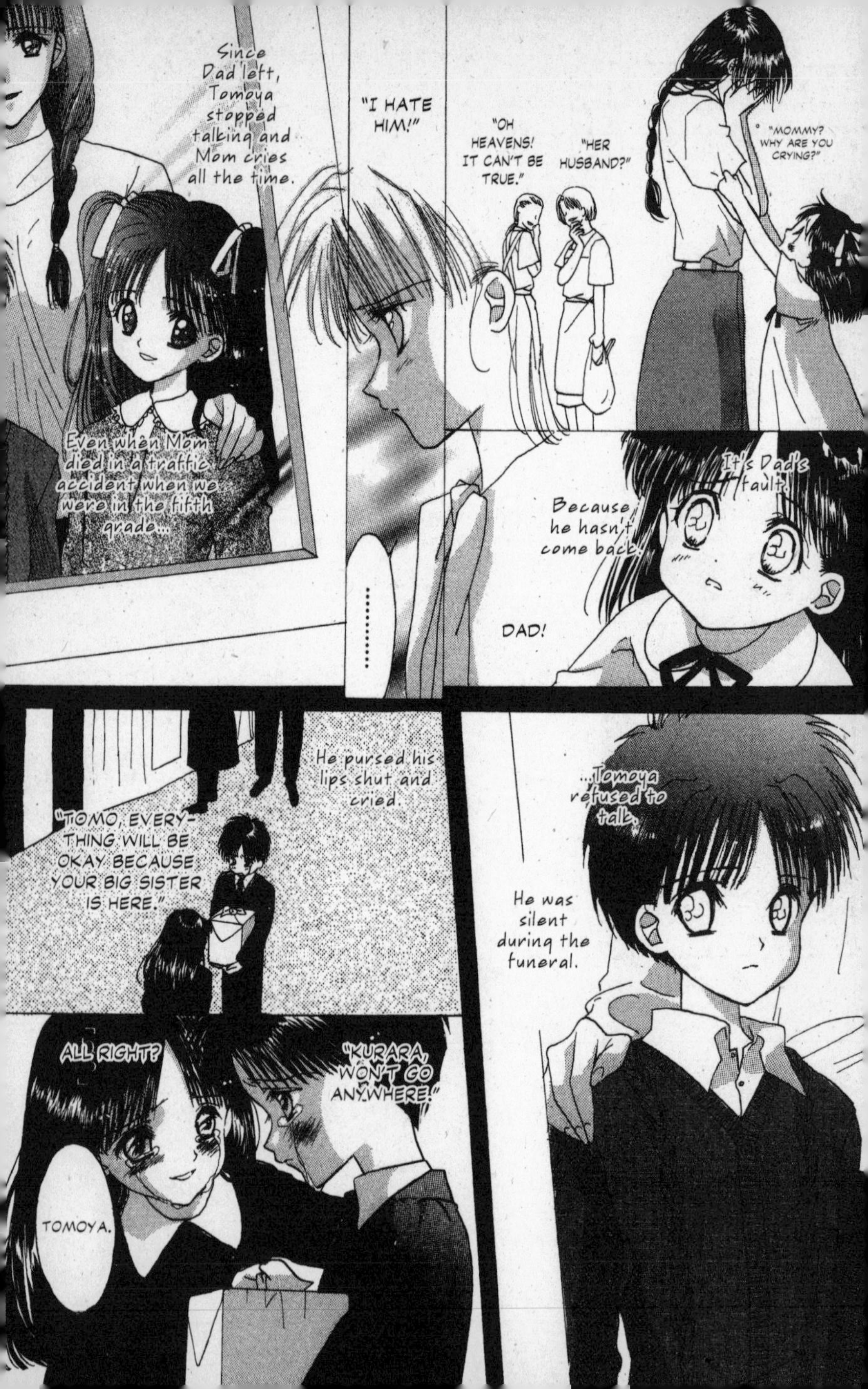
"MOMMY? WHY ARE YOU CRYING?"
"HER HUSBAND?"
"OH HEAVENS! IT CAN'T BE TRUE."
It's Dad's fault.
Because he hasn't come back.
DAD!
"I HATE HIM!"
......
Since Dad left, Tomoya stopped talking and Mom cries all the time.
Even when Mom died in a traffic accident when we were in the fifth grade...
...Tomoya refused to talk.
He was silent during the funeral.
He pursed his lips shut and cried.
"TOMO, EVERY-THING WILL BE OKAY BECAUSE YOUR BIG SISTER IS HERE."
"KURARA, WON'T GO ANYWHERE."
ALL RIGHT?
TOMOYA.

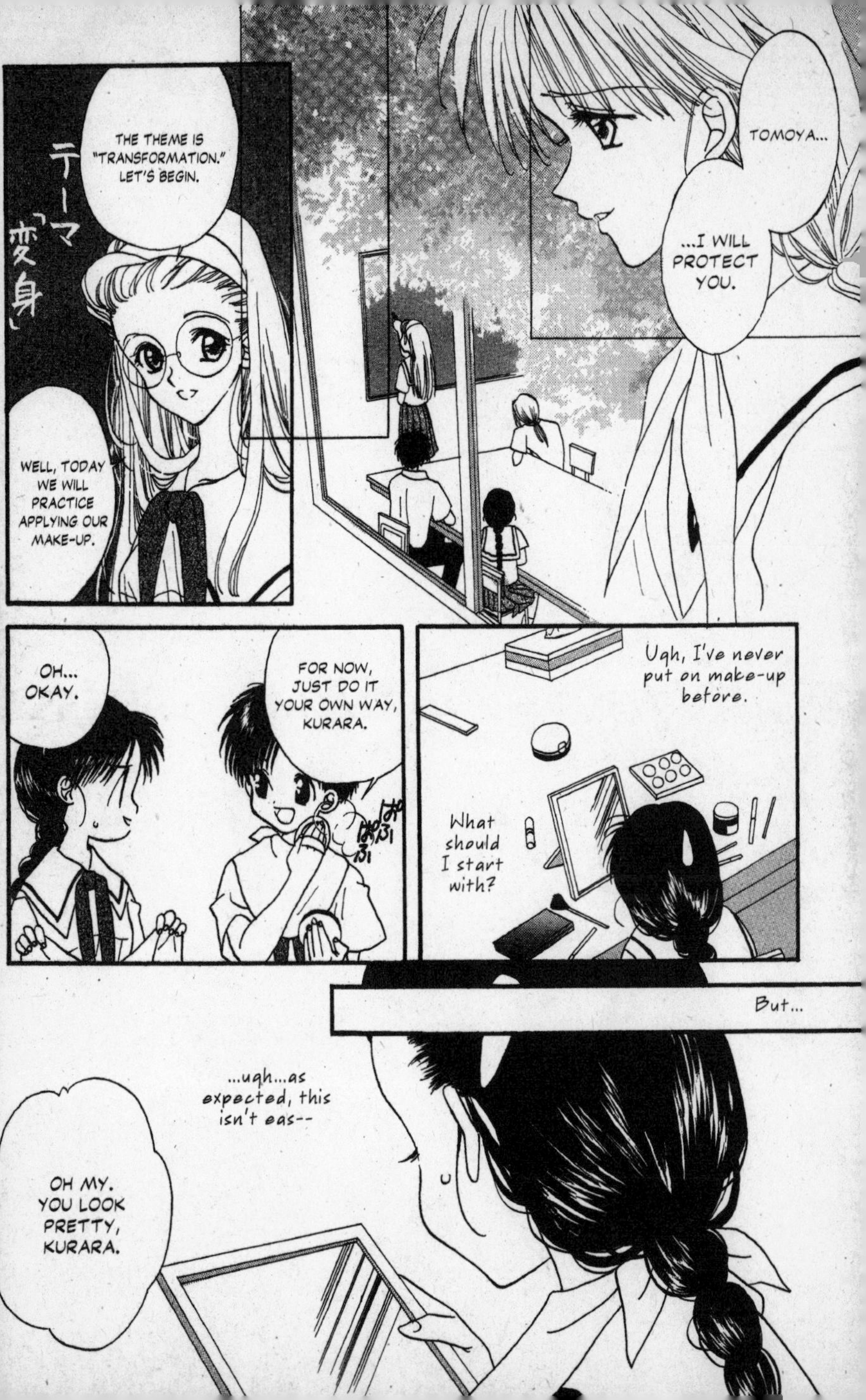
TOMOYA...
...I WILL PROTECT YOU.
THE THEME IS "TRANSFORMATION." LET'S BEGIN.
テーマ「変身」
WELL, TODAY WE WILL PRACTICE APPLYING OUR MAKE-UP.
Ugh, I've never put on make-up before.
What should I start with?
FOR NOW, JUST DO IT YOUR OWN WAY, KURARA.
ぱふぱふ
OH... OKAY.
But...
...ugh...as expected, this isn't eas--
OH MY. YOU LOOK PRETTY, KURARA.

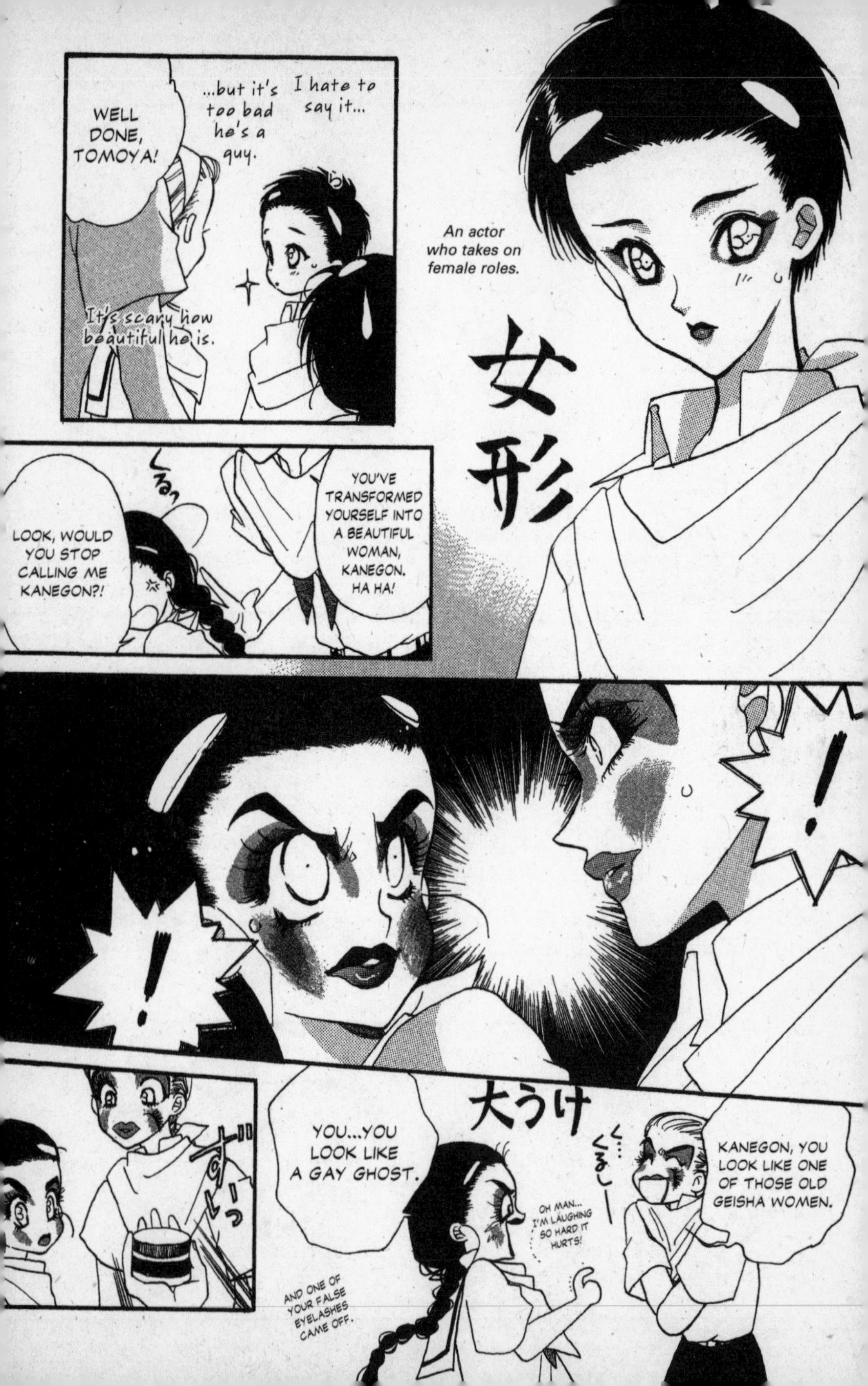
女形
An actor who takes on female roles.
I hate to say it...
...but it's too bad he's a guy.
WELL DONE, TOMOYA!
It's scary how beautiful he is.
YOU'VE TRANSFORMED YOURSELF INTO A BEAUTIFUL WOMAN, KANEGON. HA HA!
くるっ
LOOK, WOULD YOU STOP CALLING ME KANEGON?!
!
!
大うけ
KANEGON, YOU LOOK LIKE ONE OF THOSE OLD GEISHA WOMEN.
く…くるしー
OH MAN... I'M LAUGHING SO HARD IT HURTS!
YOU...YOU LOOK LIKE A GAY GHOST.
AND ONE OF YOUR FALSE EYELASHES CAME OFF.

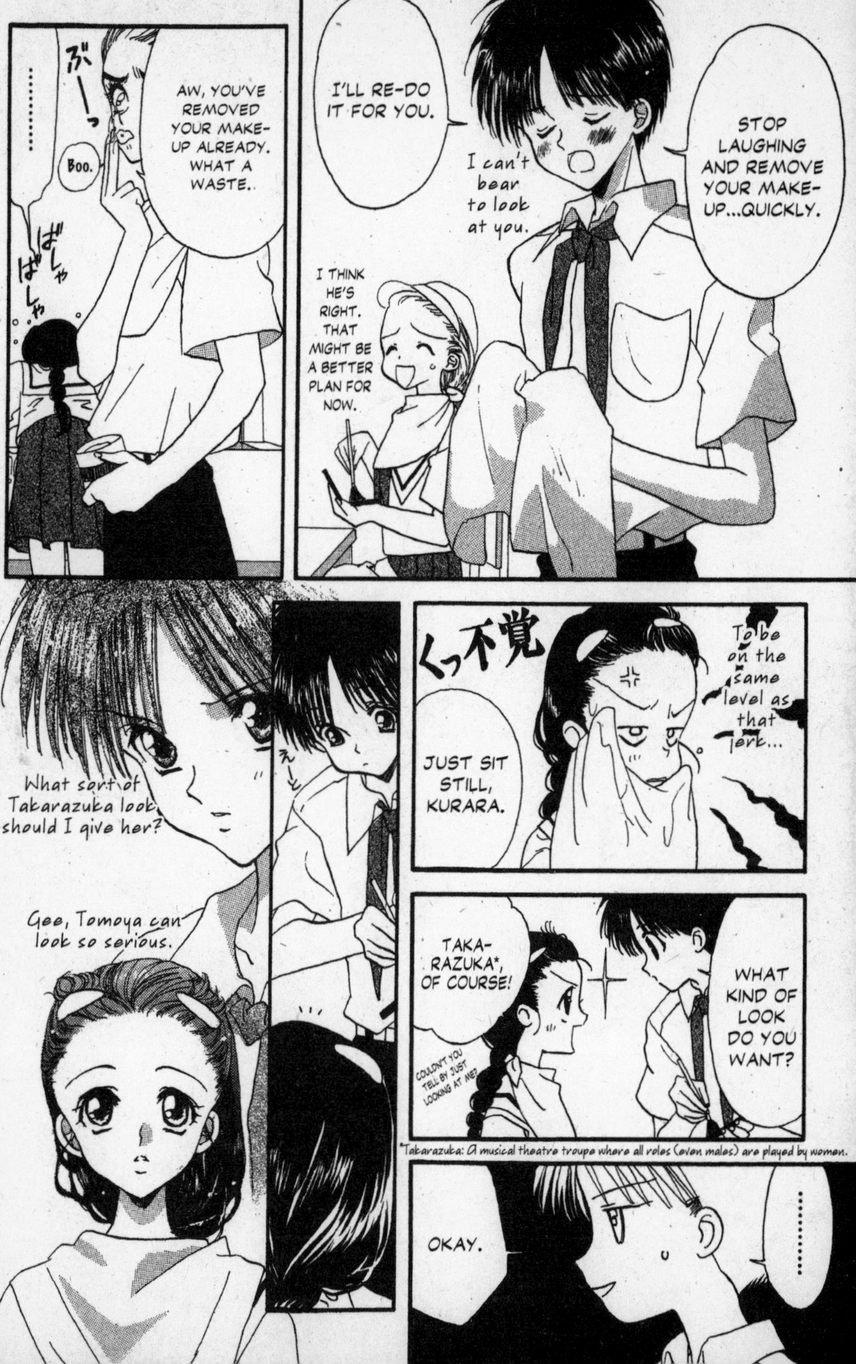
STOP LAUGHING AND REMOVE YOUR MAKE-UP...QUICKLY.
I can't bear to look at you.
I'LL RE-DO IT FOR YOU.
I THINK HE'S RIGHT. THAT MIGHT BE A BETTER PLAN FOR NOW.
AW, YOU'VE REMOVED YOUR MAKE-UP ALREADY. WHAT A WASTE..
ぶーっ
Boo.
......
ばしゃばしゃ
くっ不覚
To be on the same level as that jerk...
JUST SIT STILL, KURARA.
WHAT KIND OF LOOK DO YOU WANT?
TAKARAZUKA*, OF COURSE!
COULDN'T YOU TELL BY JUST LOOKING AT ME?
......
OKAY.
えーと
What sort of Takarazuka look should I give her?
Gee, Tomoya can look so serious.

*Takarazuka: A musical theatre troupe where all roles (even males) are played by women.

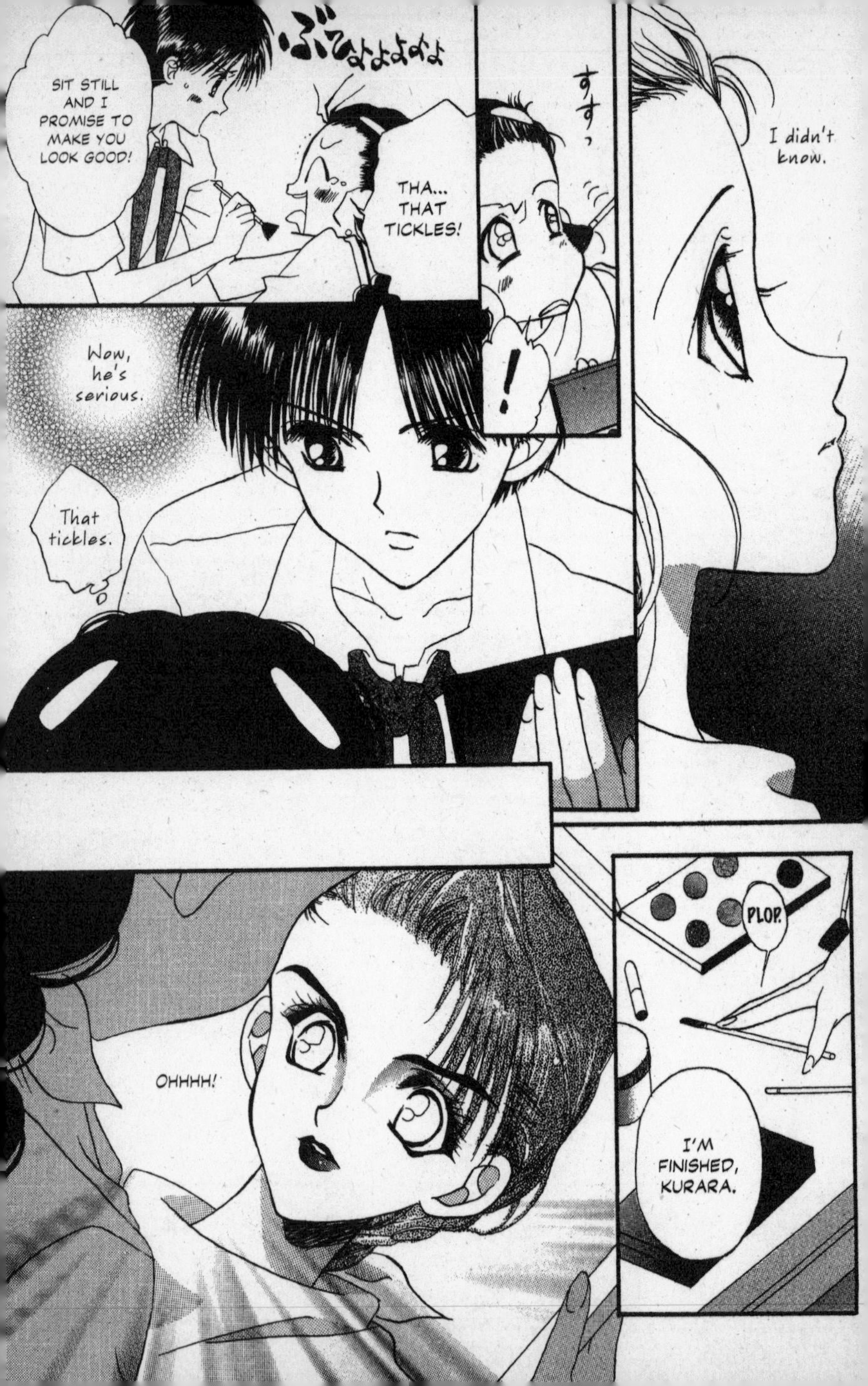
I didn't know.
すすっ
!
ぶひょよよよよ
SIT STILL AND I PROMISE TO MAKE YOU LOOK GOOD!
THA... THAT TICKLES!
Wow, he's serious.
That tickles.
PLOP.
I'M FINISHED, KURARA.
OHHHH!

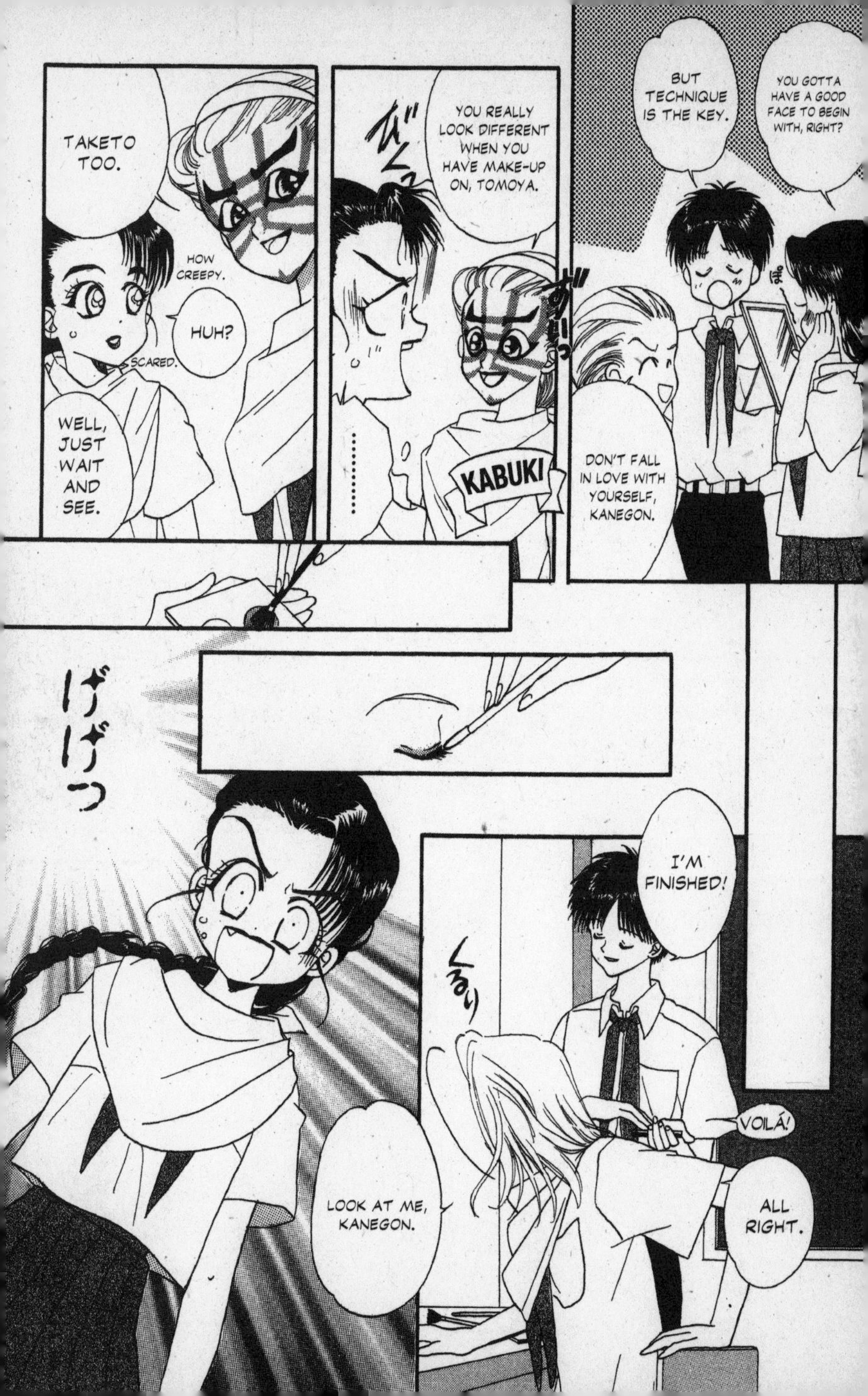
YOU GOTTA HAVE A GOOD FACE TO BEGIN WITH, RIGHT?
BUT TECHNIQUE IS THE KEY.
DON'T FALL IN LOVE WITH YOURSELF, KANEGON.
YOU REALLY LOOK DIFFERENT WHEN YOU HAVE MAKE-UP ON, TOMOYA.
KABUKI
....
TAKETO TOO.
HOW CREEPY.
HUH?
SCARED.
WELL, JUST WAIT AND SEE.
I'M FINISHED!
VOILÁ!
ALL RIGHT.
LOOK AT ME, KANEGON.

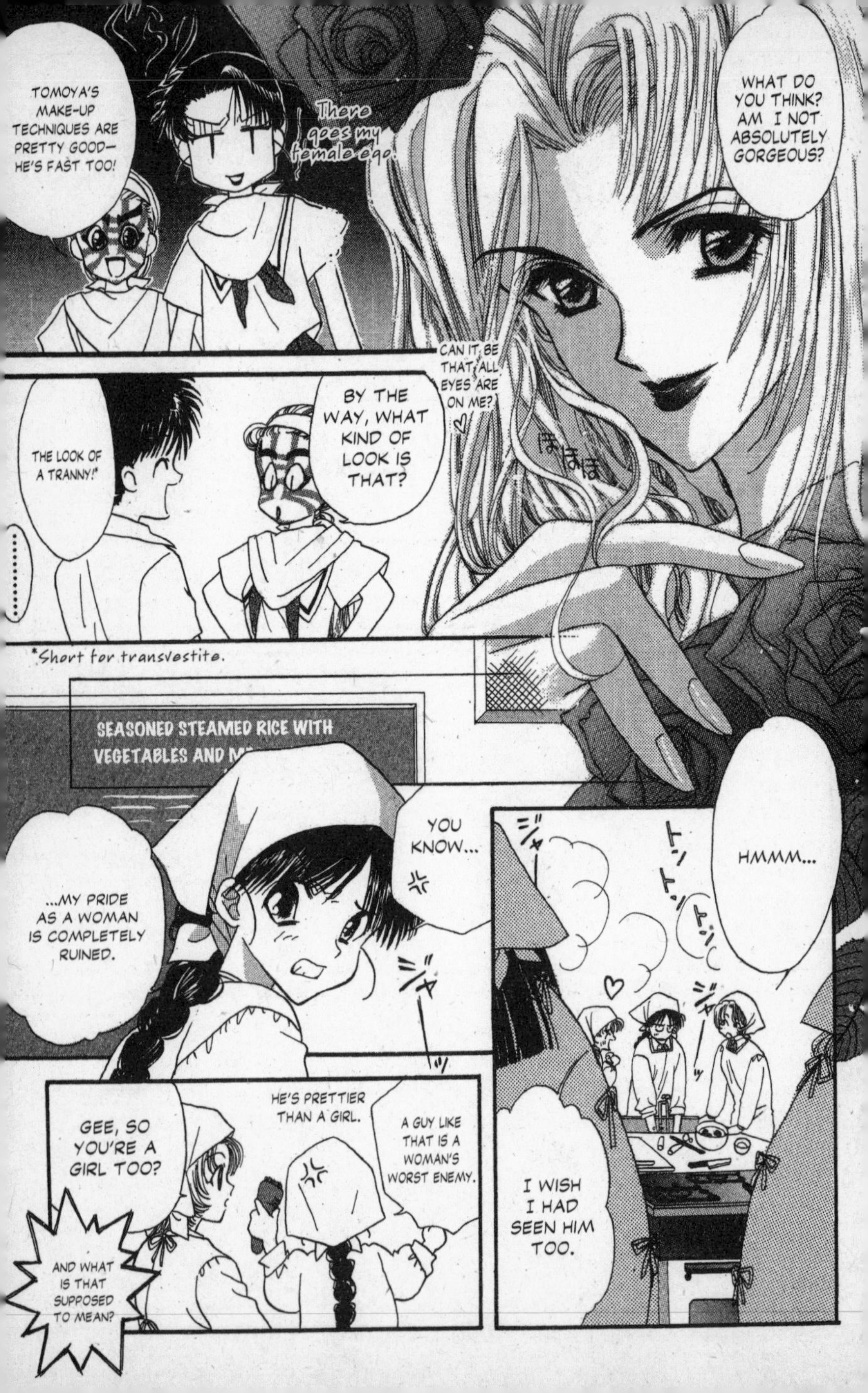
WHAT DO YOU THINK? AM I NOT ABSOLUTELY GORGEOUS?
CAN IT BE THAT ALL EYES ARE ON ME?
ほほほ
There goes my female ego.
TOMOYA'S MAKE-UP TECHNIQUES ARE PRETTY GOOD—HE'S FAST TOO!
BY THE WAY, WHAT KIND OF LOOK IS THAT?
THE LOOK OF A TRANNY!*
......
*Short for transvestite.
SEASONED STEAMED RICE WITH VEGETABLES AND M
HMMM...
I WISH I HAD SEEN HIM TOO.
YOU KNOW...
...MY PRIDE AS A WOMAN IS COMPLETELY RUINED.
HE'S PRETTIER THAN A GIRL.
A GUY LIKE THAT IS A WOMAN'S WORST ENEMY.
GEE, SO YOU'RE A GIRL TOO?
AND WHAT IS THAT SUPPOSED TO MEAN?

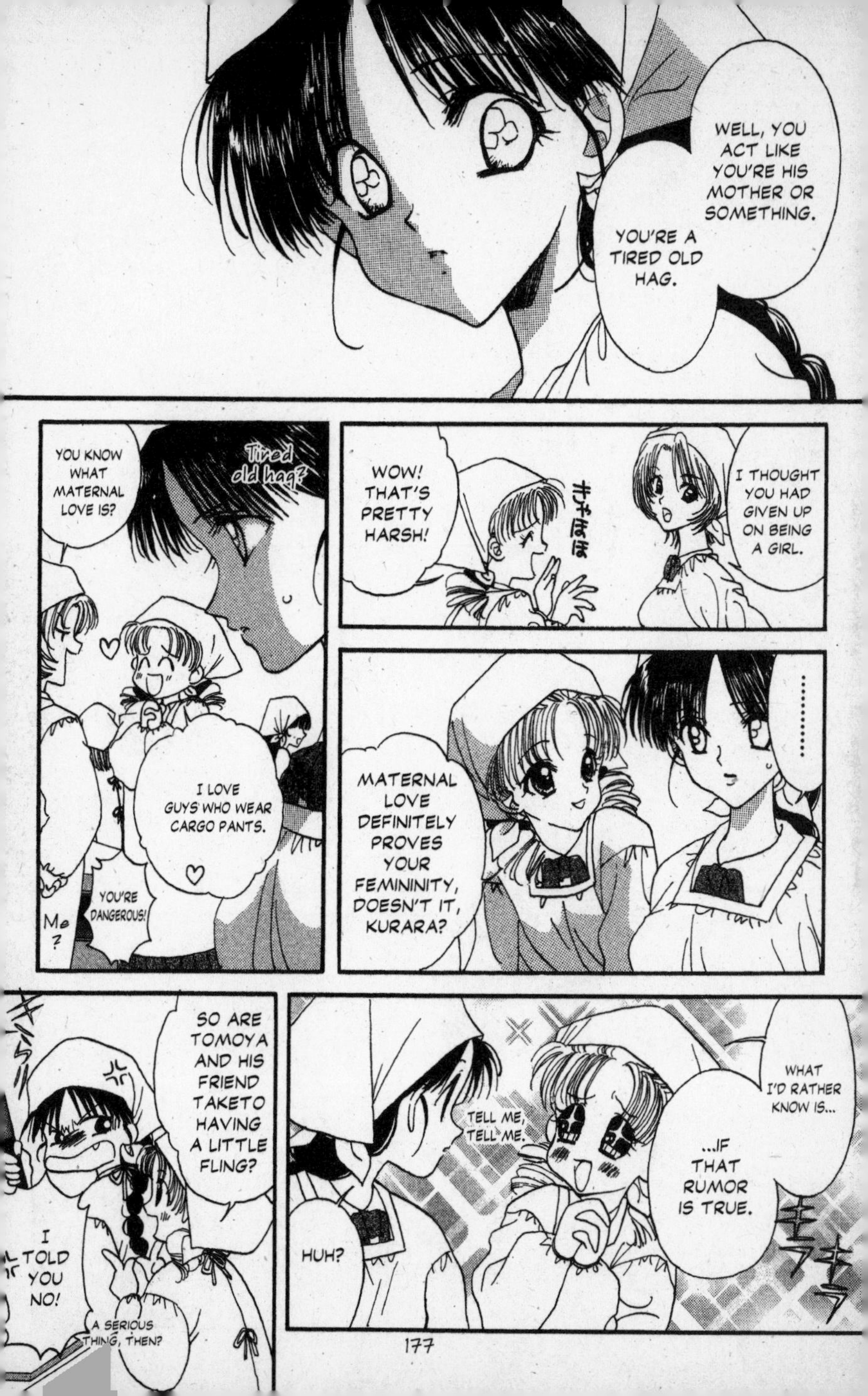
WELL, YOU ACT LIKE YOU'RE HIS MOTHER OR SOMETHING.
YOU'RE A TIRED OLD HAG.
I THOUGHT YOU HAD GIVEN UP ON BEING A GIRL.
WOW! THAT'S PRETTY HARSH!
きゃほほ
......
MATERNAL LOVE DEFINITELY PROVES YOUR FEMININITY, DOESN'T IT, KURARA?
Tired old hag?
YOU KNOW WHAT MATERNAL LOVE IS?
I LOVE GUYS WHO WEAR CARGO PANTS. ♡
YOU'RE DANGEROUS!
Me?
WHAT I'D RATHER KNOW IS...
...IF THAT RUMOR IS TRUE.
TELL ME, TELL ME.
HUH?
SO ARE TOMOYA AND HIS FRIEND TAKETO HAVING A LITTLE FLING?
I TOLD YOU NO!
A SERIOUS THING, THEN?

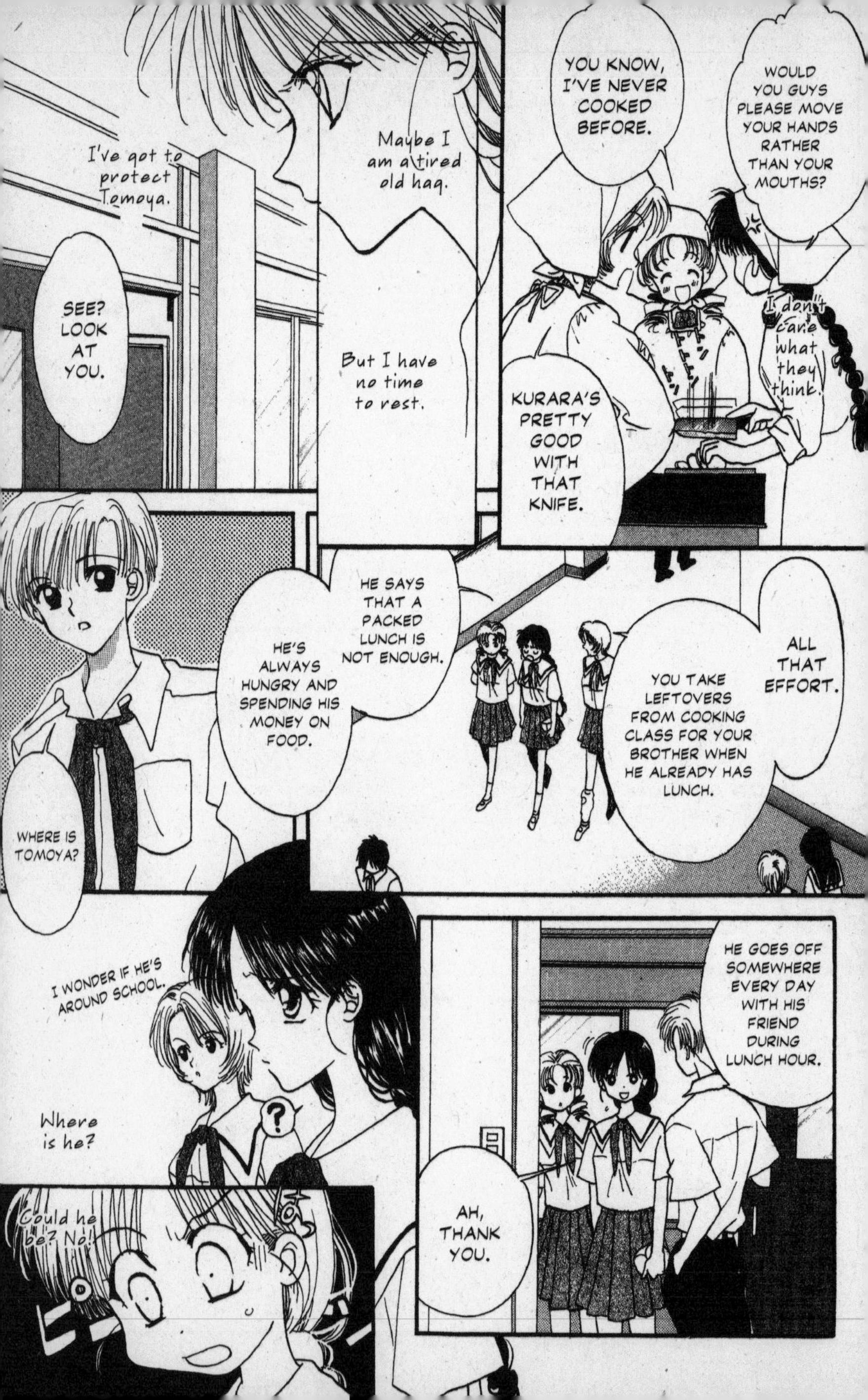
WOULD YOU GUYS PLEASE MOVE YOUR HANDS RATHER THAN YOUR MOUTHS?
YOU KNOW, I'VE NEVER COOKED BEFORE.
I don't care what they think.
KURARA'S PRETTY GOOD WITH THAT KNIFE.
Maybe I am a tired old hag.
But I have no time to rest.
I've got to protect Tomoya.
SEE? LOOK AT YOU.
ALL THAT EFFORT.
YOU TAKE LEFTOVERS FROM COOKING CLASS FOR YOUR BROTHER WHEN HE ALREADY HAS LUNCH.
HE SAYS THAT A PACKED LUNCH IS NOT ENOUGH.
HE'S ALWAYS HUNGRY AND SPENDING HIS MONEY ON FOOD.
WHERE IS TOMOYA?
HE GOES OFF SOMEWHERE EVERY DAY WITH HIS FRIEND DURING LUNCH HOUR.
AH, THANK YOU.
I WONDER IF HE'S AROUND SCHOOL.
Where is he?
Could he be? No!

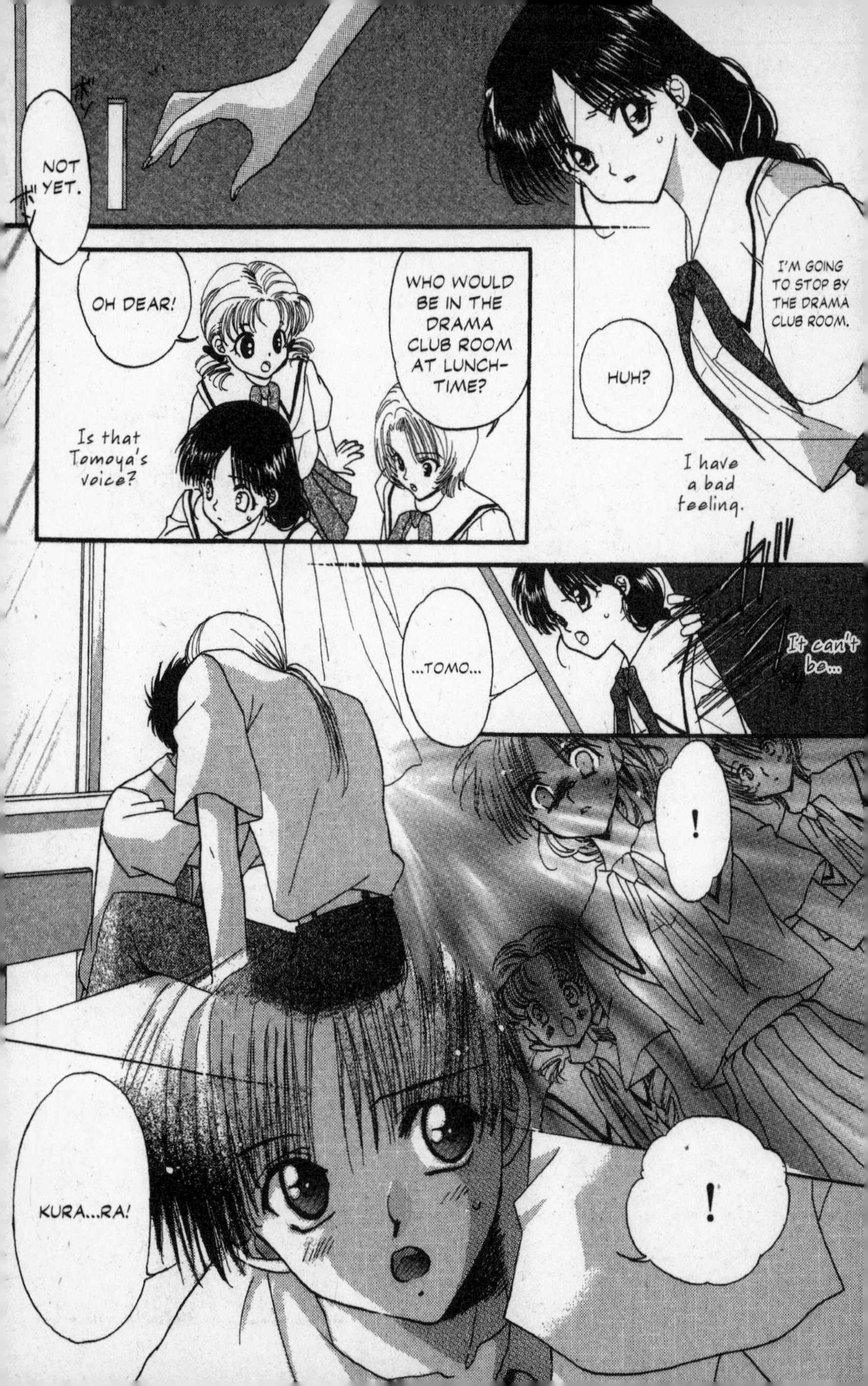
I'M GOING TO STOP BY THE DRAMA CLUB ROOM.
HUH?
I have a bad feeling.
NOT YET.
WHO WOULD BE IN THE DRAMA CLUB ROOM AT LUNCH-TIME?
OH DEAR!
Is that Tomoya's voice?
...TOMO...
It can't be...
!
!
KURA...RA!

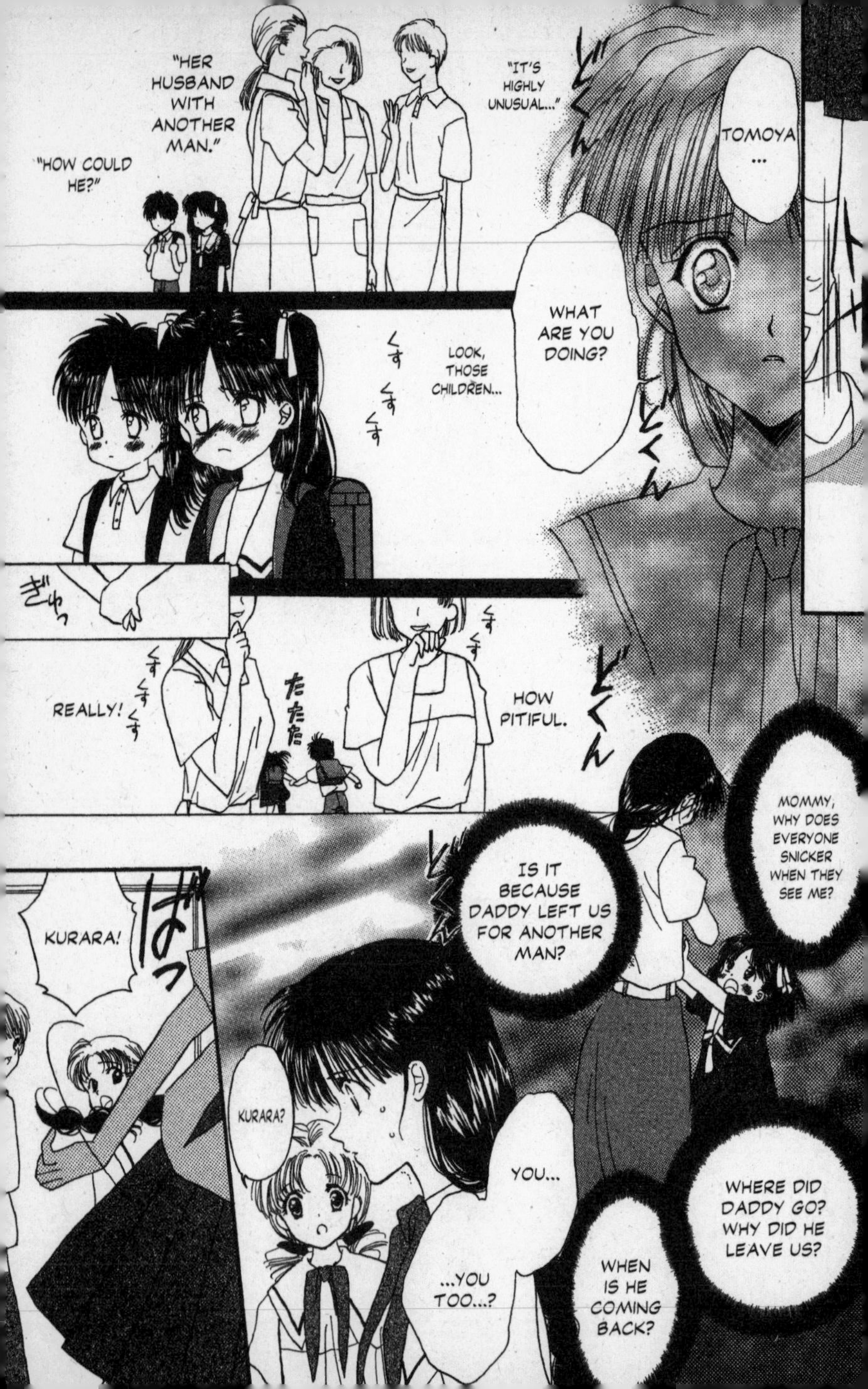
どくん
TOMOYA ...
WHAT ARE YOU DOING?
どくん
どくん
"IT'S HIGHLY UNUSUAL..."
"HER HUSBAND WITH ANOTHER MAN."
"HOW COULD HE?"
くす くす くす
LOOK, THOSE CHILDREN...
くす くす
HOW PITIFUL.
たたた
REALLY!
くす くす くす
ぎゅっ
MOMMY, WHY DOES EVERYONE SNICKER WHEN THEY SEE ME?
IS IT BECAUSE DADDY LEFT US FOR ANOTHER MAN?
WHERE DID DADDY GO? WHY DID HE LEAVE US?
WHEN IS HE COMING BACK?
YOU...
...YOU TOO...?
KURARA?
ばっ
KURARA!

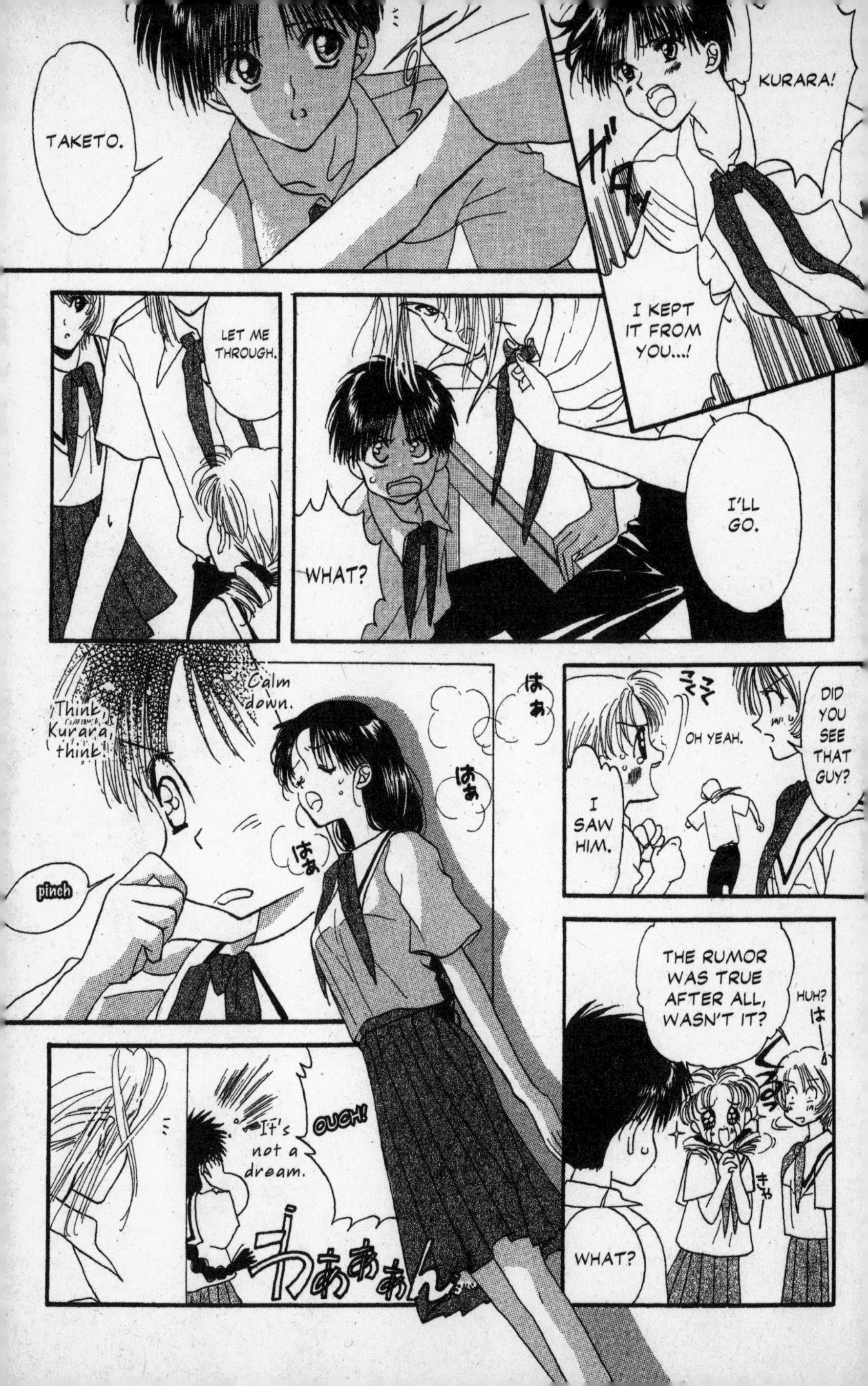
KURARA!
ガタッ
I KEPT IT FROM YOU...!
TAKETO.
I'LL GO.
WHAT?
LET ME THROUGH.
DID YOU SEE THAT GUY?
OH YEAH.
I SAW HIM.
はぁ
はぁ
はぁ
Calm down.
Think Kurara, think
pinch
THE RUMOR WAS TRUE AFTER ALL, WASN'T IT?
HUH?
は
WHAT?
OUCH!
It's not a dream.
わあああん

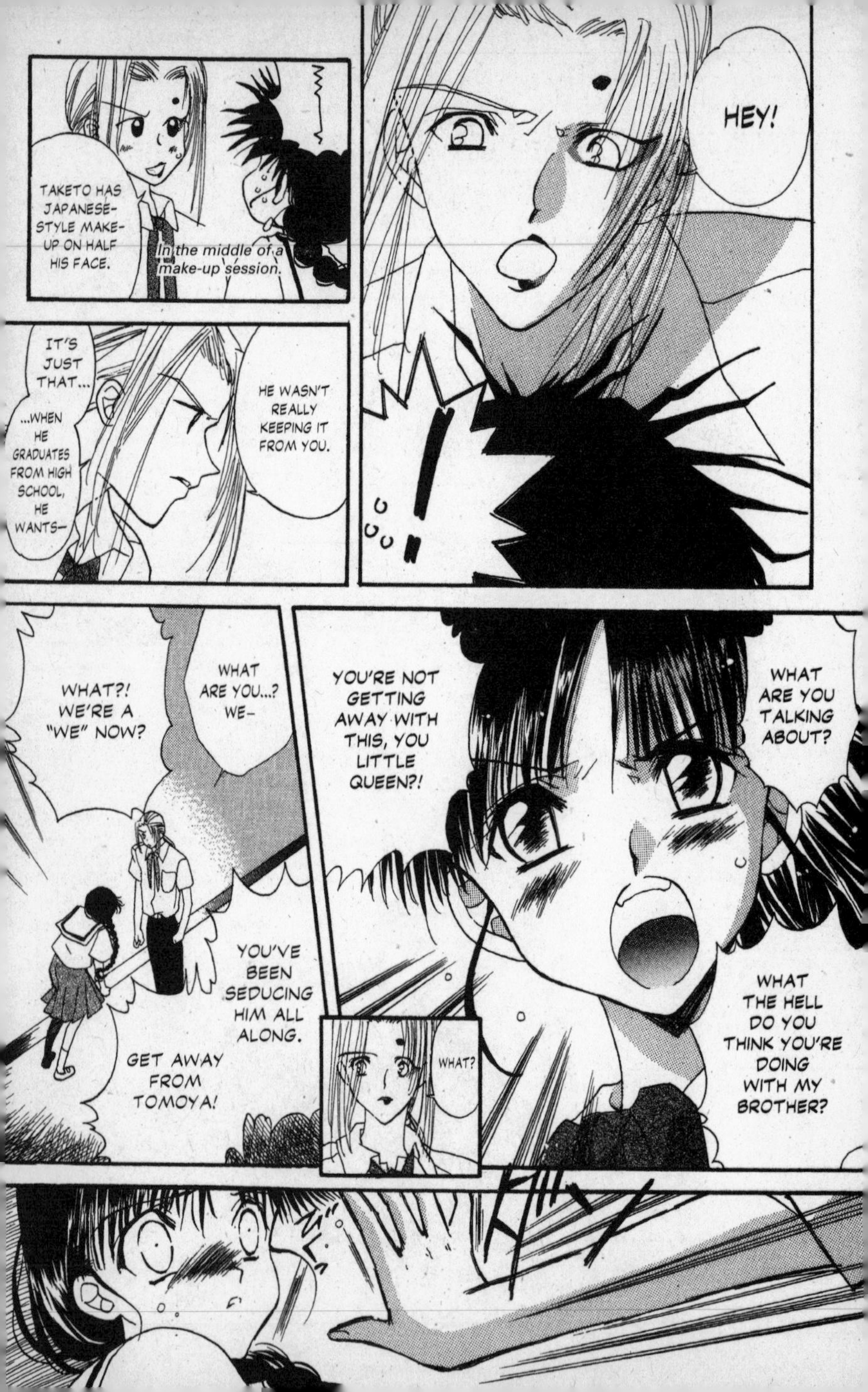
HEY!
!
TAKETO HAS JAPANESE-STYLE MAKE-UP ON HALF HIS FACE.
In the middle of a make-up session.
HE WASN'T REALLY KEEPING IT FROM YOU.
IT'S JUST THAT...
...WHEN HE GRADUATES FROM HIGH SCHOOL, HE WANTS—
WHAT ARE YOU TALKING ABOUT?
YOU'RE NOT GETTING AWAY WITH THIS, YOU LITTLE QUEEN?!
WHAT THE HELL DO YOU THINK YOU'RE DOING WITH MY BROTHER?
WHAT?
WHAT ARE YOU...? WE—
WHAT?! WE'RE A "WE" NOW?
YOU'VE BEEN SEDUCING HIM ALL ALONG.
GET AWAY FROM TOMOYA!

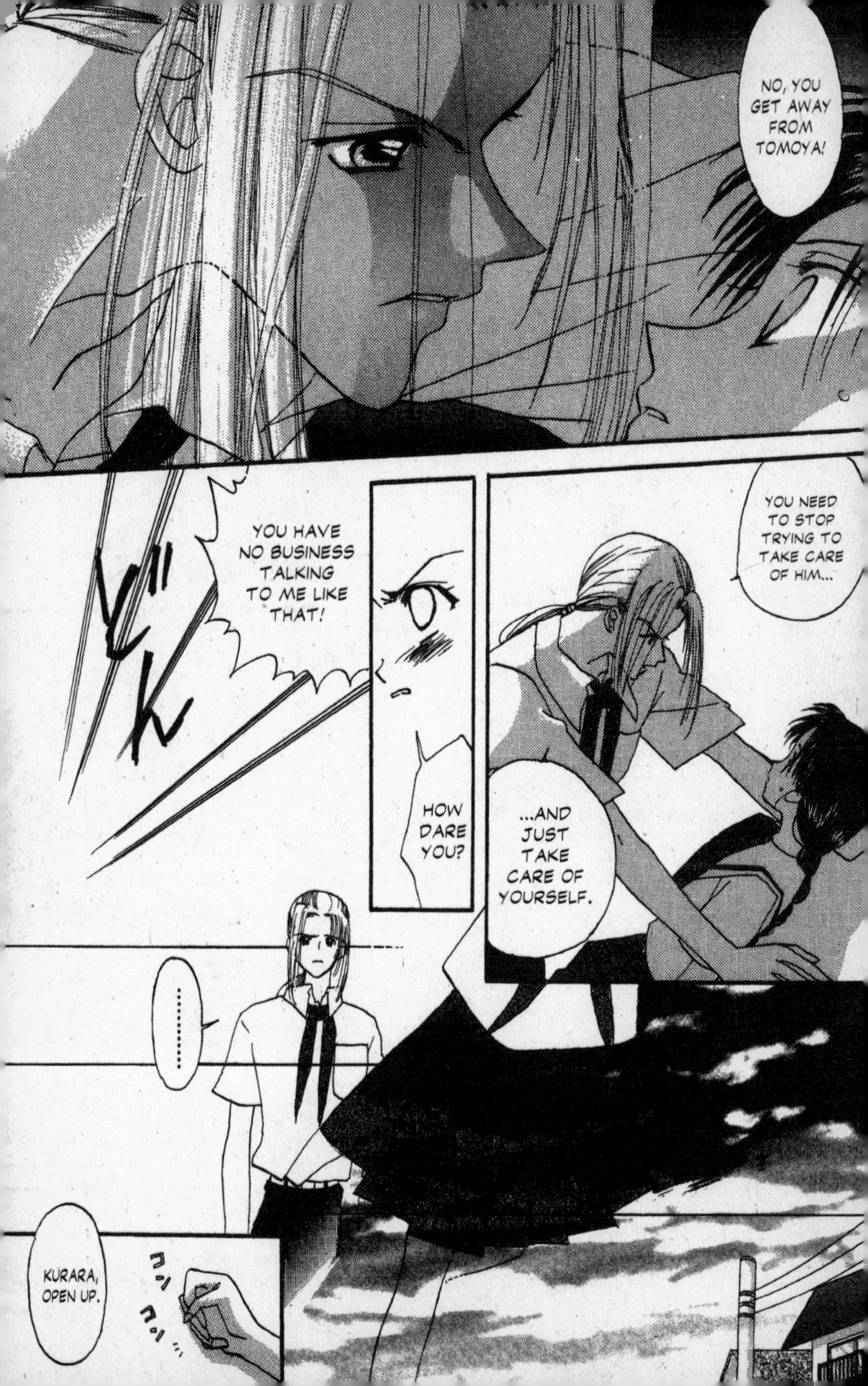
NO, YOU GET AWAY FROM TOMOYA!
YOU NEED TO STOP TRYING TO TAKE CARE OF HIM...
...AND JUST TAKE CARE OF YOURSELF.
HOW DARE YOU?
YOU HAVE NO BUSINESS TALKING TO ME LIKE THAT!
....
KURARA, OPEN UP.

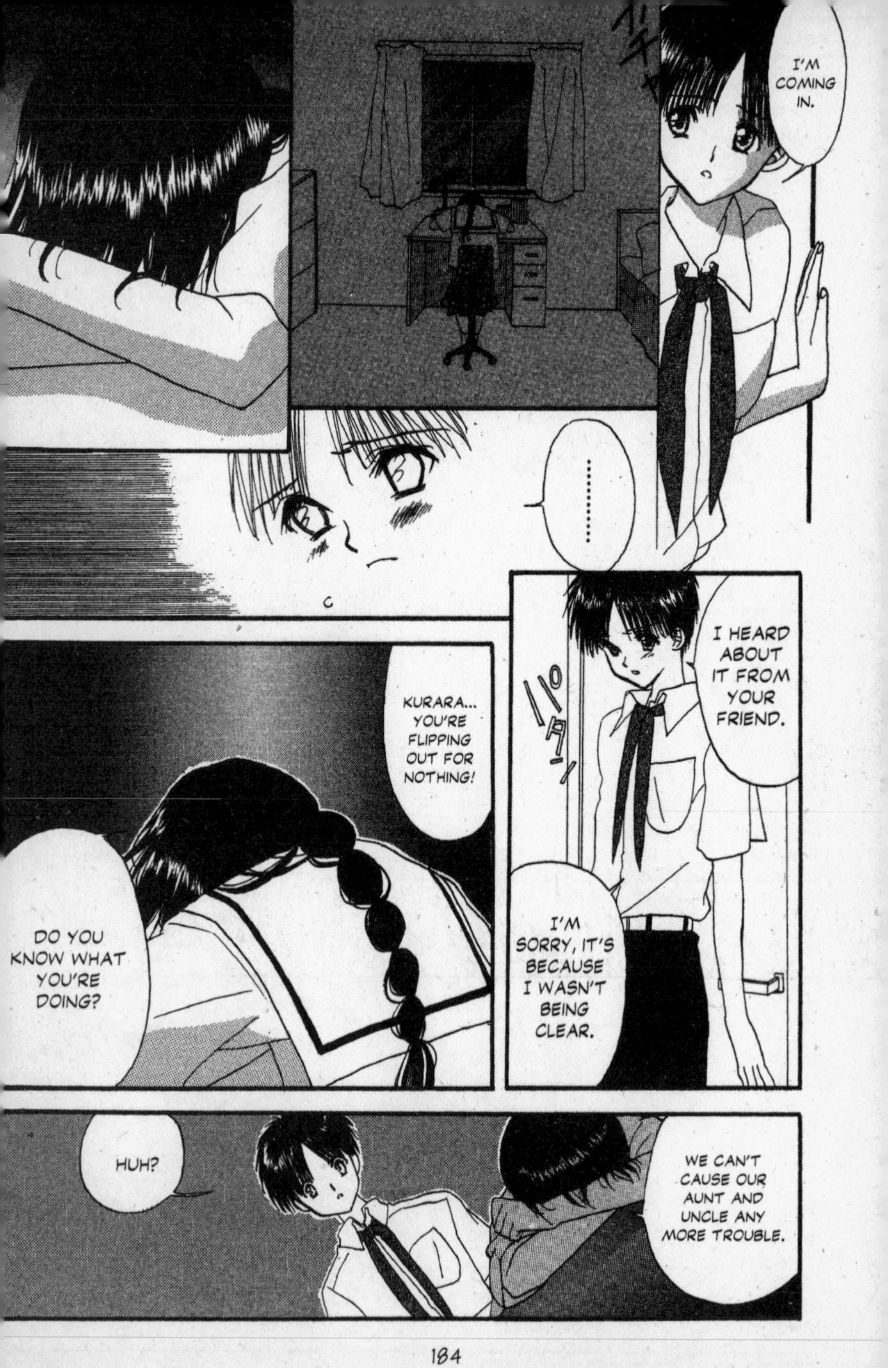
I'M COMING IN.
……
I HEARD ABOUT IT FROM YOUR FRIEND.
I'M SORRY, IT'S BECAUSE I WASN'T BEING CLEAR.
KURARA... YOU'RE FLIPPING OUT FOR NOTHING!
DO YOU KNOW WHAT YOU'RE DOING?
WE CAN'T CAUSE OUR AUNT AND UNCLE ANY MORE TROUBLE.
HUH?

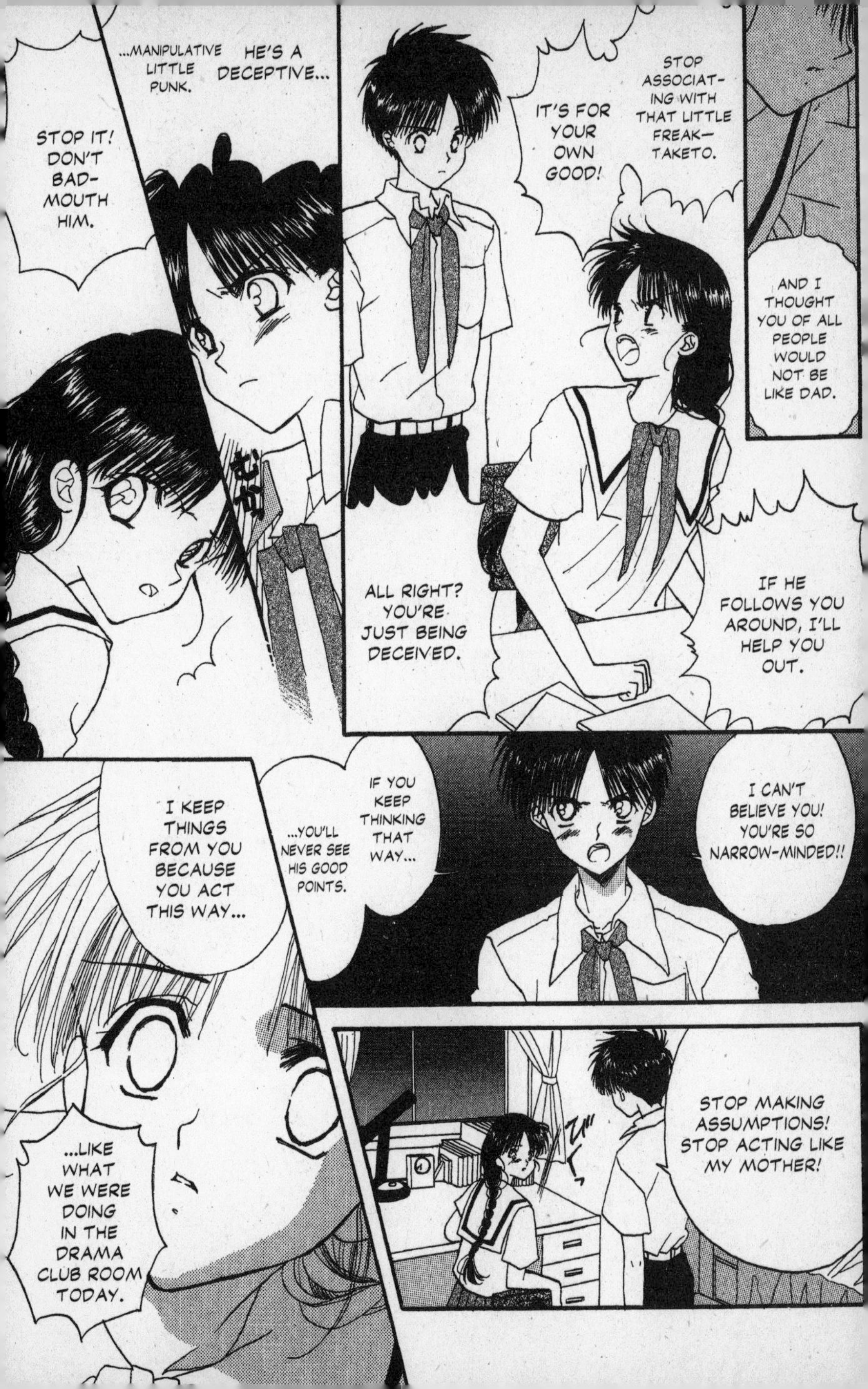
AND I THOUGHT YOU OF ALL PEOPLE WOULD NOT BE LIKE DAD.
STOP ASSOCIATING WITH THAT LITTLE FREAK—TAKETO.
IT'S FOR YOUR OWN GOOD!
IF HE FOLLOWS YOU AROUND, I'LL HELP YOU OUT.
ALL RIGHT? YOU'RE JUST BEING DECEIVED.
HE'S A DECEPTIVE...
...MANIPULATIVE LITTLE PUNK.
STOP IT! DON'T BAD-MOUTH HIM.
I CAN'T BELIEVE YOU! YOU'RE SO NARROW-MINDED!!
IF YOU KEEP THINKING THAT WAY...
...YOU'LL NEVER SEE HIS GOOD POINTS.
STOP MAKING ASSUMPTIONS! STOP ACTING LIKE MY MOTHER!
I KEEP THINGS FROM YOU BECAUSE YOU ACT THIS WAY...
...LIKE WHAT WE WERE DOING IN THE DRAMA CLUB ROOM TODAY.

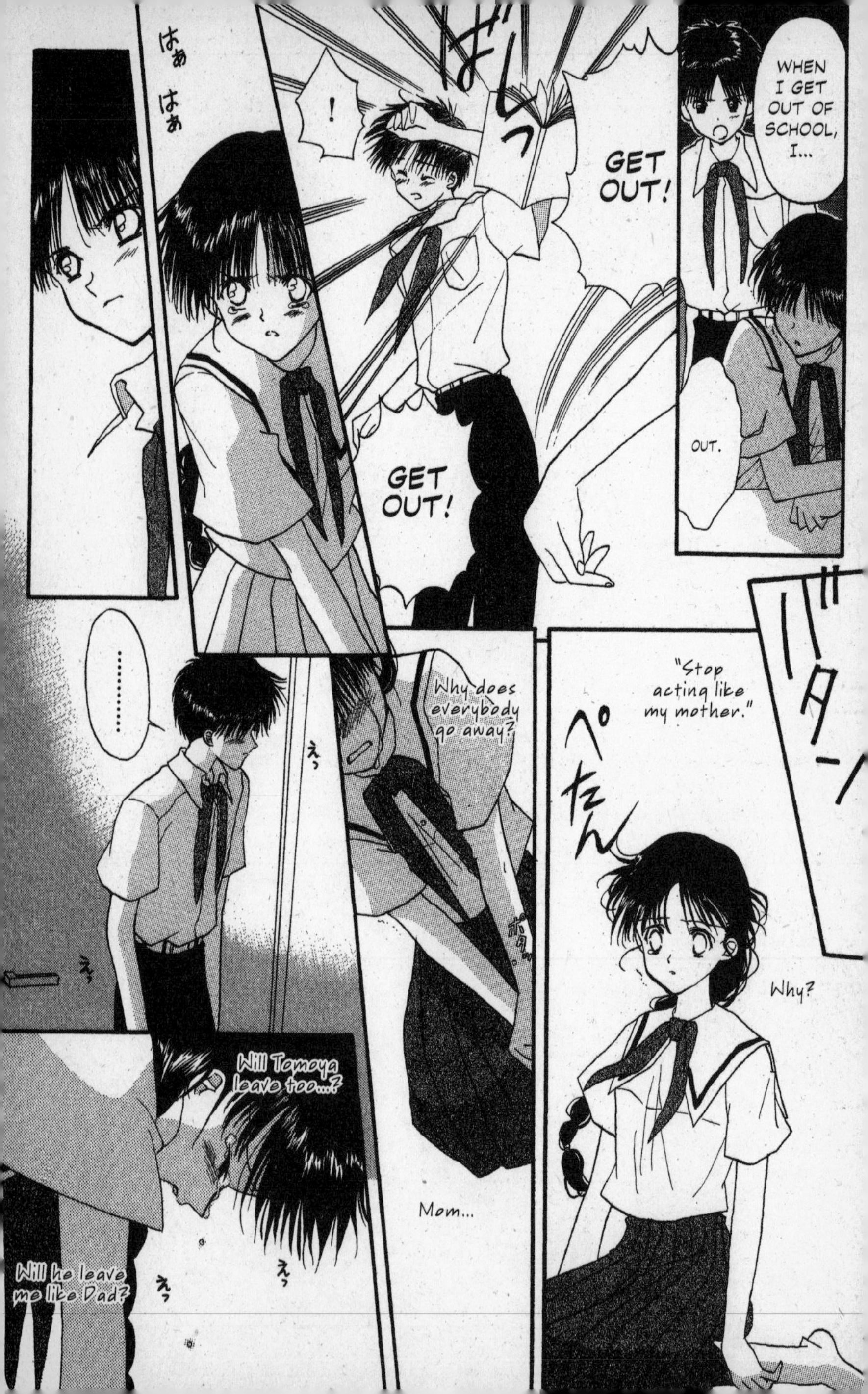
WHEN I GET OUT OF SCHOOL, I...
OUT.
ばしっ
!
GET OUT!
GET OUT!
はぁ はぁ
バターン
ぺたん
"Stop acting like my mother."
Why?
Why does everybody go away?
Mom...
えっ
......
えっ
Will Tomoya leave too...?
Will he leave me like Dad?
えっ
えっ

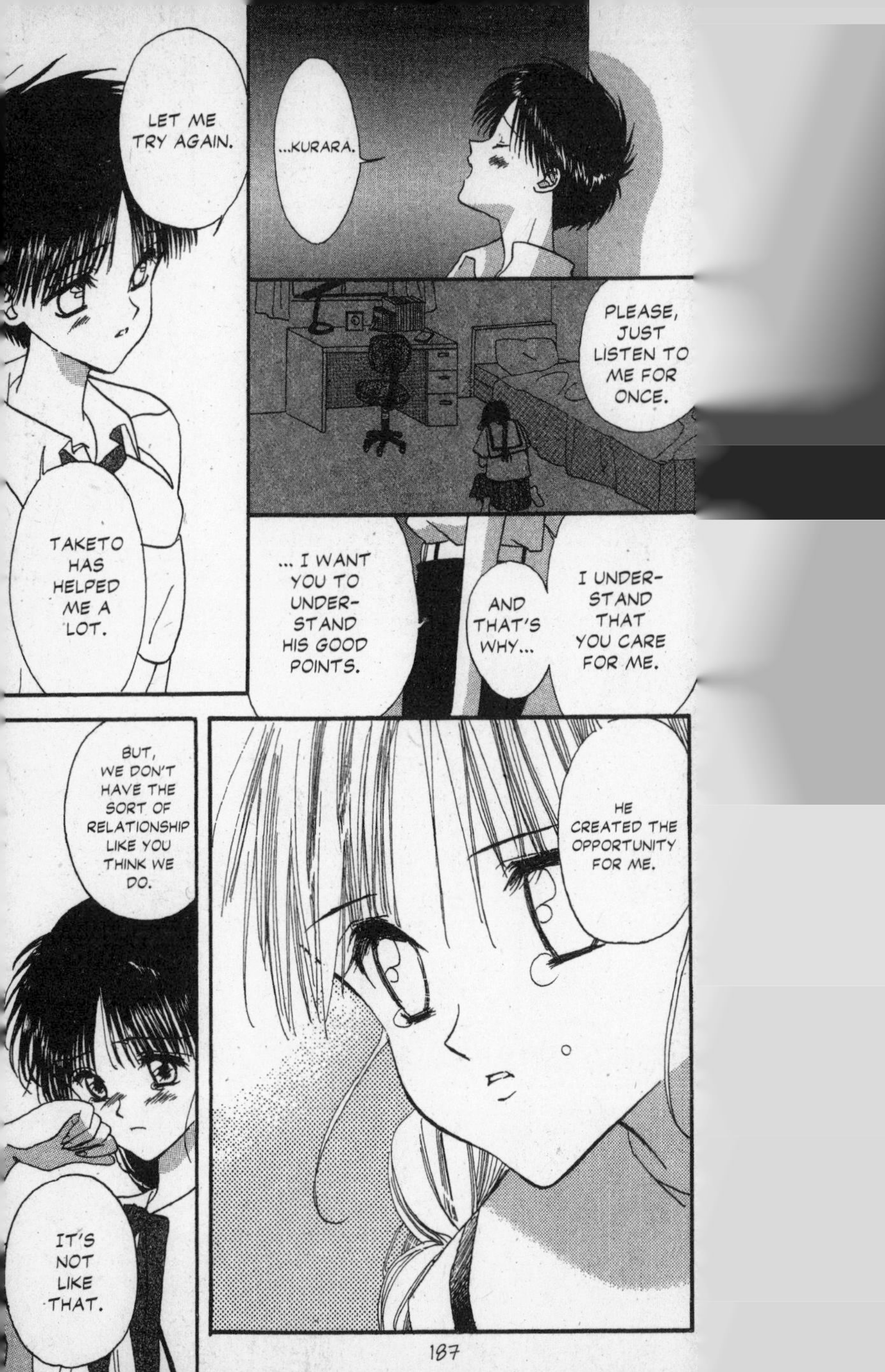
...KURARA.
PLEASE, JUST LISTEN TO ME FOR ONCE.
I UNDER-STAND THAT YOU CARE FOR ME.
AND THAT'S WHY...
... I WANT YOU TO UNDER-STAND HIS GOOD POINTS.
LET ME TRY AGAIN.
TAKETO HAS HELPED ME A LOT.
HE CREATED THE OPPORTUNITY FOR ME.
BUT, WE DON'T HAVE THE SORT OF RELATIONSHIP LIKE YOU THINK WE DO.
IT'S NOT LIKE THAT.

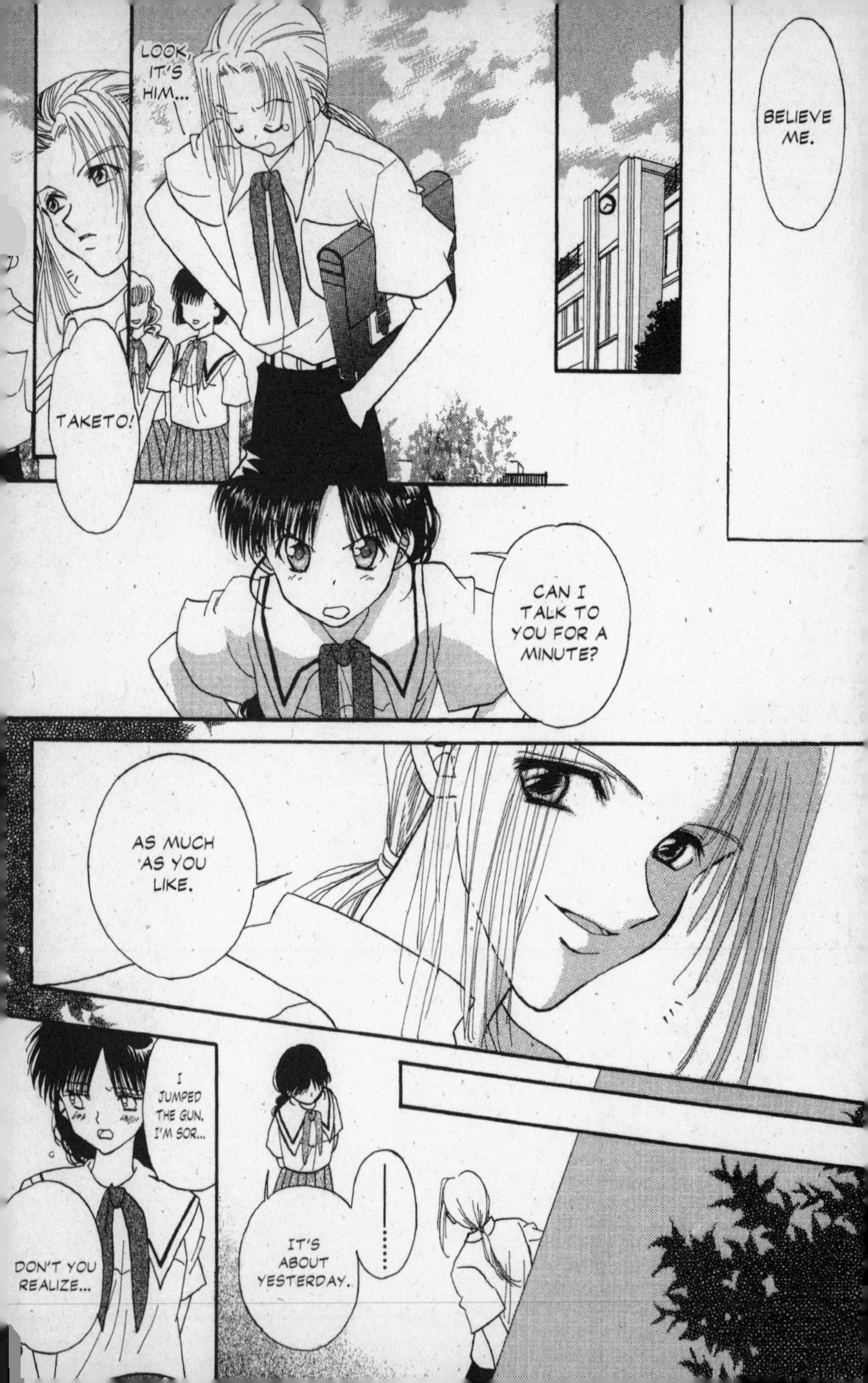
BELIEVE ME.
LOOK, IT'S HIM...
TAKETO!
CAN I TALK TO YOU FOR A MINUTE?
AS MUCH AS YOU LIKE.
......
IT'S ABOUT YESTERDAY.
I JUMPED THE GUN. I'M SOR...
DON'T YOU REALIZE...

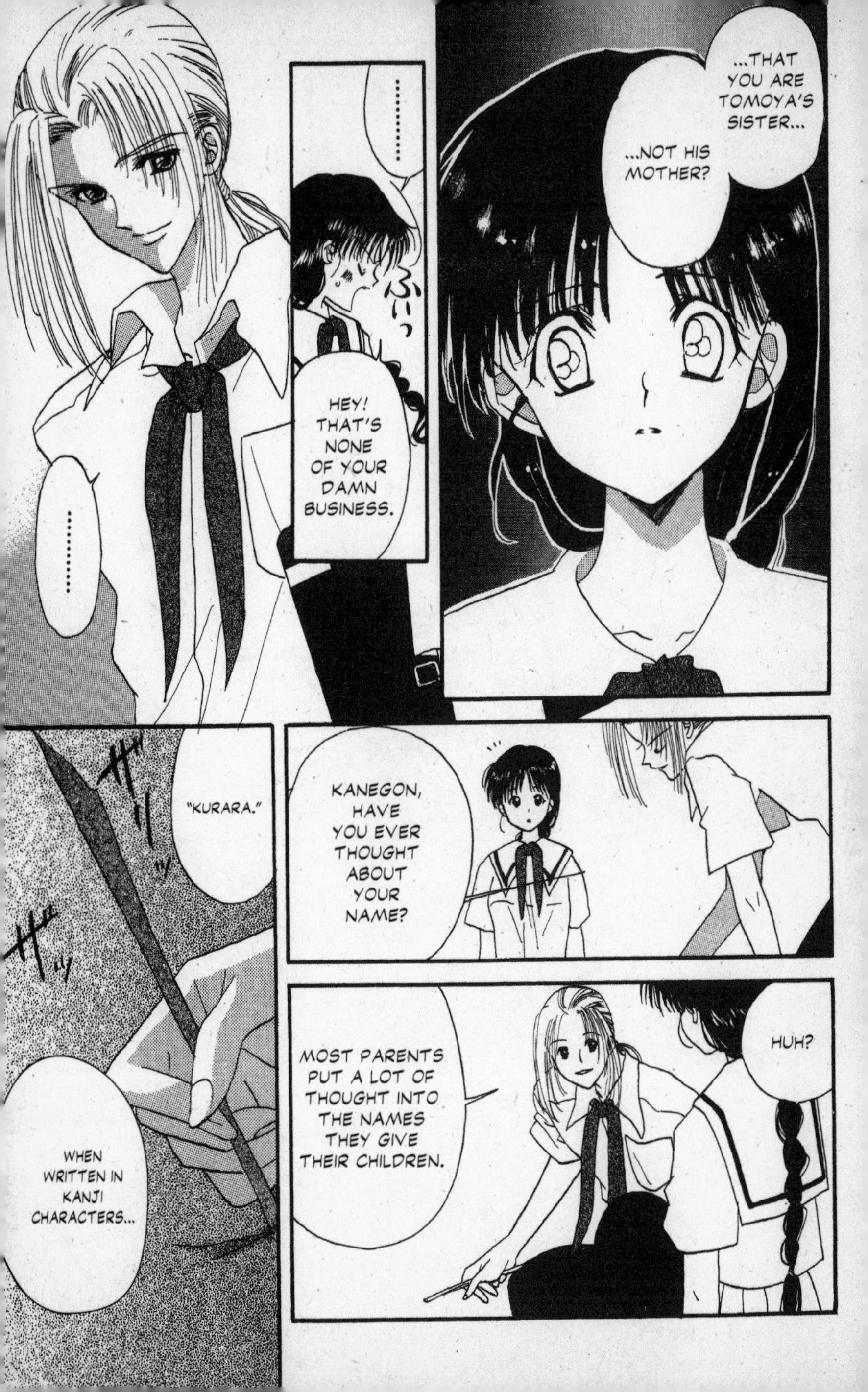
...THAT YOU ARE TOMOYA'S SISTER...
...NOT HIS MOTHER?
....
ふいっ
HEY! THAT'S NONE OF YOUR DAMN BUSINESS.
....
KANEGON, HAVE YOU EVER THOUGHT ABOUT YOUR NAME?
HUH?
MOST PARENTS PUT A LOT OF THOUGHT INTO THE NAMES THEY GIVE THEIR CHILDREN.
"KURARA."
WHEN WRITTEN IN KANJI CHARACTERS...

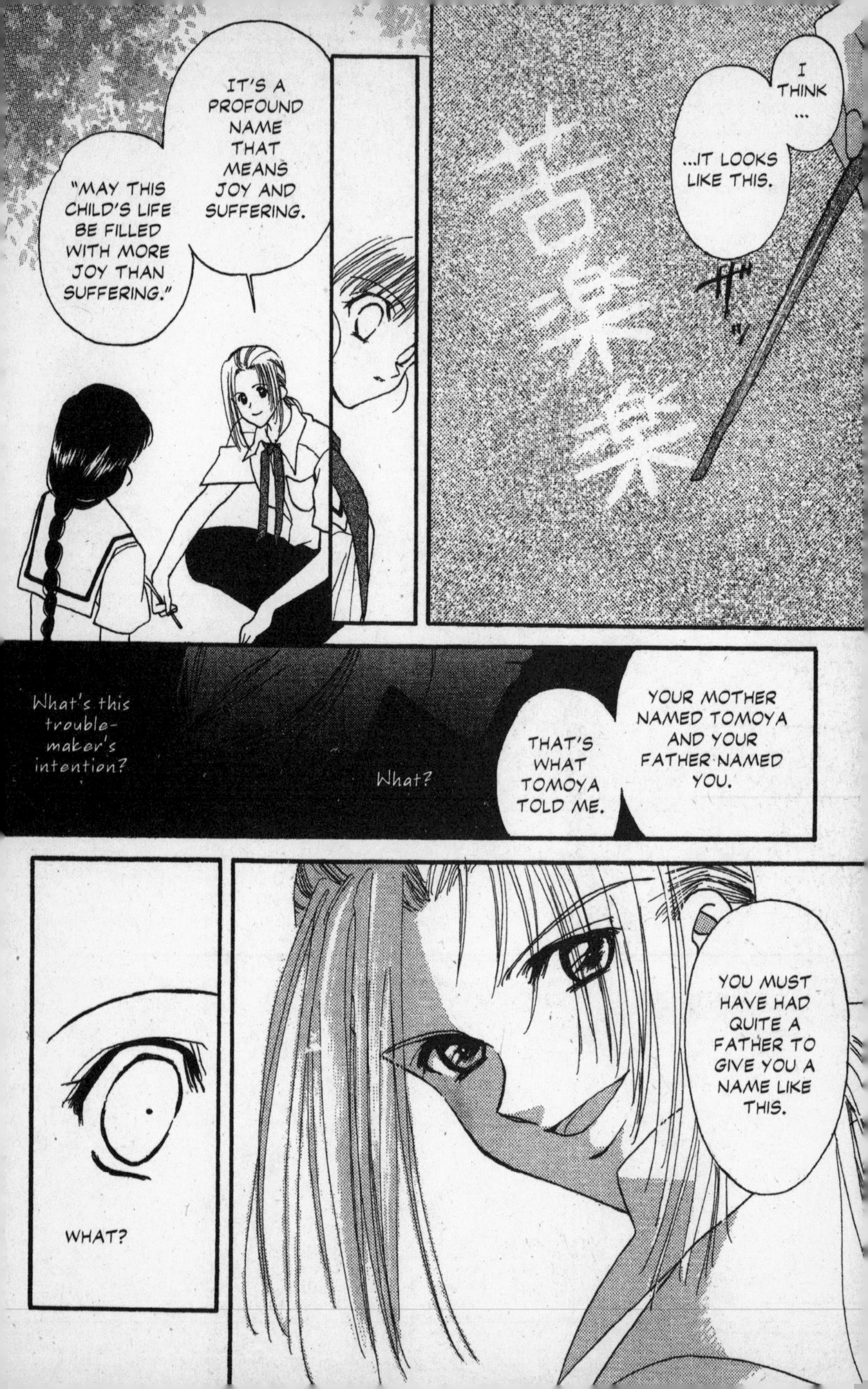
I THINK...
...IT LOOKS LIKE THIS.
ザッ
IT'S A PROFOUND NAME THAT MEANS JOY AND SUFFERING.
"MAY THIS CHILD'S LIFE BE FILLED WITH MORE JOY THAN SUFFERING."
YOUR MOTHER NAMED TOMOYA AND YOUR FATHER NAMED YOU.
THAT'S WHAT TOMOYA TOLD ME.
What?
What's this trouble-maker's intention?
YOU MUST HAVE HAD QUITE A FATHER TO GIVE YOU A NAME LIKE THIS.
WHAT?

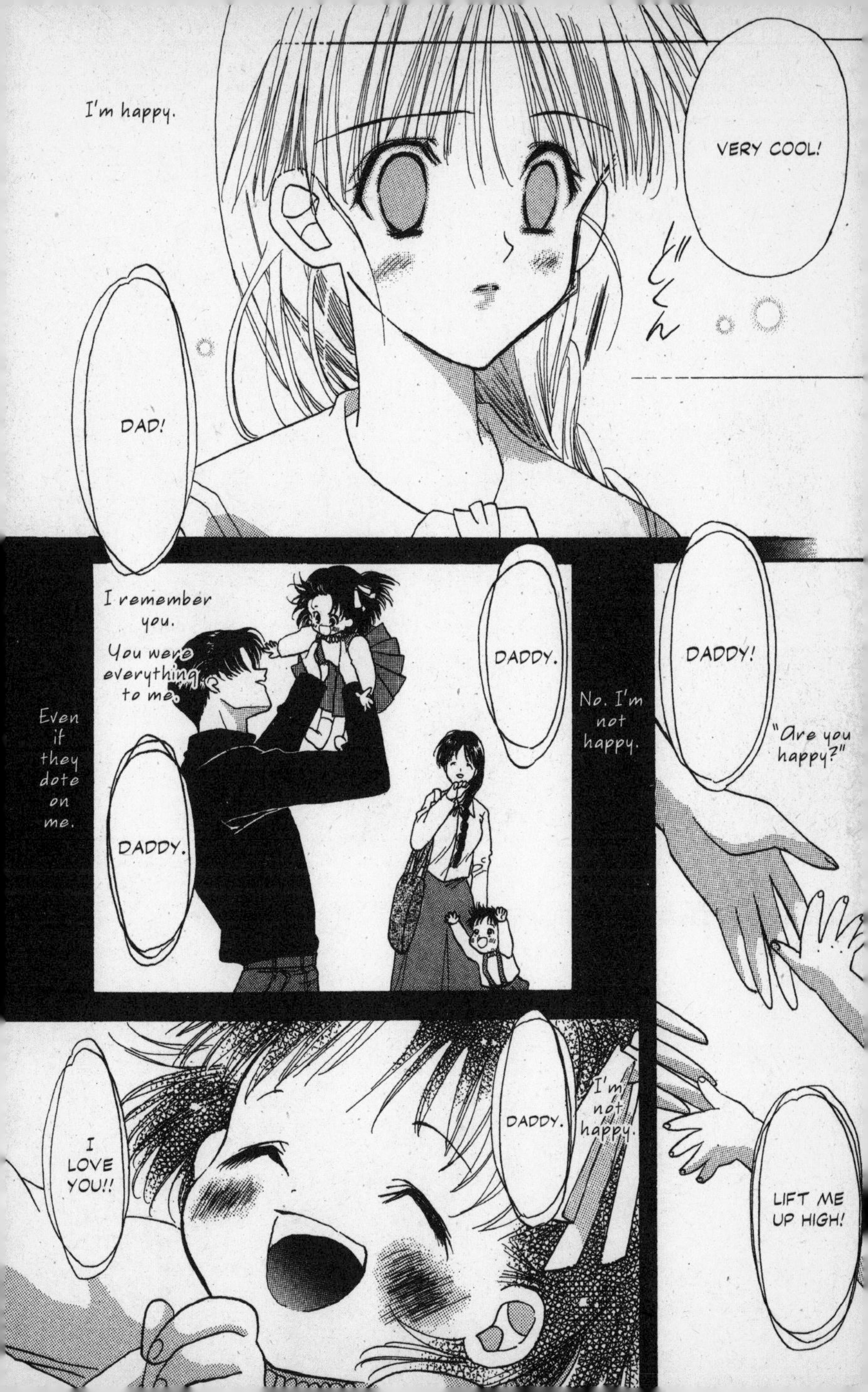
VERY COOL!
どしん
I'm happy.
DAD!
DADDY!
"Are you happy?"
No. I'm not happy.
DADDY.
I remember you.
You were everything to me.
DADDY.
Even if they dote on me.
LIFT ME UP HIGH!
I'm not happy.
DADDY.
I LOVE YOU!!

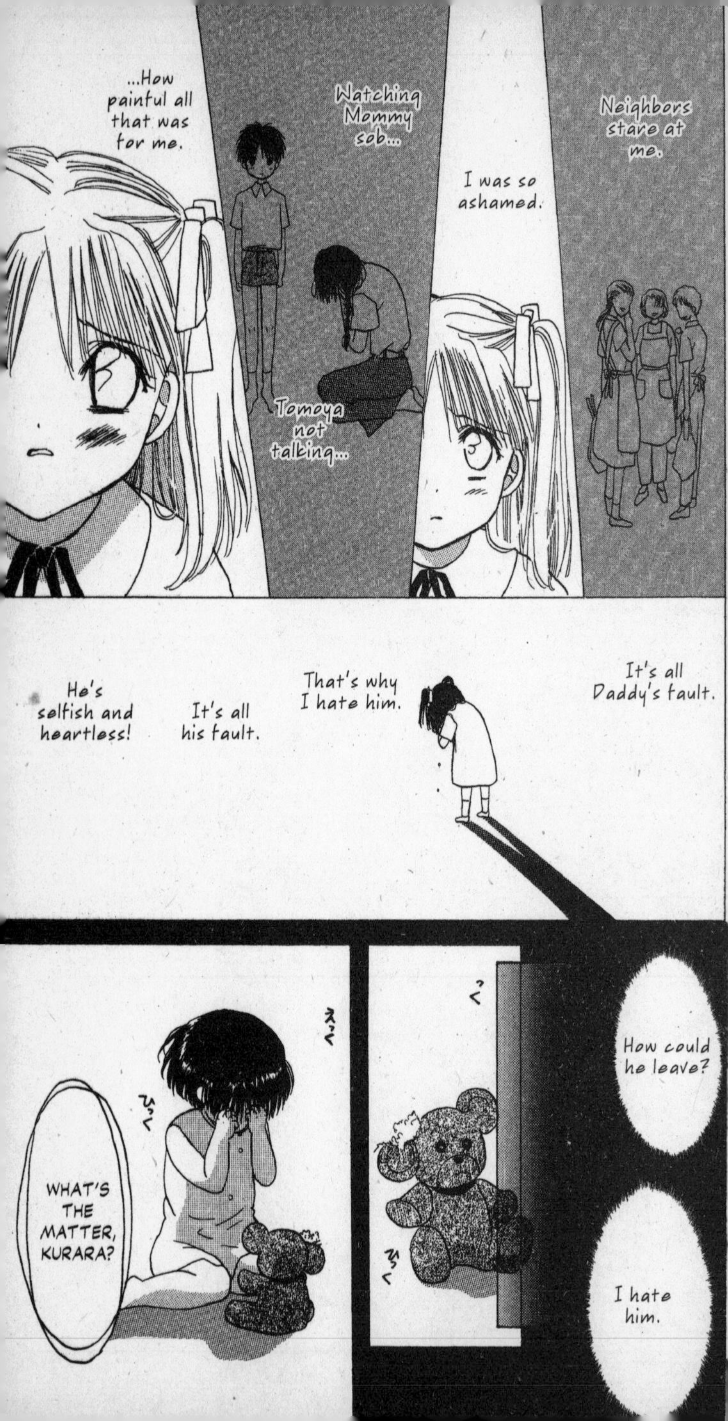
Neighbors stare at me.
I was so ashamed.
Watching Mommy sob...
Tomoya not talking...
...How painful all that was for me.
It's all Daddy's fault.
That's why I hate him.
It's all his fault.
He's selfish and heartless!
How could he leave?
I hate him.
ひっく
えっく
ひっく
WHAT'S THE MATTER, KURARA?

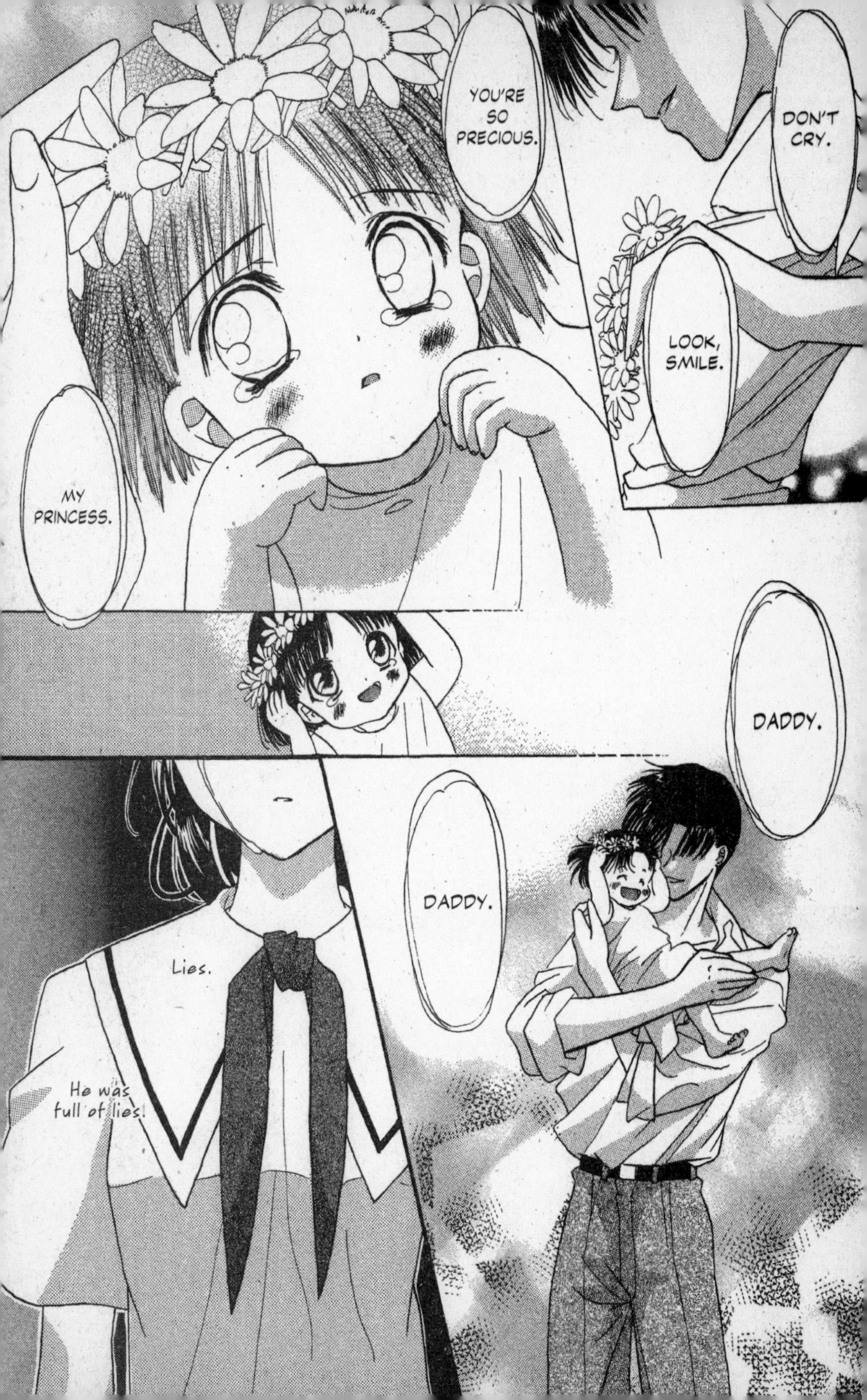
DON'T CRY.
LOOK, SMILE.
YOU'RE SO PRECIOUS.
MY PRINCESS.
DADDY.
DADDY.
Lies.
He was full of lies!

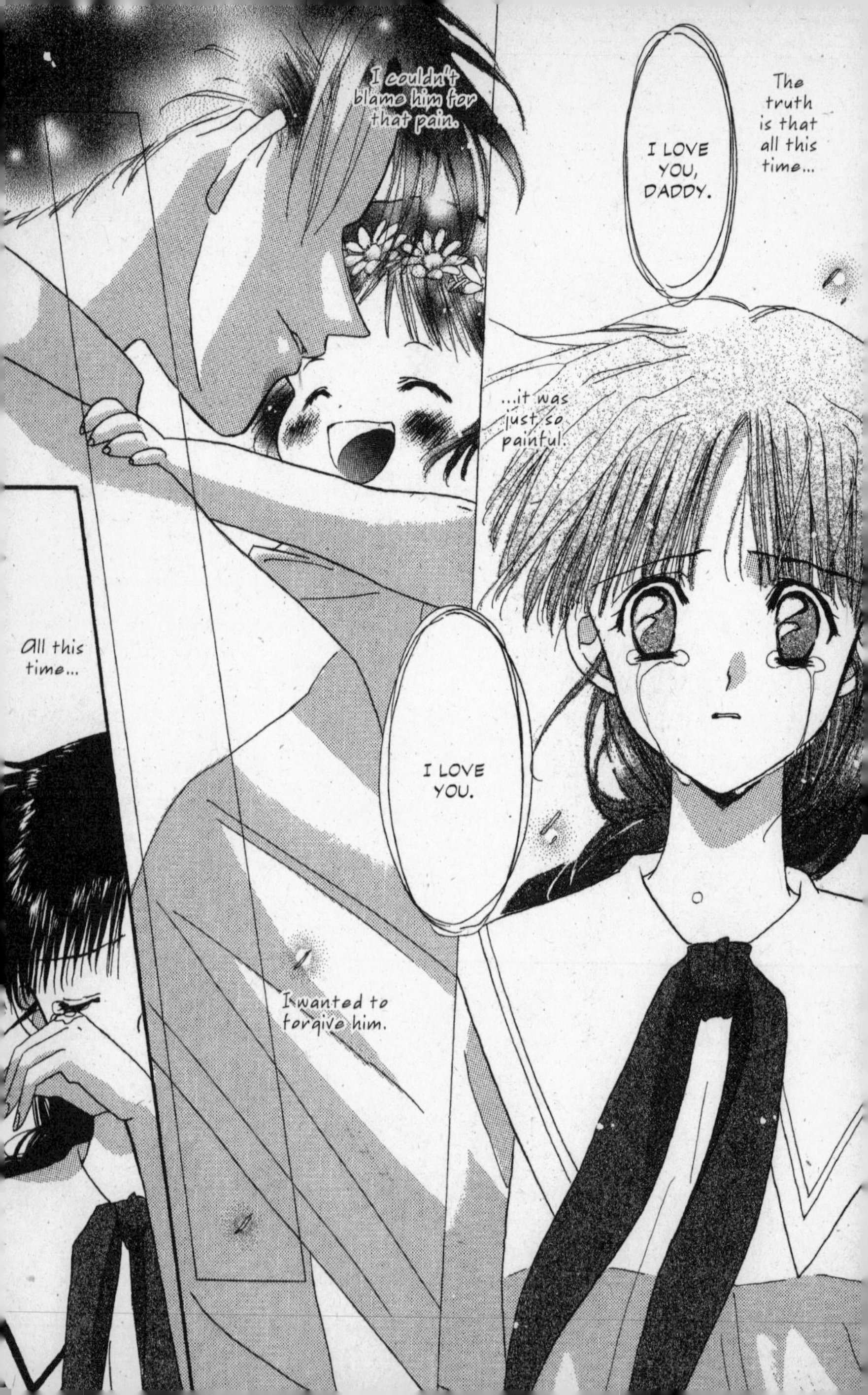
The truth is that all this time...
I LOVE YOU, DADDY.
...it was just so painful.
I LOVE YOU.
I couldn't blame him for that pain.
I wanted to forgive him.
All this time...

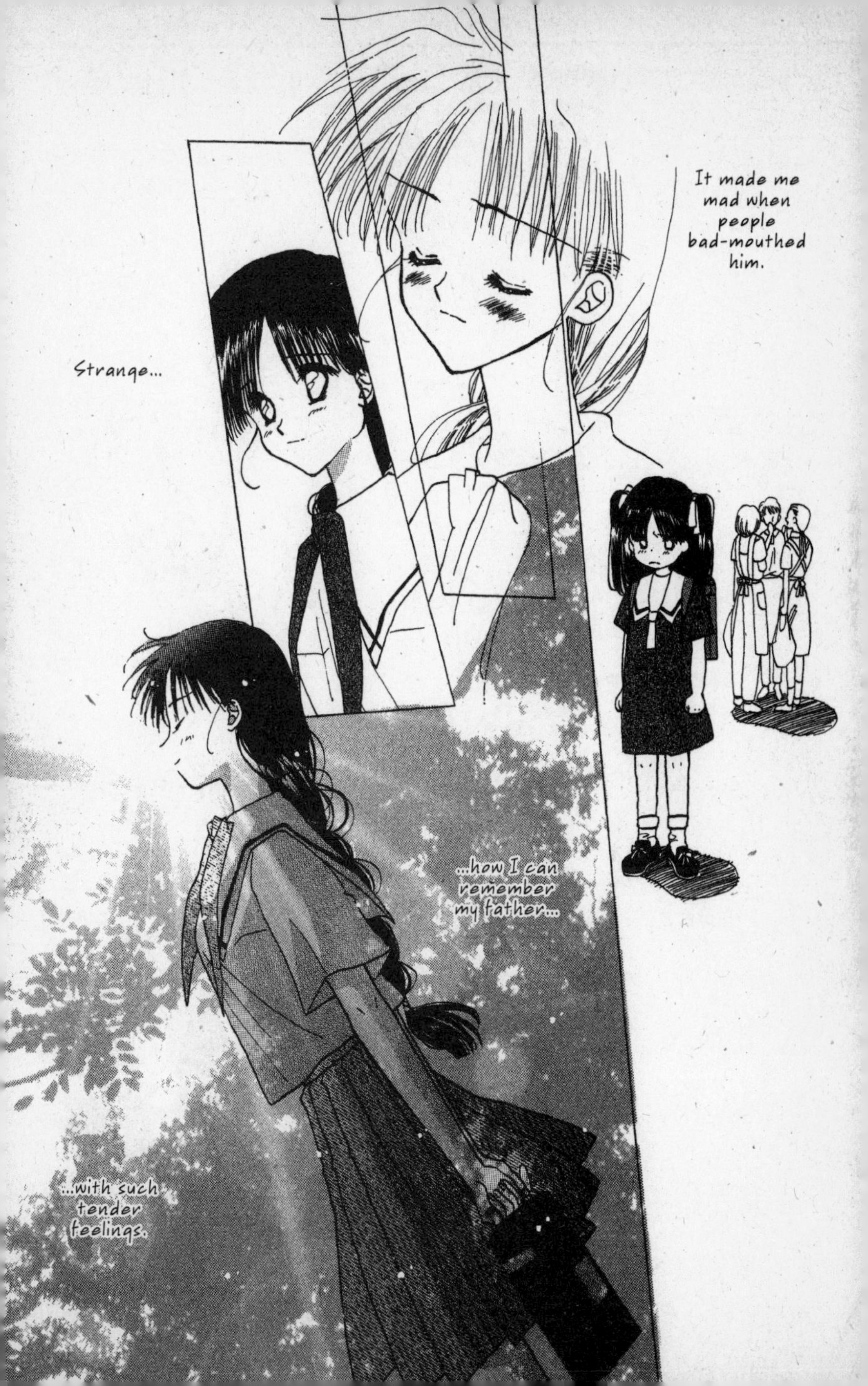
It made me mad when people bad-mouthed him.
Strange...
...how I can remember my father...
...with such tender feelings.

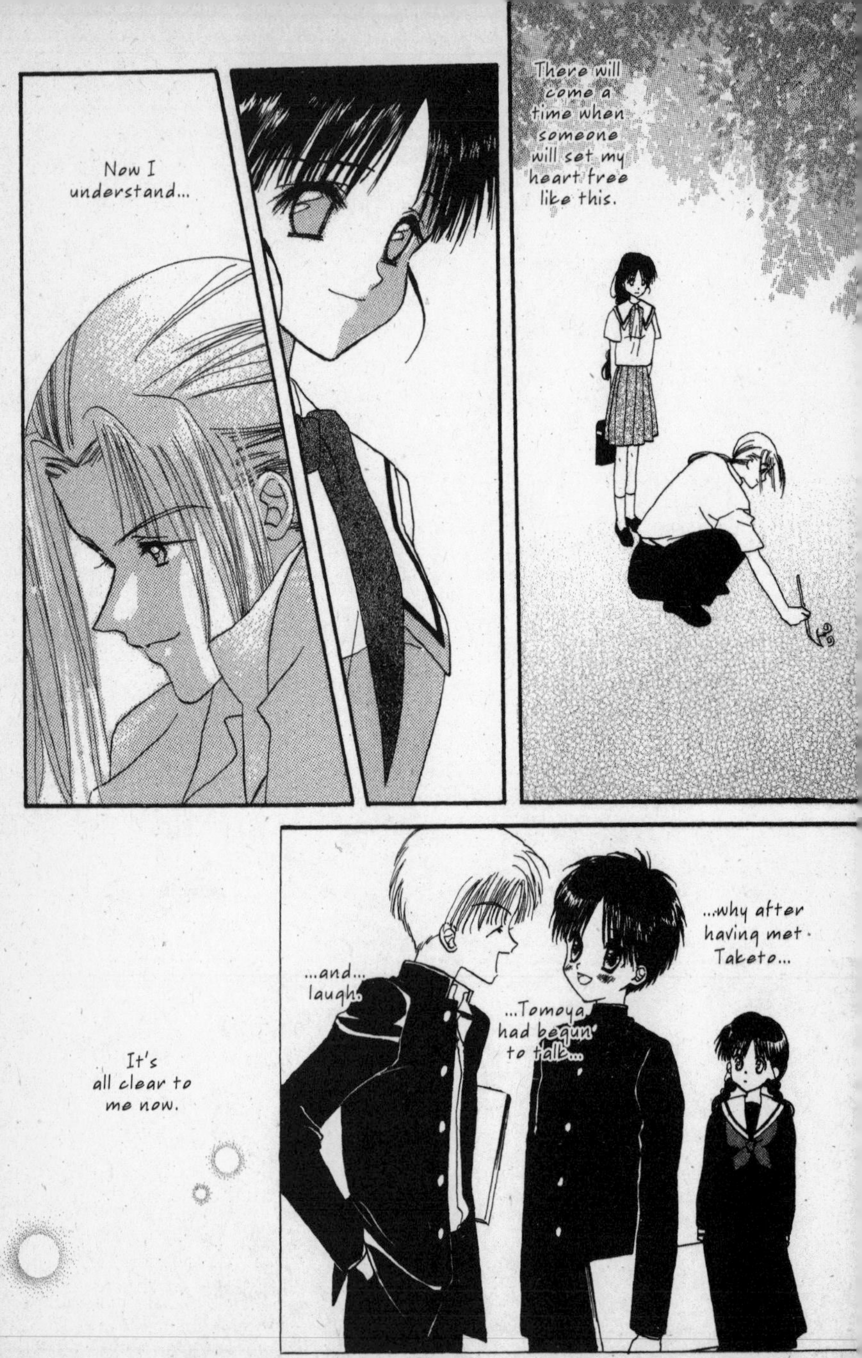
There will come a time when someone will set my heart free like this.
Now I understand...
...why after having met Taketo...
...Tomoya had begun to talk...
...and... laugh.
It's all clear to me now.

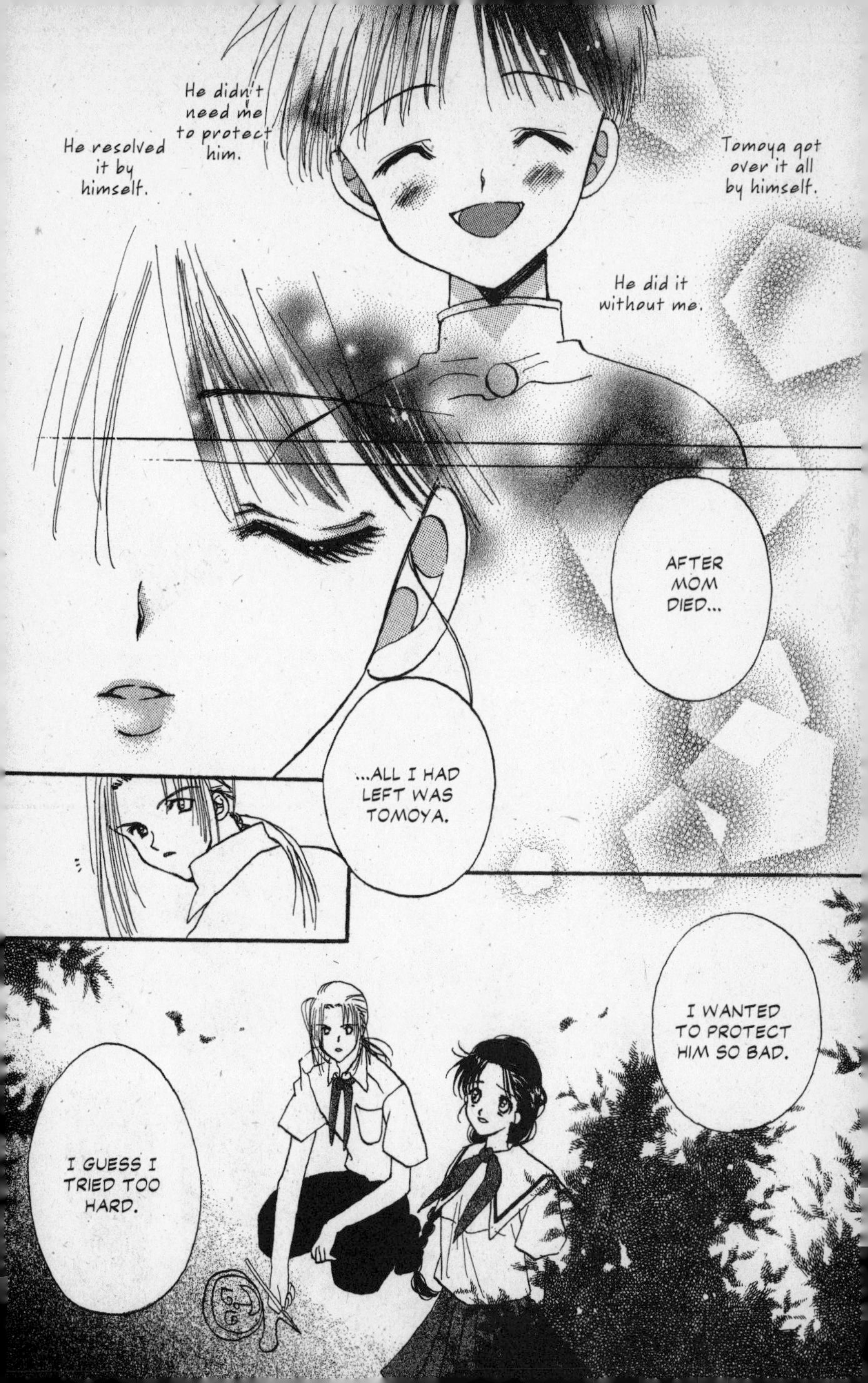
Tomoya got over it all by himself.
He didn't need me to protect him.
He resolved it by himself.
He did it without me.
AFTER MOM DIED...
...ALL I HAD LEFT WAS TOMOYA.
I WANTED TO PROTECT HIM SO BAD.
I GUESS I TRIED TOO HARD.

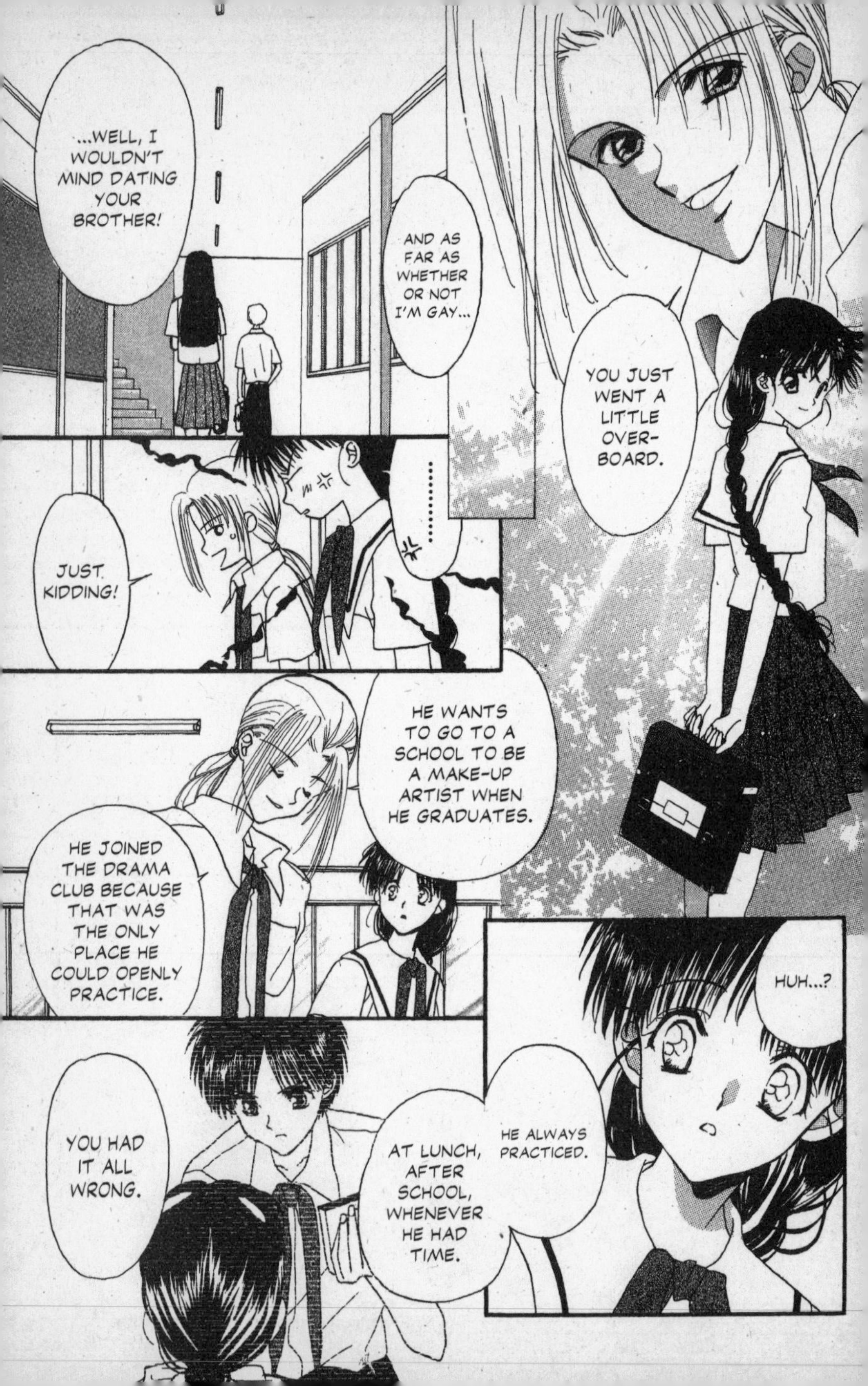
YOU JUST WENT A LITTLE OVER-BOARD.
AND AS FAR AS WHETHER OR NOT I'M GAY...
...WELL, I WOULDN'T MIND DATING YOUR BROTHER!
......
JUST KIDDING!
HE WANTS TO GO TO A SCHOOL TO BE A MAKE-UP ARTIST WHEN HE GRADUATES.
HE JOINED THE DRAMA CLUB BECAUSE THAT WAS THE ONLY PLACE HE COULD OPENLY PRACTICE.
HUH...?
HE ALWAYS PRACTICED.
AT LUNCH, AFTER SCHOOL, WHENEVER HE HAD TIME.
YOU HAD IT ALL WRONG.

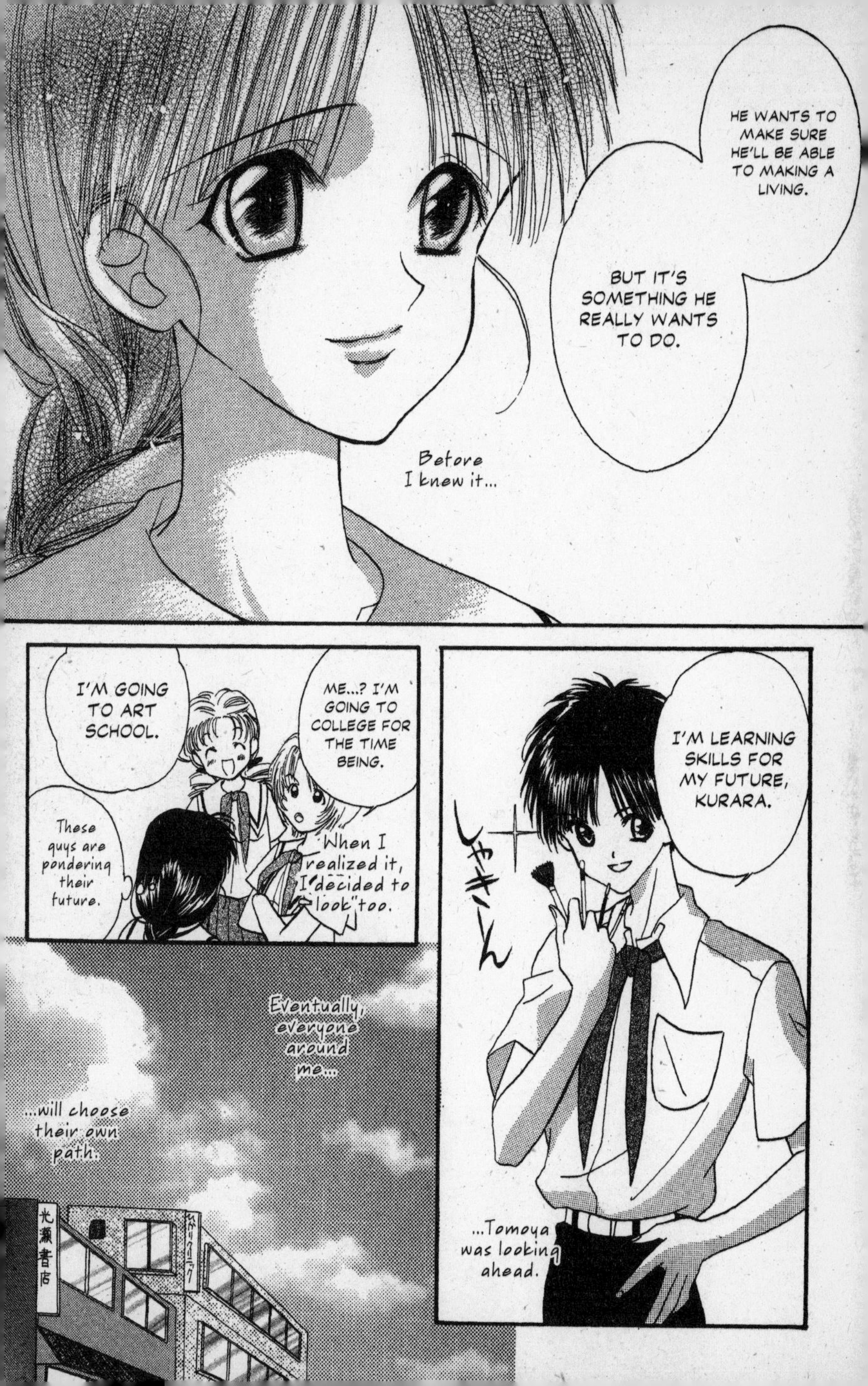
HE WANTS TO MAKE SURE HE'LL BE ABLE TO MAKING A LIVING.
BUT IT'S SOMETHING HE REALLY WANTS TO DO.
Before I knew it...
I'M LEARNING SKILLS FOR MY FUTURE, KURARA.
しゃきーん
...Tomoya was looking ahead.
ME...? I'M GOING TO COLLEGE FOR THE TIME BEING.
I'M GOING TO ART SCHOOL.
When I realized it, I decided to "look" too.
These guys are pondering their future.
Eventually, everyone around me...
...will choose their own path.
光瀬書店

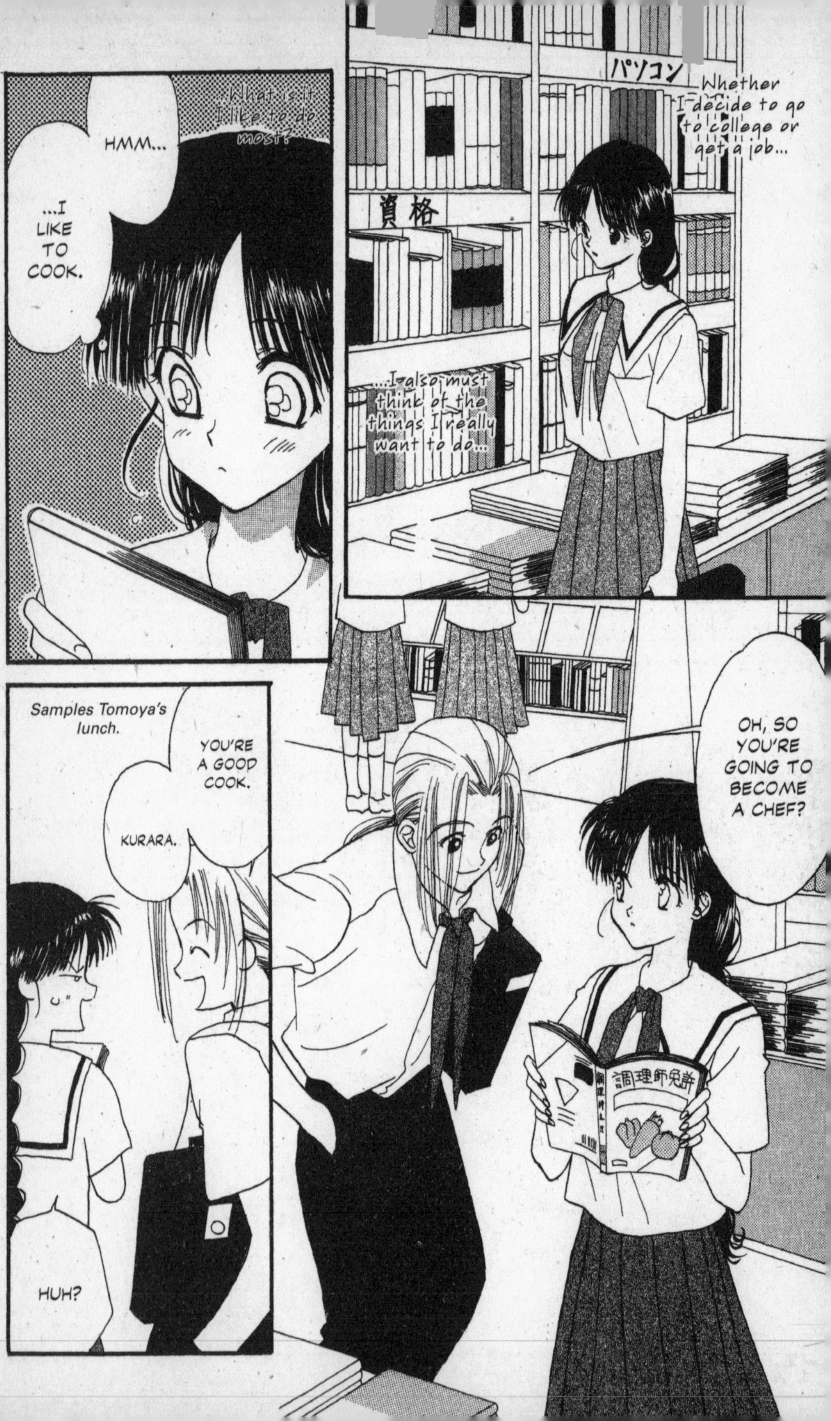
パソコン
Whether I decide to go to college or get a job...
資格
...I also must think of the things I really want to do...
What is it I like to do most?
HMM...
...I LIKE TO COOK.
OH, SO YOU'RE GOING TO BECOME A CHEF?
調理師免許
Samples Tomoya's lunch.
YOU'RE A GOOD COOK.
KURARA.
HUH?

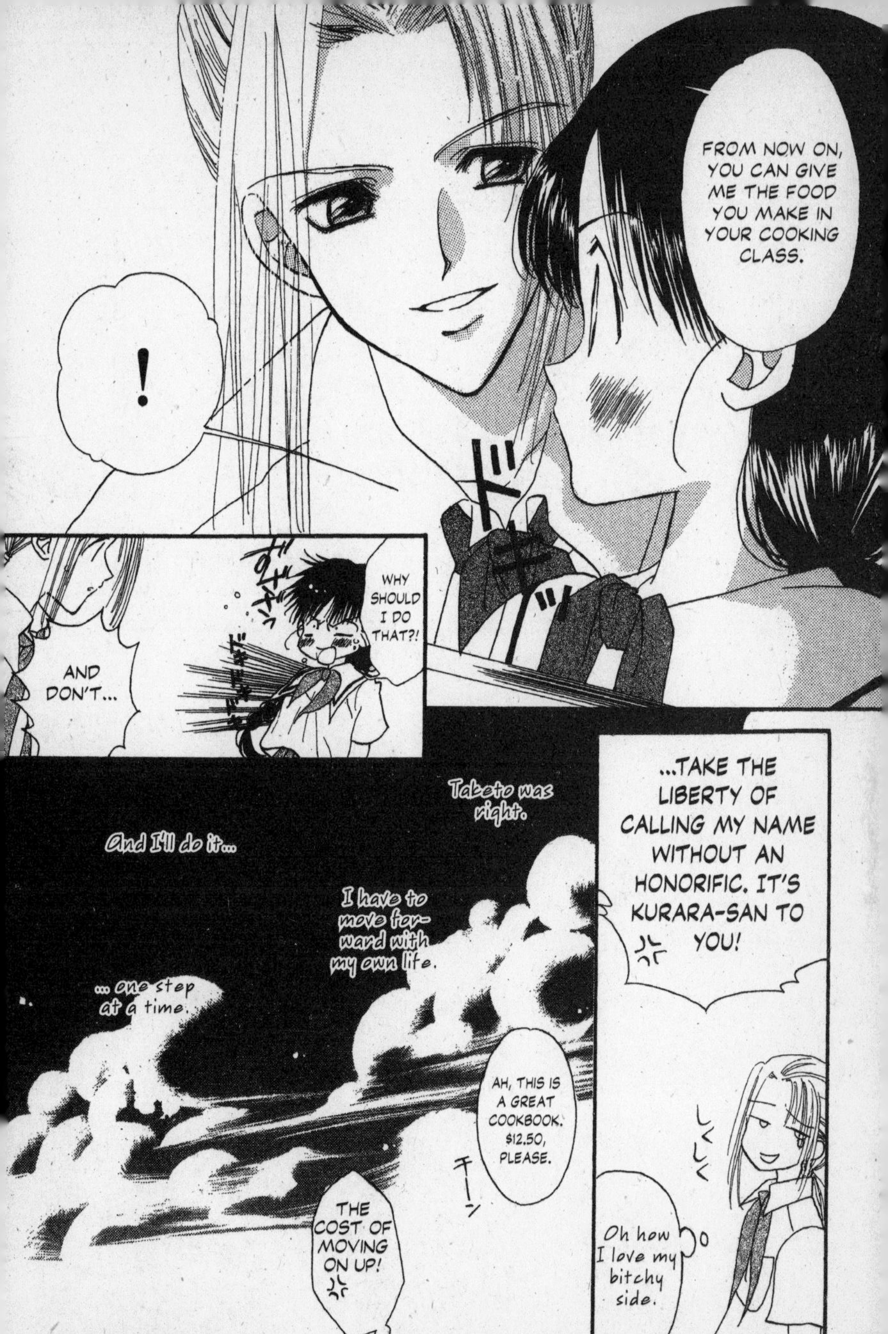
FROM NOW ON, YOU CAN GIVE ME THE FOOD YOU MAKE IN YOUR COOKING CLASS.
!
WHY SHOULD I DO THAT?!
AND DON'T...
...TAKE THE LIBERTY OF CALLING MY NAME WITHOUT AN HONORIFIC. IT'S KURARA-SAN TO YOU!
Oh how I love my bitchy side.
Tabeto was right.
And I'll do it...
I have to move forward with my own life.
...one step at a time.
AH, THIS IS A GREAT COOKBOOK. $12.50, PLEASE.
THE COST OF MOVING ON UP!

STEP END

"The past: our cradle, not our prison; there is danger as well as appeal in its glamour. The past is for inspiration, not imitation, for continuation, not repetition."

-Israel Zangwill

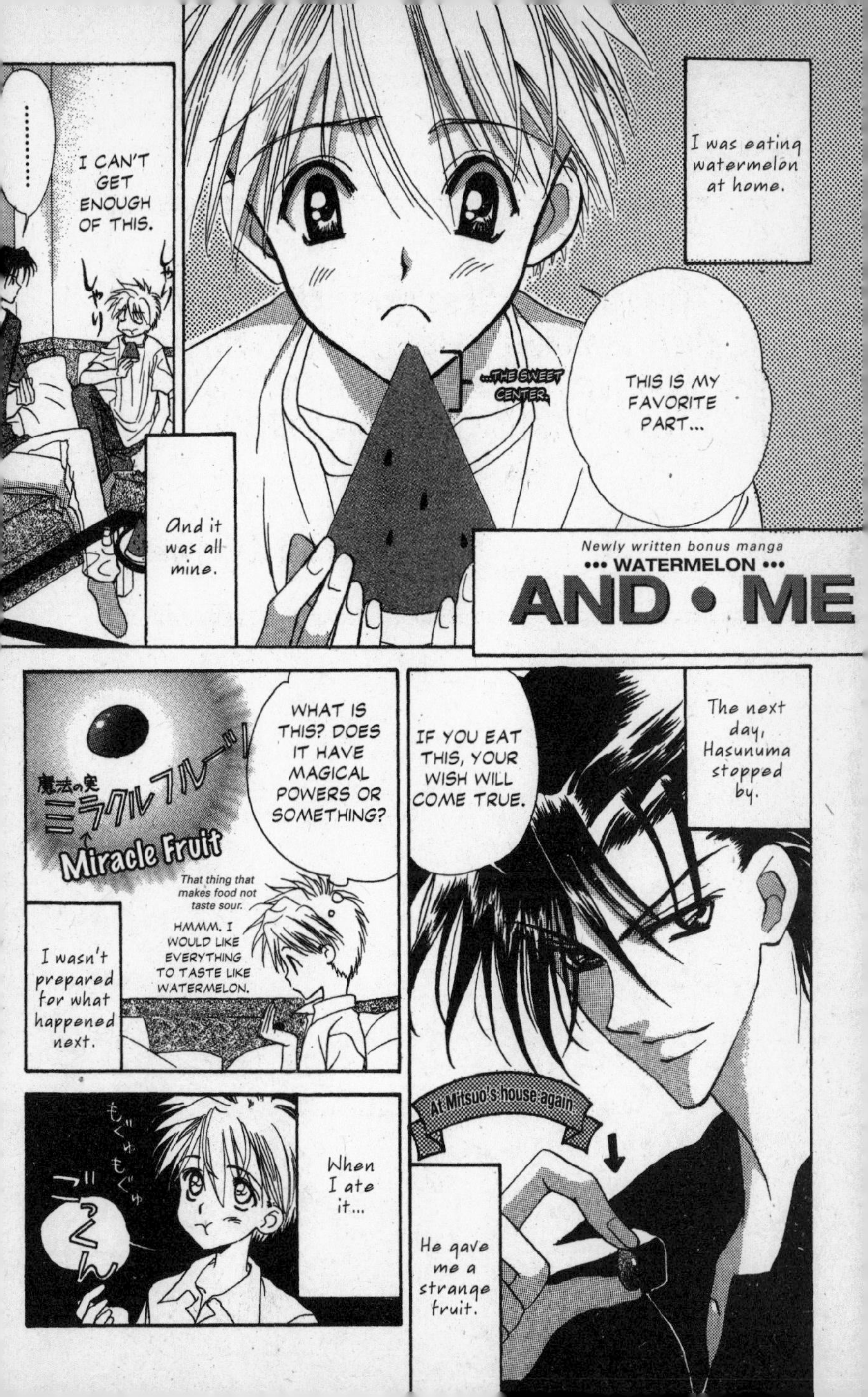
I was eating watermelon at home.
THIS IS MY FAVORITE PART...
...THE SWEET CENTER.
Newly written bonus manga
••• WATERMELON •••
AND • ME
And it was all mine.
......
I CAN'T GET ENOUGH OF THIS.
しゃり
The next day, Hasunuma stopped by.
IF YOU EAT THIS, YOUR WISH WILL COME TRUE.
At Mitsuo's house again
He gave me a strange fruit.
WHAT IS THIS? DOES IT HAVE MAGICAL POWERS OR SOMETHING?
魔法の実
ミラクルフルーツ
Miracle Fruit
That thing that makes food not taste sour.
HMMM. I WOULD LIKE EVERYTHING TO TASTE LIKE WATERMELON.
I wasn't prepared for what happened next.
When I ate it...
もぐゅもぐゅ
ごっくん

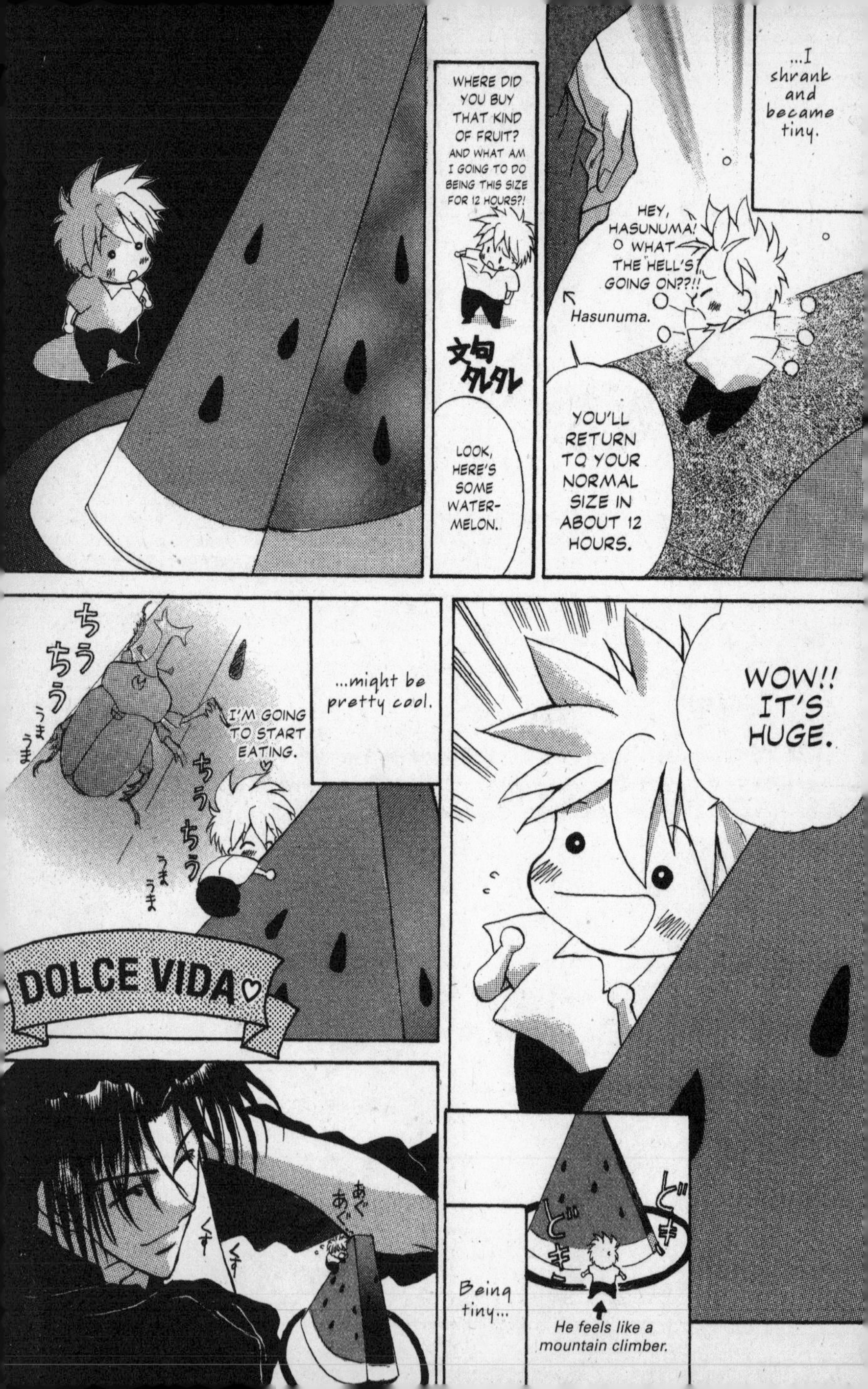
...I shrank and became tiny.
HEY, HASUNUMA! WHAT THE HELL'S GOING ON??!!
Hasunuma.
YOU'LL RETURN TO YOUR NORMAL SIZE IN ABOUT 12 HOURS.
WHERE DID YOU BUY THAT KIND OF FRUIT?
AND WHAT AM I GOING TO DO BEING THIS SIZE FOR 12 HOURS?!
文句タレタレ
LOOK, HERE'S SOME WATER-MELON.
WOW!! IT'S HUGE.
どき どき
Being tiny...
He feels like a mountain climber.
...might be pretty cool.
ちう ちう
うま うま
I'M GOING TO START EATING.
ちう ちう
うま うま
DOLCE VIDA♡
くす くす
あぐ あぐ

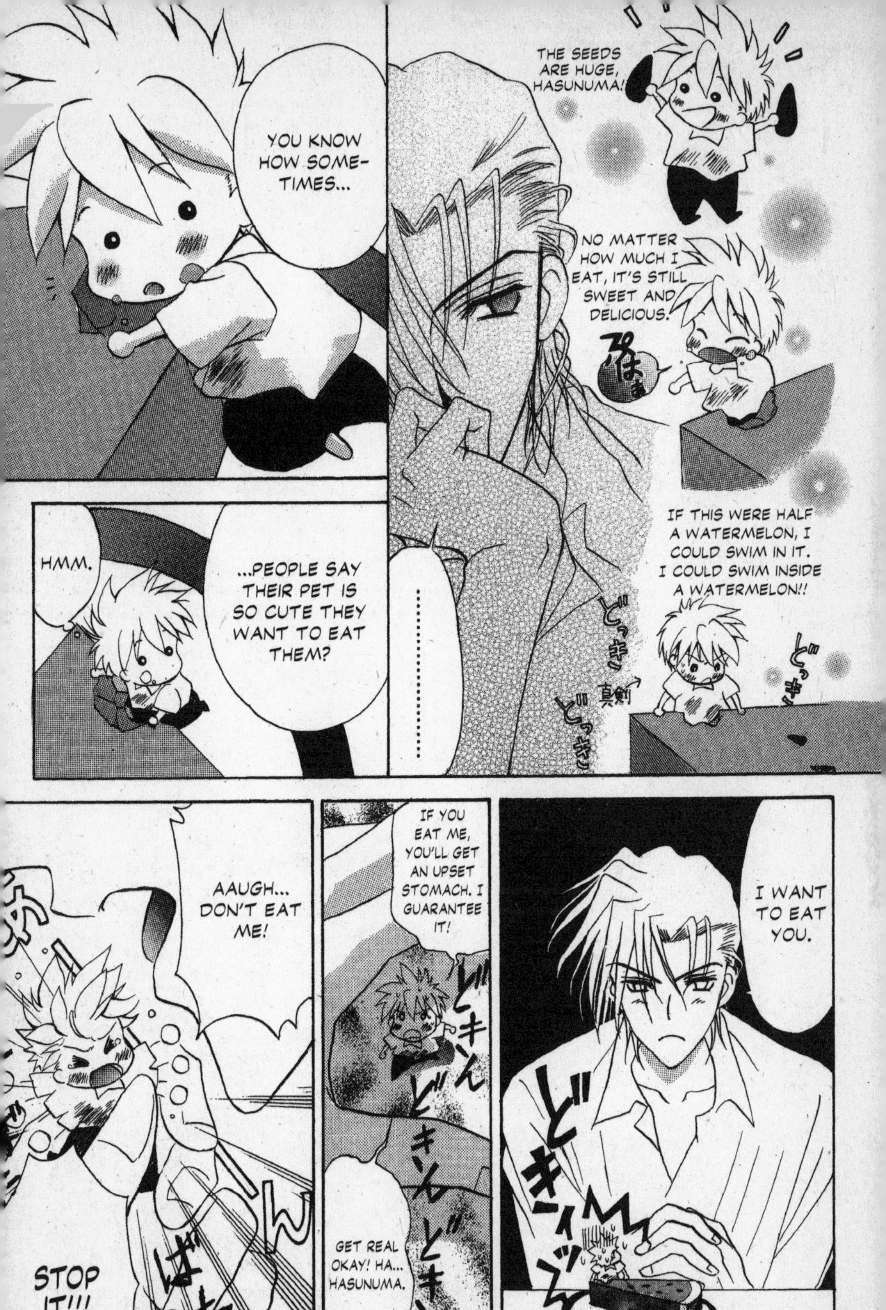
THE SEEDS ARE HUGE, HASUNUMA!
NO MATTER HOW MUCH I EAT, IT'S STILL SWEET AND DELICIOUS.
ぷはぁ
IF THIS WERE HALF A WATERMELON, I COULD SWIM IN IT. I COULD SWIM INSIDE A WATERMELON!!
どっき
......
どっき
真剣
どっき
YOU KNOW HOW SOME-TIMES...
...PEOPLE SAY THEIR PET IS SO CUTE THEY WANT TO EAT THEM?
HMM.
I WANT TO EAT YOU.
どきーッ
IF YOU EAT ME, YOU'LL GET AN UPSET STOMACH. I GUARANTEE IT!
どきん
どきん
どきん
GET REAL OKAY! HA... HASUNUMA.
AAUGH... DON'T EAT ME!
ばたん
STOP IT!!!

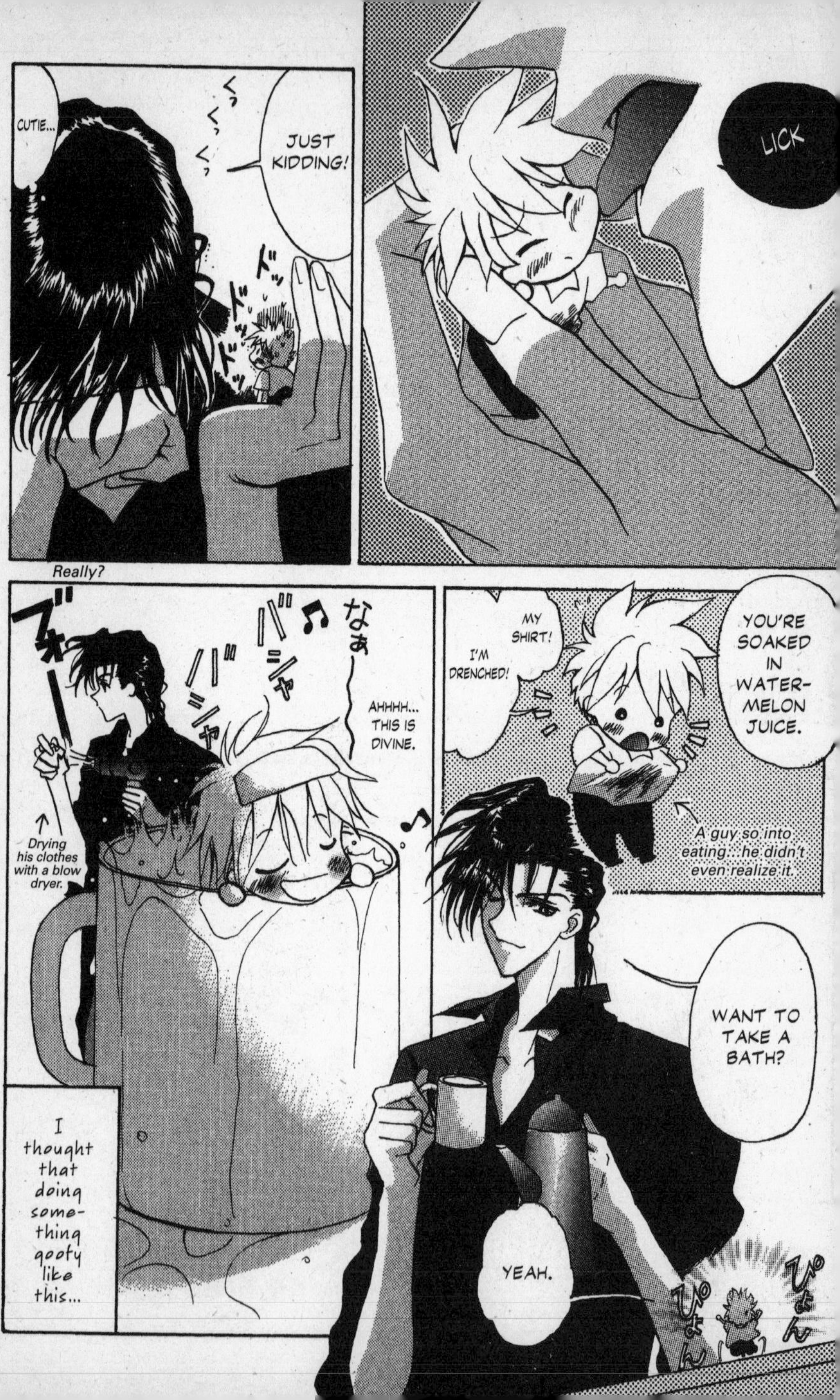
LICK
CUTIE...
くっくっくっ
JUST KIDDING!
ドッドッドッ
Really?
YOU'RE SOAKED IN WATER-MELON JUICE.
MY SHIRT!
I'M DRENCHED!
A guy so into eating... he didn't even realize it.
WANT TO TAKE A BATH?
YEAH.
ぴょん ぴょん
ぴょん ぴょん
なぁ～♪
AHHHH... THIS IS DIVINE.
バシャバシャ
ブォー
Drying his clothes with a blow dryer.
I thought that doing some-thing goofy like this...

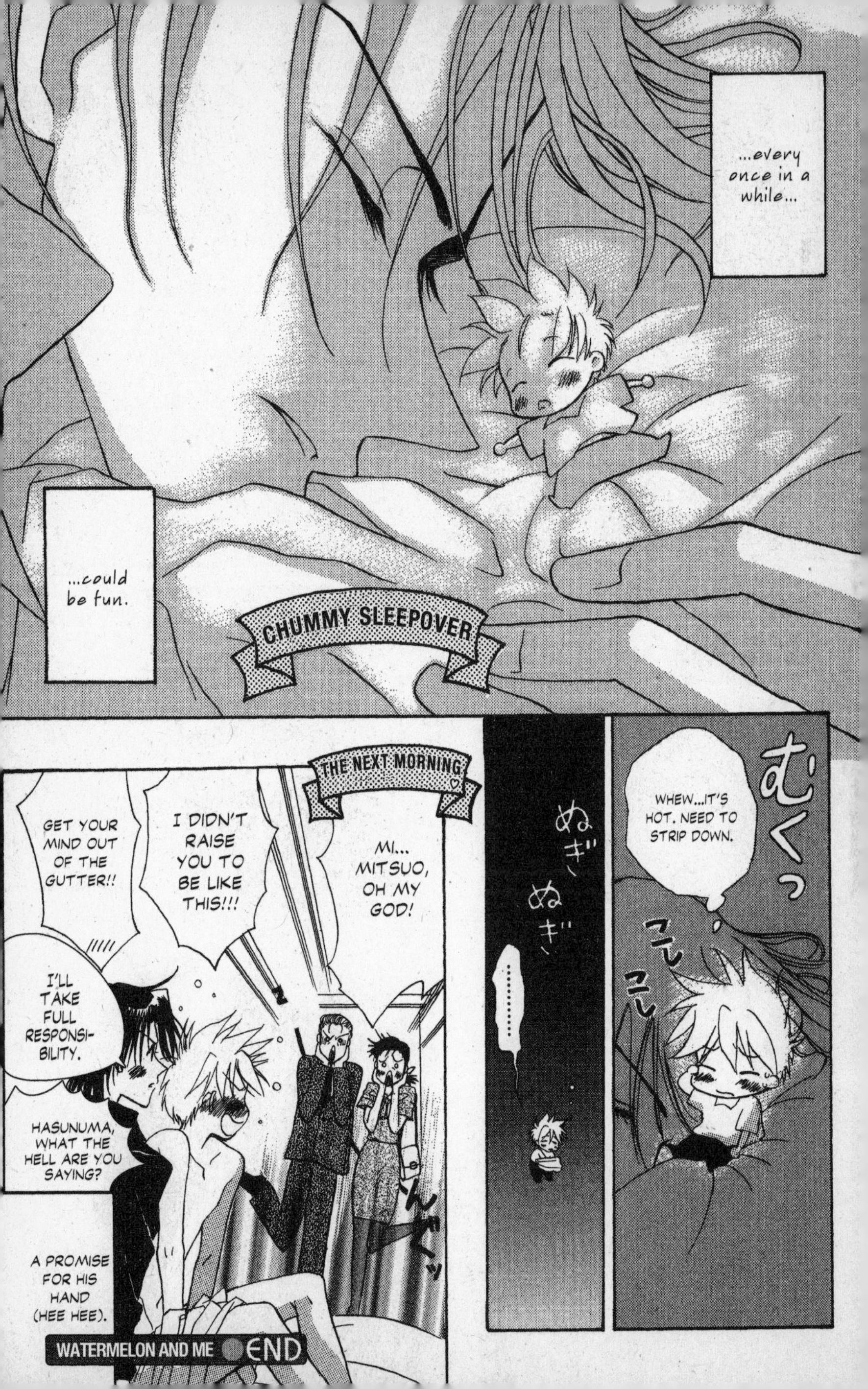
...every once in a while...
...could be fun.
CHUMMY SLEEPOVER
むくっ
WHEW...IT'S HOT. NEED TO STRIP DOWN.
こし こし
ぬぎ ぬぎ
....
THE NEXT MORNING
MI... MITSUO, OH MY GOD!
I DIDN'T RAISE YOU TO BE LIKE THIS!!!
GET YOUR MIND OUT OF THE GUTTER!!
I'LL TAKE FULL RESPONSI-BILITY.
HASUNUMA, WHAT THE HELL ARE YOU SAYING?
A PROMISE FOR HIS HAND (HEE HEE).
WATERMELON AND ME END

■ SPECIAL THANKS ♡ ■

S. HIMATSURI **SAMA** A teacher to whom I'm greatly indebted to.

M. KUBO SAMA

Y. YOSHIOKA SAMA

■ THANKS♡ ■

M. A

Y. ARAKI

H. KARUBE

E. K

K. KOBAYASHI

A. KOUSE

K. SAKAMOTO

H. S

M. SARUYAMA

E. SUEYOSHI

A. CHINONE

Y. TOUGOU

M. HURIHATA

A. HURUKAWA

And to those responsible for publishing
this book! Thank you very much.
And to my readers! I'm very grateful to you.

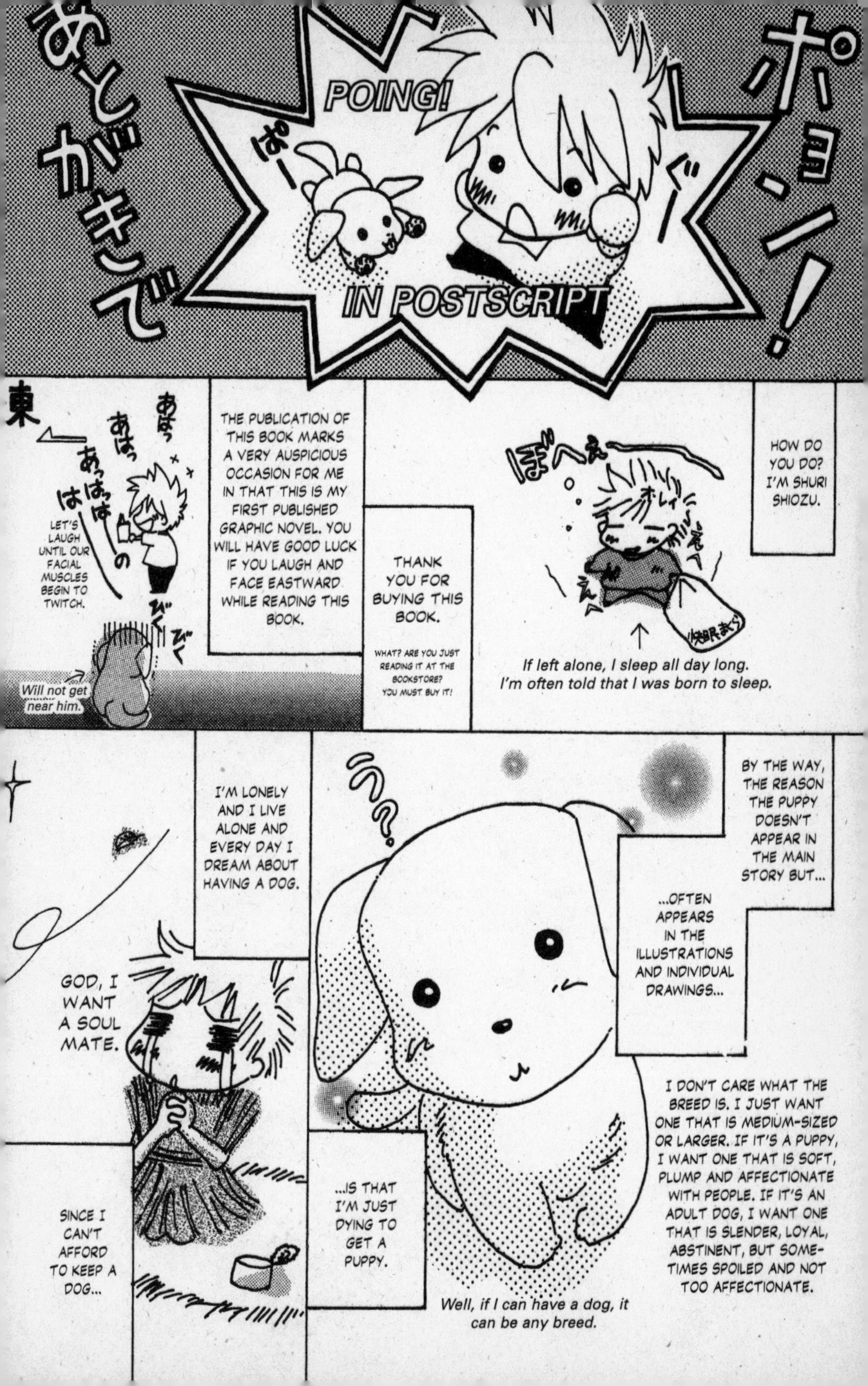
ポヨーン!
あとがきで
POING!
IN POSTSCRIPT
HOW DO YOU DO? I'M SHURI SHIOZU.
If left alone, I sleep all day long. I'm often told that I was born to sleep.
THANK YOU FOR BUYING THIS BOOK.
WHAT? ARE YOU JUST READING IT AT THE BOOKSTORE? YOU MUST BUY IT!
THE PUBLICATION OF THIS BOOK MARKS A VERY AUSPICIOUS OCCASION FOR ME IN THAT THIS IS MY FIRST PUBLISHED GRAPHIC NOVEL. YOU WILL HAVE GOOD LUCK IF YOU LAUGH AND FACE EASTWARD WHILE READING THIS BOOK.
東
LET'S LAUGH UNTIL OUR FACIAL MUSCLES BEGIN TO TWITCH.
Will not get near him.
BY THE WAY, THE REASON THE PUPPY DOESN'T APPEAR IN THE MAIN STORY BUT...
...OFTEN APPEARS IN THE ILLUSTRATIONS AND INDIVIDUAL DRAWINGS...
...IS THAT I'M JUST DYING TO GET A PUPPY.
I DON'T CARE WHAT THE BREED IS. I JUST WANT ONE THAT IS MEDIUM-SIZED OR LARGER. IF IT'S A PUPPY, I WANT ONE THAT IS SOFT, PLUMP AND AFFECTIONATE WITH PEOPLE. IF IT'S AN ADULT DOG, I WANT ONE THAT IS SLENDER, LOYAL, ABSTINENT, BUT SOMETIMES SPOILED AND NOT TOO AFFECTIONATE.
Well, if I can have a dog, it can be any breed.
I'M LONELY AND I LIVE ALONE AND EVERY DAY I DREAM ABOUT HAVING A DOG.
GOD, I WANT A SOUL MATE.
SINCE I CAN'T AFFORD TO KEEP A DOG...

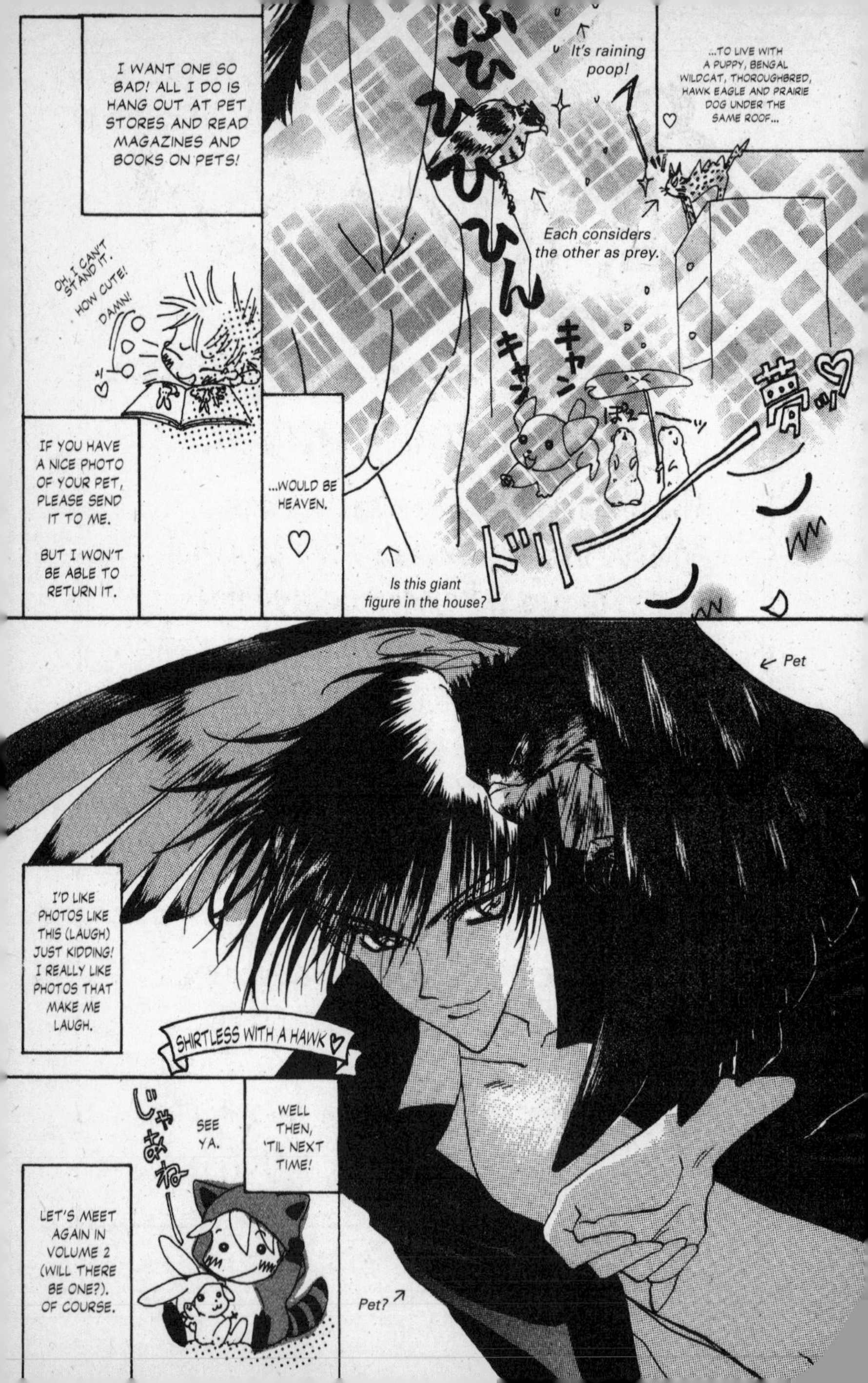
...TO LIVE WITH A PUPPY, BENGAL WILDCAT, THOROUGHBRED, HAWK EAGLE AND PRAIRIE DOG UNDER THE SAME ROOF...
It's raining poop!
ふひひひひん
Each considers the other as prey.
キャンキャン
夢
ドリー
Is this giant figure in the house?
...WOULD BE HEAVEN.
I WANT ONE SO BAD! ALL I DO IS HANG OUT AT PET STORES AND READ MAGAZINES AND BOOKS ON PETS!
OH, I CAN'T STAND IT.
HOW CUTE!
DAMN!
IF YOU HAVE A NICE PHOTO OF YOUR PET, PLEASE SEND IT TO ME.
BUT I WON'T BE ABLE TO RETURN IT.
Pet
SHIRTLESS WITH A HAWK
I'D LIKE PHOTOS LIKE THIS (LAUGH) JUST KIDDING! I REALLY LIKE PHOTOS THAT MAKE ME LAUGH.
WELL THEN, 'TIL NEXT TIME!
SEE YA.
じゃあねー
LET'S MEET AGAIN IN VOLUME 2 (WILL THERE BE ONE?). OF COURSE.
Pet?

Eerie Queerie!

Coming Soon in Vol. 2

The ghostbusters are back when Mitsuo and Hasunuma take a school field trip to a lakeside haunted hotel, where Mitsuo suddenly develops a case of non-stop hiccups, a curse by the God of Happiness that can be deadly if Mitsuo hiccups 100 times in a row! Find out in Volume 2 if the spooky sleuths can expel a ghost that's been haunting their school for the last 15 years. And when Hasunuma goes through a mysterious out-of-body experience, will Mitsuo be able to save his one and only soul mate?!

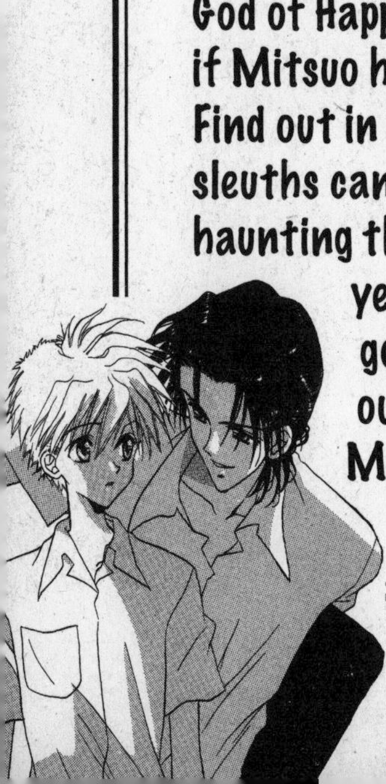

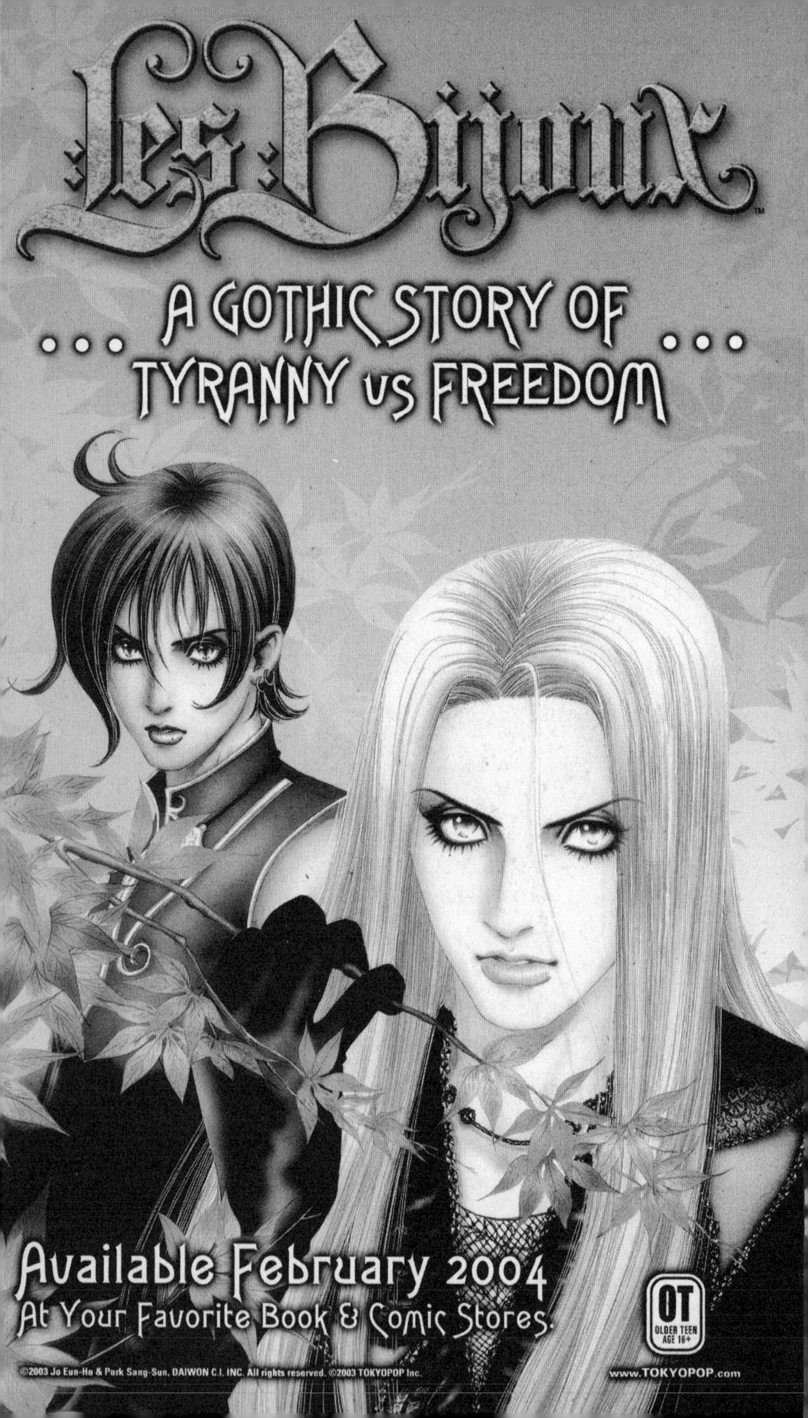
Les Bijoux™
...A GOTHIC STORY OF TYRANNY vs FREEDOM...
Available February 2004
At Your Favorite Book & Comic Stores.
OT
OLDER TEEN AGE 18+
©2003 Jo Eun-Ha & Park Sang-Sun, DAIWON C.I. INC. All rights reserved. ©2003 TOKYOPOP Inc.
www.TOKYOPOP.com

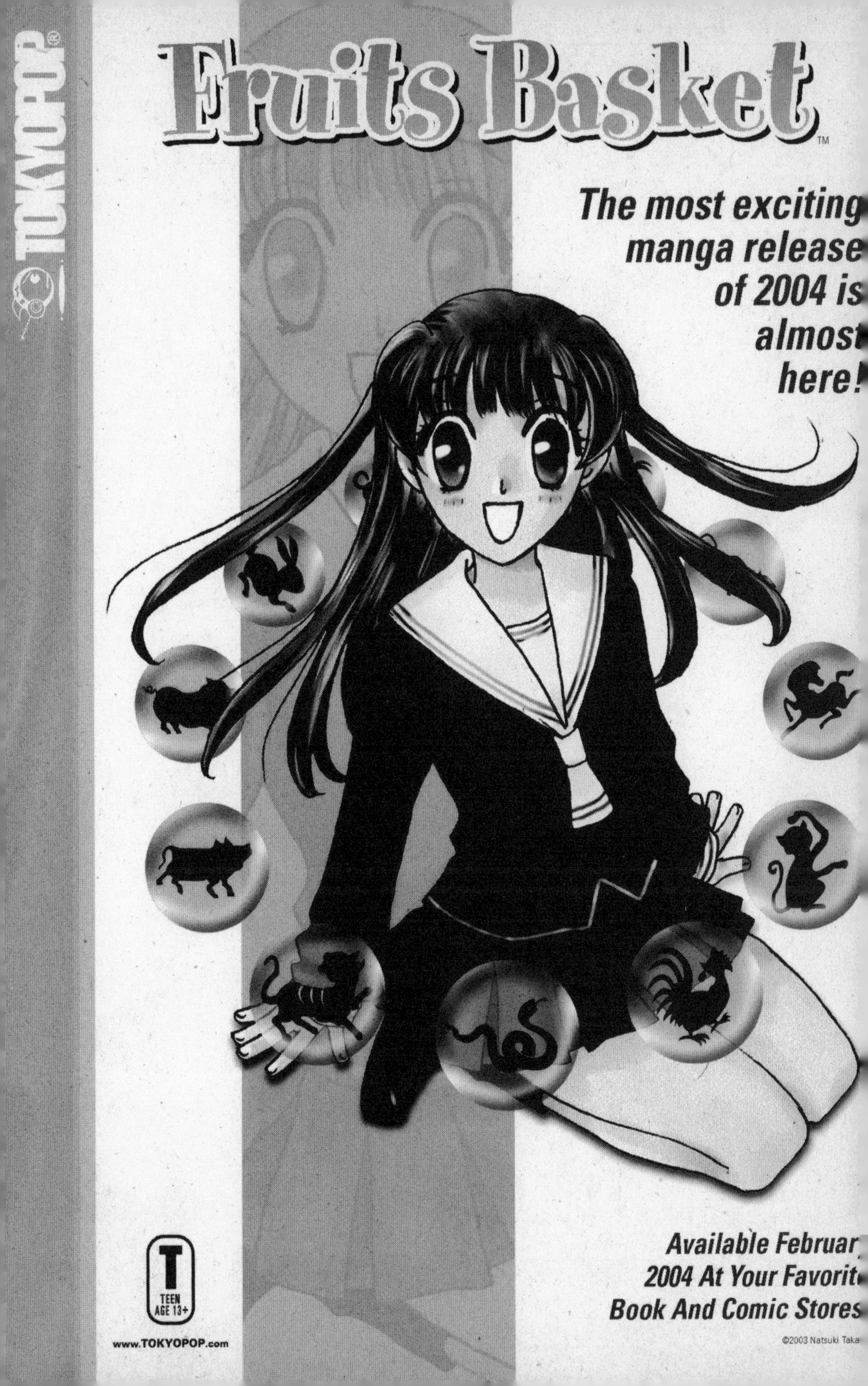
TOKYOPOP
Fruits Basket
The most exciting
manga release
of 2004 is
almost
here!
T
TEEN
AGE 13+
www.TOKYOPOP.com
Available Februar
2004 At Your Favorit
Book And Comic Stores
©2003 Natsuki Taka

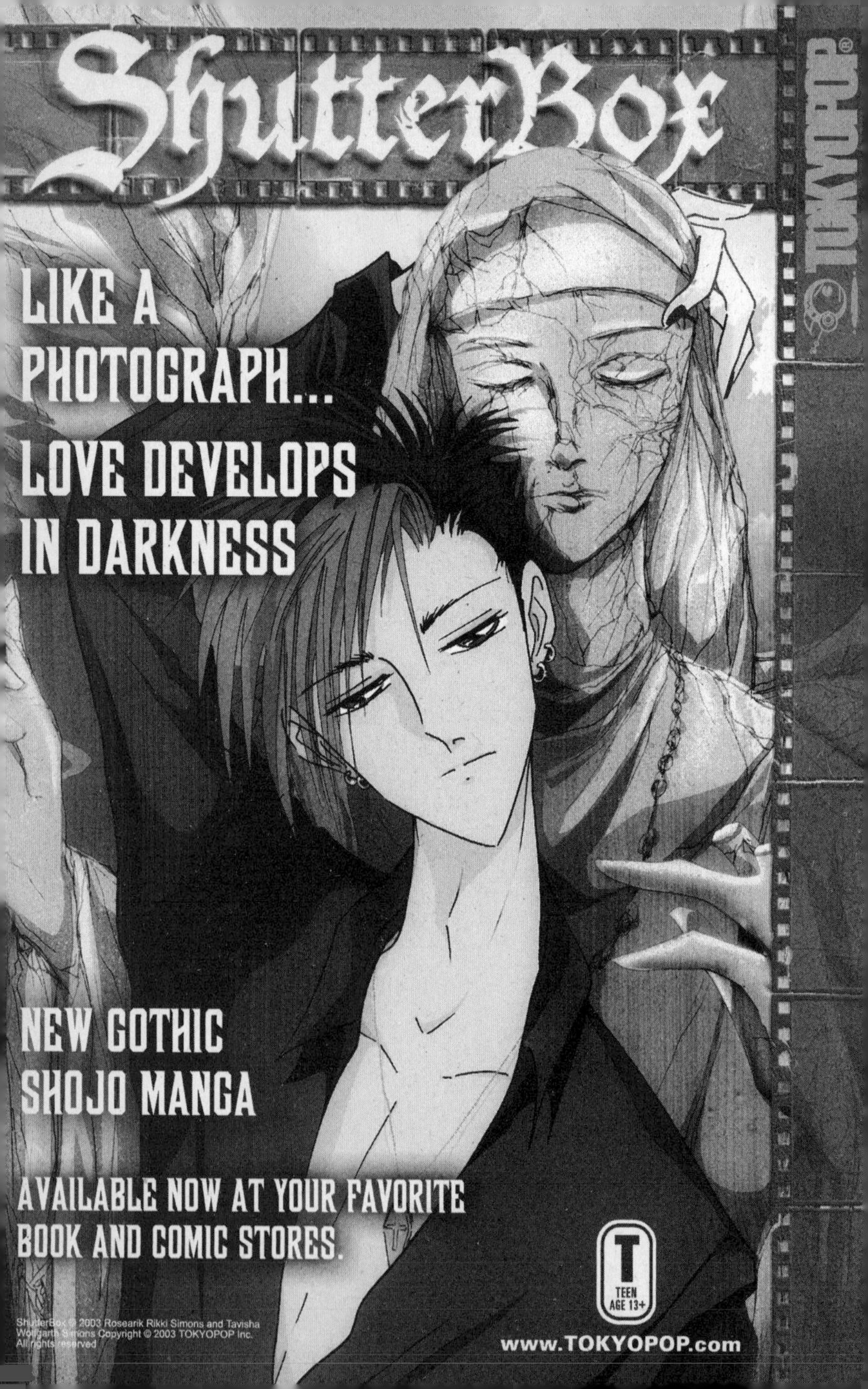
ShutterBox
TOKYOPOP
LIKE A PHOTOGRAPH...
LOVE DEVELOPS IN DARKNESS
NEW GOTHIC SHOJO MANGA
AVAILABLE NOW AT YOUR FAVORITE BOOK AND COMIC STORES.
T TEEN AGE 13+
ShutterBox © 2003 Rosearik Rikki Simons and Tavisha Wolfgarth Simons Copyright © 2003 TOKYOPOP Inc. All rights reserved
www.TOKYOPOP.com

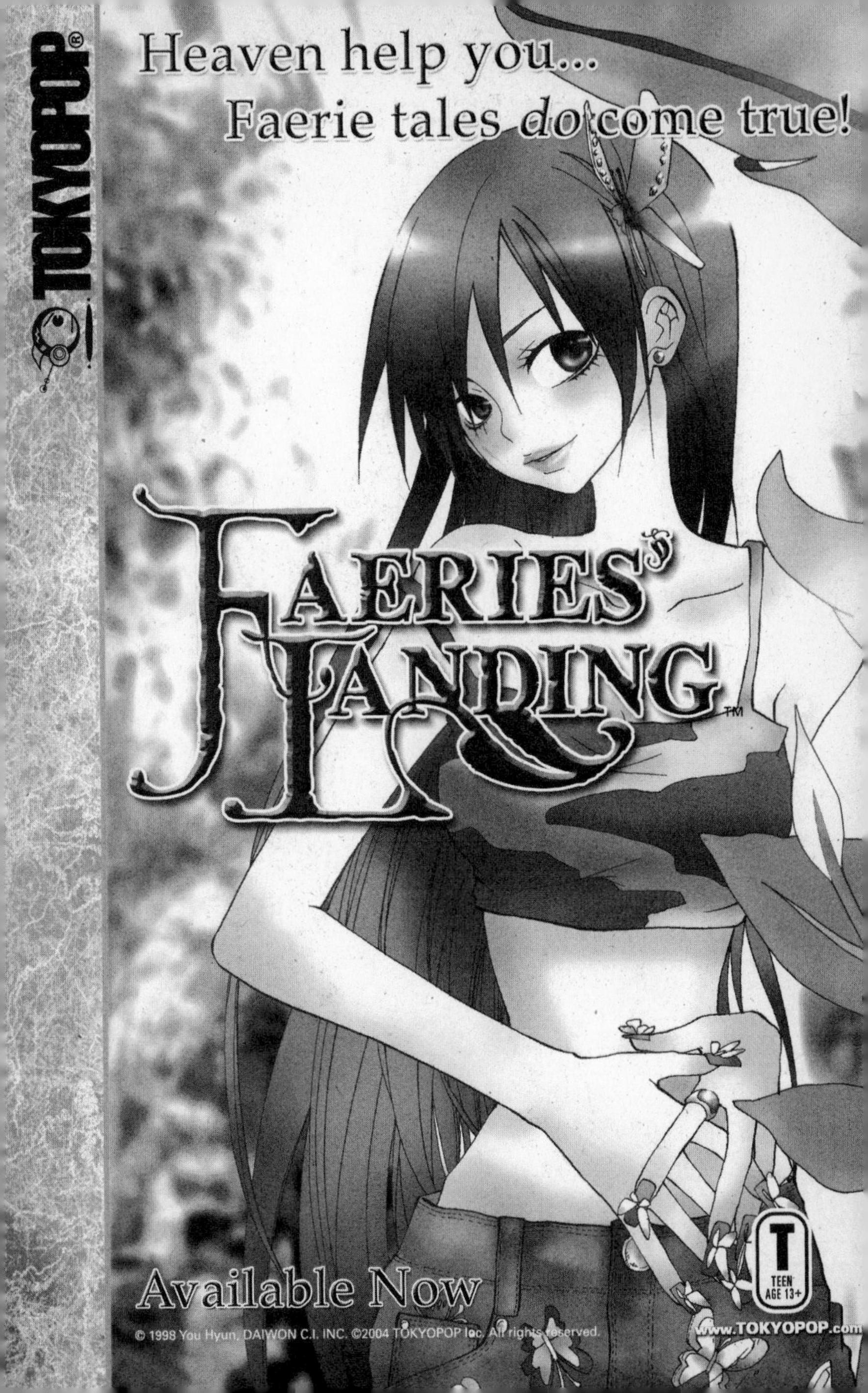
TOKYOPOP®
Heaven help you...
Faerie tales *do* come true!
FAERIES' LANDING™
Available Now
T TEEN AGE 13+
© 1998 You Hyun, DAIWON C.I. INC. ©2004 TOKYOPOP Inc. All rights reserved.
www.TOKYOPOP.com

STOP!

This is the back of the book.
You wouldn't want to spoil a great ending!

This book is printed "manga-style," in the authentic Japanese right-to-left format. Since none of the artwork has been flipped or altered, readers get to experience the story just as the creator intended. You've been asking for it, so TOKYOPOP® delivered: authentic, hot-off-the-press, and far more fun!

DIRECTIONS

If this is your first time reading manga-style, here's a quick guide to help you understand how it works.

It's easy... just start in the top right panel and follow the numbers. Have fun, and look for more 100% authentic manga from TOKYOPOP®!